(continued from front flap)

retarded now being carried o[...]
it is permissible to talk about [...]
rational planning.

The section on services for elderly people with mental disability also illustrates the fact that the groundwork of evaluation is beginning to be well-established. Professor Roth draws attention to the increasing proportion of the elderly in the population and to the fact that the vast majority of those who need help are not, and should not be, in institutions. The dangers of uprooting are emphasized. Dr Sainsbury and Dr Grad describe one of the few comparative surveys to have been undertaken. Dr Wertheimer describes the well-developed service in Lausanne and Dr Harwin discusses the various methods of screening available, particularly the use of district nurses, to identify elderly people at risk in the general population.

Miss Goldberg's contribution shows how far evaluative studies of social work practice have developed. Several careful surveys and experiments have been carried out, which indicate that the evaluative problems are much the same as those discussed in other sections. 'Much social work is based upon intuition, empathy, and exploration, following the client through all kinds of mazes and, not infrequently, getting lost with him.' Like Dr Robins's chapter, this is an excellent introduction to a field of work which is rapidly expanding. Dr Kreitman's critical review of suicide prevention programmes illustrates very well the value of a series of studies from one unit, allowing continuity and development of investigation and fruitful accumulation of knowledge. Dr Leff contributes a particularly important discussion of single-centre versus multi-centre trials of drug treatment and shows how similar the methodology of drug evaluation is to that of service evaluation. Drs Bruce and Barbara Dohrenwend discuss the difficult problem of measuring social performance. A great deal depends upon its solution.

In general, the book summarizes the progress made during the past few years towards establishing a scientific basis for service evaluation. All the contributions are critical; all are based on the assumption that, in the long run, it is better to know the truth than to rely on administrative or clinical impressions of success. Very little of the work discussed is generally known and the book is a contribution towards bringing the attention of scientists, practitioners, and administrators to bear on the problems and possibilities of rational service planning.

Roots of Evaluation

The epidemiological basis for
planning psychiatric services

Roots of Evaluation

The epidemiological basis
for planning psychiatric
services

Proceedings of the International
Symposium held at Mannheim
26–29 July 1972

EDITED BY J. K. WING and H. HÄFNER

World Psychiatric Association
Deutsche Gesellschaft für Psychiatrie
und Nervenheilkunde

360p.

Published for the
Nuffield Provincial Hospitals Trust
by the Oxford University Press
London New York Toronto
1973

Oxford University Press, Ely House, London W1

Glasgow New York Toronto Melbourne Wellington
Cape Town Salisbury Ibadan Nairobi Dar es Salaam Lusaka
Addis Ababa Bombay Calcutta Madras Karachi Lahore
Dacca Kuala Lumpur Singapore Hong Kong Tokyo

ISBN 0 19 721375 8

© The Nuffield Provincial Hospitals Trust 1973

Designed by Bernard Crossland

Printed in Great Britain by Alden & Mowbray Ltd
at the Alden Press, Oxford

Preface

The second Symposium on Psychiatric Epidemiology, held in Mannheim in July 1972, was jointly sponsored by the World Psychiatric Association and the Deutsche Gesellschaft für Psychiatrie und Nervenheilkunde. A small organizing committee, consisting of Professor H. Häfner, Dr G. Moschel, Dr W. Feuerlein, and Professor J. K. Wing, was set up to represent the two associations. The meeting followed the similar symposium held three years earlier at Aberdeen University (Hare and Wing, 1970) and the theme was the evaluation of the community psychiatric services. The present volume bears witness to the remarkable increase in evaluative work in recent years; itself an outgrowth from psychiatric epidemiology.

There are twice as many papers by psychiatrists as behavioural scientists but this ratio is already lower than at Aberdeen, where it was more than three to one, and if there is another meeting in three years' time, there will no doubt be further indications of the truth of the statement that the behavioural and social sciences are as fundamental to medicine as the biological.

In order to produce a readable and marketable book it was unfortunately necessary to leave out some of the papers discussed at the conference. The choice was made mainly on the basis of whether the work concerned was to be published in greater detail elsewhere. Several of the authors affected have contributed to another book on evaluation, published by the Oxford University Press for the Nuffield Provincial Hospitals Trust, which can be read as a companion volume to this one, since it deals mainly with the detailed assessment of one particular developing community service (Wing and Hailey, 1972). A list of the papers omitted follows the list of Contents on p. xi, together with references to the work discussed. Each of the typescripts is available from the author concerned.

J. K. WING and H. HÄFNER

Contents

Preface   v

Papers given at the Symposium but
not included in this volume   xi

List of participants   xiii

Acknowledgements   xvii

Part 1 *Introduction*   1

1 *Principles of evaluation.* J. K. Wing   3
   Evaluation and planning, 3. Morbidity, treatment,
   and need, 5. Methods of evaluation, 7. Conclusion,
   10. References, 11.

2 *Epidemiological basis for planning.*
   E. Strömgren   13

Part 2 *Statistics for planning*   21

3 *International statistics.* E. M. Brooke   23
   What statistics are collected? 23. Difficulties in
   obtaining psychiatric statistics, 25. Difficulties in
   the international comparison and interpretation of
   statistics, 26. Coverage, 26. What is being done to
   improve international statistics? 32. References,
   34.

4 *The role of a national statistics programme in the planning of community
   psychiatric services in the United
   States.* M. Kramer and C. A. Taube   35

Definitions, 37. Description of national programmes in the United States, 39. Examples of
data relevant to planning, 42. Discussion, 65.
Summary, 68. References, 69.

5   *Statistics from general practice.*   75
       B. Cooper
       Introduction, 75. The scope of general practice
       research in psychiatry, 76. Conclusion, 84. Ac-
       knowledgements, 85. References, 86.

6   *Morbidity statistics from population*
       surveys. **D. Hughes**   87
       Introduction, 87. Methodology, 89. Results, 91.
       Conclusions, 96. References, 97.

Part 3 *Evaluating services for children and*
        adolescents   99

7   *Evaluation of psychiatric services for*
       children in the United States.
       L. N. Robins   101
       The traditional method: psychotherapy, 102. Thera-
       py via teachers or mothers, 107. The recent
       innovations: education and the behaviour thera-
       pies, 110. Drug therapies, 120. Overview, 124.
       References, 126.

8   *Evaluation of psychiatric services for*
       children in England and Wales **I. Kolvin**   131
       Introduction, 131. Descriptions of services, ser-
       vice needs, and deficiencies, 134. Evaluative re-
       search: review of United Kingdom literature, 145.
       Discussion, 148. Research, 151. Summary, 158.
       Addendum, 159. References, 160.

9   *Evaluating services for adolescents.*
       M. Capes   163
       The development of adolescent psychiatry, 163.
       In-patient care, 164. Evaluating different pro-
       grammes of in-patient care, 165. Out-patient
       psychiatric clinics, 167. Varied facilities, 168.
       Other facilities, 171. Discussion, 171. Refer-
       ences, 172.

10   *Evaluation of residential services for*
       mentally retarded children. **A. Kushlick**   175
       Introduction, 175. Summary of the method used
       and progress to date, 176. The evaluative study,
       177. The research design, 178. Setting up the new

locally based units, 181. Research design developments, 195. Evaluation of Command 4683 locally based units for adults, 192. Acknowledgements, 193. References, 193.

11   *Alternatives to the hospital for the residential care of the mentally retarded.* R. D. King   **197**

The range of residential provision: present and future, 197. The quality of care: alternatives to the large hospital, 200. The need for theoretically informed research, 210. References, 211.

Part 4   *Evaluating services for the elderly*   **213**

12   *The principles of providing a service for psycho-geriatric patients.* Sir Martin Roth   **215**

The demographic background, 215. The magnitude of the problem, 216. The relationship between mental illness and duration of stay in hospital and residential accommodation, 218. Limits of safety, 222. Factors influencing admission, 223. Misclassification of individuals requiring long-term care, 224. Suggested guidelines for the provision of residential and institutional care in specific forms of psycho-geriatric disorders, 226. Problems in assessment, 227. Preventative measures and the concept of 'lines of defence', 228. Needs in the immediate future, 232. Inquiries needed for the planning and development of psycho-geriatric services, 234. Psychogeriatrics as a special branch of psychiatry? 235. References, 236.

13   *Evaluating a service in Sussex.* P. Sainsbury and J. Grad de Alarcon   **239**

Introduction, 239. The general problem, of design and methods in evaluating services, 240. The service in Sussex, 243. The aims of the evaluation, 244. Method and design, 245. Some results, 246. Effect of the service on admission rates, 248. Effect of the service on families, 251. Outcome, 252. Conclusions, 254.

14   *Evaluating a service in Lausanne.* J. Wertheimer, P. Gilliand, L. Bircher, and M. Perier   **257**

15   *Psychiatric morbidity among the physically impaired elderly in the community: A preliminary report.* B. Harwin   **269**

Introduction, 269. Design and method, 270. Preliminary findings, 271. Conclusions, 276. Acknowledgements, 277. References, 277.

Part 5   *Evaluation of some community*   279
              services

16   *Services for the family.* E. M. Goldberg   281
      Introduction, 281. Objectives, 281. Methods of
      social work, 282. Criteria of success and failure,
      283. Some field experiments with no differences in
      outcome, 284. Some criticisms of these studies,
      287. Two field experiments showing differences
      in outcome, 289. Differences in input, 291. Differ-
      ences in outcome, 292. Implications of these
      studies, 293. References, 296.

17   *Prevention of suicidal behaviour.*
      N. Kreitman   297
      Completed suicide, 297. 'Attempted suicide'
      (parasuicide), 300. Primary prevention, 301. Sec-
      ondary prevention, 304. Conclusion, 306. Refer-
      ences, 307.

18   *Development of a hospital-centred*
      community psychotherapy service
      for schizophrenic patients. Y. Alanen
      and A. Laine   309
      Starting points and the development of the service,
      309. The 1971 follow-up examination of the 1969
      patients, A. Laine, 312. Discussion, 321. Refer-
      ences, 324.

19   *Trials of preventative medication.*
      J. P. Leff   327
      Specific trials, 330. References, 335.

20   *Ability and disability in role functioning*
      in psychiatric patient and non-patient
      groups. B. S. Dohrenwend, B. P.
      Dohrenwend, *and* D. Cook   337
      Problem, 338. Procedure, 339. Results, 334.
      Discussion, 354. Conclusions, 357. Technical
      Appendix, 358. References, 359.

Papers given at the Symposium but not included in this volume

It was not possible to include in the present volume every paper circulated to participants because the resulting book would have been too unwieldy. Since the quality of papers was very even, a decision about what to omit had to be taken on the basis of criteria such as whether the material was likely to be published elsewhere, whether it contained original data and whether it would fit into the editorial scheme. Several excellent papers had to be left out and a note of the title, where the paper is being published, or where similar work by the author can be found, is appended below. Authors will be glad to supply copies of the original papers.

L. Bartak and M. Rutter, 'A comparison of three units for autistic children'. To be published in *J. Child. Psychol. Psychiat.*

G. W. Brown, 'The mental hospital as an institution'. To be published in *Soc. Sci. and Med.*

J. E. Cooper, 'Making diagnosis more reliable'. See: Wing, J. K., Cooper, J. E., and Sartorius, N. (1973). 'Measurement and classification of psychiatric symptoms' (Cambridge, at the University Press).

R. Giel, 'Referral and admission to a mental hospital in the Netherlands'.

D. Goldberg, 'Principles of rehabilitation'.

Anthea M. Hailey, 'Local case-registers'. See: Wing, J. K., and Hailey, A. M. (eds) (1972). *Evaluating a Community Psychiatric Service* (Oxford University Press for the Nuffield Provincial Hospitals Trust).

J. M. Kuldau, 'Outcome studies as a guide in the evaluation of a programme for a mixed group of chronic and relapsing patients'.

H. B. M. Murphy, 'Evaluation of the Symposium'.

H. Reimann, 'Sociology of institutions', See: Reimann, H. (1968). *Kommunikations-Systeme* (Tubingen: Mohr/Siebeck).

N. Sartorius, *The International Classification of Diseases*, Part V.

Barbara Stevens, 'Evaluation of rehabilitation for psychotic patients in the community'. To be published in *Acta Psychiatrica*.

J. K. Wing, 'Principles of evaluation'. Full version will be found in: Wing, J. K. and Hailey, A. M. (eds), op. cit.

Lorna Wing, 'Evaluating the services for children'. See: Wing, L., in Wing, J. K. and Hailey, A. M. (eds), op. cit., chap. 23, p. 398.

List of participants

Professor Yrjö O. Alanen, Department of Psychiatry, University of Turku, 20700 Turku 70, Finland.

Dr Jacqueline Grad de Alarcon, MRC Clinical Psychiatry Unit, Graylingwell Hospital, Chichester, Sussex.

Dr Tol Asuni, Neuro-Psychiatric Hospital, Aro, Abeokuta, Western State of Nigeria.

Professor Walter Ritter von Baeyer, Psychiatrische Klinik der Universität Heidelberg, 69 Heidelberg, Voßstrasse 4, FRG.

Lawrence Bartak, Department of Psychiatry, Institute of Psychiatry, De Crespigny Park, London SE5 8AF.

Dr Douglas Bennett, The Maudsley Hospital, Denmark Hill, London SE5.

Miss Ursula Binz, Psychologisches Institut der Universität Mannheim, 68 Mannheim, Schloß, FRG.

Dr Wolfgang Böker, Sozialpsychiatrische Klinik der Universität Heidelberg, 68 Mannheim, Städtische Krankenanstalten, FRG.

Dr Roy E. Bransby, Department of Health and Social Security, 14 Russell Square, London WC1 B5EP.

Miss Eileen M. Brooke, Department de Statistique Médicale, Institut de Médicine Sociale et Préventive, Hôpital Sandoz, 1011 Lausanne, Switzerland.

Dr John Brothwood, Department of Health and Social Security, Alexander Fleming House, Elephant and Castle, London SE1.

Dr George W. Brown, Bedford College Annexe, Peto Place, Marylebone Road, London NW1 4DT.

Dr Mary Capes, Wessex Regional Hospital Board, Highcroft, Romsey Road, Winchester, Hampshire.

Dr L. Ciompi, Clinique Psychiatrique Universitaire, 1008 Prilly/Lausanne, Switzerland.

Professor Rudolf Cohen, Fachbereich Psychologie an der Universität Konstanz, 775 Konstanz, FRG.

Dr Brian Cooper, Institute of Psychiatry, De Crespigny Park, London SE5 8AF.

Professor John E. Cooper, Department of Psychiatry, Nottingham University Medical School, University Park, Nottingham.

Dr John A. Corbett, The Bethlem Royal Hospital and the Maudsley Hospital, Hilda Lewis House, 579 Wickham Road, Shirley, Croydon CRO 8DR.

John B. Cornish, Department of Health and Social Security, Alexander Fleming House, Elephant and Castle, London SE1.

Dr Michael von Cranach, Psychiatrische Universitatsklinik Müchen, Nußbaumstrasse 7, 8000 Müchen 15, FRG.

Professor Rudolf Degkwitz, Psychiatrische und Nervenklink der Universität Freiburg, Hauptstrasse 5, 78 Freiburg, FRG.

Dr Horst Dilling, Psychiatrische Klinik und Poliklinik der Universität München, Nußbaumstrasse 7, 8000 München 15, FRG.

Professor Barbara S. Dohrenwend, Department of Psychology, The City College, New York, NY 10031, USA.

Professor Bruce P. Dohrenwend, Department of Psychiatry, Social Psychiatry Research Unit, Columbia University, 100 Haven Avenue, New York, NY 10032, USA.

Dr Annalise Dupont, Institut for Psykiatrisk Demografi, Statshospitalet ved Aarhus, 8240 Risskov, Denmark.

Dr Robin Eastwood, Clarke Institute of Psychiatry, 250 College Street, Toronto 28, Canada.

Professor Helmut Ehrhardt, Institut für Gerichtliche und Sozial-Psychiatrie, Ortenbergstrasse 8, 355 Marburg (Lahn), FRG.

Dr Wilhelm Feuerlein, Max-Planck-Institut für Psychiatrie, Kraepelinstrasse 10, 8000 München, FRG.

Dr Asmus Finzen, Universitäts-Nervenklinik, Osianderstrasse 22, 7400 Tübingen, FRG.

Dr Margit Fischer, University of Aarhus, 8240 Risskov, Denmark.

Professor Robert Giel, Algemeen Provinciaal, Stads- en Academisch Ziekenhuis, Psychiatrische Kliniek, Sociale Psychiatrie, Groningen, Oostersingel 59, Netherlands.

Dr David Goldberg, Department of Psychiatry, University of Manchester, University Hospital of South Manchester, West Didsbury, Manchester M20 8LR.

Miss E. Matilda Goldberg, National Institute for Social Work Training, Mary Ward House, 5-7 Tavistock Place, London WC1 H9SS.

Professor Heinz Häfner, Sozialpsychiatrische Klinik der Universität Heidelberg, 68 Mannheim, Städtische Krankenanstalten, FRG.

Dr Wiltrud Häfner-Ranabauer, Sozialpsychiatrische Klinik der Universität Heidelberg, 69 Heidelberg, FRG.

Mrs Anthea M. Hailey, MRC Social Psychiatry Unit, Institute of Psychiatry, De Crespigny Park, London SE5 8AF.

Dr Brian G. Harwin, GP Research Unit, Institute of Psychiatry, De Crespigny Park, London SE5 8AF.

Professor Hanfried Helmchen, Psychiatrische Klinik II der Freien Universität Berlin, Nußbaum-Allee 36, 1 Berlin, FRG.

Dr Steven Hirsch, Institute of Psychiatry, De Crespigny Park, London SE5 8AF.

Dr Dafydd Hughes, The Welsh National School of Medicine, University of Wales, Department of Psychological Medicine, Whitchurch Hospital, Cardiff CF4 7XB.

Dr Anthony D. Isaacs, The Bethlem Royal Hospital and the Maudsley Hospital, Denmark Hill, London SE5.

Professor Niels Juel-Nielsen, Department of Psychiatry, University of Odense, Denmark.

Dr Heinz Katschnig, Psychiatrisch-Neurologische Universitätsklinik, Allgemeines Krankenhaus der Stadt Wien, Spitalgasse 23, Wien, Austria.

Professor Henry B. Kedward, Clarke Institute of Psychiatry, 250 College Street, Toronto 28, Canada.

Dr Roy D. King, Department of Sociology and Social Administration, University of Southampton, Southampton SO9 5NH.

Dr I. Kolvin, Nuffield Child Psychiatry Unit, Hospital for Sick Children, Great North Road, Newcastle upon Tyne NE2 3AX.

Dr Morton Kramer, National Institute of Mental Health, Department of Health, Education, and Welfare, 5454 Wisconsin Avenue, Chevy Chase, Maryland 20015, USA.

Dr Burkhard Krauß, Nervenkliniken der Universität Göttingen, Neurologische Klinik und Poliklinik, von Siebold-Strasse 5, 34 Göttingen, FRG.

Dr Zivko Kulcar, Croatian Institute of Public Health, Zagreb, Yugoslavia.

Dr Norman Kreitman, University Department of Psychiatry, MRC Unit for Epidemiology, Royal Edinburgh Hospital, Edinburgh EH10 5HF.

Dr Heinrich Kunze, Max-Planck-Institut für Psychiatrie, Deutsche Forschungsanstalt für Psychiatrie, Kraepelinstrasse 2 und 10, 8 München 23, FRG.

Dr Albert Kushlick, Wessex Regional Hospital Board, Highcroft, Romsey Road, Winchester, Hampshire.

Professor Hans Lauter, Nervenkliniken der Universität Göttingen, Psychiatrische Klinik und Poliklinik, von Siebold-Strasse 5, 34 Göttingen, FRG.

Dr Julian Leff, MRC Social Psychiatry Unit, Institute of Psychiatry, De Crespigny Park, London SE5 8AF.

Dr A. R. May, World Health Organization, Regional Office for Europe, 8 Scherfigsvej, DM 2100 Copenhagen Ø, Denmark.

Professor Joachim Meyer, Nervenkliniken der Universität Göttingen, Psychiatrische Klinik und Poliklinik, von Siebold-Strasse 5, 34 Göttingen, FRG.

Dr Alexander G. Mezey, Department of Psychological Medicine, North Middlesex Hospital, Silver Street, Edmonton, London N18.

Dr John H. Morris, Medical Research Council, 20 Park Crescent, London W1N 4AL.

Dr Günther Moschel, Sozialpsychiatrische Klinik der Universität Heidelberg, 68 Mannheim, FRG.

Professor Christian Müller, Clinique Psychiatrique Universitaire, Hôpital de Cery, 1008 Prilly/Lausanne, Switzerland.

Professor Henry B. M. Murphy, Section of Transcultural Psychiatric Studies, McGill University Montreal, Beatty Hall, 1266 Pine Avenue West, Montreal 109, Qué, Canada.

Professor Ørnulv Ødegaard, Overlege ved Gaustad Sykehus, Vinderen, Gaustad, Oslo 3, Norway.

Professor Manfred Pflanz, Institut für Epidemiologie und Sozialmedizin der Medizinischen Hochschule Hannover, Roderbruchstrasse 101, 3 Hannover, FRG.

Professor Horst Reimann, Lehrstuhl für Soziologie, Universität Augsburg, Memminger Strasse 6/14, 89 Augsburg, FRG.

Dr Helmut Remschmidt, Klinik für Kinder- und Jugendpsychiatrie der Universität Marburg, Hans-Sachs-Strasse 6, 355 Marburg (Lahn), FRG.

Dr Eibe Rudolf Rey, Deutsche Forschungsanstalt für Psychiater, Kraepelinstrasse 2/10, 8 München 23, FRG.

Professor Lee N. Robins, Department of Psychiatry, Washington University Medical School, 4940 Audubon Avenue, St Louis, Mo. 63110, USA.

Dr Raymond Sadoun, Institut National de la Santé et de la Recherche Médicale, 3 Rue Léon-Bonnat, Paris 16ᵉ, France.

Dr Norman Sartorius, Mental Health Unit, World Health Organization, 1211 Geneva 27, Switzerland.

Dr Hilde Seelheim, Landschaftsverband Westfalen-Lippe, Landeshaus, 44 Münster (Westf.), FRG.

Dr Ctirad Škoda, Psychiatric Research Institute, Prague 8 (Bohnice), Czechoslovakia.

Professor Erik Strömgren, Psychiatric Institute, University of Aarhus, 8249 Risskov, Denmark.

Professor Hans Strotzka, Institut für Tiefenpsychologie und Psychotherapie, Daringergasse 16/24, 1190 Wien, Austria.

Dr Hilchen Sundby, Child Psychiatry Unit, University of Oslo, Vinderen, Norway.

Professor Mervyn Susser, School of Public Health and Administrative Medicine, Columbia University, Division of Epidemiology, 600 West 168th Street, New York, NY 10032, USA.

Dr Zena Susser (Stein), School of Public Health and Administrative Medicine, Columbia University, Division of Epidemiology, 600 West 168th Street, New York, NY 10032, USA.

Dr J. Váňa, World Health Organization, Regional Office for Europe, 8 Schersigsvej, DM 2100 Copenhagen Ø, Denmark.

Dipl. Psych. Wendeler, Deutsches Institut für Internat. Pädagogische Forschung, 6 Frankfurt/Main, Schloss-Strasse 29, FRG.

Dr Jean Wertheimer, Clinique Universitaire de Lausanne, 1008 Prilly/Lausanne, Switzerland.

Professor John K. Wing, MRC Social Psychiatry Unit, Institute of Psychiatry, De Crespigny Park, London SE5 8AF.

Dr Lorna Wing, MRC Social Psychiatry Unit, Institute of Psychiatry, De Crespigny Park, London SE5 8AF.

Dr Detlev von Zerssen, Max-Planck-Institut für Psychiatrie, Forschungsanstalt für Psychiatrie, Kraepelinstrasse 2 und 10, 8 München 23, FRG.

Acknowledgements

The meeting was held at the Municipal Hospital of Mannheim, Federal Republic of Germany, by kind permission of Herr K. Kihm, Director of the Hospital. Thanks are due to Frau Käte Strobel, Federal Minister of Youth, Family, and Health, and to Frau Annemarie Griesinger, Minister of Employment and Social Affairs of the State of Baden-Württemberg, for their generous financial assistance and for their personal support of the conference. Acknowledgement is also due to Dr Hans Reschke, Mayor of the city of Mannheim, and to Dr Hans Martini, Head of the Department of Health and Social Affairs of the city, who gave a reception for the participants at the Rittersaal, Mannheim Castle, and who contributed in many other ways to the success of the meeting. The work of Dr Gunther Moschel, Secretary of the Programme Committee, and of his colleagues in the Organizing Committee and at the Municipal Hospital, both in preparing for the Symposium and in ensuring its smooth running, deserves especial recognition.

Contributions towards the costs of publication were made by: Byk Gulden, Konstanz; Ciba–Geigy AG, Wehr/Baden; Cilag-Chemie GmbH, Alsbach; Gebr. Guilini GmbH, Ludwigshafen; Chem. Fabrik von Heyden GmbH, Munchen; Hoffmann La Roche AG, Grenzach; Janssen GmbH, Dusseldorf; Knoll AG, Ludwigshafen; Krewel-Werke GmbH, Koln; Med. Pharmazeutische Studiengesellschaft e.V., Frankfurt; Nordmark-Werke GmbH, Uetersen/Holstein; Pharma-Stern GmbH, Wedel.

Part 1　*Introduction*

1 *Principles of evaluation*

J. K. WING

This is a summary of the paper given at Mannheim. The
full version may be found in chapter 2 of Wing J. K., and
Hailey, A. M. (1972).

Evaluation and planning

Planning consists of anticipating the problems that are likely to arise when
trying to achieve a given aim, and of working out in advance some means
of solving them. The more systematic and intelligent the anticipation, the
more successful the decisions are likely to be when plans are put into
effect. In planning health services the over-all aim is to decrease morbidity
(illness and disability) and mortality as far as possible. There may be
problems in deciding priorities between different methods of carrying this
out, for example between the relative proportion of available resources
which should be devoted to heart transplants or to hostels for the mentally
retarded, but whatever decision is made will need to be evaluated in terms
of the extent to which morbidity actually is decreased. Thus the aims of
planners and evaluators are fundamentally the same but each group has a
separate role. Planners make decisions concerning the priority to be
accorded different developments but they must then be prepared for
independent evaluation of the results; it is an unusual planner who can
objectively evaluate the results of his own decisions. Evaluators are
concerned with the extent to which services carry out their function of
reducing or containing morbidity and the experience thus gained will
enable them to make recommendations for changes; but they cannot make
the decisions themselves. Philosophies of planning are fundamentally
political while philosophies of evaluation are fundamentally scientific.

Most national and local planning committees have only limited
information available to them; their own experience, the advice of clinicians
and administrators, some *ad-hoc* statistics, and a set of institutions and
agencies with in-built traditions and prejudices. Most begin with a few
generally accepted principles. The chief aim of the health services is to
decrease or contain morbidity, firstly in patients, secondly in the patient's
immediate family, thirdly in the community at large. Each service agency

has a combination of diagnostic, therapeutic, rehabilitative, and preventive functions, but prevention is better than cure. Primary, secondary, and tertiary preventive methods should be used to stop disease occurring in the first place, to detect and treat illness at an early stage, to limit development of chronic disabilities following an acute illness, and to prevent the accumulation of secondary handicaps if clinical disabilities are unavoidable. All this can be summarized as the 'containment' of morbidity and mortality.

In order to achieve these ends different models of service have been proposed. One which has been quite widely accepted in principle assumes that health service authorities should accept responsibility for the population of a given geographical area so that everyone needing treatment should be able to obtain it locally. The range and variety of agencies should be adequate, the staff should be skilled and not overworked, and there should be proper communication between all parts of the service so that no blocks or delays occur when a patient moves from one agency to another. These principles are conveniently summarized as the provision of a responsible, comprehensive, and integrated community service.

Evaluative work could therefore begin with the question, 'Is the community service responsible, comprehensive, and integrated?' Behind this question, however, is the more fundamental one, 'Does the service, or any given section of it, contain morbidity or not?' Only when this question is satisfactorily settled is it permissible to go on to consider the most economical and efficient ways of containing morbidity. Thus evaluative work needs to be carried out at many different levels and will usually involve several branches of scientific work. It must be concerned with the organization of community services, the management of particular institutions (including perhaps the committee structure), the morale and training and skilfulness of staff, the extent and quality of various specific forms of service, the attitudes of local residents, and the carrying out of specified clinical functions such as diagnosis, treatment, rehabilitation, or prevention.

Clearly much evaluative research will be *ad hoc* and piecemeal but a basic strategy can be outlined in the form of six questions (Wing, Wing, and Hailey, 1970).

1. How many people are in contact with the various services that already exist, what patterns of contact do they make, and what are the temporal trends in contact rate?

2. What are the needs of these individuals and of their relatives?

3. Are the services at present provided meeting these needs effectively and economically?

4. How many other people, not in touch with services, also have needs, and are these needs different from those of people already in contact?

5. What new services, or modifications to existing services, are likely to cater for unmet needs?

6. When innovations in service are introduced, do they in fact help to reduce need?

In each case, the criterion is firstly whether the service reduces or contains morbidity or mortality and secondly whether it does so efficiently and economically.

The first question can be answered by the use of descriptive statistics, particularly those provided by case-registers. The second requires the definition of morbidity and of treatment; the relation of one to the other gives an estimate of need. The third is the question of value; do the existing services meet the needs of those in touch with them? The fourth is an extension of the second but requires surveys of the population not in touch with existing services. The fifth involves planning innovations on the basis of the answers to the earlier questions. The sixth returns to evaluation, this time of the innovations. Thus a cycle of evaluation–planning–reevaluation–replanning is set up. This strategy proceeds from the known to the unknown; from the routine collection of statistical data concerning services which already exist, to morbidity in the general population and the planning and evaluation of new services.

Morbidity, treatment, and need

It has been suggested that the main aims of planners and evaluators are complementary. Planners wish to ensure the reduction or containment of morbidity and mortality through the provision of appropriate services; evaluators wish to know whether the services actually carry out this function and, if not, how to improve them. Morbidity, however, is often measured in terms of contact with services. This is attractively simple but becomes a circular process if it is assumed that anyone who makes contact is ill or disabled and anyone who does not make contact is well. In fact, there are at least three components in psychiatric morbidity, each of which has its own implications for evaluating psychiatric services. The first component consists of the biological or psychological abnormalities of the illness itself, or the primary residual impairments caused by the illness (slowness or thought disorder in schizophrenia for example). The second component consists of the adverse attitudinal and behavioural reactions which accumulate secondarily whenever primary impairments are present (for example lack of confidence in ability to obtain a job, maladaptive attitudes or personal habits). Institutionalism is largely a matter of secondary reactions. The third consists of handicaps which exist independently of any illness, such as a lack of occupational or social skills due to poverty or a poor education or a lack of 'coping ability'. The combined effect of these three types of handicap on the social performance of an individual creates a condition called 'disablement' which is defined in

Introduction

purely social terms, according to the degree to which an individual falls short of the level of social performance expected of him within a given subgroup of society.

The measurement of these three components of morbidity has been discussed elsewhere (Wing, 1972) and no further consideration will be given to them here except to say that the measurement and classification of morbidity is of the essence of good evaluation, since this is the criterion against which services will be judged. The extent of the patient's co-operativeness must, of course, also be considered under this heading, since it is useless having an effective therapy for a condition of known morbidity if the patient cannot be persuaded that he ought to have it.

Medical treatment may be generally defined as any procedure which directly results in a decrease in the severity of symptoms or clinical disabilities or in the prevention of an increase. It thus includes many rehabilitative or preventive procedures. Biological and psychological treatments need no special commentary but the term 'social treatment' does give rise to confusion in evaluative work. There can now be little doubt that the social environment has a direct and marked effect on the course of many psychiatric illnesses, including some such as schizophrenia, which formerly were thought to have an inviolable natural history. The significance of this fact for evaluative work is that a distinction has to be made between the ward or unit providing the treatment and the processes which make up the treatment itself. Concepts such as 'administrative therapy' (Clark, 1964) or 'the therapeutic community' (Rapoport, 1960; Jones, 1962) involve many such processes and confusion is inevitable unless some attempt is made to distinguish one from another. Sometimes the processes seem to be very specific as in the reduction of certain severe and chronic primary handicaps of schizophrenia by an increase in social stimulation (Wing and Freudenberg, 1961; Wing and Brown, 1970). Even the process of attitude-change in order to reduce secondary disabilities can be very specific although some rather general social processes are.involved (Wing, 1966). Naturally the two kinds of handicap interact with each other and also with the third or 'pre-morbid' kind. Schizophrenic patients are particularly vulnerable to institutionalism in the social conditions found in many mental hospitals. Institutionalism, in schizophrenia, may be largely due to the fact that patients with a tendency towards apathy, because of the illness, do not use all their faculties spontaneously and, in crowded and understaffed wards, it is difficult to give the attention which would keep residual mental and physical functions at an optimum level. The necessary characteristics that a community should have in order to make it 'therapeutic' for such patients can be fairly precisely specified. Evaluation then consists in making the appropriate measurements of morbidity in order to see whether the aims are achieved. It would be useless, however, trying to test out these ideas in a 'therapeutic community' set up for a completely different group of patients.

Having discussed morbidity and treatment it is possible to approach the difficult concept of 'need'. Matthew (1971) gives clear and economical definitions of the terms 'need', 'demand', and 'utilization' as they are used in a medical context.

A need for medical care exists when an individual has an illness or disability for which there is effective and acceptable treatment or care. It can be defined either in terms of the type of illness or disability causing the need or of the treatment or facilities for treatment required to meet it. A demand for care exists when an individual considers that he has a need and wishes to receive care. Utilization occurs when an individual actually receives care. Need is not necessarily expressed as demand and demand is not necessarily followed by utilization, while, on the other hand, there can be demand and utilization without real underlying need for the particular service used.

It might perhaps be added that a demonstrated need for care still has to be assigned a priority as compared with other needs; it cannot be automatically translated into provision of the appropriate service. The allocation of priorities is a very complex and insufficiently considered process (Minns, 1972).

This definition of 'medical' need is only as useful as the definitions of morbidity and its treatment that it depends upon. It can be applied fairly reliably to conditions such as schizophrenia or dementia or anxiety state but much less so to 'social inadequacy', 'heavy drinking', or 'personality disorder'. Criteria can be set up in all these cases, as in the case of delinquency or unemployment or destitution, but the lack of reliability in definition leads to a very wide range of value judgements concerning the need for extra provisions, whether made by politicians or by the officials or professional people who are in day-to-day charge of services. Some of the dimensions involved have been dissected out by Bradshaw (1972). The principles of evaluation, however, remain the same.

Methods of evaluation

If the strategy for evaluative research outlined in the first section of this chapter is taken by way of illustration, it is clear that a considerable range of research designs and techniques is likely to be necessary. The *first* of the six questions mentioned earlier, which concerned the numbers of people already in contact with existing services, can be answered in terms of various kinds of descriptive statistics (cf. Part 2 of this book; Baldwin, 1971; Wing, Hailey, *et al.*, 1972). It is, of course, never possible to be purely descriptive. In effect, all routine statistics are judged in the context of clinical or administrative experience, against norms laid down elsewhere or in the light of what is regarded as good practice in areas with services of exceptionally high quality.

There is a danger in using descriptive data too readily in this way; the danger of 'instant evaluation', which can be quite as harmful in its effects as 'instant planning'. The mere observation of a figure or of a trend over time gives no information as to its value. It summarizes the cumulative results of clinical and administrative decisions without indicating whether they are the right ones. The author very often adds an element of evaluation by building in his own value-judgements, whether explicitly or not. Indeed, this is the commonest form of evaluative research and it can have its uses, particularly when the author is experienced, has collected data systematically and reliably, and has no axe to grind. Even under these conditions, however, descriptive work provides only a ground-clearing process for further evaluation. When the author is describing the results of his own clinical or administrative innovations, or when a government department is describing the effects of some official policy, there is much to be said for keeping an open mind until the results of independent evaluations are available. These will nevertheless depend to some extent upon value-judgements for their recommendations. However, the data they collect will be of more use to those whose final responsibility it is to make decisions if the appropriate design is used. Such a wide range of designs is available, from comparative statistics, 'natural experiments', sub-group comparisons, longitudinal studies, controlled trials, epidemiological surveys, and combinations of these, that it is not feasible to attempt a discussion. In general, research workers make too much of the difficulties in the way of using experimental designs and they have not given sufficient attention to replicating their findings.

The *second* of the six questions, concerning the definition of need, has already been discussed but the *third*, 'Are the services meeting the need effectively and economically?', requires consideration. Each element in a comprehensive service has to be organized and managed in such a way that the effectiveness of therapeutic and preventive techniques is maximized. This is true of a hospital ward, a day-hospital, a workshop, an out-patient clinic, or a hostel. These units themselves have to be co-ordinated into an efficient service and, ultimately, precisely the same criteria must be applied to a government department. At each organizational level there are problems of management and leadership and how these are decided will help to determine the effectiveness of treatment.

At the simplest level, the leader of a unit determines its policy, its morale, and the efficiency of its organization. At its most complicated, there is a complex committee structure, with several professional hierarchies represented and a wide distribution of personal responsibility, so that it is difficult to identify the unit with any particular individual. The more complicated the service the more likely are evaluative procedures to lose their way and miss their ultimate goal of assessing reduction of morbidity.

Hyman (1962) has dealt in detail with the principles of evaluation of a specified agency. He spends a good deal of time considering the problem of how to get the agency's aims clear, what to do when these objectives are ambiguous or unstated and how to take into account the unanticipated effects of the agency's policies. The logic of the present argument goes further, however, since it is assumed that the final aim of any sociomedical service must in the long run be to diminish morbidity. Whatever its stated aims and policies, therefore, the evaluator must set up his own criteria against which to measure success, as well as including criteria based upon the agency's stated or implicit goals.

The assessment of treatment procedures requires an evaluation of numbers of staff, their training, morale, and functions, and the extent to which they are actually carrying out their duties. Some of the most fundamental problems facing the helping professions are likely to be discovered when the roles of psychiatrist, psychologist, social worker, nurse, occupational therapist, occupational supervisor, house parent, hostel warden, teacher, and GP are contrasted, compared, and evaluated. King, Raynes, and Tizard (1971) have pointed the way in their comparison of house mothers and nurses looking after mentally retarded children. Bartak's study of three schools for autistic children (1971) and some of the investigations of social work have also been particularly interesting (Reid and Shyne, 1969; Goldberg, 1970). In all such work, the staff concerned must feel themselves under investigation and this introduces a new dimension into evaluative work; one not present in a simple drug trial. The evaluator should always try to give due weight to views concerning the results which conflict with his own. At this point, he can no longer pose as totally disinterested; he does not like having his conclusions challenged any more than the agency likes being told it is not as successful as it thought. It will usually be wise to obtain the reactions of those concerned before making the final report, although it may not be possible after due consideration to take them into account.

The *fourth* question concerned the extent of unmet need in the general population. Some surveys have taken the view that anyone who can be shown to have even the most minor psychiatric incapacity requires specialist help (Srole *et al.*, 1962). This is to equate need with morbidity (albeit morbidity defined in rather a loose fashion). Matthew's definition is sterner than that; it defines need in terms of morbidity for which there exists an acceptable and effective treatment (and, in parenthesis, which will not get better reasonably quickly on its own).

Shepherd and his colleagues (1966) estimate that some 15 per cent of the population have a form of psychiatric disorder during one year, but only 2 per cent are actually in contact with a psychiatrist (Wing and Bransby, 1970). It is not yet possible to pick out in any precise way which people would actually benefit from referral. Eastwood (1971) has pointed out the difficulties involved in screening a population for psychiatric illness, particularly the neuroses; the criteria adopted for assessing a screening programme in other fields of medicine (Wilson, 1971) could certainly not be met. There are no valid ways of detection at a presymptomatic stage, the value of early treatment has not been securely established and the proportion of false positives or false negatives is unacceptably high.

Thus, although the 'path to the hospital' usually lies through the GP's surgery, it is too early yet to say, from general practice studies, which patients will get more effective and acceptable treatment from a specialist than from the family doctor. Matthew's criteria of need are not, therefore, met.

So far as the more severe psychotic disorders are concerned there is less likelihood of cases being missed in areas with reasonably good services. Some of the most sensitive indices of unmet need are indicators of various forms of social deprivation; homelessness in particular. Among the destitute population, who sleep 'rough' or live in common lodging houses or reception centres, there is a remarkably high rate of untreated morbidity, particularly alcoholism, schizophrenia, and personality disorder (Tidmarsh and Wood, 1972). This is due, in part, to gaps in the existing services, particularly in after-care facilities and in sheltered accommodation (what used to be called 'asylum'). Some areas are therefore likely to contain more patients than others and knowing the characteristics of a local population (particularly its housing) can give a clue as to which types of morbidity can be expected to be most prevalent. An inner working-class urban area from which the slums have only recently been cleared will have and will need a different pattern of services to a middle-class commuter suburb or a rural county.

The *fifth* and *sixth* questions concerned the introduction of new services in order to meet the needs which have been discovered at earlier stages and the further evaluation of these services. A cycle of new planning and new evaluation is set up which should continue indefinitely. If an area with responsible, comprehensive, and integrated services were to reach this stage of evaluation and planning, it would indeed have a model service. So far as evaluation goes, most areas at the moment are still in an elementary phase of stage 1. If high-quality planning were ever developed, very sophisticated machinery for monitoring, feedback, and estimating further change would be needed. Automated records systems and standardized clinical data would be mandatory and clinicians and administrators, as well as research workers, would appreciate the need for accurate recording. The very mention of the idea that clinicians would be concerned with precision in record-keeping indicates that we are now in the realm of science fiction.

Conclusion

Evaluation is no different from any other scientific work except that its results may sometimes be immediately useful to administrators, and this introduces special problems. Much of it is long-term and strategic, and administrators will only become aware of any practical value towards the closing stages of the research. The immediacy of contact with planners carries opportunities and dangers (Dainton, 1971; Rothschild, 1971). The danger is that freedom of inquiry and criticism may be limited, even if unconsciously, in the circumstances of investigating services which engage the energies and emotions of planners, administrators, and professional staff and whose success means a great deal to all concerned. When a scientist is undertaking a laboratory experiment he can remain objective in the face of his own desire to get a certain result, if only because he knows the experiment will be repeated elsewhere. In evaluative work the pressures are greater and the likelihood of independent replication considerably less. The need for visible independence and objectivity is therefore proportionately the greater. Another danger is that there will gradually be a shift of balance from strategic to tactical research, which would be tantamount to killing the goose that lays the golden eggs. The opportunities, in my view, outweigh the dangers.

REFERENCES

Baldwin, J. A. (1971). *The Mental Hospital in the Psychiatric Service: A Case Register Study* (Oxford University Press for the Nuffield Provincial Hospitals Trust).

Bartak, L., and Rutter, M. (1971). 'Educational treatment of autistic children', in Rutter, M. (ed.), *Infantile Autism; Concepts, Characteristics and Treatment* (London: Churchill).

Bradshaw, J. R. (1972). 'A taxonomy of social need', in McLachlan, G. (ed.), *Problems and Progress in Medical Care*. Seventh Series (Oxford University Press for the Nuffield Provincial Hospitals Trust).

Clark, D. (1964) *Administrative Therapy* (London: Tavistock).

Dainton, F. (1971). 'The future of the Research Council System', in *A Framework for Government Research and Development,* Cmnd 4814 (London: HMSO).

Eastwood, M. R. (1971). 'Screening for psychiatric disorder', *Psychol. Med.* **1,** 197.

Goldberg, E. M. (1970). *Helping the Aged* (London: Allen and Unwin).

Hyman, H., Wright, H., Charles, R., and Hopkins, T. K. (1962). *Applications of Methods of Evaluation* (Berkeley and Los Angeles: University of California Press).

Jones, M. (1962). *Social Psychiatry: in the Community, in Hospitals and in Prisons* (Springfield: Thomas).

King, R., Raynes, N., and Tizard, J. (1971). *Patterns of Residential Care* (London: Routledge).

Matthew, G. K. (1971). 'Measuring need and evaluating services', in McLachlan, G. (ed.), *Portfolio for Health, Problems and Progress in Medical Care,* Sixth Series (Oxford University Press for the Nuffield Provincial Hospitals Trust).

Minns, R. (1972). 'Homeless families and some organisational determinants of deviancy', *Policy and Politics,* **1,** 1–22.

Rapoport, R. N. (1960). *Community as Doctor* (London: Tavistock).

Reid, W. J., and Shyne, A. W. (1969). *Brief and Extended Casework* (New York: Columbia University Press).

Rothschild, Lord (1971). 'The organisation and management of government R and D', in *A Framework for Government Research and Development,* Cmnd 4814 (London: HMSO).

Shepherd, M., Cooper, B., Brown, A. C., and Kalton, G. (1966). *Psychiatric Illness in General Practice* (London: Oxford University Press).

Srole, L., Langner, T., Michael, S. T., Opler, M. K., and Rennie, T. A. C. (1962). *Mental Health in the Metropolis* (New York: McGraw-Hill).

Tidmarsh, D., and Wood, S. (1972). 'The Camberwell Reception Centre', in Wing, J. K., and Hailey, A. M. (eds), *Evaluating a Community Psychiatric Service* (Oxford University Press for the Nuffield Provincial Hospitals Trust).

Wing, J. K. (1966). 'Social and psychological changes in a rehabilitation unit', *Soc. Psychiat.* **1,** 21–28.

—— (1972). 'Principles of evaluation', in Wing, J. K., and Hailey, A. M. (eds), *Evaluating a Community Psychiatric Service* (Oxford University Press for the Nuffield Provincial Hospitals Trust).

—— and Bransby, R. (eds) (1970). *Psychiatric Case Registers,* DHSS Statist. Rep. Ser. no. 8 (London: HMSO).

—— and Brown, G. W. (1970). *Institutionalism and Schizophrenia* (Cambridge: University Press).

—— and Freudenberg, R. K. (1961). 'The response of severely ill chronic schizophrenic patients to social stimulation', *Am. J. Psychiat.* **118,** 311.

—— and Hailey A. M. (eds) (1972). *Evaluating a Community Psychiatric Service* (Oxford University Press for the Nuffield Provincial Hospitals Trust).

—— Wing, L., and Hailey, A. M. (1970). 'The use of case registers for evaluating and planning psychiatric services', in Wing, J. K., and Bransby, R. (eds), *Psychiatric Case Registers,* DHSS Statist. Rep. Ser. no. 8 (London: HMSO).

Wing, L. (1971). *Autistic Children* (London: Constable).

Wilson, J. M. G. (1971). 'Screening in the early detection of disease', in McLachlan, G. (ed.), *Portfolio for Health, Problems and Progress in Medical Care,* Sixth Series (Oxford University Press for the Nuffield Provincial Hospitals Trust).

2 Epidemiological basis for planning

ERIK STRÖMGREN

The title chosen for this paper seems to indicate that results of epidemiological research can be used as one of the bases for health planning. There are different kinds of planning, so where does epidemiology come in as a useful tool?

Different types of health planning are described in the fourteenth report of the WHO expert committee on health statistics; *Statistical Indicators for the Planning and Evaluation of Public Health Programmes*. This report distinguishes between four types of planning: deductive, inductive, impressionistic, and idealistic planning.

In 'deductive planning', according to the report, 'broad policies and objectives are established at the highest level of the organization and detailed proposals for implementation flow downwards to those who provide services'. This is obviously not the place for application of epidemiological results.

About 'inductive planning' it is said, on the other hand, that 'local experiences, services, and practices are identified and efforts are made to coordinate and consolidate them so that greater benefit can be made more widely available'. Epidemiological studies do not seem to be of special importance for such planning, and the importance must be even less in 'idealistic planning', where 'the aims of the plan are stated only in the form of unattainable ideals. Action is encouraged by exhortation, but precise objectives or methods of achieving them are not specified.' Thus, for epidemiology only 'impressionistic planning' is left. About this type of planning the report says that 'this is the type of *ad hoc* professional and institutional decision-making to which most clinicians and administrators have been accustomed in the past. Decisions and choices are made on the basis of experience, pressures, minimal information and rough estimates of needs and possibilities. The process is more intuitive and political in character than rational or scientific and can scarely be regarded as planning in the strict sense of the term.' This description sounds most familiar to those who are in contact with current mental health planning and have witnessed the fate which solid epidemiological facts can have when politicians and administrators apply them in planning.

The results of epidemiological research can be applied in so many different ways. When plans are made for the mental health services it seems obvious that knowledge of the prevalence of mental illness in the population is essential. In many populations such information is available from psychiatric population surveys. These prevalence figures do not, however, say anything about that which should be essential to administrators and politicians, namely the need of the population for psychiatric care. For each group of mental illnesses it has to be decided to what extent the members of the group are in need of treatment and nursing. As soon as this has been established for all groups it will become obvious that available resources are not nearly sufficient to provide the amount of care which is supposed to be necessary. The next step is, therefore, the creation of a system of priorities.

Priorities can, however, be defined in different, incommensurable ways. Should available resources be concentrated on those who suffer most, even if this would imply that only a very small fraction of all the mentally ill could at all be treated? Or should the resources be applied in such a way that a maximum number of individuals could profit from their application? Is complete cure the goal to aim at in all cases, or is it more rational to help the mentally ill just to the point where they can adapt to society, regardless of their being cured or not?

It is quite all right for psychiatric epidemiologists to answer such questions but it is far more complicated when they are supposed to answer other questions which are *not* asked. These other questions are not asked because they are not decent questions, in spite of the fact that the answers are really those which decide the actions of politicians.

For some politicians the main goal of their activities within the field of mental health planning is not the reduction of the prevalence of psychiatric disorder in the population. Their main interest may be to reduce the costs of mental illness. What is expected by some politicians from mental health programmes is first of all that the problem should be reduced in the view of the public. Reduction of the number of hospitalized patients is a spectacular feature in this respect. The undesired consequences of such a policy are not nearly so visible.

In different countries, different types of social system may cause varying attitudes of politicians towards the care of the mentally ill. I can mention an example which has turned out to be important in Denmark. It is a very popular idea among local politicians that the overcrowding of hospitals is a consequence of the presence there of patients who are not real hospital cases, but rather nursing cases. Such politicians are against building new hospitals and very much in favour of building nursing institutions instead. This seems reasonable, although everybody knows that when these patients are transferred to a nursing institution, the cost of residence there will be exactly the same as the cost in hospital. What differs is the fact that, as long as a patient is in a general hospital run by a local authority, the state will pay only 35 per cent of the costs to the local authority, whereas for nursing institutions the state contribution is 50 per cent or more. No wonder that administrators and politicians quite often approach those engaged in psychiatric epidemiological research with questions concerning how many patients in hospitals could be transferred to nursing institutions.

Now, enough of this disenchanting talk. In the following, such decisive political facts will be disregarded.

It seems natural that I should mention some of the applications of epidemiology which have been made in recent years in Danish mental health service planning. Such planning has become especially needed in Denmark, because four years ago the Danish government decided that the responsibility for psychiatric treatment, which had traditionally been a matter for the state, should be handed over to local authorities (counties) instead. The care for the physically ill had always been a matter for local authorities, and it was now thought that the desirable integration of mental and physical health services could be best carried out if both were under the same administration.

This step would imply a complete remodelling of mental health services. Denmark has five million inhabitants. In addition to the municipality of Copenhagen there are thirteen counties, most of which have 200,000 to 600,000 inhabitants. As the psychiatric state hospitals usually serve more than one county there are several counties which have no psychiatric hospital of their own at present. For such counties it seemed especially important to create as soon as possible a comprehensive plan for the development of mental health services.

Although, as mentioned, the government had decided that local authorities should take over psychiatric services, the government had not said anything about when this should happen. An unwanted consequence of this was that now neither the state nor the local authorities felt psychiatric services to be their responsibility, and no planning whatever was undertaken, either by the state or by the counties.

In this deplorable situation the Danish Psychiatric Association felt obliged to prepare plans for developments which should take place as soon as the counties took over psychiatric services. The result of these efforts was a huge report, published in 1970, which contained a complete plan for the development of psychiatry in general and for all the different branches of psychiatry.

It was felt that as far as possible the conclusions and the planning should be based on empirical data. Fortunately, quite a lot of relevant material was available. First of all, in Denmark, complete statistics of psychiatric institutions have been collected for decades. All admissions to and discharges from psychiatric institutions are reported to a central register. In addition, every five years a census study is performed of the population in psychiatric institutions. Furthermore, a number of more detailed studies in certain localities have been carried out, comprising also those cases which are not admitted to psychiatric institutions. One of these studies is the so-called 'Samsø-study' which concerns the 6,000 inhabitants of the island of Samsø. On this island psychiatrists from the Department of Psychiatry of the University of Aarhus have, since 1967, been in continuous co-operation with the GPs. The aim of this project has been to ascertain all psychiatric cases and to offer them any kind of psychiatric treatment they might need. In this way, a reasonably complete picture of the mental health status of the population has been built up, and as the population of the island can be assumed to be relatively representative of the rural population of Denmark, some generalizations are permissible.

Two census studies have been performed, during which information was gathered about every single inhabitant of the island. The 1964 census gave the result that no less than 1,656 out of 6,013 inhabitants could be stated to present or to have presented psychiatric problems, ie 27 per cent. It was, of course, of great importance to make an estimate concerning the need for psychiatric care which these mentally abnormal cases represented. It was found that 29 per cent of the abnormal cases had already contacted psychiatric services; in addition to these cases, some 14 per cent were estimated to be in need of such attendance, whereas the remaining 58 per cent could probably do as well without any psychiatric help.

These prevalence figures can then be supplemented by incidence figures. During each of the first six years of operation of the project, about 2 per cent of the population were referred for psychiatric examination. During the rest of the period, the figure has been about 1·5 per cent, the decrease probably indicating that during the first years after the start of the project there was an accumulated need for psychiatric assistance. Of the first 500 cases referred only 11 per cent were regarded as being in need of admission to a psychiatric institution. Forty-six per cent needed psychiatric out-patient treatment, and the remaining 43 per cent were regarded as being best served through treatment by their GP.

These studies and a few other field studies recently carried out in Denmark supplemented the hospital statistics in such a way that plans for the mental health services for certain population units could be designed. First, a general plan was made for a unit comprising 30,000 inhabitants. It had been estimated that for the non-metropolitan areas of Denmark there would be a need for 2·0 psychiatric hospital beds per 1,000 inhabitants, 0·5 bed per 1,000 in psychiatric nursing homes, and facilities for 0·5 day-places per 1,000 inhabitants. This would mean that for the 30,000 inhabitants, 60 hospital beds would be required, 15 of them intended for patients who would only spend a few days or weeks in hospital, 15 beds for patients staying for a few months up to one year, and 30 beds for chronic patients. The unit should, in addition, have 15 day-patients and access to about 15 nursing home beds.

These figures, being average figures for the non-metropolitan population of Denmark, should of course be subjected to modifications according to local demographic and social circumstances. An intensive analysis of conditions in each county needs to be carried out. First of all, a radical difference can be anticipated between counties in which there is already a well-developed mental health service, and counties which have until now mainly relied on services placed in neighbouring districts. When these latter counties establish their own services the inclination to seek psychiatric assistance will increase to a considerable degree. No final plan can be constructed on the basis of demands for psychiatric services which have previously been registered in such a population.

Nevertheless, statistics of the psychiatric contacts made by the population during the past decade must serve as the starting point for the calculations. More basic demographic features also need to be taken into account; the present age distribution and its likely future projection for example. Migration is a most important variable; if the population is shrinking because of out-migration, the residual group left behind is likely to have a correspondingly higher morbidity.

Some epidemiological data can give rise to conclusions which at first glance may seem paradoxical. It is, for example, a general experience that schizophrenic patients have a greater chance of discharge if they have relatives. It might therefore be expected that of schizophrenics living in the community those living alone would need more assistance than those living with relatives. The reverse may, however, be true. Nystrup, who recently performed a large-scale follow-up of discharged schizophrenics, found that patients living alone had the best mental status. This was obviously due to the simple fact that schizophrenics who can be discharged to live alone are a selection of patients with a better 'spontaneous' prognosis. This shows how simple epidemiological data can be interpreted and misinterpreted.

For each of the different groups of patients the appropriate number of psychiatric sessions has been calculated, and it was estimated that there would be a need for two senior psychiatrists on the permanent staff, two younger specialists, and two to four residents in psychiatric training. Fifty per cent of the psychiatrists' time should be used for out-patient work. It is a definite trend in the Danish health services that there should be close co-operation with social institutions. Some of the psychiatrists should spend a large amount of their time in such institutions, thus serving as connecting links between social and medical institutions.

A unit of this type with seventy-five patients is regarded as the smallest unit which can function in a rational way. It is, on the other hand, preferable if a number of such units can be placed together. A design has been made for the structure of the psychiatric services for a population of 250,000 inhabitants, corresponding to the size of quite a number of the Danish counties. There would be a need for eight such units which could very well be neighbours to each other and, of fundamental importance, neighbours to the general hospital of the district. It is obvious that co-operation between a number of such units would be rational because they could use the same facilities in many areas. In principle, each of the units should have its own geographical district, thus acting as the centre for community mental health services of that population. On the other hand, when a number of such units are co-operating, there is a possibility that one or two of them, for example units for adolescents or geriatric wards, may be specialized.

It is quite clear that the realization of these plans would imply an increase of staff. It could be estimated that a doubling of the number of doctors working within psychiatry would be necessary. The number of doctors in Denmark will increase quite rapidly in the years to come, and a considerable fraction of them will probably be interested in psychiatry. It is, therefore, not at all unrealistic to believe that the numerical goal can be reached in some ten or fifteen years. The necessary number of psychologists, social workers, and occupational therapists can probably also be reached within a reasonable time. The greatest difficulty will be within the large groups of nursing staff, especially because the number of geriatric patients will increase rapidly. Will it be possible at all to obtain the necessary increase in nursing staff? This again is, partly, a question for demographic research. It can be predicted with reasonable accuracy what the balance between disabled persons and healthy persons will be in, say, fifteen years. Quite recently a survey has been made of the probable development in Denmark of the health and social service systems during the period until 1985. Even on a modest estimate the increase in demand for staff within these sectors will exceed the increase of the total population within the age-groups from which these professions are drawn. This means, obviously, that not only all increase in the population in these age-groups will be absorbed within the social and health sectors, but in addition a number of individuals must be recruited from the so-called productive professions. These grim facts are not very popular among politicians. Nobody has a solution to the problem. It is, of course, a good idea to try to find out how institutions for the disabled can be designed in such a way that the need for staff running them can be reduced as much as possible. All kinds of mechanical equipment should, of course, be available. That most of the problems could be solved by means of a reversal of the general trend towards reduction of the number of working hours per individual is a thing which could not possibly be mentioned, let alone be taken seriously. Not yet, at least. Other solutions may be contemplated vaguely in the background of some people's minds. Is there any connection between the obvious increase of problems of care for the disabled and the fact that in recent years public discussions of the problem of euthanasia are taking place quite frequently? Of course not.

We are all perfectly aware of the great difficulties encountered in epidemiological research and of the care needed whenever results of such research are applied as the basis for health service planning. These problems are, on the other hand, negligible in comparison to the problems caused by some irrational forces which are far more decisive for the development than are the humble facts which can be supplied by epidemiological research.

I may have stressed this side of the problems rather too much in my paper. I hope, however, that this may be permissible in an introductory communication.

Part 2   Statistics for planning

3 International statistics

EILEEN M. BROOKE

What statistics are collected?

Studies recently made by the World Health Organization have confirmed the impression that a great deal of work has been invested in descriptive statistics of mental hospital populations. To get an over-all view of what countries are doing, a questionnaire was sent out by WHO headquarters to member states, asking them whether or not certain simple types of patient statistics were being collected, what was their coverage and on what definitions they were based. Seventy-five countries replied to the questionnaire, of whom 70 produced psychiatric statistics. Of these 70 countries, 63 had data on in-patient admissions and 70 on discharges and deaths, while 52 had statistics of out-patient attendances. Even where such services existed, few states had any statistics about attendances at day-hospitals, day-care centres, or patients who visited the hospital as day-patients. Only 59 countries took a census of patients in hospital on a given day, although such censuses, especially when compared over time, can give valuable information about changes in the short-, medium-, and long-stay populations (Arentsen and Strömgren, 1959; Juel-Nielsen and Strömgren, 1963; Brooke, 1967). Such studies answer questions about the number of beds being blocked by long-stay elderly patients for whom other services might be planned. They also show the rate at which a new potentially long-stay population is being built up under modern conditions and methods of treatment.

The three items of information most commonly obtained for patients admitted or discharged were sex, age, diagnosis, and for discharges, the length of stay. The number of countries concerned is shown in Table 1.

Other data concerned ethnic origin, nationality, country of birth, number of sibs, religion, and occupation, all variables which are extremely difficult to record in a meaningful way and whose effect on mental health is hard to evaluate within any country, let alone internationally.

A second statistical inquiry on an international scale has been developed by the European Regional Office of WHO under the direction of Dr A. R. May. Eight countries were involved in this study when it began in 1969 and an additional 10 in 1970. In 1971 the scheme was extended to all member

Table 1.

	Admissions	Discharges
Sex	51	60
Age	35	40
Diagnosis	42	51
Length of stay		33

states of WHO in the European Region and 31 replies to the questionnaire were received, from 24 independent states, from England and Wales, Scotland, and Northern Ireland separately, from the Federal Republic of Germany and also Bavaria, Baden-Württemburg, and North Rhine-Westphalia.

The aims of the inquiry were to

enable the regional office to build up a picture of mental health services structure and organisation in the individual countries in the Region which ... would be useful in deciding where and in what form WHO assistance could best be applied and would also be of value in the countries concerned if they were able to relate their own problems and experience to those of others [May, 1969].

Information was asked for under three main headings, how the mental health services were organized, what establishments and facilities were provided and what were the manpower resources in terms of personnel and their training. The replies showed that many of the 31 countries were well-informed about manpower. All 31 respondents had data about the total number of psychiatrists and 27 knew the total number of physicians. Twenty-four had statistics of qualified nurses and 20 for auxiliary nurses. In the same way, 29 countries knew the total number of health facility beds and 28 of psychiatric beds. For the ambulatory services, 28 respondents knew the number of out-patients' clinics, 21 the number of attendances made, but only 12 knew how many psychiatrists worked in these services. For day-patients there were data on the number of establishments, and the number of places available from 22 respondents, but on the number of attendances or patients from only 8.

Since all countries have psychiatric hospitals, even if they do not have day facilities, it is perhaps surprising that 14 respondents did not know how many psychiatrists were working in psychiatric hospitals, that 22 had no data on their long-stay patients and 11 no information about the number of admissions; such wide gaps in statistical knowledge do not point to well-developed mental health information systems in the region as a whole, especially since the almost complete information about medical personnel is likely to have been obtained from their professional organizations. Under such conditions planning for the future becomes very difficult.

Table 2. *Number of authorities responsible for the care of psychiatric patients and collection of statistics in thirty member states (or parts of federated territories) of the European Region of WHO.*

Coverage	Number of responsible authorities							Total states
	1	2	3	4	5	6	7	
All services together	—	—	6	7	12	4	1	30
Mentally ill	10	10	4	5	—	1	—	30
Mentally retarded	2	9	10	6	2	1	—	30
Children and adolescents	9	8	7	5	1	—	—	30
Aged	9	10	2	2	—	1	—	24*
Alcoholics	14	7	4	3	—	1	—	29*
Addicts	13	7	5	1	1	—	—	27*
Offenders	10	16	2	1	1	—	—	30
Statistics	11	10	4	3	1	—	—	29

* Not treated separately in some countries.

Difficulties in obtaining psychiatric statistics

Among the chief difficulties of obtaining statistics in the mental health field is the number of organizations involved in the collection of statistics. Not only may different authorities be responsible for the care of the mentally retarded as opposed to the mentally ill, but other authorities again may be concerned with special groups of patients, as Table 2 shows.

Table 2 suffices to show, in the first place, the extraordinary complexity of the organization of mental health services and leads one to wonder whether efficient co-operation exists between the responsible authorities to ensure effective management and the best utilization of resources. Table 2 also points to the difficulty of collecting comprehensive psychiatric statistics at the national level and the even greater one internationally of understanding and interpreting the official statistics published by individual countries. When the European study was being inaugurated, most of the countries in the region were visited either by Dr May or the present writer so that the purpose of the questionnaire could be explained and the interpretation of individual questions discussed on the spot. It was disheartening to find the official statisticians did not always know which sections of their own ministry were responsible for different parts of the psychiatric services, whether these sections were collecting statistics or not, and whom to approach to get the data.

In two-thirds of the countries either one or two authorities are responsible for the collection and presumably publication of statistics. The WHO inquiry referred to above in which data were obtained from 70 countries showed that in 39 countries a government department such as a ministry of health and welfare had the sole responsibility, and in 7 others a government statistical office. In 5 countries they had joint responsibility, for example one collecting and the other publishing the data. In these 51 countries it should be less difficult to introduce internationally agreed definitions and even forms of tabulation, since at the most 2 government institutions were involved. There were, however, 15 countries in which responsibility for publication was shared by 2 or even 3 organizations such as a ministry of health, a university or research department, a central statistical office, or the administrators of a sickness insurance fund. Since each of these will be looking at a different aspect of the provision of psychiatric care, probably using different definitions and covering different sectors of the national population, international comparison of the resulting statistics will be a formidable task. The complexity of the services and difficulties of data collection all too frequently result in statistics being two to three years out of date at the time of publication. In some cases, such as the services for drug-dependent persons, planning cannot wait for the routine statistics and weekly returns may be needed.

Difficulties in the international comparison and interpretation of statistics

One of the chief problems facing those who wish to make international comparisons is how to obtain the data. People do not know where to obtain the statistical publications of other countries, what titles to ask for and how to get the currency needed for payment. This applies also to WHO publications and how to better disseminate statistical data is being actively discussed at the present time. Then there is also the problem of language.

Although countries can learn a great deal by comparing their own statistics of mental health services with those of others, it is essential that each should clearly understand what the others' data represent. There are several major difficulties in the way of such understanding.

Coverage

One of the chief difficulties in comparing statistics is a lack of uniformity in coverage. Although most of the seventy countries in the first WHO study had private psychiatric services, few had any data about them as will be seen from Table 3.

It would be extremely difficult to compare statistics between countries without having any idea of the proportion of beds or places not covered by the statistics. There is an extra problem with federated countries, since the constituent territories may have different reporting systems so that data on the same variables may not be obtained by all.

Method of counting transferred patients

Another source of distortion in the statistics arises from the way in which patients are counted who are transferred from one psychiatric establishment to another. Some count these as discharges from one

Table 3.

For the whole country	In-patients	Out-patients	Day-patients
Both public and private establishments	13	4	1
Public establishments only	20	17	6

hospital and admissions to another. As there is no break in hospitalization involved, such a method falsifies the distribution of length of stay, while inflating the admission and discharge rates. Unfortunately, 48 of the 70 countries in the WHO study counted transferred patients as admissions and discharges, compared with only 16 who counted them separately as transfers out and in.

First admissions

Although many patients admitted to psychiatric hospitals have already been treated in out-patient departments, countries still make a distinction between first and non-first hospital admissions. In the WHO inquiry 37 of the 70 member states involved did so, but only 27 gave their definition. The two main alternatives were either a first admission to a psychiatric hospital in the country or else a first admission to the hospital of admission. Even where care has been taken to lay down a definition of a first admission the extent of error can be considerable. Brooke (1967) found that among 48,000 admissions described as 'first', 1 in 12 had in fact already been admitted to a psychiatric hospital or unit in England and Wales.

Diagnosis

Perhaps the greatest difficulty in international comparisons is related to diagnosis. Kramer (1961) drew attention to the differences in first admission rates between England and Wales and the United States for three main diagnostic groups which accounted between them for 62 per cent of first admissions in England and Wales and 52 per cent of those in the USA (Table 4).

Although applied in this case to the American and British statistics, the following questions will arise wherever there are diagnostic differences in statistics between countries.

1. Are the diagnostic differences real, the American hospital patients being more likely to be schizophrenic and the British depressive?

2. Is there a different type of selection for hospitalization, so that some schizophrenic British and some depressive Americans are treated in other services than psychiatric hospitals?

3. What is the diagnostic effect of the patient's admission being his first? In subsequent admissions would more of these same British patients be diagnosed schizophrenic rather than depressive?

Table 4. *The 1960 age-adjusted first admission rates per 100,000 standardized to the 1950 USA population.*

	England and Wales	USA
Schizophrenia	17·4	24·7
Major affective disorders	38·5	11·0
Manic depressive reaction ⎫	35·7	3·3
Psychotic depressive reaction ⎭		2·9
Involutional psychotic reaction	2·8	4·8
Disorders of the senium	12·9	16·4
Due to cerebral arteriosclerosis	1·8	10·9
Senile psychosis	11·1	5·4

4. Is there a difference between the diagnostic habits of psychiatrists in the two countries, resulting in patients with rather similar symptomatology being called schizophrenic in the USA and depressive in England and Wales?

To evaluate even the hospital services by means of international comparisons it is essential that we should know what kinds of patients are being given hospital care in various countries. There have been three major attempts on an international scale to elucidate the problems relating to diagnosis, which may be recalled here. The US–UK Diagnostic Project answered the questions posed by Kramer (Zubin, 1969; Cooper *et al.*, 1969). The study supposed that diagnostic differences of the size observed fell into two groups:

1. Real differences in the clinical states of the patients from whom the statistics originate (due to differences of prevalence, in the utilization of alternative public or private facilities or to differences in community tolerance of abnormal behaviour).

2. Differences in the diagnostic concepts and terms used by the hospital psychiatrists to describe the patients and by the recording and coding procedures used in the preparation of the statistics.

From the investigation of patients at an American and a British hospital, Cooper and his co-workers concluded that 'both of these influences are operating and to different extents for different diagnoses'.

The International Pilot Study of Schizophrenia being carried out by WHO (Sartorius, Brooke, and Lin, 1970), is a more extensive and ambitious study designed to show whether the diagnosis of schizophrenia represents the same kind of pathology between as well as within countries, and whether this diagnostic group is significantly distinguished from the group of affective disorders. Nine centres are participating in the study, which has the further advantages of collecting data about the patients' psychiatric history and social conditions and also of following up the patients at one-

and two-yearly intervals from their first psychiatric examination with a view to the possible confirmation of the diagnosis.

The WHO programme on diagnosis, classification, and statistics. This work has been carried out in annual seminars, each of which has been devoted to one of the main areas of psychopathology. The methodology, consisting partly of written diagnostic exercises and partly of diagnosing from videotaped interviews, was developed for the first seminar held in London in 1965 and is described by Shepherd *et al.* (1968). Seven seminars have so far been held, and the results, to be subsumed at the next meeting in September 1972, will be used to draw up proposals for the next revision of the *International Classification of Diseases.*

The most important part of this programme is the development of an internationally agreed Glossary of Psychiatric Terminology which could be issued for use with the next revision of the *ICD*. Such a system would not mean that any country had to sacrifice, for internal use, its own national system of classification of mental disorders, but that for statistical purposes, diseases showing certain syndromes would, by common agreement, be assigned to specific categories of the classification. The advantages for planning and evaluation would be great, since if, for example, one country claimed to treat half of its schizophrenic patients in the ambulatory services, others would have a much clearer idea than at present of the type of illness involved.

The psychiatric bed

One of the most hotly debated topics in all countries is that of the requisite number of psychiatric beds. Where the ratio of beds per 1,000 is low, the question arises whether to build more hospitals or to rely on ambulatory services. Where the ratio is high, other countries will ask what is happening (or not happening) in these countries, that makes them need so many beds. Before this question can be tackled it is necessary to define a psychiatric bed and then to make sure that everyone is using the same definition. There would no doubt be general agreement that beds in psychiatric hospitals, including those for the mentally retarded, and in special psychiatric wards in general hospitals, should be classed as psychiatric beds. There are, however, a whole range of 'fringe' beds, for which it is necessary to decide whether to count them as psychiatric beds or not. Are they to be defined as psychiatric beds if they are in a psychiatric hospital but are not used for psychiatric patients? Are they to be counted as psychiatric beds if used by psychiatric patients, no matter where they are? How are beds in hostels for ex-patients to be counted, or beds in day-hospitals used for ECT sessions?

In order to bring home to psychiatrists, medical administrators, and others working in the field, the difficulties in counting psychiatric beds and

Table 5. *Total beds regarded as psychiatric beds by forty-three persons working in the mental health field.*

Total beds	Type of worker				
	All	Psychiatrist	Medical administrator	Other medical	Non-medical
101–50	3	2	1	—	—
151–200	4	—	1	—	3
201–300	2	2	—	—	—
301–400	2	2	—	—	—
401–500	6	3	1	—	4
501–50	8	3	1	—	4
551–600	8	6	—	1	1
601–50	7	7	—	—	—
651–700	3	2	1	—	—

the need for uniform definitions if comparable data are to be obtained, an exercise was devised which listed various facilities in a fictitious town called Highwood. These included Highwood General Hospital (for which 8 wards or units are described), the District Hospital for Nervous and Mental Diseases (4 units), an institute for mentally retarded patients (3 units), a facility for autistic children, a convalescent home for ex-patients who will return to hospital before discharge, a day-hospital giving ECT sessions, a half-way house, and two hostels for ex-patients visited weekly by a psychiatric social worker. In all a total number of 798 beds was mentioned, and those who did the exercise had to say in each case how many beds they would count as psychiatric beds.

The exercise has been done by 43 people, including 27 psychiatrists, 4 medical administrators, 3 other medically qualified persons, and 9 lay persons, sociologists, statisticians, or administrators. Their geographical distribution was as follows:

One each for Algeria, Austria, Bulgaria, Czechoslovakia, Denmark, England, Ireland, Morocco, Norway, Sweden, Turkey, USSR, Yugoslavia.

Two each for Belgium, Greece, Holland, Italy, Roumania, Spain (one of whom did the exercise twice with a fifteen-month interval).

Four for Switzerland.

Six for France.

Seven for the Federal Republic of Germany.

Table 5 indicates wide differences of opinion on what is a psychiatric bed. An interesting example of this was the interpretation placed upon 'a ward of 10 beds for tuberculous mental patients under the care of a specialist in chest diseases'. This item was listed for both the General Hospital and the Hospital for Nervous and Mental Diseases. Twenty persons counted 10 psychiatric beds in each hospital, 3 counted the beds as psychiatric only in the General Hospital, 11 only in the Hospital for Nervous and Mental Diseases, 8 did not count them as psychiatric beds in

Table 6. *Distribution by number of beds for mental illness per 1,000 population.*

Population (000s)	Beds	Population (000s)	Beds
<1	3	3·00–3·49	2
1·00–1·49	6	3·50–3·99	1
1·50–1·99	1	4·00–4·49	2
2·00–2·49	3	4·50–4·99	3
2·50–2·99	4	>5	1

either place, and the remaining respondent, with some ingenuity, counted 5 in each hospital.

The exercise, adapted for Holland, has now been done by a group of Dutch psychiatrists, sociologists, and GPs. Firstly each participant used his own definition, then there was a general discussion, a definition was agreed upon and the exercise done again. Although there was some improvement, agreement remained far from complete when the definition was taken into account.

The study referred to above, being carried out by the European Regional Office, purports to include all beds used for psychiatric patients no matter where located, so as to give an indication of the total resources for each country. For twenty-six countries or parts of federated territories the distribution by number of beds for mental illness per 1,000 population was as shown in Table 6.

The countries with less than 2 beds per 1,000 fell into two groups, one comprising some less economically favoured countries and the other a group of eastern European countries with the dispensary system and socialized medicine. To balance their low bed ratios, these countries had highly developed out-patient services as measured by the number of out-patient attendances per 100 in-patient days, which ranged from 27·7 to 11·5. The countries with 2 but less than 4 beds per 1,000 constitute a band running roughly from north to south through western and central Europe. Highly industrialized and wealthy and with heavy urban concentrations of population, their out-patient services are less developed than those of their eastern neighbours. Finally there is the group with 4 beds per 1,000 or more, which includes the Scandinavian countries, Scotland, Ireland, and Belgium, with out-patient indicators ranging from 0·8 to 7·6. In most of these countries geographical factors are likely to influence the development of out- and day-patient care.

At one end of the scale is Turkey with 0·22 psychiatric beds per 1,000 population and a total of 1·9 beds for all health services combined, and with 2·0 out-patient attendances per 100 in-patient days, while at the other extreme is Ireland with 5·96 psychiatric and 20·4 total health service beds per 1,000 and an out-patient attendance index of 2·4. It is very clear that none of these figures can be adequately interpreted without a detailed knowledge of the socio-economic and demographic characteristics of the countries concerned. It is also essential to relate the psychiatric services to other health services. A high ratio of psychiatric beds where a large proportion of resident patients is aged 65 years or more may merely indicate a lack of suitable accommodation for geriatric patients.

What is being done to improve international statistics?

It may be deduced from what has already been said, that there are many dangers and difficulties in the way of using psychiatric statistics for international comparison. One of these is due to a wide range of data descriptive of patients being collected, compared with few data on the working of the services or the socio-demographic background in which mental illnesses develop. One method of improvement would be to persuade countries to produce a limited number of data with standardized definitions. And here I would draw attention to Brooke's Law, which says that the amount of data required for the management and evaluation of psychiatric services varies inversely as the size of the unit to which the data relate. At the level of the individual patient a very large amount of information is required for treatment, rehabilitation, and maintenance. To run a hospital or ambulatory service, far less is needed. The administrator at the national level needs less data again while at the international stage it is only worthwhile comparing a few carefully selected items of information obtained in a systematic and standardized way.

Many of the difficulties of cross-national comparisons of mental health statistics stem indeed from a lack of standardized definitions. Hence one method of improvement would be to try to persuade countries to first agree to such definitions and then to use them. That this would be a heavy task can be judged from the time it took to formulate and introduce a standard definition of a still-birth. Another method of trying to improve psychiatric statistics while at the same time showing member states their value in planning has been adopted by the European Regional Office of WHO. In connection with the long-term programme in mental health developed by Dr May, uniform data collection for special groups of patients is being carried out.

The first of these experimental studies began in 1970, when representatives from ten countries agreed upon a data collection sheet for the out-patient services. Subsequently two other countries joined the study, which was carried out in a wide variety of specialized and non-specialized clinics, both in faculties of medicine and other psychiatric services. The results of this pilot inquiry were shown to a general meeting of countries in the European Region in 1972, and a second group of countries is now being formed which will carry out the same exercise. A similar study relating to psycho-geriatric patients has now started in another group of countries, again using standard data sheets and instructions agreed upon by the countries concerned, while an exercise on the mentally subnormal will follow on in the series.

In these statistical exercises, not only the patients but also the clinics or other facilities involved are being studied simultaneously, and in particular for the psycho-geriatric patients, alternative services are being examined. The results of all these studies will be extremely useful when meetings on the methodology of evaluating services come into the programme of the Regional Office.

One may ask, however, how such studies, and the general collection of statistics, can influence the development of the psychiatric services in any country, and here it is essential to state that only the responsible authorities in a country can take this decision; it is not possible for an outsider to tell any country what it ought to do. The development of any form of health service is influenced by an enormous number of factors and even if some of these appear irrational, there is nothing to be done. However, most people are interested in what their neighbours are doing and especially in the results obtained.

For this reason it is proposed to establish in the European Region, certain model reporting centres for the examination and evaluation of psychiatric services. These centres will be in countries with differing types of psychiatric services, administered in different ways, and served by psychiatrists and other workers coming from different schools of training. Nevertheless, each will be typical of a number of other countries or centres. In each centre an area will be defined and the social, economic, geographic, and demographic characteristics determined. The health resources of the chosen area in terms of establishments and personnel will also be assessed. It will be necessary to establish a psychiatric register, ensuring the follow-up of patients, and to analyse the data in a meaningful way with regard to the evaluative purpose for which the register has been established. Such centres, by reason of the existence of background data, will be suitable for the development of studies in depth. The establishment of the centres and collection of information will be a long and difficult but also extremely worthwhile task. Their ultimate purpose, as envisaged by Dr May, is that any inquirer visiting one of the centres can be told: 'Here we do this, that and the other, for such kinds of patients, in such and such a setting and these are the results.' Those coming from other countries will be better able to see what they might like to adopt or adapt for their own services. Instead of the present tendency to urge everyone to adopt community psychiatry or group therapy or industrial work, a psychiatric shop-window will be developed, filled with goods that have been tested and can be guaranteed.

REFERENCES

Arentsen, K., and Strömgren, E. (1959). 'Patients in Danish psychiatric hospitals', *Acta Jutlandica*, **31**, 1, Medical Series 9 (Copenhagen: Munksgaard).

Brooke, E. M. (1963). *A Cohort Study of Patients first admitted to Mental Hospitals in 1954 and 1955*, GRO Studies on Medical and Population Subjects no 18 (London: HMSO).

—— (1967) *A Census of Patients in Psychiatric Beds, 1963*, Ministry of Health Reports on Public Health and Medical Subjects no. 116 (London: HMSO).

Cooper, J., Kendell, R., Gurland, B., Sartorius, N., and Farkas, T. (1969). 'Cross-national study of diagnosis in the mental disorders', *Am. J. Psychiat.* supplement, **125**, 10.

Juel-Nielsen, N., and Strömgren, E. (1963). 'Five years later', *Acta Jutlandica*, **35**, 1, Medical Series 15 (Copenhagen: Munksgaard).

Kramer, M., Pollack, E., and Redick, R. (1961). 'Studies of the incidence and prevalence of hospitalised mental disorders in the United States: current status and future goals', in Hoch, P., and Zubin, J. (eds), *Comparative Epidemiology of the Mental Disorders* (New York: Grune and Stratton).

May, A. R. (1969). *The Application of Mental Health Statistics in the European Region of WHO*, EURO 0192/3 (Copenhagen: WHO Regional Office for Europe).

Sartorius, N., Brooke, E. M., and Lin, T. Y., (1970). 'Reliability of psychiatric assessment in international research', in Hare, E. H., and Wing, J. K. (eds), *Psychiatric Epidemiology* (Oxford University Press for the Nuffield Provincial Hospitals Trust).

Shepherd, M., Brooke, E. M., Cooper, J., and Lin, T. Y. (1968). 'An experimental approach to psychiatric diagnosis', *Acta Psychiat. Scand.* supplement 201.

Zubin, J. (1969). 'Cross-national study of diagnosis of the mental disorders: methodology and planning' *Am. J. Psychiat.* supplement, **125**, 10.

4 The role of a national statistics programme in the planning of community psychiatric services in the United States

MORTON KRAMER and CARL A. TAUBE

INTRODUCTION

During the past decade increased emphasis has been placed on the use of rational and scientific methods in planning health services and evaluating their effectiveness. The activities of WHO in national health planning illustrate action at the international level to stimulate this development (WHO Expert Committees: Health Statistics, 1967, 1969, 1971; Hospital Administration, 1968; National Health Planning, 1970). Recent legislation passed in the US for construction and staffing of community mental health centres (Public Laws PL 88–164, 1963; Amendments PL 89–105, 1965; PL 90–31, 1966; PL 90–574, 1968; PL 91–211, 1970) and comprehensive health planning (PL 89–749, 1966) illustrate actions taken at the national level within the US to require administrators of health programmes to engage in systematic health planning and evaluation activities.

Although there are differences of opinion as to how best to utilize demographic data, health, vital, morbidity, social, and economic statistics and inventories of health facilities in the health planning process, there is essentially universal agreement on the need for such data for this purpose. Thus, the Eighteenth World Health Assembly (1965) emphasized that the types of data just enumerated are an essential prerequisite for health planning.[1] The WHO Committee on Health Statistics stated that statistics are needed:

1. Report of the technical discussions at the Eighteenth World Health Assembly: Health Planning (1965) (Geneva: WHO) (unpublished document A181 Technical Discussions/6 Rev. 1).

... (1) to assist in the administration and coordination of health services and their effective management; (2) for the short- and long-term planning of services; (3) for measuring accomplishment in terms of effectiveness and efficiency; (4) for research purposes and to provide background information for use by the administration, legislative bodies and the public [WHO Expert Committee on Health Statistics, 1971].

With respect to the legislation in the US, the Community Mental Health Centers Act of 1963 required each State that wished to qualify for funds to construct centres to submit a State-wide plan which includes among other things:

... a program for construction of community mental health centers which is based on an inventory of facilities for the entire State ...; which will meet the requirements for furnishing needed services to persons unable to pay therefor; which will deal with the State on an 'area' basis and will rank the designated areas according to relative need; and which will state the probable location of, and the relative need for, construction projects [National Institute of Mental Health, 1965].

The regulations governing the implementation of these Acts (Code of Federal Regulations, 1971*a*, *b*, *c*) virtually require administrators, in developing their plans for construction and staffing of centres, to take into account the epidemiology of the mental disorders within the boundaries of their states and communities, the current patterns of delivery of psychiatric services, the effectiveness of such services and interrelationships between mental disorders and other social problems. These public laws and regulations demonstrate clearly that the highest legislative authorities in the US have taken seriously recommendations made over the years by epidemiologists, biostatisticians, social scientists, and other persons concerned that sound epidemiological and statistical techniques must be applied to the planning and evaluation of public health and medical care programmes.

Some of the requirements for various types of statistics for planning community mental health programmes go far beyond our current capabilities for collecting them. For example, no country in the world has as yet been able to establish a system for the collection of prevalence and incidence data on the mental disorders. The major impediments to accomplishing this have been the absence of a standard case-finding technique that can be used in a uniform and consistent fashion to detect persons in the general population with mental disorders and differential diagnostic techniques to make it possible to assign each case to a specific diagnostic category with a high degree of reliability. As Frost stated in a classic paper on epidemiology published in 1927 (Frost, 1927):

... since the description of the distribution of any disease in a population obviously requires that the disease must be recognized when it occurs, the development of epidemiology must follow and be limited by that of clinical diagnosis and of the rather complex machinery required for the systematic collection of morbidity and mortality statistics.

As a result, no health agency has yet developed a mechanism for the systematic collection of morbidity data on the mental disorders which can be used to provide reliable current estimates of the total incidence and prevalence of these disorders in the population of a state, city, county, or other geographic subdivision.

Despite the absence of basic morbidity data on the mental disorders, it is possible to develop a statistical system that will provide systematic data on the number, distribution, and characteristics of psychiatric facilities, and of patients utilizing them. Operational data obtained from administrative records on the material and personnel resources of psychiatric facilities and from records of patients under their care can provide a firm starting point for planning and evaluating programmes related to the control and reduction of disability from these disorders. Facts derived from these records, used in conjunction with data from the Census of Population, are of value in that they may be used to demonstrate the volume of services for treatment and rehabilitation of patients available to a community through these resources; the staffing of such services; the extent to which they are used and the characteristics of persons making use of them. Often they provide indications of the success or failure of programmes and delineate more clearly the additional knowledge needed to assess the effectiveness of programmes of care, treatment, and rehabilitation in the control of mental disorders (American Public Health Association, 1962).

This paper will demonstrate how data derived from such a statistical system are being used in community mental health developments in the US.

DEFINITIONS

For the statistician to be helpful in planning community mental health programmes he must understand what is meant by planning and by community mental health programmes.

Planning

For purposes of this discussion, the definition to be followed is that of the WHO Expert Committee on Health Statistics (1971). This committee has stated:

It (i.e. planning) is essentially an administrative instrument intended to provide a more rational basis for decision making. Perhaps its most important concern is with the allocation of scarce resources and with insuring that services are made available and provided in a more equitable manner. Administration is concerned with questions of allocation of resources, and planning is intended to improve decision-making in this connection. . . . The principal concern of the health planner is with the health of the population, and he is consequently also concerned with the planning of health services; the overall objectives are similar.

If these notions are applied to the planning of community mental health services, it follows that an essential function of the planner(s) of such services is to determine how to allocate resources so that necessary mental health services are made available to a population and provided in a more equitable manner. Indeed, the Community Mental Health Centers Act and its Regulations state that this must be done.

The WHO Expert Committee on Health Statistics (1971) also identified five steps that generally constitute the planning process:

1. *Situational analysis* or the description, definition, or statement of the problem, its characteristics and dimensions in relation to population and time.

2. *The formulation of alternative tactical approaches to the handling and solution of the problem;* ie, formulating alternative solutions or plans and working out their implications in terms of cost potential effectiveness and the decision-making process.

3. *Decision analyses* or the selection of a plan, based on discussions of the alternatives and the balancing of political, cultural, social, and economic considerations against estimates of the biological, psychological, and social consequences.

4. *Discussion and implementation of the plan selected,* two closely related functions which determine the procedures and actions to be carried out; their success is dependent on the acceptance of the plan by both providers and consumers of service.

5. *Evaluation of the results achieved by the services in relation to the problems, situations, or populations concerned;* ie, the measurement of the results achieved in relation to the effort expended.

Community mental health programme

Although there is no universally accepted definition of a community mental health programme, the following are conceptualizations which seem to apply to many of the situations with which we are familiar.

The application of public health principles to the promotion of mental health and to the prevention and control of mental disorders in a population has led to the development of the concept of a community mental health programme. The notion underlying such programmes is that a series of activities can be carried out by various governmental and voluntary agencies of a community and by the citizens themselves which, on the one hand, will eventually improve the mental health of the inhabitants of the community and, on the other, reduce the amount of disability caused by mental disorders. The agencies involved are those responsible for the health, welfare, educational, religious, recreational, and related activities of a community, as well as those responsible for the maintenance of law and order.

To raise the level of mental health of the community, two principal techniques are used. First, professional mental health workers provide consultative services to the personnel of the various agencies enumerated above on the utilization of techniques for improving interpersonal relationships and for developing sensitivity to factors which affect the emotional well-being of individuals. Second, mental health personnel carry out programs of mental health education in order to 'communicate knowledge regarding human personality to other professionals, to the general public and to teachers, physicians, ministers, parents, policemen and other individuals who have, because of their occupation or other relations, special responsibilities for the welfare and the mental health of other persons' (Milbank Memorial Fund, 1956).

To prevent and control disability from mental disorders, additional techniques are used. Primary prevention of a limited number of mental disorders is accomplished by applying on a community-wide basis knowledge which has been demonstrated to lower the rates at which certain disorders occur. Early diagnostic and intensive treatment services are developed to control those disorders which cannot be prevented, and various other services are developed to reduce the burden of disability among the chronically ill population. Finally, programmes are developed to rehabilitate persons who have suffered from mental disorders (Gruenberg, 1957).

Although community mental health programmes attempt to include most of the elements described above, considerable variation exists among them in the relative emphasis placed on activities related to mental health promotion, those related to prevention of mental disorders, and those related to treatment and rehabilitation. As a result of differences in community organization, of relationships between official and voluntary agencies, of availability of personnel, and of the characteristics of the population groups being served, considerable variation also exists in the way the agencies responsible for various elements of these programmes implement and co-ordinate their activities at the State, county, city, and local levels (Kramer *et al.*, 1961).

In the US the Community Mental Health Centers Program is underway which is designed to implement many of the notions described above.

DESCRIPTION OF NATIONAL PROGRAMMES IN THE UNITED STATES

For the purposes of this paper, the authors will concentrate on the role of statistics in fulfilling two of the five steps that constitute the planning process (situational analysis and evaluation) for the Community Mental Health Centers Program which has been underway in the US since 1963.

In particular, we will describe uses of data collected through the statistical system at the national level on patterns of use of psychiatric facilities, on the staffing and financing of these facilities, and types of services provided. We will then illustrate tabulations that can be generated from such a system to provide data relevant to the planning of community mental health centres and monitoring changes in the patterns of use of psychiatric services that accompany such a programme.

So that the reader will have some understanding of the relevance of the National Reporting Program to the Community Mental Health Centers Program, a brief description will be given of each.

For collection and analysis of data from mental health facilities

The main elements of the National Reporting Program are:

1. An inventory of mental health facilities which collects data on individual facilities regarding services provided, case-load, staffing patterns, and expenditures.

2. An annual census of patients which collects data on the age, sex, and diagnostic distribution of patients served in selected mental health facilities.

3. A sample survey of patient characteristics which collects detailed social and demographic data on persons served in mental health facilities.

The universe of facilities covered by this programme include: (a) psychiatric hospitals; (b) general hospital psychiatric services; (c) community mental health centres; (d) other multi-component mental health facilities; (e) residential treatment centres for emotionally disturbed children; (f) out-patient mental health facilities; (g) mental health day/night facilities; (h) transitional mental health facilities. Definitions of these different facility types are provided in the *Mental Health Directory* for the United States (National Clearinghouse for Mental Health Information, 1971).

The data generated by this programme serve several general functions such as: (a) measuring progress towards broad national mental health goals; (b) measuring the progress toward goals of specific NIMH organizational units; (c) documenting and justifying the need for various NIMH programmes; (d) providing data to persons planning mental health services and evaluating their effectiveness; (e) providing data for lay and professional education; (f) highlighting priority problems for basic and applied research on clinical, epidemiologic, demographic, and related related problems; (g) providing data necessary for the recommendation of new policy or legislation.

For Community Mental Health Centers Program

A community mental health centre is designed to provide a comprehensive co-ordinated programme of mental health services located in one or more facilities in the community (US Department of Health, Education, and Welfare, 1970). Whether the services are offered at one location or more, they comprise a unified programme permitting continuity of patient care. Centre programmes vary widely, each reflecting its community's special resources and needs. The purpose of the centre is to provide a varied range of accessible and co-ordinated services to help prevent mental illness and to treat the mentally ill. The centre's programme is designed to assist a patient in finding the type of care he needs in his own community. An essential feature is to provide patients with 'continuity of care' through a system of co-ordinated services which enables a patient to move easily from one type of service to another as his needs dictate so that the treatment he is receiving at any time is appropriate to the course of his illness. To help assure continuity of care, a central record-keeping system makes the patient's records readily available to authorized personnel of various services of the centre.

To qualify for Federal funds a centre must provide at least five essential services:

1. *In-patient care,* which offers treatment to patients who need twenty-four-hour hospitalization.

2. *Out-patient care,* which offers patients individual, group, or family therapy while permitting them to live at home and go about their daily activities.

3. *Partial hospitalization,* which offers either day-care for patients able to return home in the evenings, or night-care for patients able to work but in need of further care and who are usually without suitable home arrangements. It must include day-care, and, to the extent possible, night-care and/or weekend care.

4. *Emergency care,* which offers emergency psychiatric services at any hour around the clock.

5. *Consultation and education,* which is made available by the centre staff to community agencies and professional personnel.

In addition to the basic five essential services, a centre may offer the following for a full comprehensive programme: (6) rehabilitation services; (7) training; (8) research and evaluation; and (9) special services which may be offered particular groups such as children, the elderly, citizens, alcoholics, or the retarded. Special services may also be developed to assist in solving community problems such as drug abuse, suicide, or juvenile delinquency.

These services are to be provided on a catchment area basis. Each centre serves a defined population group of not less than 75,000 or more than 200,000 persons. For example, in an urban area a centre may serve an inner city neighbourhood of up to 200,000. In a rural area small localities or counties in one or adjacent states may join together to form a centre and share its facilities.

As of June 1971, 452 centres have been funded and 300 were in operation. The catchment areas of the operating centres include a total population of 40 million persons, or 22 per cent of the total population of the US. When the remaining funded centres are in operation, the population covered will increase to 68 million persons, or 33 per cent of the US population. However, it must be remembered that, in addition to the centres, the following major types of psychiatric facilities were also in operation throughout the US as of January 1970: 310 State and county mental hospitals; 34 Veterans' Administration neuropsychiatric hospitals; 146 private mental hospitals; 783 general hospital psychiatric facilities; 2,000 out-patient psychiatric services.

The extent to which centres co-ordinate and integrate their programmes with those of other facilities varies considerably. Developing the necessary relationships to accomplish this in a way that would optimize the delivery of mental health services to the residents of a catchment area is a matter of considerable importance. This will be discussed further below (p. 51).

EXAMPLES OF DATA RELEVANT TO PLANNING

As indicated above, the regulations for the implementation of the community mental health programme requires that essential background data on characteristics of population, distribution of mental disorders, and patterns of psychiatric care be used in the development of plans for the construction and staffing of such centres (Code of Federal Regulations, 1971*a, b, c*). In the following pages, a limited number of illustrations will be given of how data collected through the National Reporting Program can be utilized to provide background for planning (ie, to fulfill the preconditions for planning), to monitor the extent to which some of the simpler goals of the Community Mental Health Centers Program are being met and to detect problems planners must consider if programmes are to meet the needs of certain target populations. Although such data are national in scope (ie, apply to the nation as a whole and in some instances to the States), they provide prototypes for States and local areas in developing data for planning services at the local catchment area level. Other illustrations will be given as to how statisticians can assist planners in establishing goals of programmes, translating these into quantitative terms and outlining steps to be taken to obtain data for assessing the extent to which objectives are being met. In some instances, the data required are relatively simple to collect and to analyse. In others, carefully designed studies and complicated survey designs are needed to collect the relevant data.

Demographic characteristics of catchment areas

Planning requires basic information on the demography of the population to be served. The NIMH is developing basic population data for each of the 1,511 catchment areas in the US. The data are derived from the 1970 Census of Population but regrouped to conform to catchment areas. The characteristics selected for tabulation are those which studies of epidemiology, sociology, and human ecology of mental disorders have demonstrated as identifying high risk populations; that is, population groups which are characterized by high rates of social disorganization and disruption (Redick and Goldsmith, 1971).[1] These data are stored on computer tapes, and programs have been developed to abstract items from these tapes which will produce for each catchment area not only age, sex, race distributions of the population, but also a whole series of statistics on economic, social, and educational status; ethnic composition, household composition, and family structure, style of life, conditions of housing, and community instability.

These basic population data are needed to provide not only estimates of potential numbers of persons with various characteristics who are to be served, but also denominators for utilization rates specific for such characteristics. More rapid progress has been made in developing denominator than numerator data. Statistical systems collecting data on characteristics of patients are the usual source of the numerators for the utilization rates. So that patients can be assigned to various demographic categories, it is essential that their records include the relevant items defined as in the Census of Population. Otherwise, numerators derived from facility records will not be comparable to the denominators derived from the Census.

The Biometry Branch is collaborating in several pilot projects designed to develop numerator data. These projects are: (*a*) the Multi-State Information System which has developed uniform records, data collection procedures, and computer programs for storage and retrieval of patient data; (*b*) a programme developing detailed data on characteristics of patients admitted to a community mental health centre programme in the District of Columbia; and (*c*) a project being carried out in a mental health catchment area of New York City designed to provide more insight into the utilization patterns of community mental health centres versus other types of facilities specific for various demographic characteristics of patients.[2]

Patterns of use of psychiatric facilities

Many mental health programmes collect data on patterns of use of mental hospitals and other psychiatric facilities. The annual reports of ministries of health and central statistical bureaux contain numerous examples of tabulations of first admission, readmission, resident patient, discharge and death data for mental hospitals and other types of psychiatric facilities. Indeed, many of the persons present at this meeting have utilized such data to make significant contributions to our knowledge of the epidemiology of

1. Copies of this publication are available from the Biometry Branch, NIMH, 5600 Fishers Lane, Rockville, Maryland 20852, USA.

2. Descriptions of these projects, including sample forms, are available from the Biometry Branch, NIMH.

mental disorders and the fate of mental patients admitted to mental hospitals. From the point of view of community mental health programmes, patient movement data specific for age, sex, diagnosis, and various socio-economic variables must now be tabulated and analysed specific for the catchment area or other appropriate subdivision of the population for which services are being planned.

Patient care episodes

For the most part, the indexes derived from the types of patient movement data referred to above have been used to describe patterns of utilization of separate facilities. However, planning for community mental health services frequently required data that provided an overview of the utilization patterns of all facilities providing psychiatric services to the residents of a defined catchment area. Such an overview can be obtained by creating an index based on patient care episodes. Patient care episodes are defined as the number of persons under care in a specified facility as of the beginning of the year plus the total admission *actions* during the following twelve months. To obtain a measure of the volume of services provided by all the facilities, the patient care episodes for each facility can be combined. These episodes specific for type of facility, age, and sex provide a measure of the rates of utilization of that facility by specific subgroups of the population.

During 1966, a year before community mental health centres began operating in any significant number, the universe of psychiatric services defined by the State and county, Veterans' Administration and private mental hospitals, general hospitals with psychiatric services and out-patient clinics provided 2,764,089 care episodes to the population of the US, a rate of 1,427 per 100,000 population.

Fig. 1a shows the number of patient care episodes per 100,000 population specific for age and type of facility for the US during 1966. This figure emphasizes the considerable disparity among the various age-groups in the use of different facilities. The out-patient clinics provide services predominantly to persons under 35 years of age, and the mental hospitals to persons 35 years and over. The rate for mental hospitals increases with advancing age while that for out-patient clinics and general hospitals decreases. The high patient care episode rate in mental hospitals for the age-group 65 years and over is accounted for by two factors: the large number of patients in the resident population who grew old in the hospital setting (essentially patients with the functional psychoses and the brain syndromes) and the high admission rate for patients with mental disorders of the senium (brain syndromes with cerebral arteriosclerosis and senile brain disease).

The admission rates for 1966 specific for sex are given in Fig. 2. The male rates to State, county, and Veterans' Administration hospitals exceed

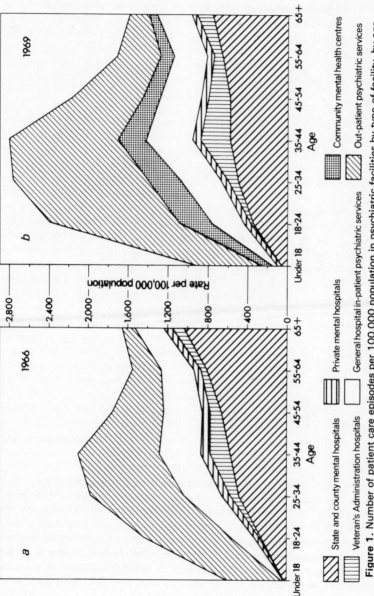

Figure 1. Number of patient care episodes per 100,000 population in psychiatric facilities by type of facility, by age, United States, 1966 and 1969.

State and county mental hospitals

Veteran's Administration hospitals

Private mental hospitals

General hospital in-patient psychiatric services

Community mental health centres

Out-patient psychiatric services

Rate per 100,000 population

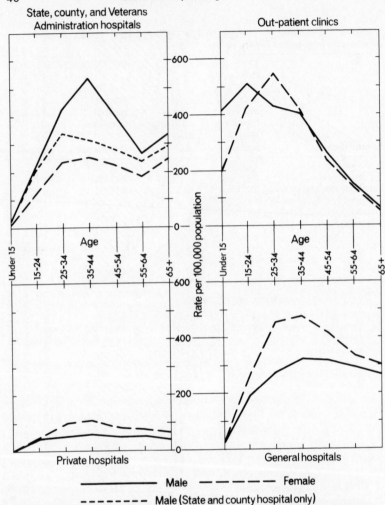

Figure 2. Number of admissions during the year per 100,000 population to public and private mental hospitals, general hospitals with psychiatric clinics by age and sex, United States, 1966.

those for females in every age-group, while in the private mental hospitals and general hospitals the female rates are higher. In the out-patient clinics male admission rates exceed the female by a considerable amount in the under 15 and 15–24 years age-groups. The female rate is higher only in the age-group 25–34 years, and in the remaining groups the male rates are slightly higher. Brain syndromes, schizophrenia, depressive, alcoholic, personality, psychoneurotic, and transient situational personality disorders are the major categories of mental disorders. The relative importance of

Table 1. *Rank order of major categories of mental disorders among patient movement categories by type of facility, United States, 1966. (Percentage of all disorders in specified facility = 100.)*

Mental disorder	TYPE OF FACILITY AND PATIENT MOVEMENT CATEGORY			
	State and county mental hospitals *First admissions*	Private mental hospitals *First admissions*	Psychiatric services general hospitals *Discharges*	Out-patient clinics *Terminations*
Brain syndromes†	1 (22%)	*	5 (11%)	*
Schizophrenia	2 (19%)	2 (19%)	3 (15%)	3 (16%)
Alcoholic disorders‡	3 (18%)	4 (8%)	4 (12%)	*
Personality disorders§	4 (11%)	5 (8%)	*	1 (23%)
Depressive disorders‖	5 (10%)	1 (33%)	1 (27%)	4 (13%)
Psychoneurotic disorders¶	*	3 (10%)	2 (15%)	5 (12%)
Transient situational personality disorders	*	*	*	2 (18%)

* Disorder not among first five for specified facility.

† Brain syndromes: excludes brain syndromes associated with alcoholism.

‡ Alcoholic disorders: includes brain syndromes associated with alcohol and the category of alcoholism from the personality disorders.

§ Personality disorders: includes all personality disorders except alcoholism.

‖ Depressive disorders: includes all affective psychoses and psychoneurotic depressive reaction.

¶ Psychoneurotic disorders: includes all psychoneurotic disorders except psychoneurotic depressive reaction.

each category of disorder varied considerably by type of facility. This is shown in Table 1 for first admissions to State and county and private mental hospitals, discharges from general hospitals in the psychiatric services and terminations from out-patient clinics in 1966. The differences in length of stay produced the distributions shown in Table 2 for resident patients in State, county, and private mental hospitals.

Time series of patient care episodes can also be useful in charting trends in patterns of use of psychiatric facilities. This is illustrated in Table 3 which shows the striking changes in the use of specific facilities from 1955, when the resident population of the mental hospitals was at its highest level, to 1969. In 1955, in-patient facilities accounted for 70 per cent of all patient care episodes while in 1969, the corresponding proportion was 47 per cent. Also, community mental health centres accounted for 10 per cent of all episodes by 1969.

Tabulations of the total additions[1] to mental health facilities by modality of care (in-patient, out-patient, and day-care services) and type of facility

1. The term additions' is used to designate the total of new admissions, readmissions, and returns from leave for a specific facility.

Table 2. _Rank order of major categories of mental disorders among resident patients of state, county, and private mental hospitals, United States, 1966. (Percentage of all disorders in specified facility = 100.)_

Mental disorder	State and county mental hospitals	Private mental hospitals
Schizophrenia	1 (48%)	1 (26%)
Brain syndromest	2 (23%)	3 (17%)
Mental deficiency	3 (8%)	*
Depressive disorders‖	4 (5%)	2 (20%)
Alcoholic disorders‡	5 (5%)	*
Personality disorders§	*	4 (9%)
Psychoneurotic disorders¶	*	5 (5%)

See Table 1 for notes *–¶

Notes to Table 3

* Patient care episodes. The sum of the two numbers: ie, residents at beginning of year or on the active rolls of the out-patient clinics, plus admission during the year, is called patient care episodes. The number of patients at the beginning of the year is an unduplicated count and is equal to the number of individual patients in this status. The number of admissions contains a certain amount of duplicaion. Since one person may be admitted to the same service more than one time per year, or to two or more different services per year, this index is not equal to the unduplicated number of individuals admitted to services and should not be interpreted as such. Special studies have indicated that of the patients admitted per year to a universe of psychiatric services, consisting of all in-patient and out-patient services in a State (excluding psychiatrists in private practice), 19 per cent were admitted to more than one service.

† Excluding federally funded community mental health centres.

‡ Includes only federally funded community mental health centres. Includes in-patient, out-patient, and day treatment services.

§ Includes both neuropsychiatric and general medical and surgical hospitals.

‖ Includes residential treatment centres for children which began reporting nationally in 1967.

¶ During the year 1965 the universe of known private mental hospitals was reviewed by the Biometry Branch, NIMH, in conjunction with the State mental health authorities and the National Association of Private Psychiatric Hospitals. In this review, it was found that of the 238 hospitals classified as private mental hospitals for 1965 and preceding years, 64 were in fact hospitals for alcoholics, geriatric hospitals, or nursing homes, or for some other reason should not be considered private mental hospitals. The apparent drop in the number of hospitals in operation and in patient care episodes in 1966 is due, therefore, to a more careful classification of facilities, rather than a change in the number of hospitals.

** The decreases in the number of patient care episodes for 1968 and 1969 are due largely to the reclassification of some general hospital in-patient units which were incorporated into and are now counted as parts of community mental health centres.

†† These estimates differ from previous NIMH published estimates in that they include an estimate for undercoverage in the known universe of hospitals surveyed.

‡‡ Total excludes 60,682 patient care episodes in other day treatment services, data for which were not available in previous years.

Table 3. Estimated patient care episodes,* number, percentage distribution, and rate per 100,000 population by type of facility, United States, 1955 and 1965–8.

Year	Total all facilities	In-patient services†				Out-patient psychiatric services†	Community mental health centres‡
		All in-patient services	State and county mental hospitals	Private mental hospitals	General hospitals/ psychiatric service	Veterans' Administration hospitals		

Year	Total all facilities	All in-patient services	State and county mental hospitals	Private mental hospitals	General hospitals/ psychiatric service	Veterans' Administration hospitals	Out-patient psychiatric services	Community mental health centres
Patient care episodes								
1969	3,589,771‡‡	1,613,371	767,115	123,850‖	535,493	186,913	1,603,303	373,097
1968	3,380,818	1,602,238	791,819	118,126‖	558,790**††	133,503	1,507,000	271,590
1967	3,139,742	1,632,321	801,354	124,258‖	578,513	128,196	1,383,000	124,421
1966	2,764,089	1,578,089	804,216	103,973¶	548,921††	112,979	1,186,000	na
1965	2,636,525	1,565,525	804,926	125,428	519,328	115,843	1,071,000	na
1955	1,675,352	1,296,352	818,832	123,231	265,934	88,355	379,000	na
Percentage distribution								
1969	100·0	44·9	21·4	3·4	14·9	5·2	44·7	10·4
1968	100·0	47·3	23·4	3·5	16·5	3·9	44·7	8·0
1967	100·0	52·0	25·5	4·0	18·4	4·1	44·0	4·0
1966	100·0	57·1	29·0	3·8	19·9	4·4	42·9	na
1965	100·0	59·4	30·5	4·8	19·7	4·4	40·6	na
1955	100·0	77·4	48·9	7·3	15·9	5·3	22·6	na
Rate per 100,000 population								
1969	1797·7	803·0	384·2	62·0	268·2	93·6	802·9	186·8
1968	1711·3	811·0	400·8	59·8	282·8	67·6	762·8	137·5
1967	1604·3	834·1	409·5	63·5	295·6	65·5	706·7	63·6
1966	1427·0	814·8	414·2	53·7	283·4	63·5	612·3	na
1965	1374·0	815·9	419·6	65·4	270·6	60·4	558·1	na
1955	1032·2	798·6	504·5	75·9	163·8	54·4	233·5	na

See opposite for notes.

Table 4. *Additions* to mental health facilities, schizophrenic disorders, by age, type of facility, and modality, United States, 1969.*

Modality and type of facility	Number of additions	Percentage distribution	Rate per 100,000 population
All modalities	473,523	100·0	237·1
In-patient services	292,627	61·8	146·5
Out-patient services	168,645	35·6	84·5
Day-care services	12,251	2·6	6·1
In-patient services	292,627	100·0	146·5
State and county mental hospitals	147,503	50·4	73·9
Private mental hospitals	17,471	6·0	8·7
VA, NP, and GM and S hospitals	37,924	13·0	19·0
Other general hospitals	76,597	26·2	38·4
Federally funded CMHC	13,132	4·4	6·6
Out-patient services	168,645	100·0	84·5
Federally funded CMHC	20,614	12·2	10·3
Other out-patient	148,031	87·8	74·1
Day-care services	12,251	100·0	6·1
Federally funded CMHC	2,675	21·8	1·3
Other day-care	9,576	78·2	4·8

* The term 'additions' is used to designate the total of new admissions, readmissions, and returns from leave for a specific facility.

for a specific diagnostic category can also be prepared. To illustrate, during 1969, about 62 per cent of the additions for schizophrenia were to in-patient services, 36 per cent to out-patient services, and about 2 per cent to day-care services (Table 4). Further analyses can be carried out by computing rates of addition specific for age, sex, and type of service (Taube and Redick).[1] Such data emphasize the magnitude of the problem presented by this severe mental disorder and show the relative role played by each service in providing care to such patients.

It must be emphasized that patient care episodes provide data on patient transactions and not on individual persons. That is, a single person can use more than one facility per year. Determination of the number of individual patients who account for the number of transactions per year requires a register which links records of individual patients over episodes of care in different services and facilities. Registers have been established in the US in Monroe County, New York (Gardner *et al.*, 1963) and in the State of Maryland (US Department of Health, Education, and Welfare, 1967); in England, in the Camberwell area of London (DHSS, 1970; Wing,

1. Taube, C. A., and Redick, R. (1970), Paper presented at Conference on Schizophrenia: Implications of Research Findings for Treatment and Teaching, Washington DC. Available from Biometry Branch, NIMH. To appear in the published proceedings of this Conference.

L., *et al.,* 1967); Salford (Susser, 1968; Susser *et al.,* 1970); and Aberdeen (Baldwin *et al.,* 1965); and in Denmark, in the county of Aarhus (Juel Nielsen *et al.,* 1961). However, it is too complex and expensive a task to establish and maintain one at the national level in the US. Indeed, maintaining a register for the State of Maryland (population 4 million) from 1962 to 1968 presented a formidable undertaking. Studies based on the Maryland Register demonstrated that during the year ending 30 June 1962, about 20 per cent of the patients known to the Register had an episode of care in more than one facility (Bahn *et al.,* 1965). If this estimate were to apply to the entire US, then the 2,764,089 patient care episodes that occurred during 1966 were generated by approximately 2,462,000 separate individuals, a rate of 1,271 per 100,000 population.

Co-ordination and integration of services

The essence of the new community programmes in the US is to effect change in the existing patterns of use facilities. Table 3 demonstrates clearly the changes that have taken place in the locale of the services. The cross-sectional data in the tables and graphs in the preceding section highlight imbalances in the use of different facilities by age, sex, diagnosis. These data are useful to the administrator in planning programmes to correct imbalances where they exist, to integrate and co-ordinate services provided by these various facilities, and to provide patients with continuity of care within and between facilities. Accomplishing this is a complex task of considerable magnitude. Those responsible for these efforts require considerable skill and ingenuity in community relations and planning, extensive knowledge of actual and potential role functioning of each of the many agencies involved, and the various relationships that exist among them. In addition, they require data on the effectiveness of the programme of each facility as a basis for determining what needs to be done to change ineffective programmes to effective ones.

Statistics related to goals of mental health centre legislation

Planning for comprehensive centres and assessing their effectiveness in reducing the burden of disability from mental disorders suffered by a community requires an explicit statement of the goals to be achieved by such centres. Clearly, centres are to serve multiple purposes, depending on the needs of the community being served. Consequently, some goals and objectives will vary from centre to centre. However, the President's message that set the stage for this legislation established several common ones for each centre programme:

... it will be possible within a decade or two to reduce the number of patients now under custodial care by 50 per cent or more. Many more mentally ill can be helped to remain in their own homes without hardship to themselves or their families. Those who are hospitalized can be helped to return to their own communities. All but a small proportion can be restored to useful life. We can spare them and their families much of the misery which mental illness now entails. We can save public funds and we can conserve our manpower resources ... [President of the US, 1963].

The following sections will deal with statistics relevant to two of these goals. The first is the reduction of the number of mentally ill in custodial care by 50 per cent within a decade or two. The message provided no definition of 'patients in custodial care', but its contents left no doubt that the patients referred to were for the most part the large number in State and county mental hospitals. The second is the development of co-ordinated and integrated services to provide patients with continuity of care and assist in maintaining them in their own homes without hardships to themselves and their families.

Reduction of population in State and county mental hospitals

The annual censuses of patients in State and county mental hospitals provide essential data for determining the extent to which the objective[1] of reduction of patients in State and county mental hospitals is being achieved as well as starting points for studies to assess possible consequences of such reductions.

Changes in the total resident patient population. During the period 1946–54, the numbers of patients in the State and county mental hospitals increased at an average annual rate of 2·1 per cent (Fig. 3). Despite changed attitudes toward the treatment of the mentally ill which resulted in more and more patients being returned to the community, the rates of net release were still not sufficiently high to counterbalance an increasing number of admissions. As a consequence, the mental hospital population continued to grow. A major turning point occurred between 1955 and 1956 when the first drop occurred in this population. This was the year during which tranquillizers were used extensively in these hospitals. The decrease in patient population has continued over the years at an increasing rate so that by the end of 1970 the resident population was 338,592, or 40 per cent less than its peak of 558,922 in 1955.

Since changes in number of resident patients during a year are

1. Health planners are attempting to differentiate between the terms 'goals' and 'objectives'. A recent bulletin from the US Department of Health, Education, and Welfare (1968) has defined these terms for the purposes of health planning as follows: '(a) *Goal:* Specifies what is to be accomplished to succeed in the direction of the mission; a long-range state of accomplishments toward which programs are directed; (b) *Health Goal:* Usually stated in terms of accomplishments to completely overcome a health problem or reduce it to a specified level; (c) *Health Objective:* Statement of a measured and specific kind of progress toward a goal during a stated time period.' In the context of these definitions, reduction of mental hospital population and return to the community are considered to be health objectives. The reduction of disability among the mentally ill and the members of their families is the *health goal* that is to be achieved.

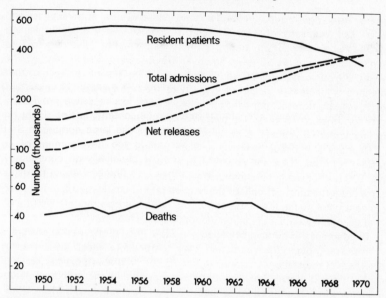

Figure 3. Number of resident patients, total admissions, net releases, and deaths in State and county mental hospitals, United States, 1950–70.

determined by the annual additions to and subtractions from the patients in residence at the beginning of the year, the total resident patient count is affected by community or intrahospital programmes that produce change in: (*a*) the number of additions; (*b*) placements on leave; (*c*) returns from leave; and (*d*) deaths (Kramer, 1969). Indeed, the major changes to be noted below have been due to the success or failure of programmes designed to modify any of these components of patient movement within various age and diagnostic groups.

Changes specific for age and diagnosis. Between 1955 and 1968, striking decreases have occurred in the number of resident patients in each of the age-groups 25 years and over, while equally striking increases have occurred in the age-groups under 25 years (Kramer, Taube, and Redick, in press). The percentage decreases in numbers varied widely, being largest in the age-group 35–44 years (45 per cent) and smallest in the age-group 75 years and over (18 per cent). The percentage increase also varied widely from 176 per cent in the age-group under 15 years to 47 per cent in the age-group 15–24 years.

The changes in the resident population also varied by diagnosis. Among the schizophrenic patients there was an over-all decrease of 27 per cent. Decreases occurred in five age-groups ranging from a high of 50 per cent in the age-group 35–44 years to 12 per cent in the age-group 65–74 years. Three age-groups (under 15 years, 15–24 years, and 75 years and over) had increases of 374, 34, and 14 per cent respectively. Marked decreases also occurred among patients with mental disorders of the senium in age-groups 55 years and over: 55–64 years, 43 per cent; 65-74 years, 39 per cent; and 75 years and over, 27·5 per cent. For all other diagnoses, decreases occurred in each of the age-groups 25 years and over, ranging from 43 per cent for patients aged 45–54 years and 19 per cent for those of 75 years and over. Marked increases occurred in the age-groups under 15 years (138 per cent), and 15–24 years (58 per cent).

Changes also occurred in the resident patient rates; ie, the number of residents in the State and county mental hospitals at the end of the year per 100,000 of the general population. Relative changes in resident patient rates are a function not only of the relative rate of change in the number of resident patients (ie, the numerator of the rate), but also the relative rate of change in the general population (denominator of the rate).

The decrease in number of patients in State and county mental hospitals in the age-groups 65 years and over, particularly those with mental disorders of the senium (brain syndromes with cerebral arteriosclerosis and senile brain disease), has, for the most part, been the result of sharp reductions in first admissions for patients of 65 years and over. Many State hospital systems adopted policies that restricted admissions of certain types of aged patients and encouraged increased use of nursing homes and related facilities for such patients. As a consequence, between 1962 and 1965, the first admission rate for the age-group 65 years and over dropped by 9 per cent for males, 12 per cent for females, and 11 per cent for both sexes combined. Between 1965 and 1969 the corresponding decreases were 19 per cent for males, 43 per cent for females, and 31 per cent for both sexes combined (Kramer, Taube, and Redick, in press).

The situation was quite different for patients under 15 years of age. The sharp increase in first admissions for these patients indicated that factors other than the increase in general population for this age bracket were operating; such as, increases in the number of mentally ill children, increased recognition of need for services for severely disturbed children and inadequate and/or inappropriate services at the community level to meet these needs.

The total percentage change in resident patients that occurred between 1955 and 1968 masked the striking changes observed in the average annual rates of change during this period. The rate of decrease was more rapid during the latter part of that period (1962–8) than during the earlier part (1955–61). To illustrate, the annual relative rate of decrease in total number of patients for all ages and all diagnoses was 0·87 per cent during 1955–61, but 4·15 per cent during 1962–8.

It is of interest to consider what the implications of the 1962–8 rate of decrease of the resident patient population are for achieving the 50 per cent reduction within the decade or two specified in the President's message (1963). A theoretical determination was made of the average annual rate of decline required to reduce the 1962 year end population by 50 per cent within ten years (by 1972) and within twenty years (by 1982), assuming a constant annual rate of decrease. Achievement of such a reduction by 1972 requires an annual rate of decrease of 6·7 per cent; by 1982, one of 3·4 per cent. The actual annual rate of decrease of the entire population in the interval 1962–8 was 4·2 per cent. If this rate continues, then a 50 per cent decrease will be achieved by the end of 1979. Similar computations may be made for various diagnostic groups specific for age. For example, consider the population of schizophrenic patients. The average annual rates of decrease in the age-groups 35–44 years (6·9 per cent) and 45–54 years (6·9 per cent) are such that 50 per cent reductions in their year end 1962 population should occur by 1972. The corresponding rates of decrease in the age-groups 25–34 (4·6 per cent), 55–64 (3·4 per cent), and 65 years and over (3·0 per cent) are such that reductions of this magnitude would occur by 1977, 1983, and 1985, respectively. Indices such as these provide hospital administrators with a basis for evaluating programmes directed toward various target populations. Studies can be designed to determine reasons for the differences in the rates of decrease and the results can be used as a basis for planning programmes to accelerate the decrease provided, of course, that such action is deemed desirable. Or, as in the case of the populations under 15 and 15–24 years, which are increasing at annual rates of 5·4 per cent and 1·2 per cent respectively, programmes would be needed to reverse the trends.

The future role of the State mental hospital

Although the period 1955–68 was one of marked decline in the resident population of State mental hospitals, it was, as already indicated, one of marked increase in the establishment and use of a variety of community based facilities: out-patient clinics, day-care facilities, community mental health centres, half-way houses, and psychiatric services in general hospitals. In addition, nursing homes appeared in increasing numbers. Indeed, the downward trend in the mental hospital population is closely related to the upward trend in the availability and use of these other facilities. For example, the out-patient clinic or general hospital service served as alternatives for treatment which either prevented or at least delayed the admission of certain types of patients to mental hospitals. Out-patient clinics also provided a resource for follow-up care, and thus facilitated the earlier discharge of some types of patients from the mental hospital. The use of nursing homes accelerated the reduction of mental hospital populations in two ways. The admission to these homes of large numbers of aged mentally ill directly from the community reduced the admissions to mental hospitals. The transfer of chronic long-term patients to nursing homes reduced the resident population of the mental hospitals.

The above changes were encouraged and catalysed not only by the Federal and State community mental health legislation but also by certain developments in private and national health insurance benefits. Many private insurance carriers expanded their coverage to include payment for mental health services so that increased numbers of persons could afford such care. This accelerated the growth of psychiatric services in general hospitals and increased the numbers of admissions for these services (Giesler *et al.*, 1966). The Social Security Amendments of 1965 also provided insurance benefits for the care of the aged mentally ill (PL89–97, 1965). The benefits under Section A of Title XVIII of this Public Law encouraged the use of general hospitals, extended care facilities, and services provided by home health agencies. The supplementary medical insurance benefits of Part B provided additional coverage for out-patient psychiatric services and for home health services. These benefits undoubtedly increased the number of aged mentally ill admitted to general hospitals and to nursing homes. Another part of this legislation (Title XIX) also provides grants to States for medical assistance for aged persons in mental institutions.

The rapid changes taking place in the size and composition of the State mental hospitals have intensified the debate on their future role. Some argue that State mental hospital systems should be abolished, while others recommend integration of these hospitals with the community and the expansion of their research, training, and community functions. Still others recommend that the State hospital should provide specialized services on a regional basis. Additional analyses of national data provide further information on the current status of the State hospitals which may help planners in defining their future role. Some of these facts are:

1. State hospitals are not a homogeneous group of hospitals; in fact, there are at least four distinct groups: children's hospitals, hospitals for criminally insane, county hospitals, and the traditional State mental hospitals.

2. Some States have introduced new State hospitals, while others have closed some. Between 1961 and 1969, 43 new hospitals were created[1] in 20 States, while 14 were closed in 7 States.

3. Although the resident population of all State hospitals in the US combined has decreased between 1955 and 1970, from 559,000 to 339,000 or by 29 per cent, their patient care episodes decreased only 6 per cent during the same period (from 818,000 to 767,000).

1. This number includes some newly constructed hospitals, others converted to a mental hospital from a hospital used for other purposes (for example, tuberculosis hospitals) and several that resulted from the division of a single large mental hospital into two or more administratively distinct hospitals.

4. As a result of the sharp reductions in resident population, the median size of the State hospitals has decreased from 1,474 beds in 1961 to 850 beds in 1970.

5. Many of the State hospitals provide a wide range of services, including out-patient and day-care programmes, and about 50 State hospitals, or one-sixth of the total are serving as the primary in-patient unit for a federally funded community mental health centre.

6. Between 1962 and 1969 first admissions increased 26 per cent, while readmissions increased over 50 per cent. Of the total annual admissions in 1969 over half were readmissions (Taube, 1971).

7. Striking changes have occurred in the diagnostic composition of first admissions. Alcohol disorders accounting for 15 per cent of the total in 1962 now account for 18 per cent. Drug abuse disorders increased from 1·3 to 3·9 per cent. Schizophrenia accounted for 21 per cent in 1962, but only for 15 per cent in 1969. Largely as a result of the decrease in admissions 65 and over, brain syndromes decreased from 26 per cent of the total admissions in 1962 to 16 per cent in 1969 (Taube, 1971).

All of these data plus those in the preceding section demonstrate clearly that State mental hospitals are still used extensively by the communities they serve and play an important role in the delivery of mental health services. This is further illustrated by Fig. 2*a* and *b* which provide a comparison of the patient care episodes specific for age and type of facility (including community mental health centres) in 1969 with the corresponding episodes in 1966.

Statisticians can provide various estimates of future size and composition of State hospitals based on prior trends and on various assumptions concerning future rates of use (Koons, 1969). However, statistics *per se* cannot determine the future size and role of the State mental hospital. What is needed are policy decisions that determine what this role shall be. These in turn determine what resources are needed to implement the policy. If the policy is to eliminate these hospitals completely by a specific date, then appropriate action should be taken to accomplish this and to provide sufficient alternative facilities and programmes to meet the needs of the patients who will be affected by such a decision. If the policy is to optimize the role of the State hospital in the provision of community mental health services, then appropriate actions should be taken to accomplish this. Without such decisions, statistics of trends in patterns of use of State hospitals will merely reflect the results of community inaction rather than of positive action directed toward resolving this issue.

Maintaining patients in the community

Much emphasis is being placed on providing services at the local level to maintain patients in their home, and to protect their links with their families and communities. The planning and implementation of such programmes require data on characteristics of patients specific for the composition of the households and families in which they live. Systematic health, vital and social statistics that provide descriptions of the frequency of occurrence of disease and disability specific for such variables are quite limited. The most generally available type of data relevant to this problem are rates of morbidity, mortality and use of psychiatric facilities (particularly mental hospitals) by marital status (Kramer, 1967). Although marital status data are useful in pinpointing high-risk groups, they do not provide sufficiently detailed information for planning home and community care programmes for the ill. Data on the physical characteristics of the household in which the patient resides, on the characteristics of the individuals living in the household and their relationship to each other are much more relevant. As indicated, one of the major goals of the Community Mental Health Services Program was to develop co-ordinated and integrated services which will provide patients with continuity of care and assist in maintaining them 'in their own homes without hardship to themselves or their families' (President of the US, 1963).

Planning for these programmes emphasized that answers were needed to questions such as the following:

1. Does the patient have a home?

2. Does the patient have family members or other persons who are willing to assume responsibility for him and who are well enough physically and financially able to provide the necessary care?

3. Are the patterns of organization and interpersonal relationships in the patient's household such as not to impede or prevent his recovery or rehabilitation?

4. Does the family have sufficient understanding of the patient's illness and expected behaviour so as to develop attitudes that assist rather than retard recovery and rehabilitation?

5. Are the patient's behaviour and needs such that his presence in the household does not produce undue hardships for other members of the household and does not precipitate secondary attacks and disability in these members?

6. Are appropriate medical, psychiatric, nursing, social work, and related services readily accessible to meet the changing needs of the patient and his family; or, if the patient does not have a family, of the patient and his caretaker?

It was clear that answers to all of these questions could not be obtained quickly. However, to obtain some basic information relevant to these issues, the NIMH contracted with the Bureau of the Census to prepare tabulations from the 1960 Census of Population on persons by age, sex, marital status, and characteristics of the households and families of which they are members (US Bureau of the Census, 1964). Although such data were not prepared for each State, special tabulations were obtained for Maryland and Louisiana where studies were carried out to provide some information on the relationship of household composition to the rates of admission to psychiatric services (Pollack *et al.,* 1968).

The Bureau of the Census now publishes data for the US on the numbers of persons by marital status, age, sex, living arrangements,[1] and socio-economic status (US Bureau of the Census, 1969, 1970, 1971). Such data can be used to pinpoint high-risk groups with respect to mental disorders and use of psychiatric services. As indicated above (p. 42) the NIMH has made similar tabulations available on a catchment area basis to assist State and local authorities in their planning activities.

An important area for evaluation in community programmes for the care of the mentally ill is that related to the burden such care may place on the families of the mentally ill. It is essential that research be initiated at the catchment area level to measure changes over time in 'burden on family' resulting from such programmes. Although considerable research has been carried out on this problem in Britain (Brown *et al.,* 1962, 1966; Grad and Sainsbury, 1963, 1966; Sainsbury and Grad 1962, 1966; Wing *et al.,* 1964), relatively little has been done in the US. Statisticians can serve an important function for administrators and programme planners in designing research protocols related to this problem by assisting them in formulating precise objectives, translating these into operational terms, developing statistical measures to determine whether objectives are met, specifying the data needed to compute the statistical measures, and devising the appropriate procedures for their collection.

Assessing the extent of use and working of various services

A variety of supporting programmes and facilities have been established to assist in returning mental hospital patients to the community, as well as in preventing admissions to these institutions. Data from the National Reporting Program, as well as from other surveys and studies, can be used to monitor the extent to which such facilities are being used. Certain indexes may suggest under-utilization of one service and over-utilization of another. Other indexes raise questions as to whether the numbers of personnel are sufficient and their training is appropriate to meet the needs of patients entrusted to their care. Such information pinpoints programmes that require intensive, systematic study to determine whether a problem exists and, if so, what should be done to change the situation. Morris (1964) characterizes such studies as *operational research* which he defines

1. Classification of living arrangements is based on whether a person lives in a household or in group quarters. Persons who live in households are classified as to whether they: (*a*) are members of a family, and, if so, by their relationship to the head of the family (for example, wife, child, other relative); (*b*) live alone; (*c*) live with non-relatives. Persons who live in group quarters are further classified by the type of institution.

as '... systematic study of the working of health services with a view to their improvement'. He further states that:

Operational research translates knowledge of community health in terms of needs and demand. The supply of services is described and how they are utilized; their success in reaching standards and in improving health ought to be appraised. All this has to be related to other social policies and to resources. Knowledge thus won may be applied in experiment, and in drawing up plans for the future.... The regular supply of information on health and health services is itself a key service needing as much scrutiny as any.

Any of a number of examples can be selected from the material already presented to illustrate this use of national data. However, for purposes of this section, three examples will be chosen because of their relevance to programmes designed to reduce mental hospital populations: (1) use of day-care services, (2) use of half-way houses, (3) use of nursing homes.

Day-care services

Day-care services are considered to be important for maintaining certain types of patients in the community. Despite general acceptance of the needs for such programmes, day-care has been slow to catch on. While there was a 400 per cent increase in the number of day hospitalization programmes between 1963 and 1967 (from 110 to 500), less than 1 per cent of the total admissions to all mental health facilities in 1967 occurred in these programmes. Between 1967 and 1969, day-care programmes increased in number from 500 to 757, an increase of almost 50 per cent, and the estimated number of admissions to these services increased two-fold: from 27,000 to 50,000. Still patient care episodes for day-care services accounted for only 2 per cent of the total patient care episodes to all facilities (Taube, 1972).

It is important to determine why the level of use of these services appears to be relatively low at a time when so many patients are being maintained in the community. Also, surveys could be carried out to determine who in the community may be in need of day-care services, how many are not using these services, and why.

Half-way houses

The half-way house is another facility that is considered an important resource for assisting patients in making the transition from hospital to community. As of 1969, there were 7,876 half-way house beds for patients with mental disorders in the US. This corresponds to 16 half-way house beds per 1,000 discontinuations[1] from State and county mental hospitals. This index varied from 9 per 1,000 in the East South Central States to a high of 54 per 1,000 in the Mountain States (Table 5).

1. The term discontinuations is used to designate the total of discharge and placements on leave.

Table 5. *Number of half-way house beds and beds per 1,000 discontinuations* from State and county mental hospitals by geographic region, United States, 1969.*

Geographic division	Total half-way house beds†	Discontinuations* State and county mental hospitals	Half-way house beds per 1,000 discontinuations
United States	7,876	491,952	16
New England	633	48,661	13
Middle Atlantic	933	75,535	12
South Atlantic	1,443	82,182	18
East North Central	1,128	97,455	12
East South Central	260	30,076	9
West North Central	491	42,210	12
West South Central	746	42,888	17
Mountain	691	12,868	54
Pacific	1,551	60,077	26

* Includes all persons who were discharged, placed on extended leave, escaped or otherwise discontinued receiving in-patient service during the year.

† Includes only half-way house beds for psychiatric patients, alcoholics, or combinations of these.

Source. Cannon, Mildred, 'Halfway houses—a growing mental health resource', paper presented at a Kansas Conference on Transitional Living Programs at Topeka, Kansas, 13 April 1972.

While there are no clear-cut rules for determining what the actual number of half-way house beds should be, certain assumptions can be made to estimate the potential demand for such services. For example, consider the population of persons discharged or placed on leave during 1969 from State and county mental hospitals (492,000 persons), and assume that half-way house beds would be appropriate for one-quarter of these persons. On the basis of certain assumptions about the average length of stay in half-way houses of this number of persons discharged from the State hospital, it is estimated that from 1·5 to 2·5 times the number actually available would be needed (NIMH, 1971). Such estimates suggest that the current half-way house resources meet at most one to two-fifths of the potential demand. Here again surveys are needed to determine why there is such variation in the actual volume of such services and the extent of their use; how well the services are functioning; and whether there is a large unmet need for them in various parts of the US.

Services for the aged mentally ill

The role of nursing homes in accelerating the reduction of the patient population 65 years and over in mental hospitals has already been discussed. As a result of the increase in the number of these facilities and their increased use for care of patients who would in former years have been admitted to mental hospitals, a situation has developed where more aged mentally ill are now in nursing homes and related facilities than in mental hospitals (Kramer *et al.*, 1968).

Table 6. *Percentage of nursing staff who had attended a course on mental or social problems.*

Type of personnel	Accredited course	Short course or workshop
Registered nurses	4·8	11·9
Licensed practical nurses	4·3	15·3
Nurses' aides	0·7	4·2
Other professional staff	4·9	15·9

A variety of indicators point to the problems of providing care to patients in nursing and personal care homes. Characteristically, their personnel consists of a relatively small number of physicians and other professional and technical staff and a very large proportion of nursing staff (Taube, 1966). As of May 1964, there were 281,000 employees in these homes. Of this number, 56 per cent were nursing staff, 7 per cent administrators (many of whom performed other tasks), about 1 per cent occupational and physical therapists, dietitians, and social workers combined, and 0·3 per cent physicians. The remaining 35 per cent were non-professional.

Other data indicate that only a small proportion of employees of any type in nursing homes have had any special training with respect to the problems of the mentally ill. Data from a 1964 survey indicated that the percentage of staff which had special training related to mental or social problems of the aged or chronically ill was as shown in Table 6 (Taube and Bryant, 1967).

Another problem revolves around the difficulties in obtaining reliable data on the diagnostic characteristics of patients in nursing and personal care homes. A survey of the prevalence of chronic conditions among residents of the facilities in 1967 indicated a lack of precise data on mental disorders in this patient population. Thus, among patients 65 years and over, 214,203 were reported to have had a condition which was coded as shown in Table 7.

The data in Table 7 plus others that can be produced on the social and demographic characteristics of the aged not only in nursing homes but in other institutions and in the non-institutional population, emphasize the complexity of the problem of providing adequate psychiatric services to the aged. Here, again, the statistician can provide data which point to problems that need to be solved and, occasionally, can suggest solutions. It is the task of the administrator and planner to use these data and other relevant information to develop the programmes needed to change and, hopefully, to improve the situation and to develop the strategies for gaining the necessary approval, funds, staff, and whatever else may be required to implement the necessary programmes.

Table 7. _Diagnosis given to patients aged 65 years or more in nursing and personal care homes._

Diagnoses	Number
Chronic brain syndrome with senile brain disease with psychosis _(ICD_ 304)*	118,259
Senility without mention of psychosis (_ICD_ 794)	26,528
Other specified mental disorders without mention of senility (_ICD_ 300-303; 305-329)	5,740
Mental or nervous trouble ill-defined _(ICD_ 327, 780.7, 780.8)	63,676
Total	214,203

* These rubrics are from the _International Classification of Diseases,_ Seventh Revision (World Health Organization, 1957).

Indicators of need to modify existing legislation

Facts generated from the National Reporting Program also point to additional legislation that may be required to achieve certain programme goals. The following example, related to Federal legislation for funding community mental health centres in poverty areas, will be used as an illustration.

One of the major goals of the Community Mental Health Centers Program is to insure that centres become self-supporting; that is, they do not have to depend on Federal funds for continued support. The intent of the programme was to use Federal funds as 'seed money' to start centres going. Once they were underway, it was expected that they develop a broad base of community support so that they would eventually become self-supporting. Data collected annually in the inventory of federally funded community mental health centres, relating to source of funds for annual operating expenditures, help to monitor progress towards this goal. These data, along with others, have also indicated problem areas which have led to programme redirection. For example, it was noted that centres located in extreme poverty catchment areas were having difficulty developing the State and local support within the fifty-two months described by the existing legislation, after which Federal funds are terminated. Legislation was introduced and passed, to extend this period to eight years for centres located in poverty areas (Public Law PL 91–211, 1970). This illustrates important gains that can be achieved through the collaboration of the statistician, the planner, and those responsible for recommending and drafting new legislation.

Projections of future needs for facilities and staff

Another use of data derived from the National Reporting Program is in the projection of future needs. While the calculations may be crude, their results can alert administrators and planners to emerging problems that need immediate attention. The following is an illustration of this use. Pre-

Table 8. *Estimated US populations, 1970 and 1985* by age and colour† (population in 1,000s).*

Age	1970 Total	White	Non-white	1985 Total	White	Non-white
Under 18	70,656	59,882	10,774	73,307	61,363	11,944
18–24	24,589	21,432	3,157	28,423	23,975	4,448
25–34	25,315	22,310	3,005	40,699	35,109	5,590
35–44	22,961	20,339	2,622	31,384	27,657	3,727
45–64	41,817	37,800	4,017	42,941	38,398	4,543
65+	19,585	18,031	1,554	24,977	22,925	2,052
Total	204,923	179,794	25,129	241,731	209,427	32,304

* Future population estimates are made on the basis of four different sets of projections (Series A, B, C, D). The four series differ wholly with respect to assumptions relating to fertility, with only one set of assuptions regarding mortality and immigration applying to all four series. The fertility assumptions for Series A, B, C, D assume that, on the average, women will bear 3·35, 3·10, 2·78, and 2·45 children respectively, during their lifetime. The mortality assumption implies only slight increases in survival rates between 1963 and 2000 and immigration assumption is that net civilian immigration for all classes will amount to 400,000 a year. Since the four series of projections are based only on differences in fertility, only the populations in the younger age-groups vary between the four series. The Series D projection was used in this paper since this implies the lowest birth-rate which is in keeping with current trend in birth-rates in the US.

† *Source.* US Bureau of the Census, *Current Population Reports, Summary of Demographic Projections,* Series P-25, no. 388, Tables 2 and 6 (Series D projection).

vious surveys have identified the higher utilization rate of State and county hospitals and out-patient psychiatric services by the non-white population (Taube, 1970, 1971*a*). When these data are combined with projections of population change, future needs become evident. Table 8 shows the population changes between 1970 and 1985 in numbers of persons in the various age-groups of the US population by colour (US Bureau of the Census, 1968). By 1985, the population of the US is expected to be about 241·7 million as compared to 204·9 million in 1970, an increase of 18 per cent (US Bureau of the Census, 1968). The increase for whites will be 16·5 per cent (from 180 to 209 million), and for non-whites 29 per cent (from 25 to 32 million). Non-whites are expected to constitute about 13 per cent of the population in 1985.

Large relative increases are expected in every age-group for both whites and non-whites, but the increases for the non-whites are much larger as may be seen in Table 9.

The basic population data for 1970 and 1985 in Table 8 can be used in conjunction with age-specific admission rates to mental hospitals and to out-patient psychiatric services to estimate expected admissions to these facilities in 1985. A conservative estimate can be made by assuming that the admission rates to such facilities in 1970 and 1985 will be the same as

Table 9. *Percentage increases in population, 1970–85, by age.*

Age-groups (years)	1970–85	
	White	Non-white
<18	2·5	10·9
18–24	11·9	40·9
25–34	57·4	86·0
35–44	36·0	42·1
45–64	1·6	13·1
65+	27·1	32·0

in 1969. Such an assumption would result in the white admissions to State and county mental hospitals increasing by 21 per cent (from 316,000 in 1970 to 383,577 in 1985), and those for the non-white population by 45 per cent (from 63,891 to 92,649). The corresponding increases to out-patient clinics would be 21 per cent for whites (from 777,213 to 939,183) and for non-whites 37 per cent (from 137,742 to 188,595). Developing various options to meet such increased demands in terms of facilities and personnel, and strategies that might conceivably prevent the problems that lead to as well as result from these demands is an essential part of planning.

DISCUSSION

Sources of additional data: records of other health, social, educational, and related agencies

The preceding sections have illustrated ways in which data from a national programme of collection and analysis of data on the care of the men-tally ill in the US, from the Decennial Census and other sources, can be used in planning of community mental health programmes. However, there are other sources of information which might provide the planner with relevant data for his activities.

Birth, death, and marriage certificates and records from a large variety of health, social, and welfare agencies can be used to supplement records of patients admitted to psychiatric facilities as starting points for studies of mental disorders, the problems they create, and the effectiveness of efforts made to prevent and control such disorders. A partial list of these agencies includes:

1. Health departments, including poison-control and accident-prevention centres.

2. Businesses and industries with health and safety programmes.

3. Public and private schools.

4. Special hospitals for tuberculosis, crippled children, chronically ill, alcoholism.

5. Nursing homes.

6. Boarding homes.
7. Police courts and legal institutions.
8. Counselling agencies.
9. Adoption agencies.
10. Health insurance plans.
11. Workmen's compensation.
12. Records of private psychiatrists and GPs.

Techniques for gathering additional data

Another point that administrators and planners should keep in mind is that frequently sources of existing data are not appropriate to their needs for planning and evaluation. Consequently, it is necessary to carry out surveys, special studies, and controlled clinical trials (Kramer, 1969). The precise techniques to be used depend on the kinds of questions to be answered, the manpower required to design and carry out the survey and the amount of money available for such purposes. So that the activities of the statisticians and planners can be better interrelated and mutually supportive, it is essential for them to establish close working relationships. As stated by the WHO Expert Committee on Health Statistics (1971):

It is now universally recognized that the biostatistician must be involved at the earliest stages in the conception and design of a research study. The same relationship should be created and fostered in the case of health statisticians and health planners.

Needs for international collaboration

The composition of this conference brings to the foreground the problem of international comparisons of health data used for planning and evaluation purposes. Much needs to be done to improve the comparability of statistics on the utilization of mental health services both within and between countries. Designing and carrying out activities to achieve better international comparability presents many difficult but not insuperable problems. The accomplishments of several activities relevant to improving comparability of diagnostic statistics on mental disorders provide testimony to this. This includes such projects as the US–UK Bilateral Pilot Study of Diagnostic Comparability (Kramer *et al.,* 1969; Gurland *et al.,* 1970; Cooper, 1970; Cooper *et al.,* 1972) and the WHO activities on the International Pilot Study of Schizophrenia (Sartorius *et al.,* 1970; WHO, 1973), seminars on Standardization of Psychiatric Diagnosis, Classification, and Statistics and the Draft Glossary of Mental Disorders.

If better standardization of morbidity statistics on the mental disorders relevant to the planning and evaluation of community mental health services is to be achieved, much more remains to be done over and above that of improving the reliability and comparability of psychiatric diagnoses. The following are just a few of the needs:

1. Uniformity in terms used to designate facilities for the provision of psychiatric services. Many terms are now used to designate facilities for the provision of psychiatric services. The following are examples: mental hospital, sanatoria, psychiatric service in a general hospital, out-patient psychiatric clinic, comprehensive community mental health centre, day-care centre, night-care centre, half-way house, dispensary beds, nursing home, observation stations, psychiatric colonies, hostels, etc.

Some countries combine neurological and psychiatric disorders in their mental health statistics; mental deficiency may or may not be included. It is essential, therefore, that persons in one country who are studying developments in other countries should have a clear understanding of similarities and differences between the types of facilities designated by these various terms. In addition, several countries have now developed classifications and definitions of types of mental health facilities. *To achieve greater comparability in statistics from these facilities, it would seem necessary to have an internationally accepted classification and glossary of mental health service facilities and the services they render.*

2. Procedural standards for published statistical reports from different countries. A review of the published statistical reports from different countries on the characteristics of the mentally ill emphasizes additional problems that must be solved in order to produce uniform international statistics on the mental disorders. The following procedural standards need to be developed:

1. Standard lists of mental disorders based on Section V of the *ICD* for publishing detailed and summary diagnostic distributions for patients under care in specific kinds of facilities.

2. Standard age-groups of patients for use in such tabulations.

3. Uniform definitions of specific movement categories of patients.

4. Uniform definitions of specific types of facilities.

5. Minimum sets of tabulations that should be generally available from all countries on the characteristics of patients under treatment in specified types of facilities.

6. Standards for the computation of various indices used to describe the movement of patients into and out of psychiatric facilities.

The availability and use of such standards would assist materially in correcting many of the current deficiencies in national and international statistics of the mental disorders.

3. Establishment of various classifications for producing uniform data relevant to planning and evaluation. It is generally recognized that the *ICD* meets only one need for uniform statistics on the mental disorders, that related to diagnostic data. However, other classifications are needed. To illustrate, the seminars on Standardization of Diagnosis, Classification, and

Statistics have highlighted the need for a classification of psychosocial factors in the aetiology of mental disorders (see p. 66). Still others are needed on types and degrees of psychiatric disability, impairment of social functioning, etc.

Availability of standardized classifications of degree of psychiatric disability, impairment of social functioning, etc., would assist materially in developing uniform data on such problems.

Research on measurement of need for psychiatric services

Repeatedly, planners and evaluators are handicapped by lack of systematic data on the prevalence and incidence of mental disorders in the non-institutionalized population and on specific needs of persons with such disorders for psychiatric and related human services. Agencies responsible for planning and implementing programmes to prevent and control mental disorders require current objective reliable data on the extent of need for various types of clinical and rehabilitative services among the members of population groups for whom the services are intended. Indeed, standard techniques and procedures are long overdue for carrying out psychiatric clinical examinations in the non-institutionalized population in a manner that would make it possible to determine with a high degree of reliability and validity not only the presence or absence of psychiatric disorders, but also the type of psychiatric disorder, degree of impairment, and specific types of services needed by the patient. Such surveys should also provide other information required to plan appropriate treatment and rehabilitation services for a patient. This includes information on his physical status; his met and unmet requirements for specific types of medical, social, and other services; his social adjustment and living arrangements. *Techniques that would provide such comprehensive data on individual patients would be eminently useful at this time by providing basic information required for planning comprehensive and integrated services at both the institutional and community levels.*

SUMMARY

This paper illustrates uses of statistics derived from the Census of Population and from a national programme for collection and analysis of data on patterns of use of psychiatric services in the planning of community mental health services in the US. These national statistics provide prototypes for development of similar data for use at the local catchment area level. The examples given are those that have relevance to the development of various plans for co-ordinating and integrating services at the local level, monitoring and assessing the functioning of various aspects of community programmes, and determining the extent to which certain limited goals are being attained. Recommendations are made concerning some needs for developing more uniform and comparable national and international statistics for use in planning and evaluating community mental health programmes, for developing additional classifications that can be used in the collection and analysis of data for these purposes and for determination of needs for psychiatric services.

REFERENCES

American Public Health Association. Program Area Committee on Mental Health (1962). *Mental Disorder: A Guide to Control Methods* (New York: American Public Health Association).

Bahn, A. K., Gorwitz, K., Klee, G. D., Kramer, M., and Tuerk, J. (1965). 'Services received by Maryland residents in facilities directed by a psychiatrist', *Publ. Hlth Rep.* **80,** 405–16.

Baldwin, J. A., *et al.* (1965). 'A psychiatric case register in North-East Scotland', *Br. J. prev. soc. Med.* **19,** 38.

Brown, G. W., Monck, E. M., Carstairs, G. M., and Wing, J. K. (1962). 'Influence of family life on the course of schizophrenic illness', ibid. **16,** 55–68.

—— Bone, M., Dalison, B., and Wing, J. K. (1966). *Schizophrenia and Social Care,* Maudsley Monograph no. 17 (London: Oxford University Press).

Code of Federal Regulations Title 42: Public Health Revised as of 1 January 1971 (Washington, DC: US Government Printing Office).

  (a) Par. 54.204: 'State plan; areas; determination of relative need; priorities', p. 110.

  (b) Par. 51.104 g: 'State plan requirements, scope and quality of services', p. 78.

  (c) Par. 54.305 *(a):* 'Submittal of application', p. 119.

Cooper, J. E. (1970). 'The use of a procedure for standardizing psychiatric diagnosis', in Hare, E. H., and Wing, J. K. (eds), *Psychiatric Epidemiology,* pp. 109–32 (Oxford University Press for the Nuffield Provincial Hospitals Trust).

—— Kendell, R. E., Gurland, B. J., Sharpe, L., Copeland, J. R. M., and Simon, R. J. (1972). 'Psychiatric diagnosis in New York and London. A comparative study of mental hospital admissions', Maudsley Monograph (London: Oxford University Press).

Department of Health and Social Security (1970). *Psychiatric Case Registers,* DHSS Statist. Rep. Ser. no. 8 (London: HMSO).

Frost, W. H. (1927). 'Epidemiology', in *Nelson Loose Leaf System. Public Health Preventive Medicine,* vol. 2, chap. 7, pp. 163–90 (New York: Thomas Nelson and Sons). (Reprinted in papers of Wade Hampton Frost, MD, *A Contribution to Epidemiologic Method* [ed. Maxcy, K. F. (1941)], pp. 493–542 [New York: Commonwealth Fund].)

Gardner, E. A., *et al.* (1963). 'All psychiatric experience in a community. A cumulative survey: report of first year's experience'. *Arch. Gen. Psychiat.* **9,** 369.

Grad, J., and Sainsbury, P. (1963). 'Mental illness and the family'. *Lancet, i,* 544–7.

—— (1966). 'Evaluating the community psychiatric services in Chichester: results', in Gruenberg, E. M. (ed.), *Evaluating the Effectiveness of Community Mental Health Services,* pp. 246–77 (New York: Milbank Memorial Fund).

Gruenberg, E. M. (1957). 'Application of control methods to mental illness', *Am. J. Publ. Hlth,* **47,** 944.

Gurland, B. J., Fleiss, J. L., Cooper, J. E., Sharpe, L., Kendell, R. E., and Roberts, P. (1970). 'Hospital diagnosis and hospital patients in New York and London', *Compr. Psychiat.* **11,** 18–25.

Juel-Nielsen, N., Bille, M., Flygenring, J., and Helgason, T. (1961). 'Frequency of depressive states within geographically delimited population groups: 3. Incidence (The Aarhus county investigation)', reprinted from *Depression, Acta Psychiat., Scand.,* supplement 162, **37,** 69–80.

Koons, G. F. (1969a). 'Predictions of the resident patient population in public mental hospitals based on a gompertz curve', Statistical Note 1, January 1969 (Rockville, Maryland: Biometry Branch, National Institute of Mental Health).

—— (1969b). 'Projected age-diagnostic composition of the resident patient population in State and county mental hospitals—1973'. Statistical Note 8, July 1969 (Rockville, Maryland: Biometry Branch, National Institute of Mental Health).

Kramer, M. (1967). 'Epidemiology, biostatistics and mental health planning', in *Psychiatric Epidemiology and Mental Health Planning,* Psychiatric Research Report no. 22, pp. 1–63 (Washington, DC: American Psychiatric Association).

—— (1969). *Application of Mental Health Statistics* (Geneva: WHO).

—— Pollack, E. S., Locke, B. Z., and Bahn, A. K. (1961). 'National approach to the evaluation of community mental health programs', *Am. J. Publ. Hlth,* **51,** 969.

—— Taube, C. A., and Starr, S. (1968). 'Patterns of use of psychiatric facilities by the aged: current status, trends, and implications', in *Aging in Modern Society,* Psychiatric Research Report no. 23, pp. 89–150 (Washington, DC: American Psychiatric Association).

—— —— and Redick, R. W. (in press): 'Patterns of use of psychiatric facilities by the aged: past, present and future', in *Task Force Report on Aging* (Washington, DC: American Psychological Association).

—— Zubin, J., Cooper, J. E., Gurland, B. J., *et al.* (1969). 'Cross national study of diagnosis of the mental disorders', *Am. J. Psychiat.* **125,** 10, supplement.

Lin, T. (1967). 'The epidemiological study of mental disorders', *World Health Organisation Chronicle,* **21,** 509.

Milbank Memorial Fund (1956). *The Elements of a Community Mental Health Program,* p. 30 (New York: Milbank Memorial Fund).

Morris, J. N. (1964). *Uses of Epidemiology,* 2nd edn (Baltimore: The Williams and Wilkins Co.).

National Clearinghouse for Mental Health Information (1971). *Mental Health Directory, 1971,* Public Health Service Publication no. 1268 (revised 1971), pp. 8–9 (Washington, DC: US Government Printing Office).

National Institute of Mental Health (1965). *Guidelines for State Plans to be submitted under the Community Mental Health Centers Act of 1963* (Washington, DC: US Government Printing Office).

—— (1971). *Halfway Houses serving the Mentally Ill and Alcoholics, 1969–70,* Publ. no. (HSM)-72-9049 (Washington, DC: US Government Printing Office).

Ødegaard, Ø., and Astrup, C. (1970). 'Continued experiments in psychiatric diagnosis', *Acta Psychiat. Scand.* **46,** 180–210.

Pollack, E. S., Redick, R. W., and Taube, C. A. (1968). 'The application of census socio-economic and familial data to the study of morbidity from mental disorders', *Am. J. Publ. Hlth,* **58,** 83–89.

President of the United States (1963). 'Message relative to mental illness and

mental retardation', 5 February 1963, 88th Congress, House of Repre-
sentives, Document no. 58 (Washington, DC).

Public Law 88–164–88th Congress, S. 1576, 31 October 1963. Mental Retardation Facilities and Community Mental Health Centers, Construction Act
of 1963.

―― 89–97–89th Congress, H.R. 6675, 30 July 1965. Social Security Amendments of 1965.

―― 89–105–89th Congress, H.R. 2985, 4 August 1965. Mental Retardation
Facilities and Community Mental Health Centers Construction Acts Amendments of 1965.

―― 89–749–89th Congress, S. 3008, 3 November 1966. Comprehensive Health
Planning and Public Health Services Amendments of 1966.

―― 90–31–90th Congress, H.R. 6431, 24 June 1967. Mental Health Amendments of 1967.

―― 90–574–90th Congress, H.R. 15758, 15 October 1968. Public Health Service Act, Amendment.

―― 91–211–91st Congress, S. 2523, 13 March 1970. Community Mental
Health Centers Amendments of 1970.

Redick, R. W., and Goldsmith, H. F. (1971). *1970 Census Data used to In-
dicate Areas with Different Potentials for Mental Health and Related
Problems,* National Institute of Mental Health, Mental Health Statistics
Series C no. 3, Public Health Service Publication no. 2171 (Washington,
DC: US Government Printing Office).

Rutter, M., Lebovici, S., Eisenberg, L., Sneznevskij, Sadoun R., Brooke, E., and
Lin, T. (1969). 'A triaxial classification of mental disorders in childhood. An
international study', *J. Child Psychol. Psychiat.* **10,** 41–61.

Sainsbury, P., and Grad, J. (1962). 'Evaluation of treatment services', in *The
Burden on the Community,* chap. vi, pp. 69–116 (Oxford University Press
for the Nuffield Hospitals Trust).

―― (1966). 'Evaluating the community psychiatric service in Chichester: aims
and methods of research', in Gruenberg, E. (ed.), *Evaluating the Effectiveness of Community Mental Health Services,* pp. 231–9 (New York: Milbank Memorial Fund).

Sartorius, N., Brooke, E. M., and Lin, T. (1970). 'Reliability of psychiatric
assessment in international research', in Hare, E. H., and Wing, J. K. (eds),
Psychiatric Epidemiology, pp. 133–47 (Oxford University Press for the
Nuffield Provincial Hospitals Trust).

Shepherd, M., Brooke, E. M., Cooper, J. E., and Lin, T. (1968). 'An experimental approach to psychiatric diagnosis'. *Acta Psychiat. Scand.,* supplement 201.

Susser, M. W. (1968). *Community Psychiatry. Epidemiologic and Social Themes,*
pp. 175–82 (New York: Random House).

―― Stein, Z., Mountney, G. H., and Freeman, H. L. (1970). Chronic disability
following mental illness in an English city. Part 1. Total prevalence in and
out of mental hospital', *Soc. Psychiat.* **5,** 63–69; 'Part II. The location of
patients in hospital and community', ibid. **5,** 69–76.

Taube, C. A. (1966). *Employees in Nursing Homes United States, May–June
1964.* National Center for Health Statistics, Public Health Service Publication no. 1000, Series 12, no. 5 (Washington, DC: US Government
Printing Office).

―― (1970). *Differential Utilization of Outpatient Psychiatric Services by Whites
and Non-whites, 1969,* Statistical Note 36, December 1970, DHEW Publication no. HSM 72-9012 (Rockville, Maryland: Health Services and Mental
Health Administration, National Institute of Mental Health).

—— (1971*a*) *Admission Rates to State and County Mental Hospitals by Age, Sex, and Color, United States, 1969,* Statistical Note 41, February 1971. DHEW Publication no. HSM 72-9012 (Rockville, Maryland: Health Services and Mental Health Administration, National Institute of Mental Health).

—— (1971*b*). *Changes in Age-Sex Diagnostic Composition of First Admissions to State and County Mental Hospitals—1962 to 1969.* Statistical Note 55, May 1971, DHEW Publication no. HSM 72-9012 (Rockville, Maryland: Health Services and Mental Health Administration, National Institute of Mental Health).

—— (1972). *Distribution of Patient Care Episodes in Mental Health Facilities, 1969,* Statistical Note 58, January 1972, DHEW Publication no. HSM 72-9012 (Rockville, Maryland: Health Services and Mental Health Administration, National Institute of Mental Health).

—— and Bryant, E. E. (1967). *Employees in Nursing and Personal Care Homes: Number, Work Experience, Special Training and Wages. United States, May–June, 1964,* National Center for Health Statistics, Public Health Service Publication no. 1000, Series 12, no. 6 (Washington, DC: US Government Printing Office).

US Bureau of the Census (1964). *Census of Population: 1960 Subject Reports. Persons by Family Characteristics* (Washington, DC: US Government Printing Office).

—— (1968). Current Population Reports Series P-25, no. 388. *Summary of Demographic Projections* (Washington, DC: US Government Printing Office).

—— (1969). Current Population Reports Series P-60, no. 68, December 31, 1969. *Poverty in the U.S. 1959–68* (Washington, DC: US Government Printing Office).

—— (1970). Current Population Reports Series P-20, no. 198, 25 March 1970. *Marital Status and Family Status, March 1969* (Washington, DC: US Government Printing Office).

—— (1971). Current Population Reports Series P-20, no. 212, 1 February 1971. *Marital Status and Family Status, March 1970* (Washington, DC: US Government Printing Office).

US Department of Health, Education, and Welfare (1968). *Health Planning. A Programmed Instruction Course,* BHS programmed instruction Series no. 2, Public Health Service Bulletin no. 1846 (Washington, DC: US Government Printing Office).

—— National Institute of Mental Health and Maryland Department of Mental Hygiene (1967). *Maryland Psychiatric Case Register: Description of History, Current Status and Future Uses* (Rockville, Maryland: Biometry Branch, National Institute of Mental Health).

—— PHS, HSMHA, National Institute of Mental Health, (1970). *The Community Mental Health Center. Grants for Construction and Staffing,* Public Health Service Publication no. 2136 (revised 1970) (Washington, DC: US Government Printing Office).

Wing, J. K., *et al.* (1964). 'Morbidity in the community of schizophrenics discharged from London mental hospitals in 1959', *Br. J. Psychiat.* **110,** 10–21.

Wing, L., Wing, J. K., Hailey, A., Bahn, A. K., Smith, H. E., and Baldwin, J. A. (1967). 'The use of psychiatric services in three urban areas: an international case register study', *Soc. Psychiat.* **2,** 158.

World Health Organization (1957). *Manual of the International Statistical Classification of Diseases* (1955 revision) (Geneva: WHO).

—— Expert Committee on Health Statistics (1963). 'Eight Report', *Wld Hlth Org. Techn. Rep. Ser.,* **261**.

—— Expert Committee on Health Statistics (1967). 'Twelfth Report'. ibid. **389**.

—— Expert Committee on Health Statistics (1969). Ibid. **429**.

—— Expert Committee on Health Statistics (1971). 'Statistical indicators for the planning and evaluation of public health programs', ibid. **472**.

—— Expert Committee on Hospital Administration (1968). Ibid. **395**.

——— Expert Committee on Mental Health (1960). 'Epidemiology of mental disorders', ibid. **185**.

—— Expert Committee on National Health Planning in Developing Countries (1967). Ibid. **350**.

—— Expert Committee on Training in National Health Planning (1970). Ibid. **456**.

—— Mental Health Unit (1968). 'Psychiatric diagnosis, classification and statistics', *Fourth World Health Organization Seminar,* Moscow (Mimeographed Report MH/70.8).

—— Mental Health Unit (1969). 'Psychiatric diagnosis, classification and statistics', *Fifth World Health Organization Seminar,* Washington, DC (Mimeographed Report MH/70.2).

—— Mental Health Unit (1970). 'Psychiatric diagnosis, classification and statistics', *Sixth World Health Organization Seminar,* Basel (Mimeographed Report MH/71.7).

—— Mental Health Unit (1971). 'Psychiatric diagnosis, classification and statistics', *Seventh World Health Organization Seminar,* Tokyo (Mimeographed Report, in press).

5 Statistics from general practice

BRIAN COOPER

Introduction

The significance of general practice statistics from any country will depend largely upon the structure and organization of its medical services. In Great Britain, the system of registration with family doctors under the NHS provides a valuable sampling-frame for epidemiological research. Under this system, the GP acts as the point of first contact for most illnesses which are brought to medical care. Since all hospital contacts made by his patients are reported to the GP, his case-files constitute a register of the illness-experience of a defined population.

In countries which lack such comprehensive schemes, general practice data cannot be accorded the same importance; nevertheless, they may be extremely useful both as a supplement to hospital statistics and as a basis for operational studies.

General practice statistics should not be regarded as a substitute either for area prevalence surveys or for local case-registers. Each approach has its own well-defined advantages and disadvantages; their respective merits will vary both with the type of morbidity under investigation and with the prevailing social conditions. Ideally, all three methods should be used in conjunction, with ample opportunity for comparing and also for pooling data from each individual source.

The advantages of the GP's position can be stated succinctly. First, his services are economical, since he can act as a case-finding and recording agent while carrying out his daily work. The average British practitioner, for example, sees about 70 per cent of his registered patients in the course of one year, and probably over 90 per cent within two years (Kessel and Shepherd, 1965). Secondly, by virtue of his medical training and experience, he possesses distinct advantages over the lay interviewer. Thirdly, his relationship with his patients can be of the greatest help in gaining their co-operation, and thus in securing full coverage of the population at risk. Finally, the continuity of medical care which he provides lends itself to the requirements of longitudinal studies. In short, the GP is

Table 1. *Distribution of psychiatric patients by type of medical care and supervision, England and Wales.*

Type of care	Mentally ill	Mentally retarded
Hospitals	140,000	60,000
GPs	310,000	40,000
Local authorities	40,000	80,000

Source. Office of Health Economics (1965).

uniquely placed to observe the changing patterns of morbidity in the wider community.

The scope of general practice research in psychiatry

At any given point in time, only a minority of the psychiatric cases in a population will be under specialist care: a point repeatedly confirmed by surveys in Europe and North America. Table 1, based on data from the British health services, provides a fairly typical estimate.

Global estimates of this kind, while affording a useful perspective, may conceal important differences between the diagnostic groups. In planning services, it may be more realistic to consider psychiatric morbidity under the two broad headings of 'major' and 'minor' disorder: bearing in mind the limitations of this dichotomy. In the former category, which includes the major organic and functional psychoses, severe mental retardation, chronic alcoholism, and narcotic addiction, the patient manifests conspicuous abnormality and social impairment. In the latter group, comprising the neuroses, most character disorders and the milder forms of mental retardation, the patient usually remains a viable social unit. Although, for obvious reasons, type of morbidity cannot be equated with type of medical care, the division does correspond roughly to that between psychiatric specialist and general medical services; hence, it serves as a reminder of the scope and limits of general practice statistics.

It may be doubted whether general practice data can add substantially to our knowledge of the prevalence and incidence of major mental disorders. Fairly good information on this topic is now available from a number of area surveys and from cumulative case-registers; nor can it be said that general practice surveys to date have revealed any unsuspected reservoir of cases. They have, however, influenced our perception of psychotic illness by demonstrating the presence in the community of milder analogues, as for example of 'endogenous' depression (Watts, 1966), and of post-partum psychosis. Moreover, they have closed some of the gaps left in the recorded history of chronic or recurrent mental illness, and have thrown new light on the events leading up to such crises as hospital re-admission (Parkes *et al.*, 1962). Each of these contributions

Table 2. *Psychiatric referral rates from general practice and community surveys in England and Wales.*

Authors	Year	Size of population	Survey period (years)	Referral rate per 10,000 at risk	Proportion of psychiatric cases referred
Bodkin *et al.*	1953	14,000	1	72·9	—
Hopkins	1956	1,400	3	160·6	—
Martin *et al.*	1957	17,250	1	29·0	5·3
Fry	1959	5,500	1	61·8	5·0
Rawnsley and Loudon	1961	18,500	9	17·7	—
Taylor and Chave	1964	40,000	3	31·5	5·4
Shepherd *et al.*	1966	15,000	1	71·4	5·1

Source. Kaeser and Cooper (1971).

may have long-term significance for the planning and evaluation of services.

Undoubtedly, however, the most important aspects of psychiatric research in general practice are those dealing with the minor disorders. Even today, the great majority of these conditions remain outside specialist care. Table 2, again derived from British data, summarizes the findings of a number of general practice investigations; these indicate that, in any one year, only about one in twenty of identified cases are referred to psychiatric agencies.

The inference may be drawn that hospital and clinic statistics are unlikely to be representative; for scientific study of the neuroses and related conditions, general practice and community studies will be essential. Meanwhile, two propositions can be made with regard to service planning. First, in a situation where the patients under specialist treatment constitute only a small fraction of those potentially eligible, the processes governing selection for such treatment merit careful attention. There is some reason to suspect that, even where free medical services are provided, non-clinical factors continue to play an important part in selection. Why, for example, do GPs send relatively few elderly patients to psychiatric agencies? (Kessel and Shepherd, 1962; Hopkins and Cooper, 1969). Operational studies in general practice could usefully examine the factors underlying this kind of bias.

Secondly, it is clear that the hospital services could not hope to carry the whole burden of psychiatric care, even were that considered desirable. The central problem must remain one of equipping the general medical services, together with public health and social agencies, to deal as effectively as possible with most minor mental disorders. Here again, operational and evaluative studies are badly needed.

In this still largely unexplored field, it is not to be expected that epidemiological research will generate such firm recommendations for service provision as have come, for example, from surveys of severe mental

Table 3. *Use of medical services during a three-year period by a psychiatric group and a matched control group.*

Item of medical service	Index group (N = 170)	Control group (N = 170)
GP consultations		
Total	4,182	1,915
Mean	24·6	11·3
Standard deviation	21·1	8·5
(t = 7·8; p<0·001)		
Specialist referrals		
Total	235	151
Mean	1·38	0·89
Standard deviation	0·91	0·94
(d = 4·25; p<0·001)		
Hospital admissions		
Total	71	44
Mean	0·42	0·26
Standard deviation	0·70	0·50
(d = 2·53; p<0·02)		

Source. Harvey-Smith and Cooper (1970).

handicap (Kushlick, 1966). Information is first required as to the types of service needed, and how they can be most effectively deployed. Here, a useful start has been made in the delineation of high-risk groups: notably where controlled studies have pointed to the medical and social correlates of psychiatric morbidity. Three examples will be cited from work undertaken by our research unit at the Institute of Psychiatry. In each study, the basic research tool was a standardized psychiatric interview of known reliability, designed specifically for this type of investigation (Goldberg *et al.,* 1970).

Psychiatric and physical morbidity

General practice surveys have shown repeatedly that patients with psychiatric diagnoses consult more frequently than average, and maintain relatively high levels of demand for medical care. Table 3 summarizes the findings of a controlled study which examined this point.

Here, as in similar studies, the neurotic patients' high use of services could not be accounted for in terms of psychiatric treatment: it appeared that they also presented more physical symptoms than the controls, and were more often referred to medical and surgical departments.

Findings of this kind are open to a number of interpretations. One cannot assume the presence of disease merely on the evidence that the patient has consulted. Neurotic patients, given the same experience of physical morbidity as others, may be more likely to regard themselves as sick, and to seek medical treatment. Conversely, patients who habitually consult

Table 4. *Distribution of ischaemic heart disease among psychiatric patients and matched controls, by sex (percentage).*

Physical status	Males Psychiatric	Control	Females Psychiatric	Control
Illness-free	70·3	89·2	77·0	88·5
Probable coronary heart disease	10·8	2·7	3·4	—
Possible coronary heart disease	18·9	8·1	19·6	11·5
Total	100·0	100·0	100·0	100·0
Number of patients	37	37	87	87
	Chi-squared 4·10 $p<0.05$		Chi-squared 4·03 $p<0.05$	

Source. Eastwood and Trevelyan (1971).

their doctors frequently will tend to be labelled 'neurotic', whatever the nature of their ailments.

That these tendencies do not entirely account for the reported association between physical and psychiatric illness was indicated by a recent study which formed part of a health screening survey in general practice (Eastwood, 1970). Here, the setting of the investigation was especially valuable because it permitted the patient's physical status to be assessed independently of any subjective complaints.

Those invited to participate comprised one-half, randomly selected, of all patients aged 40 to 65 years registered with a large group practice. Of a possible total of 2,200 patients, just over two-thirds took part. Each underwent a battery of tests, including morphological measurements, blood-pressure readings, ventilatory function tests, electrocardiogram, and a number of blood and urine tests. In addition, a questionnaire including twenty items selected from the Cornell Medical Index was completed by each patient. Two weeks later, the patient was physically examined by his GP, who by this time had received a report of the test results.

At their first attendance, patients whose questionnaire scores suggested possible psychological disturbance were given the standardized psychiatric interview; as a result, 124 (8·2 per cent) were classed as confirmed cases. A control group, matched with these 124 patients by sex, age, marital status, and social class, was drawn from among the patients whose questionnaire responses gave no indication of mental disturbance; any 'false negatives' were excluded at the interview stage.

When the two matched groups were compared in respect of the screening survey findings, the index group proved to have a significant excess of major physical disease. With the small numbers available, few conclusions could be reached about individual diagnoses; however, Table 4 suggests an association between psychiatric disorder and ischaemic heart disease.

Table 5. *Comparison of social adjustment ratings* for neurotic patients and matched controls: weighted mean area scores.*

Area of social adjustment	Males		Females	
	Index (N = 20)	Control (N = 20)	Index (N = 61)	Control (N = 61)
Income and finances	50·0	8·3	53·0	15·3
Occupation	124·0	22·2	76·1	37·1
Living conditions	95·6	45·5	64·4	28·5
Social and leisure activities	117·5	61·3	112·3	64·3
Personal interaction	113·6	66·2	99·0	54·2
Parenthood	38·9	29·6	98·5	44·9

* Positive ratings in every case denote social problems or difficulties.

Whatever the causes of this association between psychiatric and physical morbidity, it cannot be ascribed simply to the patients' self-perception or demand for medical services. While it is too early to speculate on causal relationships, there is a *prima-facie* case for arguing that, among the middle-aged, clinically defined neurotic illness is linked with an increased risk of organic disease.

Social correlates of chronic neurotic illness

The standardized psychiatric interview was also employed in a controlled study of the social adjustment of patients with chronic neurotic disorders (Cooper *et al.*, 1970). For this inquiry, the index group was drawn from a sample of attending patients in eight London general practices, each practitioner keeping a special record of all consultations during one month. Of 185 potential index patients, 24 (13·0 per cent) either refused interview or failed to attend; of the 161 who were interviewed, 46 (28·6 per cent) were discarded as unsuitable, mostly because they had not had psychiatric symptoms continuously for at least one year. Thus, the index group comprised 115 confirmed cases of chronic neurotic illness: mainly depressive and anxiety neuroses.

The first 81 index patients were matched individually by sex, age, marital status, social class, employment status, ethnic group, and type of living group, with mentally healthy people drawn from the same pool of attending patients. Of 138 potential controls selected for this purpose, 34 (24·6 per cent) refused interview or failed to attend; of the 104 interviewed, 23 (22·1 per cent) were discarded as unsuitable, mostly because they had some psychiatric disturbance.

Both index and control patients were then rated for various aspects of social adjustment, on the basis of a standardized, semi-structured social interview carried out in each patient's home.

In analysing the findings, the social ratings were combined in two ways. First, they were grouped as 'area' scores each corresponding to a major aspect of the patients' lives, namely: income and finances; occupation; living conditions; social and leisure activities; personal interaction (including marital adjustment); and parenthood. Secondly, each rating was assigned to one of three broad categories designated respectively material conditions, social management, and role-satisfaction. Each of these latter groupings cuts across the 'area' totals; thus, the score for material conditions comprises ratings for income, housing conditions, handicaps to leisure activities, etc.

Large differences were found between the index and control groups on both sets of scores. Table 5, which summarizes the 'area' scores, shows that the differences extended to all aspects of the patients' life-activities, though the neurotic men were more obviously characterized by occupational difficulties, and the neurotic women by problems of child management.

These differences indicate a positive association between neurotic symptoms and the somewhat nebulous variable of social adjustment.[1] Examination of the second set of scores provided a slightly better definition of the concept, in so far as differences between the index and control groups were much smaller (though still significant) for material conditions than for social management and role-satisfaction. Similarly, within the whole psychiatric group of 115 patients, ratings of clinical severity correlated significantly with those for social management ($r = +0.37$) and role-satisfaction ($r = +0.32$), but not with that for material conditions ($r = +0.13$).

The findings here outlined agree broadly with those on the social role-performance of depressed women, reported by an American research group (Weissman *et al.*, 1971). They do not, of course, give any indication of how far the social dysfunction is primary, how far secondary to the mental disturbance: cohort studies are needed to answer this question. In any event, by the time the illness has become chronic one must expect to find a complex interaction between behavioural and environmental variables.

In the present study, re-examination of the psychiatric patients after one year revealed that, while their over-all levels of social adjustment were little altered, such change as had occurred in the ratings correlated positively with clinical changes. The findings summarized in Table 6 suggest that it may be possible, by systematic attention to the social adjustment of chronic neurotic patients, to effect a measurable improvement in their clinical condition. Nevertheless, only a small proportion of the total clinical variance could be explained in terms of the relatively static characteristics measured by the social interview.

1. Since the number of patients who could be rated varied for each item, no statistical test could be applied directly to the grouped scores shown in Table 5. Differences in individual item scores were significant, at least at the 5 per cent level, for 20 of the 26 items.

Table 6. *Correlation between clinical and social changes in a sample of chronic neurotic patients over a one-year interval (N = 97).*

Social adjustment (category mean scores)	Psychiatric interview ratings		
	Reported symptom scores	Manifest abnormality scores	Total weighted scores
Material conditions	0·156	0·067	0·125
Social management	0·243*	0·161	0·246*
Role-satisfaction	0·281†	0·330†	0·352†
Over-all mean score	0·358†	0·297†	0·380†

* = significant at 0·05 level.   † = significant at 0·01 level.

Clearly, other determinants of clinical change must be involved. Leaving aside for the moment the influence of medical treatment, and also of any endogenous change in the patient, one must consider the possible effects of any recent environmental changes which might not have been recorded in an interview focused on current social adjustment. It is a plausible hypothesis that patients selected on the basis of recent medical consultation will tend to be passing through a phase of increased social difficulties. This hypothesis has yet to be tested for chronic neurotic patients, but some supporting evidence comes from a small unpublished study of new neurotic illness-episodes.

Social correlates of new illness-episodes

The key studies of environmental precipitating factors are those by Brown and Birley (1968, 1970), who demonstrated that the weeks prior to the onset of acute psychiatric episodes are characterized by a sharp increase in the numbers of life-changes and events experienced by the patients; and that this observation holds good even for events of a kind which could hardly be influenced by the patient's mental state or personality.

While the original findings of Brown and Birley related to schizophrenia and severe depressive illness, they have obvious relevance to the minor psychiatric disorders. Moreover, research in general practice offers an opportunity to refine the methodology in two ways: first, patients can be identified at an earlier stage of the illness than in hospital studies; secondly, the technique of individual matching from the general practice population, already described, provides the basis for more exact comparisons between psychiatric and normal groups.

With these considerations in mind, a study was undertaken of the precipitants of new neurotic illness-episodes in a general practice population. The research design was basically similar to that outlined for the study of chronic neurosis. Eight practitioners each in turn kept a record of all new psychiatric cases seen during one month, a new episode being operationally defined as the first consultation for psychiatric symptoms for at least one year. In five of the practices, a special record was also kept of all patients who consulted during the month, providing a sampling-frame from which to select controls. To ensure comparability of exposure to life-changes and 'events', the index and control patients were matched individually by sex, age, marital status, social class, employment status, ethnic group, number of children, and number of persons in the household.

Psychiatric status for index and control cases was assessed by means of the standardized psychiatric interview used in the other studies. Experience of 'events' was investigated by means of the Precipitating Events Schedule developed by Brown and Birley, the social research worker who carried out the home interviews having previously trained in the use of this instrument with their research group. At the time the study was undertaken (1967–8), both research instruments were still at a formative stage; for this reason, and because of the small numbers involved, it represents a pilot rather than a definitive study.

Altogether, the GPs reported 112 psychiatric illnesses new to them. Of these, 12 patients failed to attend for the clinical interview and 5 refused the home visit; hence, altogether 17 patients (15·2 per cent) were lost through non-co-operation. Of the 100 patients interviewed, 42 (42·0 per cent) were rejected as unsuitable, mostly because their symptoms were of more than three months' duration. In this way, a fairly homogeneous group of 53 patients with new episodes of neurotic illness was obtained. Depressive neurosis was overwhelmingly the most frequent diagnosis (79·2 per cent), the remainder consisting of acute anxiety states together with two acute hysterical reactions. The average duration of illness at the time of key consultation was between two and three weeks.

Individually matched controls were selected for the first 34 psychiatric patients, before the study had to be terminated. Of 58 potential control patients who were approached, 13 (22·4 per cent) were lost through failure to co-operate and 8 out of 47 interviewed (17·0 per cent) were rejected because they had psychiatric symptoms.

The events schedule inquired about the period of three months prior to the onset of psychiatric symptoms (or, in the case of the control patients, prior to key consultation). In Table 7, the distribution of 'independent' and 'possibly independent' events, during the four consecutive three-weekly periods before onset, is given for the whole index group of 53 patients.

Thus, a clear trend was evident, both for 'independent' events only and for all reported events, towards increasing frequency as the onset of psychiatric illness approached. The pattern was similar to that reported by Brown and Birley for more severe affective disorders.

From Table 8, in which the findings for the thirty-four matched pairs of patients are summarized, it can be seen that the index patients had a higher incidence of events during the relevant period. The proportion of index patients who experienced at least one event during this period also tended

Table 7. *Percentage of new psychiatric cases with at least one re-ported event in each of the four three-weekly periods prior to the onset of illness (N = 53) (percentage).*

Type of event	Three-weekly periods prior to onset (Furthest)			(Nearest)
	4th	3rd	2nd	1st
Independent	15·1	9·4	18·9	37·7
	(Chi-squared for trend 11·09; *p*<0·01)			
Possibly independent only	5·7	17·0	20·8	30·2
All events	20·8	24·5	35·8	54·7
	(Chi-squared for trend 15·12; *p*<0·01)			

to be higher than the corresponding proportion of control patients; though not significantly so when only 'independent' events were considered.

Given the small size of sample, these differences are so marked as to suggest that frequency of 'events' may be an important variable. The implications for treatment or prevention are not yet clear, but some clues are to be found in the nature of the reported events. Apart from one case of acute febrile illness, all were more readily definable in social than in medical terms. Most carried at least the possibility of changes in personal status or interaction or in family interaction; and most could be regarded as threatening or unpleasant rather than the reverse. It appeared, therefore, that the research method had served to identify short-term social stress-factors, much as that used for the chronic patients had identified long-term factors.

Conclusion

The findings I have outlined suggest that psychiatric illness in the community is composed largely of minor affective disorders; that in the middle age-groups it is associated with a raised expectation of physical morbidity, including major disease; that the more chronic forms are also associated with long-term problems of social adjustment; and that new episodes are often precipitated by events in the family and social orbit. These findings are in conformity, both with the theoretical concept of 'illness-proneness' (Hinkle and Wolff, 1957; Hinkle, 1961) and with the work of Holmes and his colleagues on the significance of life-change (Rahe *et al.*, 1967). They point to the need for co-ordination between mental health, general medical, and social services in the management of patients with a consistently high experience of morbidity.

Further research in this field calls for cohort studies, and for experimental projects in which various methods of medical and social intervention can be evaluated. It is not difficult to envisage the kind of medical service which would lend itself most readily to such investigations. The doctors concerned would provide general medical care for a defined

Table 8. *Frequency of reported events for matched psychiatric and control patients during the three months before onset of illness.*

	Index (N = 34)	Control (N = 34)	Test of significance
Number of all events			
Total	61	24	
Mean	1·80	0·71	$t = 3·40; p < 0·01$
Number of 'independent' events			
Total	36	14	
Mean	1·06	0·41	$t = 2·55; p < 0·01$
Number of patients with at least one event	26	13	Chi-squared = 4·69 $p < 0·05$
Number of patients with at least one 'independent' event	18	9	Chi-squared = 1·90 $p > 0·05$

population; preferably, in urban areas at least, they would be combined in groups serving fairly large numbers, say 15,000 to 20,000 each. Specialist referral would as a rule be arranged by the GPs on behalf of their patients; moreover, facilities would be provided in each practice for some specialists (notably psychiatrists, geriatricians, and paediatricians) to attend regularly, both to examine patients and to discuss difficult problems. Each group would have attached public health nurses, whose work would include routine home-visiting of certain risk-categories of patient. The findings already cited lend some support to the view, now gaining ground, that the balanced health team would also include a social worker, at least in a part-time capacity. Emphasis would be placed on the need for preventive care, such as periodic health screening and routine patient follow-up. To encourage this approach, medical remuneration would be arranged by salary or capitation fee, rather than on an item-for-service basis. In short, the requirements for evaluative research in community medicine are well fitted by modern concepts of the primary medical care unit.

The immediate prospects for large-scale development of this type of service are not entirely favourable, even in countries which already possess the basic structure. In Great Britain, for example, it has been observed that the medical profession, asked to swallow a comprehensive health service on top of ideas about preventive and psychological medicine, is suffering agonies of indigestion (Vickers, 1965). Nevertheless, there is an increasing number of model services which incorporate most of the features I have listed: some have been set up by university departments; others are being actively supported by the DHSS. Their potential value for evaluative research can hardly be over-stated.

Acknowledgements

The research outlined in this paper, which formed part of the programme of the General Practice Research Unit, Institute of Psychiatry, was supported by grants from the Mental Health Research Fund and the Department of Health and Social Security, London. The unpublished studies were undertaken in collaboration with Dr M. R. Eastwood, Dr H. B. Kedward, Miss J. Sylph, and Mrs R. Fitzgerald.

REFERENCES

Brown, G. W., and Birley, J. L. T. (1968). 'Crises and life changes and the onset of schizophrenia', *J. Hlth soc. Behav.* **9**, 203.
—— (1970). 'Social precipitants of severe psychiatric disorders', in Hare, E. H., and Wing, J. K. (eds), *Psychiatric Epidemiology* (Oxford University Press for the Nuffield Provincial Hospitals Trust).
Cooper, B., Eastwood, M. R., and Sylph, J. (1970). 'Psychiatric morbidity and social adjustment in a general practice population', in ibid.
Eastwood, M. R. (1970). 'Psychiatric morbidity and physical state in a general practice population' in ibid.
—— and Trevelyan, H. (1971). 'Stress and coronary heart disease', *J. psychosom. Res.* **15**, 289.
Goldberg, D. P., Cooper, B., Eastwood, M. R., Kedward, H. D., and Shepherd, M. (1970). 'A standardized psychiatric interview for use in community surveys' *Br. J. prev. soc. Med.* **24**, 18.
Harvey-Smith, E. A., and Cooper, B. (1970). 'Patterns of neurotic illness in the community', *Jl R. Coll. Gen. Practit.* **19**, 132.
Hinkle, L. E., and Wolff, H. G. (1957). 'Health and the social environment: experimental investigations', in Leighton, A. H., Clausen, J. A., and Wilson, R. N. (eds), *Explorations in Social Psychiatry* (London: Tavistock).
—— (1961). 'Ecological observations of the relation of physical illness, mental illness and social environment', *Psychosom. Med.* **23**, 289.
Hopkins, P., and Cooper, B. (1969). 'Psychiatric referral from a general practice', *Br. J. Psychiat.* **115**, 1163.
Kaeser, A. C., and Cooper, B. (1971). 'The psychiatric patient, the general practitioner and the out-patient clinic: an operational study and a review', *Psychol. Med.* **1**, 312.
Kessel, N., and Shepherd, M. (1962). 'Neurosis in hospital and general practice', *J. ment. Sci.* **108**, 159.
—— (1965). 'The health and attitudes of people who seldom consult a doctor', *Med. Care (Lond.),* **3**, 6.
Kushlick, A. (1966). 'A community service for the mentally subnormal', *Soc. Psychiat.* **1**, 73.
Office of Health Economics (1965). *The Cost of Mental Care* (Leeds: Waddington).
Parkes, C. M., Brown, G. W., and Monck, E. M. (1962). 'The general practitioner and the schizophrenic patient', *Br. med. J.* **1**, 972.
Rahe, R. H., McKean, J. D., Jr., and Arthur, R. J. (1967). 'A longitudinal study of life-change and illness patterns', *J. psychosom. Res.* **10**, 355.
Vickers, G. (1965). 'Medicine, psychiatry and general practice', *Lancet*, **i**, 1021.
Watts, C. A. H. (1966). *Depressive Illness in the Community* (Bristol: John Wright).

6 Morbidity statistics from population surveys

DAFYDD HUGHES

The studies reported were conducted by the psychiatric epidemiology team at the Medical Research Council, Llandough, Glamorgan, Wales, under the direction of Professor K. Rawnsley. Dr J. Ingham of the Medical Research Council, a member of the team, has undertaken most of the data evaluation.

Introduction

This paper describes some of the findings from sampling surveys studying morbidity and attitudes in contrasting areas in Wales, which are hitherto largely unpublished. The inquiries followed studies of treated case prevalence in the same areas.

The population studied lived in two contrasting areas in the same county in Wales: a densely populated industrial coal-mining valley, where mining had undergone a rapid decline and where there was a 9 per cent rate of unemployment, and a relatively prosperous rural area in the lowlands near the coast some miles away (Fig. 1). The areas were served by the same psychiatric hospital and services; diagnostic criteria would therefore be comparable.

Studies of specialist-treated psychiatric cases from these areas over two periods of time (nine years apart) had shown considerable differences in rates between area and sex and marked differential increases from one period to the other. Sex ratios, however, appeared to be remarkably constant (Table 1).

Table 1. *Five-year period prevalence (specialist treated) rates per 1,000 and female/male sex ratios in period I and II showing percentage increase over period I rates.*

	1951–5 (period I)			1960–4 (period II)		
	M	Sex ratio	F	M	Sex ratio	F
Industrial (Rhondda)	15·5	1·14	17·7	26·4 (70%)	1·08	28·6 (62%)
Rural (Vale)	9·2	1·58	14·5	20·4 (122%)	1·56	31·9 (120%)

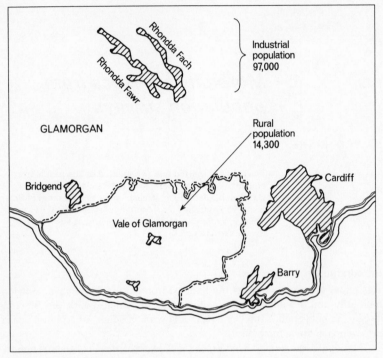

Figure 1. Map showing Rhondda Fach, Rhondda Fawr, and Vale of Glamorgan.

It was likely in the main that these considerable rate differences were caused by differential selection factors in a fractionation process. However, it did appear that despite the selection factors there might well be actual differences in morbidity between these groups. Conspicuously for example the rural males appeared to have relatively low morbidity, whereas the industrial males particularly in the 30–44 age-group appeared to suffer a high level of morbidity. Rural females in this age-group had the highest rate of all (Fig. 2).

Objectives

1. To examine differences in specialist-treated case rates in the light of various indices of morbidity.

2. To delineate further the contribution of actual morbidity differences as against selection factors in determining treated case rates.

3. To explain the apparent constancy of sex ratios despite differential rate variations.

4. To seek further evidence of the role of factors suggested by the declared case such as unemployment and coal-mining.

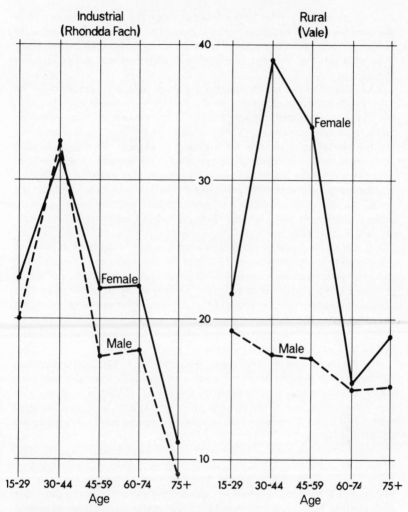

Figure 2. Five-year period prevalence rates by age-group for the Rhondda Fach (industrial) and the Vale of Glamorgan (rural).

Methodology

In attempting to evaluate the extent of selection factors, it is important to devise methods of estimating morbidity which are as free as possible from observer bias. We can then see how these observations tie up with those derived from conventional more bias prone methods. As the boundary between sickness and health is ill-defined and subject to bias, we therefore included morbidity indices which avoided sick/healthy dichotomies and in the main avoided global judgements of morbidity. The language of separate symptoms was used, structured to minimize observers' preconceptions. Thus what was lost in terms of relevance to diagnosis was gained in terms of objectivity.

The difficulty then lay in the conversion of data thus obtained to the currency of clinical psychiatry, how to correlate such morbidity rates with the rates of declared cases. To aid this conversion two validation procedures were used; (*a*) we interviewed psychiatric clinic patients in a manner similar to that used for the random sample, (*b*) the population samples were reinterviewed by a psychiatrist for a global assessment of psychiatric disorder. These validation procedures might also be considered as producing valid morbidity estimates in their own right. In addition the family doctors of the members of each random example were asked to make a judgement as to whether they considered a person to be psychiatrically disordered or not.

We were able, therefore, to compare the following subgroups in terms of the symptom morbidity indices: (*a*) Entire random samples by sex, (*b*) that subgroup of each sample considered psychiatrically disturbed by the family doctor, (*c*) that subgroup considered disordered by a psychiatrist in a clinical interview, (*d*) the group of psychiatric clinic patients from the industrial area. The psychiatrists and family doctors used different criteria. The family doctors' 'disordered' group would be expected to contain larger numbers of mildly disordered persons.

The random samples which were obtained from an MRC private census contained 581 persons from the rural area and 300 from the industrial valley (divided about equally between the sexes). The sample of more or less consecutive psychiatric out-patient clinic patients from the industrial area consisted of 35 men and 38 women. All groups were confined to the 25–45 age-range.

Two methods of examining symptoms were used. Firstly a modification of the CMI containing 102 questions (Rawnsley, 1966) was presented on cards in a face-to-face interview and for each symptom reported the respondent was asked whether he had had the symptom in the past year and whether he had sought advice. Of the many advantages of such a system, the main one is that it provides an index relevant to psychiatric disorder. The main disadvantages are that (*a*) it is open to response bias (acquiescence set) and (*b*) the yes–no nature of the answers gave no indication of symptom severity. In order to compensate for these two disadvantages, symptom scales were used which eliminated acquiescence set and which gave a measure of severity. Paired statement choices were converted to a twelve-point severity scale. The symptoms measured were backache, fatigue, depression, headache, and anxiety (Ingham, 1965). The validation procedures consisted of a comparison between a (healthy) ran-

Table 2. *Mean symptom scores.*

	Rural (Vale)			Industrial (Rhondda)		
	M	F	F-M	M	F	F-M
CMI						
Physical	4·5	5·8	+1·3	6·1	7·6	+1·5
Psychological	3·7	6·7	+3·0	5·2	8·7	+3·5
Total	8·8	12·7	+3·9	12·0	16·6	+4·6
Symptom scales						
Backache	2·2	3·3	+1·1	2·9	3·8	+0·9
Fatigue	3·5	4·0	+0·5	3·6	4·5	+0·9
Depression	2·3	2·6	+0·3	2·5	3·0	+0·5
Headache	2·6	3·8	+1·2	2·6	4·5	+1·9
Anxiety	4·4	5·1	+0·7	4·5	5·6	+1·1

dom sample group and the psychiatrically disordered groups (viz: clinic patients and those determined by a psychiatrist at clinical interview).

Results

The mean symptom scores (Table 2) as expected showed differences between sex and area. The female rates were higher than the male on all indices and in both areas. The rural males consistently scored the lowest. The differences were nearly all significant. Whereas in the specialist-treated case-study, the female/male ratios were 1·5 : 1 (rural) and 1 : 1 (industrial), according to these indices the sex ratio differences have largely disappeared.

To obtain a more exact comparison, we looked at the distribution of the symptom scores (Fig. 3). The predominance of female over male is seen over nearly the whole range of scores. To calculate a 'prevalence rate' from such a frequency distribution of symptom scores we need to choose a cut-off point. To obtain a 'prevalence rate' as low as that found for referred cases in this area (less than 4 per cent of the population), we need to define as 'disordered' persons with more than 51 symptoms on the CMI but this would exclude the symptom scores of 85 per cent of the psychiatric clinic patients we examined. The criterion that would include 70 per cent only of these patients would be 23 or more symptoms (or alternatively 7 symptoms for which a doctor had been consulted). 'Prevalence rates' calculated in this way (Table 3) show sex ratios of 3 : 1 rural and 2 : 1 industrial.

It is interesting to note (Fig. 3) how the position of the cut-off point influences the sex ratio of rates, and it is also interesting to note that for the industrial high scorers on the CMI there is actually a reversal of sex ratio which corresponds with the unusual finding in this age-group in the treated cases (Fig. 2). We find that the rural males, in addition to having a lower mean score, have a lower number of high scorers.

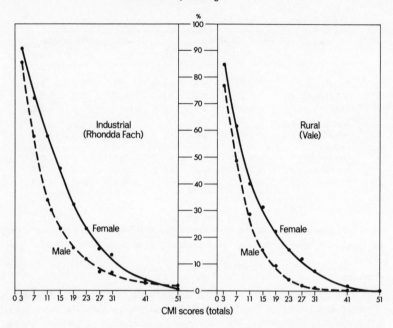

Figure 3. Cumulative frequency distributions (percentage) of total CMI scores.

It is seen that 'prevalence rates' thus calculated, differ very much from those calculated from treated case data. Accepting that the CMI provides a valid index of psychiatric morbidity, this wide difference in prevalence rates is probably explained by differential selection factors. To correspond with treated case rates (assuming an arbitrary 5 : 1 reduction factor to convert five-year rates to one-year rates), the selection ratios for sex and area shown in Table 3 would have to operate. It will be seen according to this model for example that the rural males who have the lowest prevalence rate using number of symptoms as the criterion (40 per 1,000) have the highest proportion referred (1 in 11).

To turn to the symptom scores of the various subgroups mentioned: Table 4 shows that the expected gradation is found from the group considered 'well' by the psychiatrist with the lowest scores, to the clinic patients with the highest. This also suggests that the psychiatrists were somewhat better discriminators between 'well' and 'disordered' than were the GPs. However, it should be remembered that these groups were not defined as disordered by identical criteria. Biserial correlation coefficients calculated for the relationship between symptom scores and membership of the psychiatrically disordered group, and also a physically disordered group determined by the judgement of a psychiatrist are shown in Table 5

Table 3.

	Psychiatric cases per 1,000 population		Proportion referred (to account for treated rates)	
	M	F	M	F
1. Criterion: 23 CMI symptoms				
Industrial	120	230	1:18	1:36
Rural	50	155	1:14	1:20
2. Criterion: 7 CMI symptoms (doctor consulted)				
Industrial	75	140	1:12	1:22
Rural	40	120	1:11	1:15

able 4.

	Random sample subgroups: mean CMI scores					
	Total random sample mean CMI (N = 300)	Considered 'well' by psychiatrist	Considered 'well' by GP	Considered psychiatrically disordered by GP	Considered psychiatrically disordered by psychiatrist	Clinic patients (N = 73)
Male						
psychiatric symptoms	5·2	4·2	4·5	6·6	10·3	15·7
otal symptoms	12·0	9·8	10·1	16·8	19·0	29·9
emale						
sychiatric symptoms	8·7	7·1	7·9	11·6	13·8	19·0
otal symptoms	16·6	13·2	15·3	21·0	26·2	35·7

Table 5. *Biserial correlations between scores on symptom indices and psychiatrist's classification into psychiatrically disordered, and physically disordered groups for industrial area (Rhondda)*

	Psychiatrically disordered			
	M	F	M	F
Log CMI				
Physical	0·35	0·56	0·36	0·42
Psychological	0·54	0·54	0·16	0·28
Total	0·51	0·57	0·28	0·36
Symptom scales				
Backache	0·25	0·21	0·51	0·04
Fatigue	0·29	0·30	0·20	0·39
Depression	0·18	0·24	0·00	0·07
Headache	0·69	0·28	0·40	0·02
Anxiety	0·78	0·60	0·11	0·13

Table 6. *Biserial correlations between scores on symptom indices and membership of psychiatric clinic groups versus random sample group membership (industrial [Rhondda]).*

	Clinic patients versus 'well' fraction of random sample		Clinic patients versus total random sample	
	M	F	M	F
Log CMI				
Physical	0·70	0·71	0·57	0·55
Psychological	0·84	0·72	0·74	0·59
Total	0·78	0·77	0·70	0·63
Symptom scales				
Backache	0·07	0·23	0·14	0·18
Fatigue	0·63	0·72	0·56	0·64
Depression	0·62	0·68	0·63	0·65
Headache	0·29	0·30	0·14	0·23
Anxiety	0·79	0·69	0·70	0·51

for the industrial area. These correlations are nearly all significant (especially for CMI groups).

Similarly biserial correlation coefficients between symptom indices and clinic patients as opposed to the random sample groups (industrial) were mostly positive and significant, particularly for the correlation between CMI scores and membership of the clinic patient group as opposed to that subgroup of random sample respondents considered 'well'.

The relationship between the indices and the various defining agencies is further illustrated by the way the random group and the various disordered groups are divided by the criterion of 23+ total symptoms on the CMI (Table 7). We find that the psychiatrists 'agreed' with this criterion in about half of cases, whereas the family doctors' 'disordered group' in terms of this criterion were nearer the random sample. We again have an indication of fewer severely disordered rural males.

As for the proportions of the random sample groups considered psychiatrically disordered by their own doctors, we find that about one-third of the industrial males and females and also about one-third of the rural females were judged to be disordered, whereas this is so for only one-eighth of the rural males (Table 8).

Various factors characteristic of an area have been suggested to have an influence on morbidity levels, and also that they may act as selection factors influencing the rates of treated cases. Taking the marked differences between the rural and industrial males on the symptom indices and especially in treated case rates, for example, it has been suggested that the sociological effects on the male population of a rapid decline in the coal industry with ensuing high unemployment was relevant to the high rates in this area, and conversely that the stable employment pattern and low

Table 7. *Percentage of various groups with twenty-three or more total symptoms on CMI.*

	Rural		Industrial	
	M	F	M	F
Clinic patients	—	—	70	>70
Psychiatrically disordered group (psychiatrist's judgement)	0*	54·5*	45·4	51·5
Psychiatrically disordered group (GP's judgement)	6·6	20·4	15·1	39·3
Total random sample	5	15·5	12	23

* Refers to a subsample (Social Category V) only.

Table 8. *Random sample members considered psychiatrically disordered by GPs.*

	Rural		Industrial	
	M	F	M	F
Psychiatrically disordered	30 ($\frac{1}{8}$)	74 ($\frac{1}{3}$)	33 ($\frac{1}{3}$)	33 ($\frac{1}{3}$)
Not psychiatrically disordered	247	200	107	101
No data	16	14	11	15
Total	293	288	151	149

Table 9. *Unemployment (males) in industrial (Rhondda) random sample and clinic patients.*

	Random sample	Clinic patients
Number unemployed	10	7
Number unemployed in past five years	17	11
Three jobs or more in past five years	27	12
Total	151	35

Table 10. *Coal-mining experience in industrial (Rhondda) random sample and clinic patients.*

		Random sample	Clinic patients
Coal-mining experience	Never	79	14
	Past	63 ⎱ 72	20 ⎱ 21
	Present	9 ⎰	1 ⎰
Total		151	35

unemployment in the rural area was a factor in determining its rates. We find that the numbers of the random sample unemployed approximated to the unemployment rate for that area, whereas unemployment among the clinic patients was very much higher. A fifth were unemployed at the time of interview and almost one-third had been unemployed in the preceding five years. Similarly whereas about a sixth of the random sample men had had three or more job changes in five years, this was true for a third of clinic patients. This supports the view that unemployment is related to the manifestation of psychiatric disorder.

The figures for the number of men in the random sample and among the patients from the industrial area who were at the time (or who had been in the past) coal-miners illustrate the decline of the coal industry from its position as the major employer in the area. We find that whereas less than half of the random sample men were or had been miners, this was true for three-fifths of the clinic patients furthermore. A much smaller proportion of the patients were still mining. This finding suggests the relevance of coal-mining as well as unemployment to morbidity levels in this industrial area.

Conclusion

This study looked at random population samples and psychiatric clinic patients with a combination of conventional morbidity estimating methods (psychiatric clinic and family doctor and psychiatrist-determined disordered groups) and non-diagnostic morbidity indices based on symptoms. These indices thereby served to validate each other. It is noteworthy that in this validation the symptom indices were given to psychiatric clinic cases and that conversely the random sample was examined clinically by a psychiatrist. It was found that the indices discriminated well between the disordered and non-disordered groups as determined by the various defining agencies.

The findings strengthened the indications from previous studies of treated cases that selection factors play a major part in determining treated case rates. Despite the distortion produced by these selection factors, it is nevertheless possible to discern actual differences in morbidity levels. The findings suggest, for example that the rural males who have relatively low treated case rates have morbidity levels as measured by all other indices which are even lower.

Whereas in previous treated case studies sex ratios appeared to remain the same despite great variations between area, sex, and period, these findings show that sex ratios for a population vary between different morbidity indices and that they also vary according to the position at which the threshold or cut-off point is placed on that morbidity index. The findings also supported previous indications of the relevance of certain sociological factors to treated case rates.

REFERENCES

Carstairs, G. M., and Brown, G. W. (1958). 'A census of psychiatric cases in two contrasting communities', *J. ment. Sci.* **104**, 72.

Hughes, D. (1969). 'Psychiatric case prevalence. A comparison between four areas and two periods', *Soc. Psychiat.* **4**, 144–51.

Ingham, J. G. (1965). 'A method for observing symptoms and attitudes', *Br. J. soc. clin. Psychol.* **4**, 131–40.

—— Rawnsley, K., and Hughes, D. (in press). 'Psychiatric disorder and its declaration in contrasting areas of South Wales', *Psychol. Med.*

Rawnsley, K. (1966). 'Congruence of independent measures of psychiatric morbidity', *J. Psychosomat. Res.* **10**, 84–93.

Part 3 *Evaluating services for children and adolescents*

7 Evaluation of psychiatric services for children in the United States

LEE N. ROBINS

This work has been supported in part by USPHS Grants MH–05804, MH–18864, and Research Development Program Award MH–36,598.

The topic of 'the evaluation of psychiatric services for children' could be discussed from two points of view: either as an evaluation of the delivery of service (ie, are services available for all the children requiring them and if not who fails to get them?) or as an evaluation of the effectiveness of services.

At the Aberdeen symposium on psychiatric epidemiology three years ago, I was privileged to review follow-up studies of children (Robins, 1970). One area covered by these follow-up studies was the outcome of treatment for children. At that time, the supply of careful studies of effectiveness was very small, and the results unnerving. Although most children in treatment had improved when their status was evaluated a year or more later, no study which carefully matched treated children with untreated controls was able to show any long-term advantage to treatment. In the US, there are serious social inequities in the delivery of psychiatric service to children as there are in the delivery of medical care in general. In addition to social inequities, children with poor prognosis seem to be less preferred candidates for psychiatric treatment than are children who suffer from disorders with greater likelihood of spontaneous remission. But clearly, there is little to be gained by fighting for access to psychiatric services for children on a fairer basis, unless there is evidence that these services will help the children who get them. For that reason, I would like today to discuss only one aspect of the evaluation of psychiatric services: Do they work and for which children are they effective?

At the time my last review was in preparation, a great ferment was stirring in child psychiatry. Many new methods were being introduced, but they were all so new that there had been little opportunity for evaluation. The intervening years have seen a continuing mood of openness to new techniques, but now accompanied by a corresponding interest in evaluation. There are several possible explanations for the growing attention to hard-nosed evaluation in recent years. The diversity of new treatment is itself probably one reason. When psychotherapy was considered the only truly 'first-class' treatment, to evaluate it was to throw into question the whole field of child psychiatry. When there are many treatments competing, failing to show the effectiveness of any one only encourages trying a different one. Second, some of the newer treatments have arisen from the field of experimental psychology, a field with a tradition of measurement. Finally, the National Institute of Mental Health, which has given much of the money for development of new methods in the US, has played an important role in encouraging evaluation by requiring it for both demonstration and research projects they fund. To say that evaluation has come a long way in the last few years, is not to imply that we now know with considerable precision which methods are effective and for which children. But the picture is certainly no longer so bleak.

The traditional method: psychotherapy

Individual psychotherapy

Until a few years ago the psychiatric treatment of children, at least on an out-patient basis, was virtually symonymous with individual psychotherapy. This was 'talk' therapy with older children, 'play' therapy with younger. Evaluation was chiefly by reports at the end of therapy about the proportion improved. Improvement was a global impression of the psychiatrist or other treating professional on progress during treatment, or the product of a phone call to the mother a short time after treatment to find out how the child was doing. In general, these reports were encouraging, since two-thirds to three-quarters of all child patients were found 'improved'. However, when an attempt was made to compare treated children with children with similar problems who were untreated, it was found that untreated children also improved, and at about the same rate. Levitt (1957) was an important figure in the US in pointing out the lack of hard evidence for the effectiveness of psychotherapy with children, when he reviewed those studies which provided untreated control subjects for comparison. The outcries against his review were many, with complaints centred about the criteria for the selection of controls. These were frequently children on waiting-lists. Were children on waiting-lists truly 'untreated' and were they perhaps less acute cases? In 1971, Levitt again reviewed the evidence, and found no grounds to change his initial verdict concerning the effectiveness of psychotherapy as 'not proven'. Eisenberg's review of the state of the field in 1969 leads him to the same conclusion: 'To its credit, the past decade has seen the first systematic studies of the outcome of psychotherapy for children. In general the findings have not been reassuring.'

Since 1968, which was the cut-off date for literature covered in my previous review, there have been a few additional studies of psychotherapy, but only one was found which had improved on the methodology of earlier studies. Ashcraft (1969) instead of using unspecified 'improvement' as the measure of the outcomes for children receiving psychotherapy, used Stanford Achievement Test scores collected over a five-year period. These tests were deemed appropriate because the patients were third- to sixth-graders referred with educational problems judged by psychologists to have an emotional disturbance as their cause (ie, they tested an average of seven or eight months below grade level at referral despite normal intelligence). The control subjects were children with the same problems who were referred but did not receive treatment, either because their parents did not bring them or because the clinic had a waiting-list. The treated subjects were seen in psychotherapy once a week for at least six months.

The treated children initially showed some gains in achievement test scores as compared with controls, but by the end of five years, these gains were lost. This failure to find a difference was not due to the high level of 'improvement' for controls and patients alike that had vitiated the evidence for treatment effectiveness in earlier studies. The sad fact is that neither treated nor untreated children learned at normal rates thereafter. In no single school year did either group average the expected nine-month gain. There was only one element of hope in the results: the younger children may have profited from treatment, even though only temporarily. The younger children made gains and then lost them; the older children fared no better than controls throughout. Perhaps continuing treatment could have consolidated this initial improvement for the younger students.

Other recent research in psychotherapy in the United States has compared various intensities of psychotherapy. One study has compared short- and long-term psychotherapy (Rosenthal and Levine, 1971) and another daily versus weekly psychotherapy (Heinicke, 1969). Their results are opposite. The first reports no better results for the longer treatment, while the second claims a better result for the more frequent treatment. However, both have serious methodological problems. The first study dropped from the analysis of the thirty-one short-term cases eight who were referred for further treatment after completing the experimental period. These cases might well be considered failures. The second study had only four children in each group, and results in the various tests used to evaluate outcome (academic skills as well as clinical judgement) do not consistently favour one group over the other.

In short, nothing has happened in the last four years to change Levitt and Eisenberg's verdict concerning traditional one-to-one psychotherapy with children. It remains 'not proven'.

No very recent evaluation of play therapy was located. One earlier study was found (Seeman *et al.*, 1964) in which twelve poorly adjusted second- and third-graders were evaluated after thirty-seven weekly sessions of play therapy, and compared with six similar controls who received no treatment.

Effects were measured by teacher rating scales and other children's ratings. Again results are ambiguous. Four children had dropped out of the experimental group and were not evaluated at all. Four more were included in some but not all of the later evaluations. Teachers' ratings did not show a significant change over the nineteen-month follow-up, but the children's peers showed more of a shift toward positive evaluations for the treated than for the untreated children. Both teachers and children presumably knew about the treatment experience, so that evaluations were not 'blind'. Thus, with small groups, lost cases, and no efforts to avoid observer bias, this one study's finding that popularity increased somewhat for treated children is hardly enough to give us much confidence in the effectiveness of play therapy. Again, the verdict remains 'not proven'.

Group therapy
Group therapy, originally a technique developed by psychiatrists to reduce treatment costs for their private patients and to reduce psychiatric treatment time for in-patients while still providing psychotherapy, is now also commonly conducted by school psychologists and counsellors with children who have school difficulties or behaviour problems. When counsellors were first introduced into public schools, they were only in high schools. This was thought appropriate both because of the high schools' large student bodies as compared with neighbourhood elementary schools and because high school students were considered old enough to profit from 'talk' therapy. In the last few years, however, there has been a growing realization that children who will be under-achievers, dropouts, and delinquents in high school can be detected early in their school careers. This realization, coupled with the frequent failure of the high school counsellor to modify these undesirable behaviours, has led to the introduction of counselling into elementary schools. (Such counselling as previously took place with elementary school students had been the province of the school social worker, who usually had several schools assigned to her where she also served as a consultant to the teachers, advisor to parents, and truant officer.) The use of group rather than individual therapy in the schools is a natural analogue to the usual class-room educational format.

Unlike individual psychotherapy and play therapy, group therapy has been evaluated quite objectively in sizeable, well-defined patient or subject groups, using well-matched controls. But these evaluation studies do not always provide adequate descriptions of the therapeutic manoeuvres being evaluated. Perhaps it is variation in these techniques which explain variations in outcomes. In any case, careful studies have shown all possible results: success, no effect, and harm.

The greatest success has been reported for institutionalized delinquents who received both group and individual therapy for four hours per week over a twenty-week period (Persons, 1967). Effectiveness was evaluated by comparing recidivism rates, reinstitutionalization, and employment records during an average of nine and a half months following release from the institution. Twice as many of the boys who did not receive the treatment were reinstitutionalized as boys who did (61 per cent versus 32 per cent), and parole violations were also more common among untreated boys. The controls were well matched to the treated boys with respect to age, race, IQ, and previous arrest history.

In schools, group therapy has been used with both high school and elementary school students to attempt to improve academic performance in the older children (Mezzano, 1968; Baymur and Patterson, 1960) and peer acceptance in the younger (Kranzler *et al.,* 1966; Mayer *et al.,* 1967; Hansen *et al.,* 1969). In these studies comparisons were made not only between group therapy subjects and untreated controls, but also between group therapy subjects and subjects receiving alternative treatments. In the Mezzano study, volunteering male high school students in the lower half of their classes were assigned to one of three groups: group counselling, group counselling plus individual counselling, or no treatment. Treatment lasted for at least sixteen sessions (all of which were devoted to group therapy for the first group, half spent in group therapy and half in individual therapy for the second). Shortly after treatment ended, there was no significant difference between either treatment group and the control group in grades earned, but by ten weeks later, the group-therapy-only subjects had significantly higher grade point averages than the controls, while the group-plus-individual counselling subjects were not significantly different from either group.

Baymur and Patterson studied under-achievement in both boys and girls, also in eleventh grade. One treatment group experienced group-therapy sessions; another experienced 10–12 individual therapy sessions. There was also a control, no treatment group. The evaluation was based on changes in grade point averages between the first and second semesters and on tests of personality and study habits. Both counselled groups showed grade-point-average gains, as compared with the non-counselled, whose grades actually declined. The group-counselled students did better than the individually counselled. Interestingly, grade point averages showed more change after therapy than did paper and pencil tests of personality or study habits.

Two studies compared direct group-plus-individual counselling of elementary school students unpopular with their peers with counselling their teachers about how to help them, and with no treatment. One of these studies (Mayer *et al.,* 1967) had adequate sized samples (87 in all), but evaluated the treatment outcome only once, by repeating the sociometric instrument just after treatment was completed. The treatment itself lasted 9 weeks: 6 group sessions in 3 weeks, followed by 6 individual sessions over 6 weeks. No significant gains in sociometric status occurred in either treatment. The second study (Kranzler *et al.*, 1966) used very small samples: only 19 children in all, 8 in group treatment, 4 in teacher-counselled treatment, and 7 untreated. Treatment lasted longer: a total of 18 weeks. Evaluation shortly after treatment again showed no advantage to either treatment method, but re-evaluation 7 months after the end of treatment showed gains for group counselling as compared with the other two groups combined. The tiny numbers make these results dubious, of course.

Finally, the Hansen study, also trying to improve the popularity of elementary school students, compared group counselling in which the most popular children participated as models, group counselling with unpopular children only, and an untreated group given an 'activity' period only. Treatment lasted only four weeks. Evaluation was done both immediately after termination and again after two months. In this case, the simple group counselling was ineffective, but children in groups containing sociometric 'stars' improved significantly at both testing periods, although gains were greater at the *second* period.

Although the content of the group therapies in the studies mentioned so far are not so clearly described as one would like, the illustrations suggest a permissive, supportive, teaching atmosphere. A different group atmosphere has been sought at one of the California Youth Authority institutions (1970). Here the treatment technique is confrontation in the context of a 'therapeutic community': a method modelled after drug treatment at Synanon. The delinquents must publicly acknowledge their delinquent behaviours for attack by their peers. A change in their deviant attitudes is expected to result. Effectiveness of this programme was evaluated by comparing recidivism rates in the fifteen months on parole following treatment with rates for delinquents who would have met the criteria for admission to the programme but who instead went to one of four other institutions. Failure rates during the treatment period were high: almost one-third failed to complete the programme. Graduates, as compared with matched delinquents in other programmes, fared *worse* in the fifteen months post release. Nearly three-quarters had a parole violation, as compared with 56 per cent of the controls. The greater recidivism among treated boys was especially marked among first offenders (74 per cent versus 37 per cent had parole violations).

These studies of the effectiveness of group therapy have vastly different outcomes, even though all of them have tried to minimize bias and imprecision of evaluation. They do, however, differ in ways that may help to explain their differing outcomes. First, the elapsed time between treatment and evaluation differed. It is interesting that in the three studies in which evaluation occurred at two points in time, differences between controls and treated cases were greater at the more distant time, suggesting that the effects of group therapy may be delayed. This is quite the opposite of the findings of Ashcraft's study of individual psychotherapy, in which initial differences shrank and disappeared over time.

A second difference was the duration of the treatments themselves. A look at outcome as related to the number of treatment sessions suggests that the minimum number of sessions in which a child's behaviour can be significantly modified is about sixteen. At least, the three studies with sixteen or more sessions reported positive results; the two with twelve and four sessions respectively did not. (However, the four-session treatment *did* work when 'sociometric stars' were present.)

A third difference, about which we learn too little from these reports, is the content of the treatment programme. We do know that the confrontation technique did not work, but we do not have a precise description of the effective group therapy. The fact that treatment takes place in the presence of the child's peers may well be less important than the content and duration of treatment.

These studies of group therapy, unfortunately, do not tell us to what extent a 'cure' has been effected. Because results are reported only as differences between matched treated and control groups, we do not know whether a significant difference in grade point averages implies that treated boys achieved grades within the normal range, nor whether the greater gain in popularity for treated children as compared to controls meant that their social success was now up to the average level in their classroom. We can surmise that treatment reported as highly successful in reducing the risk of arrest for delinquents did not reduce that risk to levels anywhere near those of the general young male population, since 32 per cent of the treated group were reinstitutionalized within nine and a half months. The California Youth Study adds a sombre note: group therapy may not only fail, it may do positive harm.

Where these studies compared group therapy alone with individual psychotherapy in addition to or instead of group therapy, there was again a lack of evidence for the effectiveness of individual therapy, as there had been in studies of individual psychotherapy alone.

Therapy via teachers or mothers

In the interest of serving more children at less cost in professional time, there has been a movement in the US to introduce non-professionals as therapists and to reassign the psychiatrist's role from direct treatment of children to consulting with less scarce professional and para-professional personnel. A second trend has been the training or treating of mothers instead of children. This view of the mother as patient and therapist grows out of three rather antagonistic traditions: one, the assumption of the earlier child guidance movement that the child's problems stem largely from maternal errors, two, a revulsion against that assumption, particularly as applied to infantile autism, with the view instead of the mother as a potential source of treatment for a child ill through no fault of hers; and three, the view that children's problems are not so much evidence for illness, as they are evidence of conflicts between inborn personality patterns of mother and child. The conflict can presumably be reduced by helping the mother to understand her child's basic personality better.

Whatever the philosophical and economic bases for this new interest in working with non-professionals, the result has been experiments in psychiatrists working with teachers, mothers, public health nurses, and 'teacher-moms' instead of with disturbed children.

Ashcraft's study of individual psychotherapy mentioned above divided the experimental group into those whose parents were counselled and those whose parents were not. The addition of parent counselling was associated with better grades, but differences were not significant. The relative value of direct therapy versus parent counselling could not be evaluated in this study, however, since no group received *only* parent counselling.

Two of the group therapy studies discussed previously compared counselling of teachers about how to help the children with direct counselling of the children. In both cases the direct treatment of the children was the more successful, but no significant differences were found.

One of the earliest comparisons of indirect therapy versus none was Eisenberg's (1958). He found that 44 children treated by a social worker under the guidance of a psychiatrist improved in 61 per cent of cases, as compared to only 27 per cent of 11 children for whom the psychiatrist recommended treatment but for whom it was not carried out. As the author suggests, the small sample of untreated children and the lack of information about initial differences that might account both for failure to get treatment and poor outcome in the controls make this less than a proof of the effectiveness of indirect treatment.

Another early study carried out in 1951–2 (Gildea *et al.,* 1967) compared results for white children designated as problems when they attended schools offering no mental health programme versus similar children in schools offering their parents a series of mental health education films, followed by discussions, versus similar children in schools which offered the parents the same educational film and discussion programmes plus group therapy. Evaluation of the two programmes was based on teachers' and parents' rating of the problem children over a three-year period. Over this period, teachers tended to see the children as getting worse, while parents saw them as improving, but neither's perceptions appeared to have been influenced by the parents' mental health programmes.

A somewhat similar recent study was carried out in an all-black area in Chicago (Kellam, in press; Schiff, in press). This study has been of special interest because it was designed at the request of the local community, who decided that what they most wanted from psychiatrists was school success for their children. Accordingly the psychiatrists set up a programme of guidance for teachers and parents of first-graders. The history of this programme tells us more about the difficulties of carrying out treatment and treatment evaluation when programmatic and scientific decisions are subject to review by the community than it does about the effectiveness of intervention. Each year the programme changed, sometimes focusing only on children with problems, sometimes on the whole class. Control schools refused to remain 'controls' and demanded programmes. Some teachers and parents participated; others were openly and militantly hostile: both toward the programme and toward each other. Evaluation criteria were not applied consistently from year to year. Despite this chaos, some suggestive findings did emerge. Over the years, teachers tended to give increasingly negative evaluations of the children, as they had in the all-white schools in the previously cited study. At the end of the first year, they assessed treated children as less well adapted than control children; in other years they judged them to be somewhat better adapted. One year, the experimental children did show higher IQ scores than the control children, at least suggesting that the indirect therapy may have worked, but results are inconsistent. With regard to psychiatric symptoms no effect was found.

One of the more impressive accounts of successful intervention with mothers is a programme in which public health nurses worked with twenty-three very young, unmarried, poor black mothers from before the birth of their first child until the child was 3 (Brooks, no date). The nurses provided toys and taught the mothers how to encourage the child to use the toys and how to stimulate the child to learn, explore, and communicate. As compared with twenty-two control children of mothers with equal IQs, the experimental children had higher IQs at age 2. Unfortunately, we are not told whether this programme was sufficient to compensate for the deprivation such children suffer compared to middle-class whites: only that it made a significant difference. Nor do we learn how it compares with the more expensive solution of day-care, which provides direct care to the children rather than to their mothers.

One study, at least, suggests that trained parents may be as effective as professionals in helping seriously handicapped children make gains in self-care and socially acceptable behaviour (Mira, 1970). Parents of half of eighty-two children suffering from psychosis, severe mental retardation, or physical handicap were able to modify two or more of the children's problem behaviours after training in behaviour therapy, and 60 per cent modified at least one. A group of more professional trainees, teachers, social workers, and psychiatrists, was no more successful than the mothers. (However they were also no more 'professional' in the particular therapeutic techniques used.) Evaluation was by records of the target behaviours kept by the parent and professional trainees, using systematic recording to reduce bias.

The League School, a day-school for autistic children, has experimented with training parents to handle severely disturbed children at home when there are no places available in the school (Doernberg *et al.*, no date). Parents in the experimental group both observed teachers working with their children one hour a week for thirty sessions and met for group therapy sessions. Objective tests showed that children in the experimental group made greater gains than control children, similarly on the school waiting-list, in social adjustment and various self-help behaviours. Although offered as an example of the effectiveness of parent training, this study might also be seen as showing the effectiveness of once-a-week professional therapy for autistic children.

One of the advantages claimed for group therapy over individual therapy is a more efficient use of the therapist's time. In this connection, it is noteworthy that Mira found, in the study mentioned above, that *more* professional time was required per measured item of altered behaviour in the children when mothers were trained in groups than individually. This finding suggests that the common-sense view that group treatment is the more economical way to achieve treatment goals needs to be subjected to the test of cost-benefit accounting.

Whether 'therapy at one remove' works as well as direct treatment has really not been evaluated. Settling this issue is important, since indirect therapy is the currently fashionable solution to the shortages in professional personnel in outreach mental health programmes for underprivileged children. We need to know whether these programmes are in fact offering the poor second-class care.

The five studies of parent and teacher counselling in which a non-specific kind of counselling of mothers or teachers was attempted were all negative. Thus indirect therapy shows no measurable effect when it is similar to direct individual psychotherapy in trying to achieve goals of general improvement through a permissive, responsive role on the part of the professional therapist. The successes were all when parents were directly taught specific techniques for addressing, encouraging, and controlling the children. These highly specific techniques are among the recent innovations in child psychiatry, to which we now turn.

The recent innovations: education and the behaviour therapies

The last few years have seen extended to the treatment of psychiatrically ill children methods developed for adult psychiatric patients, drugs, desensitization, aversion therapy, as well as techniques used mainly in educational and reformatory settings for academically handicapped children: tutoring and reinforcement therapy. The excursion into techniques not originally designed with patients in mind reflects the blurring that is taking place in distinctions among psychiatric illness, emotional maladjustment, minimal neurological dysfunction, visual-motor defects, misbehaviour, and cultural deprivation. Children whose behaviour receives any of these labels have in common difficulties in getting along at home and in school. Indeed, the specific label chosen probably tells us more about the discipline in which the labeller received his training than it does about the particular set of problems shown by the child. As Tjossen pointed out (Tjossen *et al.*, 1962), educational difficulties are strongly associated with somatic complaints, behavioural disturbance, and emotional distress in children. Educational therapies make sense whether they are thought to attack the underlying cause of the disorder, when behavioural and somatic symptoms are thought to follow the experience of academic failure, or whether the educational handicap is thought secondary to an underlying cultural, neurological, or psychiatric liability. Appealing to men of both aetiological philosophies, therapies based either on traditional educational techniques or on 'behaviour modification' techniques, which are educational methods more precisely defined and more self-consciously related to learning theory, constitute a major movement in child psychiatry in the US today. Psychologists and educators have helped both to develop and deliver these techniques. Perhaps as a result of roots in experimental and educational psychology, educational techniques have been more systematically evaluated than other treatment methods.

Educational methods
Educational methods have come into prominence through efforts to overcome the educational retardation typical of minority group and underprivileged children. A major government effort, 'Head Start', has provided for 4-year-old low-income children the kind of nursery school enrichment that many middle-class children received in private schools. Hailed originally as a way of equalizing educational opportunity by counteracting the depression of IQ scores caused by understimulation at home, long-term evaluation has shown that any IQ gains disappear within a short time in regular school, either because the ordinary kindergarten experience is sufficient for children without the Head Start experience to catch up, or because ordinary schools do not provide the stimulation necessary to maintain the gains. Typical of these discouraging findings is a report from Lubbock, Texas (Cartwright *et al.*, 1967) where 295 children enrolled in Head Start during the summer of 1965 were evaluated at the end of the first grade against classmates matched for sex, ethnic group, and socio-economic status. No significant difference was found in grades, behaviour, or attendance. Indeed, with respect to the first two criteria, control children did a bit better.

Most Head Start programmes have mimicked middle-class nursery schools, with an emphasis on permissive exposure to educational toys, storytelling, and field trips to zoos and fire stations, but little effort to impart specific subject matter or to demand evidence of mastery on the part of the children. Programmes instituting more structured and demanding curricula have been able to demonstrate more impressive gains in learning.

An individual tutorial programme with 4-year-olds which gives fifteen-minute daily training in handling abstract ideas such as causation, inference, exclusion, and fantasy produced IQ gains of about fifteen points after four months, as compared with gains of only two points for children receiving fifteen minutes of individual attention only and one point for children in school but not getting any special programme (Blank and Solomon, 1968). No follow-up information is available with which to estimate the permanence of these gains.

A day-care programme which included a structured teaching programme for low-income infants was able to change IQ distributions over a two-year period from a curve skewed toward low IQs to a normal distribution. However, a year after leaving the programme, much of the gain had disappeared (Caldwell and Smith, 1970).

A comparison was made among four different preschool programmes for 4-year-old disadvantaged children, one the traditional nursery school, one with a similar programme but in which the disadvantaged children were in the minority among middle-ciass children, one a Montessori-type school, which provided children access to specifically educational materials and teacher demonstrations of their use, and an academic program including language-teaching games, mathematics, science, and social studies (Karnes *et al.,* 1970). IQ tests following the programmes showed gains for all, with the academic programme showing the highest average gain, fourteen points. No significant differences were found among the other three programmes.

An academically oriented programme was developed by Bereiter and Engelmann which concentrated exclusively on language training. Children in small groups were taught intensively to speak in grammatical sentences and to use relational words such as 'above', 'over', 'alike', and 'different'. Six weeks' exposure to this programme has been shown roughly twice as effective as permissive Head Start programmes in raising performance on standard tests (Young, 1968). Fifteen black low-income 4-year-olds in this programme for seven months gained two-plus years on a standard achievement test and their IQs rose (Bereiter and Engelmann, 1966).

This intensive academic language training was compared with another cognitively oriented curriculum and a structured nursery school type programme for disadvantage 3- and 4-year-olds (Weikart, 1969). All three programmes included a bi-weekly home demonstration of the method being used. Evaluation a year later was by means of observations in the classroom, IQ tests, and teachers ratings. Children in all three programmes showed more IQ gains than did an untreated matched group. While the

Bereiter–Engelmann language training programme showed the greatest effect on the Standford-Binet score, differences among the programmes were not statistically significant, and the superiority of language training was not supported in other IQ tests. Gains in IQ scores were somewhat greater for 3-year-olds than for 4-year-olds, suggesting that the earlier the intervention the greater may be the gain. Teachers' evaluations showed no differences among programmes in the children's adjustment to school. The two more highly structured programmes were also compared by observation of behaviour in the children's classrooms. The only difference found was that children who had had language training spoke more. The near equal effectiveness of the three programmes suggests either that the home training is the essential element, or that any *structured* curriculum is effective, no matter what its philosophy.

Thus, the weight of evidence for educational programmes supports the immediate positive effects of any structured programme, with the greatest gains in IQ and achievement accorded to the most academic and most structured programme, although we do not yet know how enduring these effects are. Little is known about the effects of such programmes on non-academic behaviours.

Despite these positive finds, academically oriented nursery school pro-grammes for culturally deprived children are under fire because they are viewed as attempts to give 'white middle-class' cognitive skills to black lower-class children, robbing them of their own culture by teaching them standard English. If such a challenge is answerable by research, criteria by which to judge cognitive training will have to be agreed on not only by educators, psychologists, and psychiatrists, but also by minority group representatives. Clearly IQ tests and achievement tests standardized on white middle-class children will not be sufficient. Many other criteria could be used: acceptance by the child's black classmates, knowledge of black culture and language, creativity in areas valued by the minority culture. If child therapists do not seek to quantify and standardize such new forms of evaluation, it may be too late to save from discard on political grounds a therapy, which may be as useful in improving the emotional and creative aspects of a child's life as it is in improving his IQ score.

One response to the failure to find the striking initial gains in IQ persisting a year or two after Head Start has been to recommend extending early education programmes past preschool into the elementary school. These programmes for 5- and 6-year-olds are too new to provide much in the way of follow-up evidence as yet. However, in Ypsilanti (Radin, 1969) high IQ children who had had a preschool 'Head Start' experience were placed into one of three kindergarten programmes: a special cognitive tu-toring programme at school plus training parents to continue the cognitive tutoring in the home, a similar programme without parent training, and no special programme. All three groups showed gains in IQ, but only the twelve children experiencing both parent training and tutoring showed gains significantly greater than the children without a special programme. In this case, the control children, far from reverting to pre-Head Start levels as expected, continued to improve in IQ. Obviously, further studies of the effect of continuing cognitive training in kindergarten should concentrate on those children whose performance *does* revert after preschool ends.

One of the pioneering programmes in education as a specifically psychotherapeutic technique is Project Re-Ed, which began more than fifteen years ago. Children referred by the local mental health clinic received residential treatment for about six months, with weekends at home. Close contact with the child's schoolroom was maintained while the child was in residence, to facilitate re-entry. Treatment was exclusively by teacher-counsellors, most of whom were students in special education at the nearby teacher's college. The educational techniques used are not spelled out in detail. As in most remedial education programmes, the teachers seem to have assessed the individual child's needs and tried to tutor him in whatever areas gaps were discovered. The programme was considered so successful that it was adopted as *the* treatment modality for children by the State of Tennessee, and a number of new facilities opened. Only recently has any systematic evaluation of its success been available (Weinstein, 1969).

The first published evaluation of the programme, reporting on 250 children thus treated, showed that parents and teachers perceived significant improvement in the children's behaviour problems, but no significant movement into adequate academic achievement. These findings could mean either that educational treatment paradoxically affects mental health but *not* educational competence, or that perhaps neither is affected significantly, and we are simply seeing the spontaneous improvement so often noted in children's behaviour problems over time. Although still unpublished, data are being collected which compare children treated in Re-Ed with untreated classmates identified by their schools as having similar problems, and with normal classmates (Weinstein, quarterly reports, unpublished). These preliminary results confirm the failure of the educational programme to make up for the educational deficits with which the children entered treatment. Eighteen months after their initial evaluation, treated children and untreated disturbed children both had fallen even further behind their normal classmates in achievement test scores. However, treated children were falling behind somewhat more slowly. Both treated and untreated children's behaviour improved, although neither group reached the normal level. Treatment may have had somewhat more effect than these results suggest if treated children were initially more disturbed than controls. When levels of original disturbance were controlled, more of the treated children were in fact found improved, if not recovered.

Project Re-Ed's less striking effect on academic achievement than that reported for the structured academic programmes for nursery school children may be due not only to its less specific curriculum, but also to the fact that the children are older. Their average age was 10. A programme comparing remedial education with individual and group counselling for fourth grade (9- to 10-year-old) underachievers (Winkler *et al.*, 1965), found no greater gains in grade point averages for any one of these three methods than was found in two control groups (one with a special non-academic, non-psychotherapeutic programme and one with no programme at all). One study with positive results (Shore and Massimo, 1969) utilized remedial education as one component of a multiple-treatment approach with ten dropout or suspended delinquents who were even older (ages 15–17) than the Re-Ed children and who had gross antisocial behaviour. The boys' counsellor offered not only remedial education but also psychotherapy and help in getting and keeping a job. When the outcome of the ten treated delinquents was compared with that of ten similar untreated boys, they were found after ten months to show gains on achievement tests, while the controls showed losses, and five years later to have more often returned to school, maintained employment, and avoided arrest. Unfortunately, we are not told whether control and treated delinquents had the same achievement scores or equally severe delinquency prior to treatment.

In sum, highly structured educational methods show rapid effects on IQ scores of young children. Whether these gains are maintained without further intervention is dubious. Whether they *can* be maintained by further intervention is still untested. Educational methods also may reduce antisocial behaviour, but sufficient evidence is not yet available to be certain of this.

Operant conditioning (reinforcement)

Reinforcement therapy, which is essentially rewarding desired behaviour or approximations to it, is, of course, widely used in all educational endeavours. Often, but not always, there is also an attempt to avoid punishment and failure (negative reinforcement), partly because it is unpleasant to treater and treated alike, partly because punishment is thought to contain some covert positive reinforcement: in particular, the therapist's attention. What distinguishes operant conditioning from general educational techniques is the detailed planning of what behaviour is to be reinforced and on what schedule. In addition, the rewards are often concrete (money, toys, privileges) rather than simply praise and good grades, the classic reinforcements offered by educational institutions, and they are given immediately after the desirable behaviour is performed. The reward schedule is referred to as a 'token economy'. Typically, whenever a behaviour to be reinforced is emitted by the child, he receives a token. At the end of the day he trades in his tokens for concrete rewards. When the child is too young or too ill to understand the significance of the tokens, he gets the concrete reward, usually food, immediately. Undesirable behaviour is ignored, if possible, or if it is too disruptive to ignore, the child is isolated briefly until it subsides. If our conclusions in the previous section are correct that educational techniques are effective in proportion to their degree of structure, we should expect operant conditioning to lie at the effective end of a continuum of educational therapies.

Unlike the educational techniques described in the preceding section, operant conditioning has been used almost as much for treating psychiatric disorder in children as for improving their educational level. It has been used for profoundly psychotic and neurologically damaged children as well as for children with milder disorders.

Numerous studies have shown a close temporal relationship between the institution of 'token economies', and an increase in the ratio of desirable to undesirable behaviours. No control group is necessary to prove that it is the reinforcement that accounts for these changes, because the problem behaviours rapidly re-emerge when the reinforcement is discontinued and as rapidly disappear again when it is reinstituted. While this clear temporal association between reinforcement and behaviour demonstrates that reinforcement has an effect, it also raises two serious issues: First, does the change persist after the treatment ends? Second, does each specific undesirable behaviour have to be individually extinguished, or is there generalization to the remainder of the child's life?

Studies testing the generalization and persistence of the response to behaviour therapy are much less common than those demonstrating its immediate power.

Optimistic reports of the generalization of desirable behaviours are obtained from a programme for delinquents at the National Training School (Cohen *et al.*, 1966, cited in Krasner, 1969). A programme of rewards contingent on academic work was accompanied by a marked decrease in disciplinary problems. A second study (Staats *et al.*, 1970) found that a token reinforcement reading programme for 14—year-old educable mentally retarded black children was associated not only with improved reading but also with less truancy and higher scores on both verbal and non-verbal portions of an IQ test. This kind of evidence for the generalization of effects should not, perhaps, surprise us. If delinquents are busy doing academic work, they cannot simultaneously be creating disciplinary problems; if retarded children want to earn tokens at school they first have to be present. It is not inconceivable that behaviours thus indirectly reinforced may be more useful in the long run to the subjects of behaviour therapy than behaviours reinforced directly.

The question of the durability of the effect of treatment is a more perplexing one. Behaviour therapists hope the behaviours reinforced will eventually become self-sustaining without immediate, concrete rewards. Yet the conditioning paradigm under which token economies are initiated assumes extinction of the conditioned response if reinforcement does not occur at least occasionally. To forestall extinction, the therapist may stretch the interval between receiving the tokens and exchanging them for goods, give reinforcements on increasingly irregular schedules, or try to transfer the reinforcing value of tokens to praise or gold stars, since these will be forthcoming in the post-treatment environment. He may also train teachers and parents to continue offering reinforcements so that therapy can in fact continue almost indefinitely.

Whether extinction can be prevented by these manoeuvres is not yet known. No follow-up study of reinforcement programmes was found which failed either to continue reinforcement at a reduced level or to train parents to continue the reinforcement programme during the follow-up interval. One study of six children (O'Leary *et al.*, 1969) moved from a token system with four evaluations in two hours and prizes earnable every day to a twice daily evaluation leading to candy once a week. Good behaviour was maintained during this follow-up period for three of the six children. Among institutionalized delinquents (Phillips *et al.*, 1971), six boys who cleaned their rooms at a near 100 per cent level when a daily point system earned them privileges maintained clean rooms 80 per cent of the time when their rooms were evaluated on only 8 per cent of days. Five adolescents who originally could not be contained even in special classes had made striking academic gains and decreased antisocial behaviour under a 'Phase system' which combined earning 'points' with graduation into 'phases' requiring more and more performance to earn points (Martin *et al.*, 1968). At follow-up, these adolescents were said to be doing well. However, the number is small, their parents had been taught to reward appropriate behaviour and ignore deviant behaviour, and the follow-up period was brief: only six weeks into the next semester.

One study (Lovaas *et al.*, in press) tried to assess both generalization and persistence of improvement one to four years after the reinforcement treatment of ten severely autistic children. All improved during treatment. The four who were placed in an institution after treatment regressed to a pre-treatment level. The six who were at home did better on the average, although only two showed less self-stimulation than at intake and only two showed more appropriate verbal behaviour. All remained grossly handicapped. Three of the six who were at home had been treated as in-patients, and were then sent home to their parents after a small amount of parental training. For three who were out-patients throughout, more time was spent on training their parents to be therapists than in treating the children directly. The latter group of three showed the greater improvement. These findings, again based on very small numbers, suggest that gains are maintained only when reinforcement is systematically continued. There are suggestions that some generalization may have occurred, since IQs, sleeping behaviour, and walking all improved, although none of these behaviours was specifically reinforced. However, since we do not know whether *untreated* autistic children also improve in these respects, we cannot be sure whether these changes are generalization from the reinforcement therapy or just spontaneous improvement.

Thus, reinforcement therapy, which is most attractive in its ability to produce less psychotic-looking behaviour in extremely disturbed children, conforming behaviour in chronic delinquents, and academic effort in school-desters, has not been shown to produce any persistent effects over time when treatment is ended. Perhaps some behaviours, like learning to ride a bicycle, are never forgotten once learned. If so, short-term results may have long-term profits. And there may be the snowball effect the therapist hopes for: the normal social rewards of academic success may be enough to maintain effort in less disturbed children who, through what they have learned during behaviour therapy, are able for the first time to experience success in the classroom. As yet we simply do not know. There is much more evaluation to be done of what looks like a promising mode of treatment.

Desensitization

Beginning with Wolpe's work, reciprocal inhibition, ie, instruction in relaxation accompanied by orderly progression through hierarchies of imagined frightening experiences, has shown considerable effectiveness in dissipating phobias in adults. There are few reports of its effectiveness in children, although many children experience severe fears. Wefound no experiments using precisely the Wolpe model with children, perhaps because children are thought to be less able to participate in establishing their own hierarchies and to imagine on demand. As an alternative, children afraid of dogs (Bandura, 1971) and snakes (Ritter, 1968) have been desensitized by exposure to fearless peers as 'models' who contact the feared creatures in settings graduated according to level of threat. In Bandura's follow-up a month after treatment, fears were decreased more by watching the model interact with a dog than by exposure to the dog alone. Some small increase in effectiveness occurred if the exposure was in a 'relaxing' (party-like) atmosphere or if there were several fearless models rather than a single one. The presentation was effective 'live' or in movies. However, in treating snake phobias, Ritter got the best results in a 'live' setting, where the child himself was slowly encouraged to emulate the fearless model. When the fate of the dog phobias was evaluated after a brief elapse in time, the children had not only maintained their gains but had improved still further as compared with immediately post-treatment. Control subjects in both studies showed no appreciable decrease in fears.

These two studies made use of the gradual approach to a fearful stimulus which is one important element of Wolpe's treatment, but they did not try to teach relaxation directly. (Wolpe argues that anxiety cannot be experienced in a relaxed state.) One study of four autistic children, however (Graziano and Kearn, 1968), concentrated only on the relaxation aspect of the treatment. These children had already had two years of reinforcement therapy. Although it had succeeded in a number of areas, reinforcement therapy had not eliminated wild outbursts of excited behaviour. After the children were taught to relax during twelve-minute sessions held up to three times daily, these outbursts subsided not only during the relaxation periods but during the remainder of the day, as well. The numbers are tiny and there is no follow-up, but the short-term effects are impressive.

Aversive conditioning

Aversive therapy with adults has been used to negatively reinforce drinking and homosexuality. It has not been used widely with children: except in Anthony Burgess's imagination in *The Clockwork Orange* and in the treatment of enuresis (Baker, 1969). In treating enuresis, two foil pads are placed under the child's bedsheet. When the child wets, the electrical circuit is completed, setting off a buzzer which awakens him. Being wakened is presumably an aversive experience. The buzzer was found more effective than the child's being wakened by parents at a regular time and taken to the bathroom, a procedure which is probably equally aversive but not in temporal apposition to bedwetting. Children exposed to either the buzzer or parental wakening fared better than did a control group. Eleven out of fourteen subjects were cured during the buzzer treatment.

Lovaas (in press) has also used aversive therapy (slaps and electric shocks) to stop psychotic children from mutilating themselves and to stop self-stimulating behaviour. He argues that punishment stops self-mutilation more rapidly than does extinction by ignoring or 'time-outs'. He also feels stopping self-stimulation is a necessary precondition to an effective positive reinforcement programme. Thus he uses aversive conditioning to stop dangerous behaviours and to get the child's attention for further therapy.

Information feedback

The behaviour therapy techniques cited thus far all concentrate on the child's behaviour. Yet it is commonly observed that problem children often come from problem families. One approach developed by Kaswan (1971) applies television technology to the analysis and treatment of family interactions. This 'information feedback' technique shows the family members videotapes of their interaction and tells them how each evaluated the behaviour of the others. The therapist plays a reflexive, non-directive role. This method is similar to feedback techniques developed by Lewin and Lippitt to train group leaders, methods now commonly used to conduct 'sensitivity training'.

Kaswan compared the effectiveness of this technique with parent counselling, with psychotherapy, and with no treatment. The subjects evaluated were forty-seven school-referred children randomly assigned to the four treatment groups. Follow-up ratings were done blind by rating interaction in school and by grade point averages three to six months after completion of treatment. Feedback was superior to parent counselling, but not significantly different from psychotherapy in its effect on school interaction. It was superior to both with respect to improvement in grades.

Drug therapies

The last fifteen years have seen a great interest in the use of psycho-active drugs, particularly for hyperactive and psychotic children. Four classes of drugs are commonly used: stimulants, minor tranquillizers and sedatives, major tranquillizers, and antidepressants.

To evaluate the effectiveness of these drugs, the most satisfactory study would seem to be a comparison of the symptom level of children receiving the drug with symptom levels of similar children receiving placebos, where neither the doctor nor the observer knows which is being taken so that expectancies about their effects do not influence the results. But double-blind drug studies, attractive as they are on the drawing board, present serious difficulties in practice. The drug's side-effects may 'break the code' for the 'blind' observer. Nor can the dosage level be adjusted to the requirements of the individual patient in the double-blind procedure. Thus, the clinician may reject a drug as ineffective only because he has not been able to take differences in individual response into account. (The same phenomenon may occur in studies of non-drug therapies too, of course. Too little of the treatment may have been given to obtain beneficial effects for some children and too much for others. But so far we have no reliable way to detect the 'toxic' effects of too much psychotherapy or reinforcement!)

Stimulants

Conners and Eisenberg (1963) were among the earliest to show that stimulants are more effective than placebo for hyperactive children. Their work still provides the most solid evidence for the effectiveness of these drugs. They have shown the effectiveness of dextro-amphetamine and methylphenidate in delinquent, foster home, psychiatrically ill institutionalized children, and schoolchildren with learning problems (Connors et al., 1963, 1967, 1969). The most notable effects of the stimulant drugs were a reduction in antisocial behaviour and improved performance on IQ tests. Children on the drug appeared calmer and reported feeling happier.

A recent elegant study compares the performance of emotionally disturbed, under-achieving, and frequently antisocial 8-year-old boys on laboratory tests and classroom tasks when given methylphenidate, thioridiazine, or placebo (Sprague *et al.*, 1970). Methylphenidate was more effective than placebo or thioridiazine. This study showed some of the mechanisms through which improved learning occurs under methylphenidate treatment: less restlessness in the seat, more task-focused attention, more contact with the teacher, greater accuracy of response, and decreased response time.

In addition to these experiments applied to reasonably large groups there are many case reports that show a rapid effect following administration of the drug and an equally rapid return of problems when the drug is discontinued, a pattern that we found convincing evidence for the effectiveness of reinforcement therapy.

Despite the solid studies showing that stimulants do reduce inappropriate behaviours and foster learning in antisocial, hyperactive, and learning problem children, there is a vocal group in the US protesting their use (Witter, 1971). The substance of their complaint is that 'hyperactivity' is poorly defined and often simply a synonym for 'troublesome'; and that troublesome behaviour in children should be seen as grounds for modifying schools which are too boring, too sedentary, too irrelevant to the child's daily life, rather than for sedating the child with drugs. Stimulants for children are viewed by these critics as 'anti-joy' drugs. They cite as evidence that the causes of hyperactivity lie outside the child the fact that hyperactivity is seldom observable in the doctor's office. This seems tenuous, since the expression of many symptoms with undeniably physical bases may be suppressed in sufficiently stimulating situations. Nonetheless, there are valid issues concerning who is to decide which children need treatment, whether non-drug treatment might not be equally as effective, whether there are dangers to health and growth in long-term administration of the drug, and at what age, if ever, the drug becomes no longer effective. Whether drugs are more or less effective than other treatments is, of course, an issue that lends itself to scientific evaluation through long-term follow-up. Unfortunately there are no studies yet which investigate the relative costs in professional time or in the suffering of the hyperactive child himself, his family, his teacher, and his classmates when stimulants are given compared with attempting to change the home and school environment. However, a follow-up study by Laufer (1971) of sixty-six hyperkinetic private patients treated with amphetamines or methylphenidate approximately eleven years before follow-up does tend to allay one concern about treatment with stimulants: Those children whose parents responded to his inquiry were *not* known to have become amphetamine abusers in adolescence. Only three were reported by parents as having experimented with 'speed', and none was a habitual user. However, the stimulant was no magic cure-all. Six children had not entered high school, even though IQs were within normal limits and the minimum age at follow-up was 15. More than a third were still hyperactive, although none was still being treated with stimulants. Only 9 per cent were still in psychiatric treatment at follow-up, but one-third had had further treatment in the intervening period and 30 per cent had had some trouble with the police. Unfortunately, follow-up was achieved for only some of those treated, and there was no control group either of normal children or of non-drug-treated hyperactive children with which to compare these results. Nor do we learn how many of the diagnostic criteria for hyperactivity were originally met by these children, the length of treatment, or the level of dosage. The treatment might have appeared more effective in more rigorously diagnosed or more vigorously treated children.

The need for evaluating stimulants within uniform diagnostic groups is underscored in the work of Fish (1971). In treating hospitalized children she found stimulants helpful only in those with organic brain syndromes or minimal brain dysfunction, and not at all helpful in psychotic children without neurological signs. She cautions against confusing the symptom of hyperactivity, which can occur in grossly psychotic children, with the syndrome of hyperkinesis, which precludes psychosis.

Minor tranquillizers and sedatives
Evaluations of the effects of the minor tranquillizers in children have produced results as disappointing as they were encouraging for stimulants. After seven weeks of treatment, 21 out-patient children on placebo fared better than 19 on meprobamate or 18 on prochlorperazine (Cytryn *et al.,* 1960). No positive effects could be found within any diagnostic group. In a study of delinquents (Molling *et al.,* 1962), perphenazine was found no more effective than placebo in reducing symptoms, although *both* placebo and drug produced positive changes in behaviour.

Major tranquillizers
Much of the work with the major tranquillizers comes from investigations in psychotic child in-patients by Fish (Fish *et al.,* 1966, 1968; Campbell *et al.,* 1970, 1971). Responding to the problems cited above with double-blind studies, these studies have been 'single-blind', ie the prescribing physician is *not* blind, so that he can determine the most effective medication for each individual, but the observer is not informed as to the patient's medication status. Various phenothiazines have been tried and generally found associated with improvement, as indicated by better performance on the hospital ward and some efforts at speech in mute children. The less severely disturbed children responded more to both drug and placebo and required lower drug dosages (Fish, 1966). No drug was reported as effective enough to allow these severely ill children's discharge from the hospital.

A study in less severely disordered out-patients (Kenny *et al.,* 1968) compared chlorpromazine with mesoridazine and placebo in seventeen children, using a double-blind crossover design. Only the mesoridazine was effective, as judged by scores on behaviour rating scales given at monthly intervals. It was particularly effective in reducing hyperactivity, aggressiveness, irritability, and distractibility. No information is provided about duration of treatment, side-effects, or long-term maintenance of effectiveness. Another study of chlorpromazine (Werry *et al.*, 1966) in thirty-nine hyperactive children found it effective in reducing hyperactivity, as compared with placebo. No increment in learning was observed, however. Indeed, there was a slight decrease in WISC (intelligence test) scores. Again no long-term results have been reported.

Antidepressants

Imipramine has been used in 16 children with school phobias (Gittelman-Klein and Klein, 1971) and compared with 19 similar children on placebo. Children treated with imipramine were more often back in school after six weeks and more often rated as improved. It took more than three weeks for the effect of the drug to be noticeable. Again we lack long-term results. Imipramine has also been tried as a treatment for hyperactivity (Huessy and Wright, 1970). Two-thirds showed marked improvement, as judged by parents and school records. Although no control group was available, effectiveness is suggested by the fact that discontinuance of the drug led to relapse, with improvement again after reinstatement. Obviously, further study with adequate controls and specified criteria for improvement is necessary.

Vitamin therapy

Following the interest in vitamin treatments for adult schizophrenics engendered by Hoffer and Osmond's work, and publicized by Linus Pauling, Heeley and Roberts in England (1966) began investigating the effects of massive doses of vitamins on psychiatrically ill children. In the US, Rimland (1971) is pioneering the evaluation of vitamin treatments for psychotic children.

By mail inquiry to parents and doctors of children in his files, Rimland located fifty-seven who had been on large doses of vitamins. Over half the parents reported improvement. Rates of improvement were highest when the children had received niacinamide, ascorbic acid, pyridoxine, and pantothenic acid. Some were reported to regress rapidly to their earlier state when vitamin treatment was interrupted.

Through his survey, Rimland also located 300 parents willing to let their children try megavitamins. He eventually obtained results for 190 non-institutionalized children who received the four vitamins listed above. He sought predictors of the results of vitamin treatment among the pre-existing symptom descriptions for each child that were already in his files.

Children with the classic pattern of infantile autism seemed to be most responsive to the treatment, with 59 per cent improving.

Rimland is now replicating these findings with two groups of psychotic children: those for whom he predicts success and those for whom he predicts failure on the basis of their symptom patterns. Some of each group are receiving vitamins; others placebo. That study, still in progress, will hopefully provide a more satisfactory answer about the effect of massive doses of vitamins on psychotic children.

In summary, research on drug treatment of children already clearly shows that stimulants have a calming effect on hyperactive children and improve their ability to work and co-operate in class, while sedatives and minor tranquillizers seem ineffective. The phenothiazines appear to be of some help in managing psychotic children and perhaps help hyperactive children as well, but they are not potent enough to restore the psychotic child to anything like normal functioning. The effectiveness of antidepressants and vitamins is hardly explored as yet.

Overview

The last few years have seen a marked change in attitudes toward children's services and their evaluation. The current mood is pragmatic: 'Try anything and see if it works: drugs, psychotherapy, pain, bribes.' Not only have psychiatrists' methods diversified, their goals have as well. The goal is no longer always a complete cure via a restructuring of the personality. Rather the goal is sometimes, as it is in other chronic illness, finding the best way for the child and his family to live with a possibly incurable disorder. Sometimes the goal is to wait out a disorder that may spontaneously remit in adolescence with the least discomfort and the least chance of permanent scarring of the child during the ordeal. The goal may be to help a child to acceptance by his peers or his parents, to improve his ability to learn, to remove a specific fear, to improve his grades.

Along with the broadening of the psychiatric armamentarium and goals, there is a growing attention to systematic evaluation by brief objective observations at random intervals or by scores on standardized school tests. These are tough standards by which to judge success, but they are standards based on the impact of the child's behaviour on the real world in which he lives, rather than on the clinician's opinion of him or on the way he answers personality questionnaires.

A few of the evaluation studies cited have met generally accepted scientific standards with regard to large samples, matched control subjects, placebo controls to wipe out the effects of novelty and attention, and evaluation by 'blind' observers. This is a great step ahead, but there are three additional methodological issues that need more attention than they are getting.

First, is the question of when evaluation should take place. So little attention has been directed to this issue by the scientific community that there are still no guidelines for the evaluator. We can agree, I believe, that evaluation at termination of treatment is *not* the proper time, even though it is the most customary one. Ideally, the therapist terminates treatment when improvement has taken place, whether that improvement is due to the treatment or to unknown factors. Thus, evaluation at termination stacks the cards in favour of treatment, since the treatment failures who have not spontaneously remitted are still in treatment and do not fall into the sample. (The failure of studies to show the effectiveness of traditional psychotherapy may in part be due to the length and expense of the treatment, which makes termination a decision by the family more often than by the therapist, at the point when patience and funds are depleted rather than at the point of improvement.)

If evaluation at termination is improper, what about evaluation a number of years after treatment? This is fine when the untreated disorder is expected to have a lifelong course and the treatment is expected to cure it, but it is not proper for disorders that spontaneously remit or for treatments that control symptoms but do not cure the illness. If we tried to evaluate a cold remedy years after its administration, symptoms would be observed only in those suffering from a new cold, which the remedy tested never pretended it could prevent. Nor is there any point in evaluating the effect of insulin as a treatment of diabetes years after the last injection. Thus the proper time for evaluation depends on the natural history of the disorder being treated, and on the goal of the treatment. This makes it difficult to lay down rules for the timing of evaluation. It clearly must be at a time *independent* of clinical judgements of the therapist and it must be at a time when the treated episode could be expected to be still raging if treatment had not intervened. Thus knowing when to evaluate requires knowing the natural history of the disorder being treated and having a clear idea of how the treatment is expected to affect that course.

A second issue that should concern evaluators of psychiatric treatment much more than it has, is the danger of having dropouts from treatment destroy the comparability of the treated cases and controls. If poor prognosis cases have high treatment dropout rates, there will be a bias in favour of the treatment at follow-up; if good prognosis cases drop out, there will be a bias against the treatment. If dropouts cannot be shown to be unbiased with respect to prognosis, matched control cases should be discarded as well before evaluation takes place. I believe none of the studies reported here took this precaution.

A third issue is that new treatments should be compared not only with placebos, but also against the best available traditional treatment. A new treatment is valuable only if, at least for some children, it is more effective, produces fewer undesirable side-effects, or is more broadly available than the best existing treatment. The idea that comparisons should be against standard practice rather than against placebo alone is beginning to be accepted in adult psychiatry, where electroconvulsive therapy is seen as the yardstick against which anti-depressant drugs should be measured.

With these and other caveats, which the therapists in the audience can undoubtedly supply better than I, progress in the evaluation of therapy for children may, in the next four years, make even greater progress than it has in the last four. We look forward with hope that studies which are more carefully controlled and cover longer time-spans will confirm the impression that we take from the studies reviewed here that the new techniques of child psychiatry and psychology have a great deal to offer children with a wide variety of disabilities.

REFERENCES

Ashcraft, C. (1969). 'The later school achievement of treated and untreated emotionally handicapped children' (August) (mimeo).

Bandura, A. (1971). 'Psychotherapy based upon modeling principles', in Bergin, A. E., and Garfield, S. L. (eds), *Handbook of Psychotherapy and Behavior Change,* chap. 17 (New York: John Wiley).

Baker, B. L. (1969). 'Symptom treatment and symptom substitution in enuresis', *J. Abnorm. Psychol.* **74** (1), 42–49.

Baymur, F. B., and Patterson, C. H. (1960). 'A comparison of three methods of assisting underachieving high school students', *J. Counseling Psychol.* **7** (2), 83-89.

Bereiter, C., and Engelmann, S. (1966). 'Observations on the use of direct instruction with young disadvantaged children', *J. Soc. Psychol.* (May), 55–62.

Blank, M., and Solomon, F. (1968). 'A tutorial language program to develop abstract thinking in socially disadvantaged preschool children', *Child Develop.* **39**, 379–89.

Brooks, M. T. (nd). 'A stimulation program for young children performed by a Public Health nurse as part of well baby care', (mimeo) (Address: Child Health Center, Children's Hospital, Washington, DC 20009).

Caldwell, B. M., and Smith, L. E. (1970). 'Day care for the very young—prime opportunity for primary prevention', *Am. J. Publ. Hlth,* **60** (4), 690–7.

California Youth Authority (1970) *The Marshall Program—Assessment of a Short-term Institutional Treatment Program. Part II: Amenability to Confrontive Peer-group Treatment,* Research Report no. 59.

Campbell, M., Fish, B., Shapiro, T., and Floyd, A., Jr. (1970). 'Thiothixene in young disturbed children', *Arch. Gen. Psychiat.* **23**, 70–72.

———————— (1971). 'Study of molindone in disturbed preschool children', *Curr. Ther. Res.* **13** (1), 28–33.

Cartwright, W. J., Steglich, W. G., and Allen, S. (1967). 'Effectiveness of project Head Start', *Proceedings of the Southwestern Sociological Association,* **18**, 167–71.

Conners, C. K., and Eisenberg, L. (1963). 'The effects of methylphenidate on symptomatology and learning in disturbed children', *Am. J. Psychiat.* **120** (5), 458–64.

———————— and Barcai, A. (1967). 'Effect of dextroamphetamine on children', *Arch. Gen. Psychiat.* **17**, 478–85.

—— Rothschild, G., Eisenberg, L., Schwartz, L. S., and Robinson, E. (1969). 'Dextroamphetamine sulfate in effects on perception', ibid. **21**, 182–90.

Cytryn, L., Gilbert, A., and Eisenberg, L. (1960). 'The effectiveness of tranquilizing drugs plus supportive psychotherapy in treating behavior disorders of children: a double-blind study of eighty outpatients', *Am. J. Orthopsychiat.* **30** (1), 113–29.

Doernberg, N., Rosen, B., and Walker, T. T. (nd). 'A home training program for young mentally ill children' (League School for Seriously Disturbed Children, 567 Kingston Avenue, Brooklyn, New York 11203).

Eisenberg, L. (1958). 'An evaluation of psychiatric consultation service for a public agency', *Am. J. Publ. Hlth,* **48** (6), 742–9.

—— (1969). 'Child psychiatry: the past quarter century', *Am. J. Orthopsychiat.* **39** (3), 389–401.

Fish, B. (1971). 'The "one child, one drug" myth of stimulants in hyperkinesis', *Arch. Gen. Psychiat.* **25**, 193–203.

—— Campbell, M., Shapiro, T., and Floyd, A. Jr. (1969). 'Comparison of trifluperidol, trifluoperazine and chlorpromazine in preschool schizophrenic children: the value of less sedative antipsychotic agents', *Curr. Ther. Res.* **11** (10), 589–95.

—— Shapiro, T., and Campbell, M. (1966). 'Long-term prognosis and the response of schizophrenic children to drug therapy: a controlled study of trifluoperazine', *Am. J. Psychiat.* **123** (1), 32–39.

—— —— —— and Wile, R. (1968). 'A classification of schizophrenic children under five years', *Am. J. Psychiat.* **124** (10), 1415–23.

Gildea, Mc.-L., Glidewell, J. C., and Kantor, M. B. (1967). 'The St. Louis school mental health project: history and evaluation', in Cowen, E. L., Gardner, E. A., and Zax, M. (eds), *Emergent Approaches to Mental Health Problems.* (New York: Meredith Publishing Company).

Gittelman-Klein, R., and Klein, D. F. (1971). 'Controlled imipramine treatment of school phobia', *Arch. Gen. Psychiat.* **25**, 204–7.

Graziano, A. M., and Kean, J. E. (1968). 'Programmed relaxation and reciprocal inhibition with psychotic children', *Behav. Res. Ther.* **6**, 433–7.

Hansen, J. C., Niland, I. M., and Zani, L. P. (1969). 'Model reinforcement in group counseling with elementary school children', *Personnel & Guidance J.* **47**, 741–4.

Heinicke, C. M. (1969). 'Frequency of psychotherapeutic session as a factor affecting outcome: analysis of clinical ratings and test results', *J. Abnorm. Psychol.* **74** (5), 553–60.

Huessy, H. R., and Wright, A. L. (1970). 'The use of imipramine in children's behavior disorders', *Acta Paedopsychiatrica,* **37**, 194–9.

Karnes, M. B., Teska, J. A., and Hodgins, A. S. (1970). 'The effects of four programs of classroom intervention on the intellectual and language development of 4-year-old disadvantaged children', *Am. J. Orthopsychiat.* **40** (1), 58–76.

Kaswan, J., Love, L. R., and Rodnick, E. H. (1971). 'Information feedback as a method of clinical intervention and consultation', in Spielberger, C. D. (ed.), *Current Topics in Clinical and Community Psychology,* vol. 3 (New York: Academic Press).

Kellam, S. G. (forthcoming). 'Strategies in urban community mental health', in Golann, S. E. and Eisdorfer, C. (eds), *Handbook of Community and Social Psychology,* (Appleton Century Croft).

Kenny, T. J., Badie, D., and Baldwin, R. W. (1968). 'The effectiveness of a new drug, mesoridazine, and chlorpromazine with behavior problems in children', *J. Nerv. Ment. Dis.* **147** (3), 316–21.

Kranzler, G. D., Mayer, G. R., and Dyer, C. O. (1966). 'Counseling with elementary school children: an experimental study', *Personnel & Guidance J.* **44**, 944–9.

Krasner, L. (1969). 'Assessment of token economy programmes in psychiatric Hospitals', *Int. Psychiat. Clin.* **6** (1), 155–85.

Laufer, M. W. (1971). 'Long-term management and some follow-up findings on the use of drugs with minimal cerebral syndromes', *J. Learning Disabilities*, **4**, 519–22.

Levitt, E. E. (1957). 'The results of psychotherapy with children: an evaluation', *J. Consult. Psychol.* **21**, 189–96.

—— (1971). 'Research on psychotherapy with children', in Bergin, A. E., and Garfield, S. L. (eds), *Handbook of Psychotherapy and Behavior Change*, pp. 474–94. (New York: John Wiley).

Lovaas, O. I., Koegel, R., Simmons, J. Q., and Stevens, J. (in press). 'Some generalizations and follow-up measures on autistic children in behavior therapy', *J. Appl. Behav. Analysis.*

Martin, M., Burkholder, R., Rosenthal, T. L., Tharp, R. G., and Thorne, G. L. (1968). 'Programming behavior change and reintegration into school milieux of extreme adolescent deviates', *Behav. Res. Ther.* **6**, 371–83.

Mayer, G. R., Kranzler, G. D., and Matthes, W. A. (1967). 'Elementary school counseling and peer relations', *Personnel & Guidance J.* **46**, 360–5.

Mezzano, J. (1968). 'Group counseling with low-motivated male high school students—comparative effects of two uses of counselor time', *J. Educ. Res.* **61** (5), 222–4.

Mira, M. (1970). 'Case histories and shorter communications', *Behav. Res. Ther.* **8**, 309–11.

Molling, P. A., Lockner, A. W., Jr, Sauls, R. J., and Eisenberg, L. (1962). 'Committed delinquent boys', *Arch. Gen. Psychiat.* **7**, 70–76.

O'Leary, K. D., Becker, W. C., Evans, M. B., and Saudargas, R. A. (1969). 'A token reinforcement program in a public school: a replication and systematic analysis', *J. Appl. Behav. Analysis*, **2** (1), 3–13.

Persons, R. W. (1967). 'Relationship between psychotherapy with institution-alized boys and subsequent community adjustment', *J. Consult. Psychol.* **31** (2), 137–41.

Phillips, E. L., Phillips, E. A., Fixsen, D. L., and Wolf, M. M. (1971). 'Achieve-ment place: modification of the behaviors of pre-delinquent boys within a token economy', *J. Appl. Behav. Analysis*, **4** (1), 45–59.

Radin, N. (1969). 'The impact of a kindergarten home counseling program', *Exceptional Child*, 251–6.

Rimland, B. (1971). 'High dosage levels of certain vitamins in the treatment of children with severe mental disorders', in Hawkins, D. R. and Pauling, L. (eds), *Orthomolecular Psychiatry* (San Francisco: W. H. Freeman).

Ritter, B. (1968). 'The group desensitization of children's snake phobias using vicarious and contact desensitization procedures', *Behav. Res. Ther.* **6**, 1–6.

Robins, L. N. (1970). 'Follow-up studies investigating childhood disorders', in Hare, E. H., and Wing, J. K. (eds), *Psychiatric Epidemiology*, pp. 29–68 (Oxford University Press for the Nuffield Provincial Hospitals Trust).

Rosenthal, A. J., and Levine, S. V. (1971). 'Brief psychotherapy with children: process of therapy', *Am. J. Psychiat,* **128** (2), 141–6.

Schiff, S. K. (forthcoming). 'Free inquiry and the enduring commitment: the Woodlawn Mental Health Center 1963–1970', in Golann, S. E., and Eisdorfer, C. (eds), *Handbook of Community and Social Psychology* (Appleton Century Croft).

Seeman, J., Barry, E., and Ellinwood, C. (1964). 'Interpersonal assessment of play therapy outcome', *Psychotherapy,* **1,** 64–66.
Shore, M. F., and Massimo, J. L. (1969). 'Five years later: a followup study of comprehensive vocationally oriented psychotherapy', *Am. J. Orthopsychiat.* **39** (5), 769–73.
Sprague, R. L., Barnes, K. R., and Werry, J. S. (1970). 'Methylphenidate and thioridazine: learning, reaction time, activity, and classroom behavior in disturbed children', ibid. **40** (4), 615–28.
Staats, A. W., Minke, K. A., and Butts, P. (1970). 'A token-reinforcement remedial reading program administered by black therapy-technicians to problem black children', *Behav. Ther.* **1,** 331–53.
Tjossom, T. D., Hansen, T. J., and Ripley, H. S. (1962). 'An investigation of reading difficulty in young children', *Am. J. Psychiat.* **118,** 1104–13.
Weikart, D. P. (1969). 'Project: a comparative study of three preschool curricula' (presented at the biennial meeting of the Society for Research in Child Development, Santa Monica, California) (mimeo).
Weinstein, L. (1969). 'Project Re-Ed schools for emotionally disturbed children: effectiveness as viewed by referring agencies, parents, and teachers', *Exceptional Child,* **35** (9), 703–11.
—— (1971). Quarter reports to OE Bureau of Research, unpublished.
Werry, J. S., Weiss, G., Douglas, V., and Martin, J. (1968). 'Studies on the hyperactive child: the effect of chlorpromazine upon behavior and learning ability', in Quay, H. C. (ed.), *Children's Behavior Disorders: Selected Readings* (Princeton, New Jersey: D. Van Nostrand).
Winkler, R. C., Munger, P. F., Kranzler, G. D., and Teigland, J. J. (1965). 'The effects of selected counseling and remedial techniques on underachieving elementary school students', *J. Counseling Psychol.* **12** (4), 384–7.
Witter, C. (1971). 'Drugging and schooling', *Trans-action,* **8** (9/10), 31–34.
Young, B. W. (1968). 'A new approach to Head Start', *Phi Delta Kappa,* 368–8.

8 Evaluation of psychiatric services for children in England and Wales

I. KOLVIN[1]

INTRODUCTION

Provision of services

As the United Kingdom is a welfare state, the psychiatric services for children are provided either from local or central government sources. Under the 1946 National Health Service Act it became the duty of the Minister of Health to provide hospital specialist services. Up until this time, considerable confusion had reigned concerning provision and functioning of the various medical services designed to help psychiatrically disturbed children. Howells (1965) lists the lack of a reliable body of knowledge in this field as the single most important factor contributing to this confusion. Clinical services only slowly developed and planning was hampered by the lack of acceptable definitions and classifications of childhood behaviour disorders and lack of reliable statistics. Finally, there was confusion about whether the child psychiatric services were more appropriately based in health or education departments. Howells feels that the Blacker Report (1946) was the first significant attempt to disentangle these problems; the report clarified division of responsibility for the children's services into the child guidance clinics with a main educational component and the hospital-based child psychiatry clinics with a main clinical component. The ministries appeared to take a lead from this report. A memorandum from the Ministry of Health (1947) and a circular from the Ministry of Education (1948) underlined these responsibilities. The provision of facilities for maladjusted children became, therefore, the duty of these twin ministries.

The provision of services and allied issues became the subject of study by government committees and professional bodies. The reports produced by these have constituted important milestones in that many of their

1. This work was undertaken by: R. F. Garside, C. M. Hulbert, I. Kolvin, H. I. J. van der Spuy, F. Wolstenholme, and R. M. Wrate.

recommendations have often been embodied in government policy, becoming blueprints for the development of services in the United Kingdom and thus providing provisional norms for staffing and service.[1] Such reports have not always received general approval, for instance, the usefulness of the invaluable report produced by the Committee set up by the Ministry of Education (Underwood Report, 1955) was said to have been diminished, firstly by its limited terms of reference (being confined to the consideration of maladjustment in relation to education only); and secondly by inadequate representation of interested professional bodies and other ministries. However, such critics have often been themselves equally guilty.

The size of the problem

Before describing the services and their deficiencies it is essential to have both some idea of the size of the problem and the demand for such services. In the UK estimates of proportions of children in the community suffering from psychiatric disorder range from 5 per cent maladjustment (Underwood Report, 1955) to 17·9 per cent (Brandon, 1960). The variation has been attributed (Rutter *et al.*, 1970) to differences in ascertainment techniques and definitions of psychiatric disorder.

The most common method for estimating disturbance rates has been a preliminary screen using parent and teacher questionnaires. These have been followed by further investigation such as by psychologists (Underwood Report, 1955) with estimates of 5·4 per cent in Berkshire, a minimum of 7·7 per cent in Birmingham and 11·8 per cent in Somerset; or by psychiatrists (Rutter and Graham, 1966; Rutter *et al.*, 1970) with 6·8 per cent on the Isle of Wight. Brandon (1960) used systematic evidence gathered by health visitors (nurses) during the 'Thousand Families Study' in Newcastle and followed this up by interview with parents together with questionnaires to schools. And yet others have taken a random sample of the school population and have employed school questionnaires, parent interview, and psychiatric examination of the child (Atkins and Kolvin, 1973) giving rise to a figure of 11 per cent in infant school children in Newcastle. Pringle *et al.* (1966) in the National Child Development Study, using only Stott's Bristol Social Adjustment Guide completed by teachers, arrived at a figure of 13·4 per cent and Chazan and Jackson (1971) using a similar technique at the same age range in Wales concluded some 13–14 per cent of the children presented problems to an extent warranting attention.

While differences of definition or method could account for the wide estimated difference between the 'Thousand Families Study' and the 'Isle of Wight' study, this is less likely to be the answer for the variation in rates

1. The reports alluded to in this paper are contained in the references.

compared with the more recent Newcastle Study where there is overlap between techniques and definitions with the Isle of Wight study. Undoubtedly the latter is the most systematic, reliable, and valid of the more recent studies, and yet the estimate of disorder appears somewhat low.

This tends to suggest that regional variation may well constitute a partial explanation of the differences and so, while agreeing with Rutter *et al.* (1970) that it is not possible to arrive at any adequate summary of the findings of the above studies, we would consider a fairer over-all estimate of psychiatric disorder to be at least one child in ten.

The crucial question in relation to such rates of psychiatric disorder, is what are the service needs and the demands? Rutter *et al.* (1970) define psychiatric disorder in terms of 'abnormality of behaviour, emotions, or relationships ... sufficiently marked and sufficiently prolonged to cause handicap to the child himself and/or distress or disturbance in the family or community'. Such a definition implies that the child merits help, but after careful examination of all relevant data, Rutter and Graham (1966) conclude that of those showing psychiatric disorder a third were thought to need diagnosis and advice only, a third possibly required treatment, and a third probably or definitely required treatment.

Further, Rutter warns against simply equating prevalance with demand. Factors which determine referral are severity of the child's disorder (Wolff, 1967), intolerance of the child's behaviour, health and attitudes of the parents, family difficulties (Shepherd *et al.,* 1966*a, b*), attitudes of referral agencies such as the school and GP, and in addition the interests, theoretical orientation, and the services provided by the clinics. Indeed, only 49 per cent of the parents of the psychiatrically disordered children stated definitely that their children had a disorder, and of the children not receiving help from one or other professional agency only fifteen wanted help. Again, Rutter *et al.* (1970) points out that the low percentage of parents wanting help could partly be an index of inadequate provision. It would appear that only about 30 per cent wanted or were receiving help, and even then some of these reluctantly. They also pointed out that help could often be provided by professions other than psychiatrists. It is interesting to note, in this respect, in the city of Newcastle where a tradition exists for the paediatrician to provide a comprehensive first line service for all types of childhood disorders, that Brandon (1960) reports about 50 per cent of parents of disturbed children stated they wanted help.

While both Ryle *et al.* (1963) in a general practice survey, and Rutter *et al.* (1970) point out that only one in five children with psychiatric disorder were having some kind of help, the latter research leads to the view that 'the psychiatric services were treating an appropriate group of children who required treatment in their own right' (Rutter *et al.,* 1970).

DESCRIPTIONS OF SERVICES, SERVICE NEEDS, AND DEFICIENCES

In the UK the pattern of services which has been adopted is based on the American idea of a 'core' team consisting of the three key professional disciplines: psychiatrists, psychiatric social workers, and psychologists. Both health and educational services run out-patient clinics in which these teams function, with child psychiatry units being hospital-based and child guidance clinics run by the local education authorities. As Warren (1971) has pointed out

in some places both kinds were found, separately run and rivalling rather than complementing each other. The local authority service as a rule had closer ties with the community . . . and with the schools. The hospital based clinic was less isolated from other medical services, and better placed and oriented to deal with serious psychiatric or other ill health in children.

Each of these services has developed a different pattern of day or residential care. The health service has developed day or residential hospital units and the local educational services day or residential schools. The local education authorities in addition maintain a large number of children in private maladjusted schools. The provision and staffing of these services is the subject of the next section.

Staffing of child guidance and psychiatry services

Ratios of staff

This subject was tackled by the Underwood Committee (1955) which recommended that the ratio of the disciplines working within the psychiatric team should be: 1 psychiatrist : 1 psychologist : 2 psychiatric social workers. Where the team was to provide an educational psychological service to the school this should be supplemented by a further psychologist and social worker. Although such ratios were intended for educationally based services only, they have tended to be applied to hospital-based services as well. The report does not specify whether these ratios were to apply to senior staff only, or to all staff, nor does a more recent report (Summerfield, 1968).

Numbers of staff

The Underwood Committee (1955) made a purely practical estimate of what should be aspired to in terms of numbers of staff. The unit of population (Table 1) used in their formula was one clinic team per unit of 45,000 schoolchildren and a ten-year plan for its realization for the 6,500,000 school population in England and Wales. The achievement of this objective would have meant an expansion in the numbers of child guidance staff to approximately 140 full-time psychiatrists, 280 educational psychologists, and 420 social workers. The Committee pointed

Table 1. *Projection of numbers of staff needed in relation to number of pupils in schools, 1955–75 (England and Wales) modified from Summerfield (1968).*

	1955	1960	1965	1970/1	1975
Maintained primary and secondary schools*					
1. Pupils in school (million)	6·5	6·9	7·1	7·9	9·1
2. Staff required on basis of 1 team per 45,000 (Underwood)					
(a) Psychiatrists	145 (56)†	154 (75)	158 (110)	175 (144)	202
(b) Educational psychologists	290 (141)	308 (177)	315 (324)	349 (500)	404
(c) Social workers	435 (109)	462 (117)	473 (235)	524 (398)	606
3. Educational psychologists on basis 1 per 10,000 (Summerfield)	652	692	709	786	909
All schools (ie private and LEA)					
4. Pupils (million)	7·2	7·6	7·8	8·5	9·8
5. Staff required					
(a) per 45,000 (Underwood)	160 (56)	169 (75)	173 (110)	190 (144)	217
(b) per 35,000 (RMPA)	206	217	223	243 (144)	272
6. Psychiatrist (Underwood not specified) Consultants (RMPA)	320 (141)	339 (177)	345 (324)	379 (500)	434
7. Educational psychologists (Underwood) Psychologists (RMPA)	206 or 412	217 or 434	223 or 446	243 or 486	272 or 544
8. Psychiatric social workers (Underwood)	480 (109)	508 (117)	518 (160)	569 (398)	651
Psychiatric social workers (RMPA)	412 or 618	434 or 651	446 or 669	486 or 729	544 or 816
9. Educational psychologists (Summerfield)	720	762	776	853	977
10.Pupils treated (thousands)	31	36	54	69	

* Local education authority maintained primary and secondary schools (excludes private schools).
† Figures in brackets give full-time equivalents to staff actually in post.
Source. Underwood Report (1955), RMPA (1960), DES Forms 20M (1970), *Statistics of Education 1966*, vol. 1.

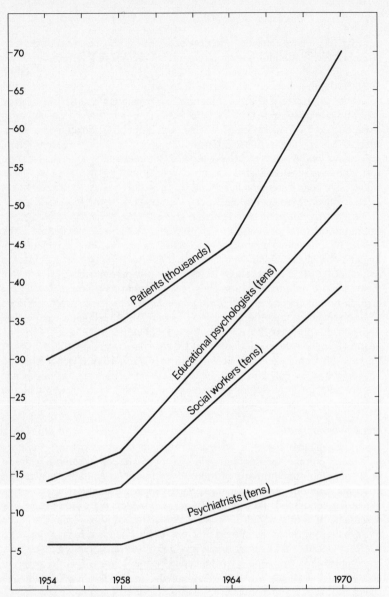

Figure 1. Profession of staff in child guidance clinics, 1954–70. *Source.* DES forms 20M: 1954, 1958, 1964, 1970.

out that this was a realistic, practical objective and in no sense was it an attempt to estimate ultimate requirements. In fact evidence from their own data, which suggested one team could only adequately cover a population of 35,000 suggests that this was a deliberate underestimate on their behalf. They also estimate the numbers of patients such a team could cope with and concluded that 300 was the largest number of new cases which could be taken on in a year. They also had at their disposal evidence that while 0·5 per cent actually attended, roughly 1 per cent of the school population would need to attend a child guidance clinic in any one year. The Underwood Committee assumed that many of the simpler cases would have been dealt with in schools by the school psychological service.

The Royal Medico-Psychological Association (RMPA, 1960) in a document *Recruitment and Training of the Child Psychiatrist* base their estimates on total population with the unit of general population to be served by one clinic team being 200,000 and the total population of England and Wales being 40 million. As the school population within each unit of 200,000 is round about 35,000, it would appear the RMPA based their estimate on smaller units. They reckoned that as a *realistic minimum* one full-time child psychiatrist with a *complementary junior* staff would be required for each team, ie 200 child psychiatrists for England and Wales. Applying this formula in 1970/1 with the population having increased to nearly 49 million the number of child psychiatrists increases to 243. If the Underwood Committee had accepted 1 team per 35,000 schoolchildren (as suggested by Essex in their evidence to the Committee) as the norm, there would be little difference between their estimates and that of the psychiatric professional body.

Manpower appraisal

Previously reliable statistics have been difficult to come by and therefore only rough comparisons are possible and these are complicated by reason of overlapping appointments of medical staff in child guidance clinics and hospitals without joint statistics being made available by the two ministries concerned. Furthermore, figures provided were not necessarily expressed in terms of full-time equivalents and in these circumstances these have had to be estimated. For the 1958 picture we have relied on RMPA (1960) statistics and for the 1970/1 picture personal communications from the two ministries. Table 1 and Fig. 1 provide an account of the steady increase in psychiatric personnel in child guidance clinics, but they do not provide an over-all picture of consultant or trainee psychiatric staff. In 1958 there were approximately 128 consultants, but we do not know what this figure consisted of in terms of full-time equivalents. At that time, there were only 10 training posts. By 1970/1 this had increased to 183 hospital employed consultants, which consisted of 149 full-time equivalents. This was supplemented by another 43

Table 2. *Education-based child guidance staff (ex Summerfield, 1968). Number of authorities achieving recommended targets by January 1967.*

School population of authorities	Psychiatrists (Underwood Target achieved)			Educational psychologists			Psychiatric Social workers		
	Yes	No	No. staff	Yes	No	No. staff	Yes	No	No. staff
Up to 45,000	32	44	26	16	18	16	19	27	54
45,000–90,000	7	25	1	15	18	0	0	23	10
90,000–135,000	2	8	0	5	5	0	0	8	2
135,000–180,000	1	4	0	1	3	0	0	2	2

psychiatrists (full-time equivalents) of unspecified status working in child guidance clinics, which we estimate includes approximately 34 full-time equivalent consultants, giving a total of 183 full-time equivalent consultants.

The then Ministry of Health, recognizing the serious staff deficiencies, has made attempts to remedy the situation by more than doubling their senior training posts from 25 in 1968 to 56 in 1971. Unfortunately, only 12 junior training posts support the senior training ones and the former are clearly insufficient for adequate recruitment to the latter. Projecting into the future, these training posts should produce 16–17 new consultants a year (Table 1).

However, the situation may be less bleak than the above figures imply. The prepublication figures obtained from the Department of Education and Science concerning staff of child guidance clinics and school psychological services are included in Fig. 1 and Table 1, and reveal a substantial increase in the recruitment of professional staff in the last twelve years. The number of psychiatrists has doubled, the social workers and psychologists trebled, and the number of children treated at child guidance clinics has doubled.

The over-all pattern of dramatic improvement of staffing is clear, but as the two ministries do not as yet produce joint figures, it is impossible to discover precisely how many of the whole-time equivalent psychiatrists working in the child guidance clinics and appointed by the local education authorities are of consultant status. Upon such information depends to what extent the original objectives delineated by the RMPA have been achieved. As the Underwood Committee did not specify consultants in their estimates of child psychiatrists, it would appear that their modest targets (Table 1) based on a school population of 6,500,000 have only recently been achieved in relation to psychiatrists.

This is also true for social workers, but their target is greatly exceeded in the case of psychologists. However, the more recent Summerfield Report

Table 3. *Regional distribution of pupils treated at child guidance clinics in 1966 expressed in ratio of pupils by region (derived from Summerfield Report, 1968).*

1:81–100	Eastern, Southern, South-Eastern, North Midland
1:101–20	South-Western, Yorkshire East and West Riding
1:121–40	London Metropolitan
1:141–60	Midland
1:201–20	Wales, Northern, North-Western
1:131	Over-all

(1968) regarding psychologists recommends one psychologist in the educational service per 10,000 schoolchildren, which is roughly double the number recommended by the Underwood Report. Hence there would still appear to be a need to build up numbers of psychologists. It is also noteworthy that in 1970 over 69,000 children were treated at child guidance clinics, (but again with considerable regional variation, Tables 2 and 3) and over 5,000 new out-patients (Brothwood, 1972, personal communication) were seen at child psychiatry clinics. There are no figures for the total children seen in hospital clinics, but obviously they would greatly swell the new and total patient attendance numbers provided in these tables. Currently at least 1 per cent of the school population is attending either child psychiatry units or child guidance clinics, compared to the 0·5 per cent described in the evidence to the Underwood Committee in 1955.

It must be noted that the Underwood Committee had not taken into consideration children under school age, the private school population, and the steady rise in birth-rate and increasing total school population. Hence by 1970/1 there was a shortfall of 31 psychiatrists (18 per cent), but if the Underwood ratio is applied to the total school population the shortfall becomes 46 (24 per cent). At this time the shortfall of psychiatric social workers was only 8 per cent (according to the Underwood estimate) but this increases to 20 per cent if we take into consideration the increased school population, and 30 per cent with the total school population. Only in the case of educational psychologists were targets in all three categories for 1970/1 surpassed, but the numbers are still below the more recent target set by the Summerfield Report.

Commentary and tentative suggestions

Some further comment is necessary on how the value of committee recommendations are seriously diminished when they persistently confine themselves to one facet of child psychiatric services when recommending ratios and targets. Such recommendations are further limited by non-consideration of population trends. We have also shown how both education and health departments, by providing separate statistics, have made it almost impossible to obtain an accurate description of the current

Table 4. *Social class and type of management.*

Social class	New out-patients	Out-patients regular psychotherapy	Day or in-patient hospital	Day/ residential maladjusted schools	Neligan NCDS,* 1961
I+II	38 (22%)	23 (20%)	8 (21%)	2 (4%)	9·9%
III	75 (44%)	46 (40%)	16 (41%)	25 (45%)	59%
IV+V	59 (34%)	46 (40%)	15 (38%)	28 (51%)	30%
Total	172 (100%)	115 (100%)	39 (100%)	55 (100%)	

* Newcastle Child Development Study.

manpower position and hence the over-all target objectives. Indeed, it would appear that only one professional body (Royal Medico-Psychological Association; later the Royal College of Psychiatrists) has appreciated the need for over-all planning for staff in relation to the total population of children. It is important that this division is not perpetuated and that future planning takes into consideration the over-all needs of maladjusted children (Tripartite Committee, 1972). Indeed, the time is ripe for a joint health and education subcommittee to be set up to consider professional staff ratios and targets in relation to child psychiatric disorders. In anticipation of the above, there is a case for a preliminary drawing together of recommendations concerning staffing estimates and ratios based on previous reports and memoranda and current available evidence. Such estimates could only be provisional, but would have the advantage of being able to ignore statutory and professional boundaries.

To recapitulate, the RMPA recommendations about numbers of psychiatrists was irrespective of their work base: they considered as a realistic minimum one full-time consultant child psychiatrist was necessary per 200,000 general (or 35,000 school) population. Then the Underwood Committee agreed that the case-load of a clinic team should maximally be 300 but we have demonstrated that currently almost 1 per cent of the school population attend child guidance clinics; this does not take into consideration children treated at hospital-based child psychiatry clinics, nor the fact that certain areas in the country have little or no child guidance staff even where there are sizeable school populations (Table 2). It is not unreasonable to suggest that if child guidance services were built up to a more even level throughout the country (Tables 3 and 4), then closer to 2 per cent than 1 per cent of children would attend for treatment. This would amount to approximately 700 out of a school population of 35,000 and implies that two rather than one consultant team and supporting cover are necessary for the above unit population. This suggests one clinic team is required for 100,000 general population. Such an estimate is supported by the latest professional committee to look into the subject (Tripartite Committee, 1972).

An analysis of Brothwood's (1972) survey data of hospital departments with attached in- or day-patient services, indicates that those which are university-based (and therefore usually have junior staff) on the average see about 170 new cases a year. There is further evidence that child guidance is falling far short of meeting known needs for diagnosis and treatment, because it cannot cope with the large number of children needing help. In addition, in 1965, the Chief Medical Officer of the Department of Education and Science reports, from a limited survey, that the waiting-list times ranged from two weeks to eighteen months, with an average of six months, and some feel that such a waiting-list policy may delay treatment until it is too late (Seebohm Report, 1968).

At this point, we would like to suggest revised estimates of unit population per child psychiatric team. The first would be a *sensible compromise* which would be somewhere between the old RMPA *realistic minimum* and the *ideal proposal* of double that figure to provide a comprehensive service. Such a compromise estimate would consist of one consultant team per 25,000 child population. This ratio would make allowances for possible modifications in the classical pattern of child guidance treatment suggested by Eisenberg (1969) and Levy (1968), hopefully leading to staff economies. Thus each region of the country would have a hierarchy of objectives in relation to staffing. Such estimates should take into consideration all children.

The Underwood proposal contained no specifications about status of each of the key professional groups under consideration. Neither the Summerfield Report nor the Seebohm Report proposed any variation of this ratio for the pure child guidance work. Clinical experience tends to support the view that this is not an unreasonable ratio for the three disciplines independent of the setting in which they work, ie hospital based or child guidance based with the following qualifications:

1. That if such ratios applied to staff of all grades, there would be adequate leeway, both for training purposes and for the newer specialized treatment and assessment services currently being established (for multiply handicapped children, deprived, delinquent, and autistic children, etc.).

2. Relating to the last point, in order to build up a pool of trained psychologists and social workers, substantial secondment to postgraduate courses will have to be embarked on.

3. Since social workers themselves now favour a 'generic' training programme leading to the 'generalist' social worker rather than the specialist psychiatric social worker, the distinction indicated in the Table 1 should be abandoned.

4. In a similar fashion, the distinction between the clinical and educational psychologist should also be abandoned.

On the above bases, in 1970/1 the *minimum* full-time equivalent/staff

Table 5.

	Consultant psychiatrists	Psychologists educational/ clinical	Social workers
Qualified	243	243	486
Training grade	68	68	136
Total	311	311	622

necessary for purely clinical psychiatric activities would be as shown in Table 5 (compare Table 1).

It is important to note with the present rate of training of about seventeen consultants a year (ignoring death, retirals, emigrations, and other contingencies) that in four years' time the RMPA realistic minimum target for 1970/1 will have been reached but not that appropriate to the year in question, ie 1974/5.

Day and residential services

Introduction

While the Education Act (1944) specified that it was the duty of the local education authorities to provide children who required it with special educational treatment, including the provision of day and residential schools and hostels, the Ministry of Health beginning in 1947 has only advised on the provision of residential services. However, hospital facilities should not be considered in isolation (Warren, 1971) but rather be related to other day and residential provision. It would appear that the persisting lack of co-ordinated planning and rationalization of day and residential services for children is a consequence of still divided ministry responsibilities.

The services

Hospital services. The build-up of hospital psychiatric services proceeded slowly. The first step was an an RMPA (1956) recommendation suggesting a scale provision of 20 beds per half-million of the population for children, the same for adolescents, and 25 beds per region for patients needing prolonged care. This recommendation seemed to have some influence on the thinking of the then Ministry of Health and was subsequently followed by a memorandum (1964) which gave advice about the scale of provision required in terms of 25 beds per million of the population for children, and that this was unlikely to represent overprovision. It also recommended an additional 25 beds per regional hospital board area would be required for children, mentally ill or seriously maladjusted, who required long-term treatment. Brothwood's (1971) survey revealed that accommodation available for children was 611–21 representing 13 beds per million population.

The figures for adolescents are 483 beds representing about 9·8 beds per million population. It is evident that by 1972 we are very far from achieving the ministry target with the greatest shortage being adolescent provision, and in addition there is substantial regional variation. Brothwood's (1971) survey led to the highlighting of some general points. As yet, no region had developed a special purpose-built unit for children requiring long-term hospitalization. Without providing figures, the hospital facilities on a day- or in-patient basis are particularly poor for certain groups such as psychotic children.

School services. While the Underwood Committee could only glean indications of the likely requirement for special schooling (in terms of a school population of 6,000 supporting a part-time special class and a school population of 10,000 a small special school) they found it impossible to estimate the numbers of places required in hostels and boarding schools. Nevertheless, the extent of need can roughly be gauged by figures provided by the Chief Medical Officer of the Department of Education and Science as for 1 January 1968. At that point in time 11,413 (14·84 per 10,000 school population) were receiving or awaiting special education; again there was considerable regional variation, ranging from 6·48 to 34·16 per 10,000 schoolchildren. With the current paucity of professional staff it would not be reasonable to suggest more than 20 places per 10,000 schoolchildren as a realistic minimum for special education of maladjusted pupils. This can be prorated to about 360 to 450 places per million general population. As the then Ministry of Health had already recommended 50 hospital beds per million for children and adolescents, it would appear that a total of 400 day and residential places could be considered as the realistic minimum target for the next decade for this unit of population. However, it must be remembered that expectation and demands from both parents and schools will rise as facilities increase, and further that there is evidence that many of the children currently in children's homes and in what were formerly approved schools (correctional schools) require psychological management for maladjustment.

Although it has been more traditional to establish residential schools, day-schools, and hostels, certain authors feel that day units or special classes (Chazan, 1972; Bartlett, 1970) are preferable, particularly where the main problems are educational or those of school refusal (Bartlett, 1970).

Hospital nursing staffing. Even when new units have been established, there are serious staffing and training difficulties. A high nurse to child ratio of 1 : 1 has been advocated (Ackral *et al.*, 1968), but Wardle (1970) in his survey found that a total of 991 in-patients and 169 day-patients were being cared for by only 821 nursing staff. Further, more than 60 per cent of these nurses had no qualifications whatsoever and less than 10 per cent had specific training in the psychological care of children. Indeed recognized training schemes (Ackral *et al.,* 1968) have only recently been established.

School staffing. The RMPA Report (1966) on Schools and Hostels for Maladjusted Children was based on the results of a questionnaire circulated to 42 special schools for maladjusted children. Though staff to pupil ratios were high (1 : 7), only a third of the teachers were trained and very few had any sort of special training, the residential being worse off than the day-schools. There was little psychiatric help available and apparently little in the way of in-service training programmes. The facilities for home contact and after-care were also rather poor.

Surveys of maladjusted schools. The same report commented on the inadequacy of information available on special educational treatment for maladjusted children and on the fact that no adequate follow-up studies had, at that time, been undertaken. Furthermore, they had the impression that a large number of these children were sent to these schools not primarily from any benefit they receive therefrom, but in order to remove them from an unsatisfactory environment. The psychodynamics within these institutions could only be dimly perceived and the committee could offer no conclusions about the relative merits of day and residential schools as they are both differently staffed and cater for different pupils. The subject of follow-up studies of children at such schools will be dealt with later in this paper.

Commentary

Shortages of hospital units, schools of various kinds, and of staff, especially with training, is obvious. Even six years after the 1966 RMPA report, the main deficiencies remain in terms of insufficient training facilities and an inadequate supply of applicants for training.

Integration of the services

The isolation of the child guidance clinics was recognized as early on as 1948 by the National Association of Mental Health and the British Paediatric Association (RMPA Memorandum, 1956) who jointly advocated a hospital-based child guidance service with links with paediatrics. As Warren (1971) points out, the Ministry of Education Circular in 1948 which advocated the appointment of medical staff to child guidance clinics by hospital boards, was the first attempt to bridge this gap. Thereafter, the debate about autonomy or integration continues right up to the recent professional committee (Tripartite Committee, 1972) who consider it crucial that the split is not perpetuated with any future planning, while pointing out that integration does not mean all child psychiatry units should be situated in hospitals: 'This is not only unrealistic, but it is also undesirable. . . . The actual siting of any department must depend on local needs and geographical considerations.' This is a position not dissimilar from that adopted by Kahn (1962) who emphasizes the importance of a variety of approaches in child psychiatry.

The Seebohm Report (Ministry of Housing and Local Government, 1968) had an unsettling effect on many child psychiatrists who saw this as another divisive measure which could fragment services which were already reasonably co-ordinated (RMPA Memorandum, 1969). If the recommendation that all social workers be employed by the new social service departments is implemented, it would appear desirable (Tripartite Committee) that those seconded to child psychiatry units and departments should work there on a long-term basis.

In the recent consultative document on the National Health Service Reorganization (May 1971) the Secretary of State advances the admirable view that the service be organized 'so that its separate parts are planned and are operated, not in fragments, but as a whole'. The Tripartite Committee points out that the inclusion of community care of the mentally disordered as part of the social service departments means that medical and social agencies caring for psychiatric patients are now divided. In other words, recent recommendations could have a divisive influence on the organization of psychiatric services for children, unless statutory safeguards and provision for liaison are built-in from the beginning. On the other hand, such unification will (hopefully) lead to the reduction of inconsistencies of status, sources of employment, renumeration, and training of staff and also to the co-ordinated regional planning of developments.

EVALUATIVE RESEARCH: REVIEW OF UNITED KINGDOM LITERATURE

Most of the evaluative research reported in the English literature emanates from the USA. The little research undertaken so far in the UK consists mainly of follow-up studies and a few drug trials. The follow-up studies are broadly of two types: follow-ups of hospital patients and of children attending maladjusted schools.

Hospital studies

Wolff (1961) followed up 43 preschool children three to six years after a first visit to a child guidance clinic. The clinic (the Maudsley) is a specialized one and it is likely the sample was selected. Not surprisingly, the outcome was found to be worse for children from broken homes, from families with overt marital discord or where the parents suffered from psychiatric disorders. Maclay (1967) similarly followed-up 424 children accepted for treatment at a London child psychiatry clinic. Only 70 per cent of the parents answered the questionnaire so that the likelihood of bias is high. Of the respondents, 68 per cent had no further difficulties. Children from larger families did worse; those with psychosomatic disorders (which category unfortunately included the most spontaneously remitting enuretic conditions) did well; but those with psychoses and organic states did poorly; and finally those who had good relations with their peers did well. Prognosis was unrelated to age at onset of symptoms, legitimacy, birth history, home state, early separation, parental ages, social class, ordinal position, family history, and length of treatment. However, there is little comment about the kinds of treatment. Whereas traditional child guidance treatment has tended to emphasize child–parent relationships (Chazan, 1972), there is evidence from this study and that of Morris *et al.* (1956) of the importance of peer relationships.

One of the more rigorous and systematic follow-up studies is that of Shepherd *et al.* (1966, 1971). They compared fifty non-delinquent and non-psychotic children attending child guidance clinics with a control group matched for type and severity of behavioural symptoms who were comparably disturbed but had not been referred. Two-thirds of each group improved markedly. The researchers were unable to relate this to treatment, but rather to environmental factors. Their results also indicated that referral to the clinic was as much related to parental reactions as to morbidity. Rutter (1970) however, questions the appropriateness of this project to answer questions about treatment as 'it assesses therapy of an unknown type and quality on a group of children with disorders of a largely unknown diagnosis'. Further, the groups were ill matched in that the clinic group contained significantly fewer children with mild disorders and more homes from where the father was absent, etc. Rutter concludes that two years is too long to study treatment of disorders with high remission rates, and hence treatments of such disorders should be assessed in terms of their power to shorten the duration of disorder and not 'cure'. Finally, the exclusion of 27 per cent of the eligible clinic cases as being unmatchable suggests that two-thirds improvement of the clinic group may well be an overestimate. However, this study has provided some clues as to factors associated with persistence of disturbance. Persistence was related to differences within the working-class group in terms of poorer outcome for those children whose fathers were in unskilled jobs, last born children, mothers who were working at the time of original interview, continued poor health of the mother, an attitude of irritation by the parents to their child's behaviour, and finally there was a marked association between failure to improve and reported stress in the family.

School studies

The value of the school studies reported in the literature is substantially reduced by their subjectivity, selectivity of intake, and lack of both control or comparison groups and hence the findings are incapable of comparability and generalization.

It is not surprising that while Shields (1962) and Shaw (1965) described over 80 per cent considerably improved or cured, Balbernie (1966) reports that over 50 per cent of the cases he followed-up had further difficulties, some of which were of a serious nature. This latter work emphasizes the importance of adequate after-care especially in difficult cases, and raises the question of whether such schools can meet the needs of such children.

The two more systematic objective studies were those of Petrie (1962) and Roe (1965). Petrie studied twenty-three 7–11-year-old children admitted to a residential school over an eighteen-month period. The children showed significant progress intellectually, educationally, and in behaviour as measured on a rating scale and projective tests. However, the observation period was short, and as again there were no controls or comparison groups, it is not possible to assess the extent of spontaneous improvement. Further, the rates of improvement were not constant in that those who improved in the first nine months did not continue to do so in the second nine. Within-sample progress was also assessed, but none of the comparisons proved significant. Finally, a key factor in prognosis appeared to be improvement in parental attitudes.

Roe studied new admissions to maladjusted boarding schools, day-schools, and tutorial classes (day units in ordinary schools). She found that in terms of their general background, age, intellectual functioning, and their initial level of disturbance, the three samples were different and therefore she doubted whether comparisons were really valid. All three groups made gains in terms of educational achievements, but in spite of the more objective nature of the measures used, the author does not indicate how significant the improvement was. In statistical analysis (due to regression to the mean) one usually finds the most disturbed showing the *greatest* improvement, but Roe found that the day-school sample (the *most severely* disturbed) showed the *least* improvement. With an objective behavioural instrument she found that the boarding school sample (severely disturbed) showed a reduction in the number of overt maladjustment 'pointers' with a significant two-way trend, with the original very high scorers tending to have reduced subsequent scores, and low scorers tending to have increased subsequent scores. But this may merely be a reflection of the regression effect. With the day-school sample there was an increased average number of maladjustment 'pointers', but with similar two-way trend. However, with the tutorial group (the least disturbed) there was a significant over-all trend in the direction of reduced maladjustment 'pointers'. It is interesting to note that the tutorial class pupils whose level of disturbance is not so severe as to precipitate exclusion from ordinary schools 'are likely to show a steady decrease in overt maladjustment pointers'. This latter finding is similar to that of Lunzer (1960) and Shepherd *et al.* (1971). Lunzer reported that spontaneous recovery occurred in rather more than half of twenty-four disturbed children attending ordinary primary schools over a period of one year. Shepherd *et al.* (1971), in their epidemiological follow-up study of children showing 'deviant behaviour' in ordinary schools utilizing relatively objective methods, describe what amounts to considerable spontaneous improvement in three-quarters of the group three years later.

An important question is whether major maladjustment can be contained in ordinary schools in special classes, both because they are said to be administratively easier to run (Chazan, 1972) and more economical than special schools. Though Bartlett (1970) reports the usual success rate (over 60 per cent) in her survey of eleven small day units, her assessments were subjective and this work therefore merits replication utilizing controls and more objective measures.

DISCUSSION

A major criticism of current attempts to estimate staffing or accommodation requirements is that they are nothing more than educated hunches or inspired guesses which are apt to be made without taking into consideration the *demand for* and *desirability of* treatment; nor are they based on objective and detailed findings resulting from operational research. Further, they have not taken into account economies that might accrue from variations of treatment or alternative ways of utilizing clinic personnel. And yet, once such estimates are given nominal approval they become the subject of emotive lobbying for their implementation.

Therapeutic intervention

In relation to the above issues are questions about what can be achieved by intervention. Lewis (1965) argues on two counts that there is a need to re-examine what is hoped to be accomplished by intervention. The first is the absence of definitive evidence that most neurotic children develop into neurotic adults (Robins, 1966) and secondly the regularity with which studies of childhood psychiatric disorders report that two-thirds of children improve regardless of treatment. This issue can mainly be decided by follow-up studies.

Robins (1970) has provided the most competent and comprehensive review of such studies. Commenting on the fact that treatment appears to make little difference, she points out that questions have been raised whether such negative findings result from initial differences in the degree of illness in treated and untreated groups, and the result of not specifying the disorders treated or treatments used. The fact that lesser degrees of disturbed behaviour which occur commonly in children frequently require no treatment (Shepherd *et al.*, 1971), leads to questions and views about how we can most efficiently use the limited services (Rutter *et al.*, 1970). To rephrase this, which children need which services, if any at all? At one extreme are those who consider all children with 'behaviour disorders' merit treatment to prevent adult emotional instability (Howells, 1965), while others suggest (Rutter *et al.*, 1970) that treatment in childhood has no demonstrable effect on the health of the adult; furthermore predicting which disorders persist is an uncertain procedure (Rutter *et al.*, 1970). Leading from this is the other extreme view that psychiatric help should be confined to chronic psychiatric disorders which are likely to extend into adult life if left unattended (Buckle and Lebovici, 1960; Shepherd *et al.*, 1966a, b). However, Rutter *et al.* (1970) point out 'quite apart from the difficulties of making this judgement, this would deny help to many children who might suffer unnecessarily and be handicapped for several years although their eventual prognosis was good'.

Central to the issue are the current concepts of treatment in relation to other branches of medicine. In certain branches of medicine the aphorism has been coined of a therapeutic philosophy to 'cure sometimes', 'palliate' often, to 'comfort' always. But unfortunately child psychiatry has been hamstrung by the concept of 'cure' as the optimistic hope of child public health measures in the prevention of adult disorders. It is therefore not surprising that other concepts have evolved which appear rational in the light of the above arguments to which future exercises of evaluation will have to be addressed. For instance, a hierarchical concept is beginning to emerge, either in terms of advice and support only for spontaneously remitting conditions (Shepherd *et al.*, 1966), or expressed differently as realistic symptomatic treatment (Lewis, 1965) with various intermediate hierarchies right through to where major resources are devoted to those chronic cases in which spontaneous remission is unlikely (Shepherd *et al.*, 1966), or those acute or chronic disorders whose duration can be shortened by intervention. In these circumstances, concepts of cure would appear to be inadequate as major criteria in justifying service estimates. It is therefore not surprising that Rutter and Graham (1966) offer the view that the following professional functions also have to be considered: diagnosis, prognostic opinion, consultation and advice, supportive therapy, etc.

Desirability of treatment

The subject of desirability of treatment merits further examination. It is well reviewed by Rutter and colleagues (1970). They point out that Lapousse and Monk (1958, 1959, 1964) have suggested that deviant behaviour, especially monosymptomatic behaviour may just be a phase of normal development. However, Shepherd *et al.* (1966*a, b*) appear to extend Lapousse and Monk's concept of a phase of normal development in relation to monosymptomatic disorders, even to severe disorders, by asserting that even extreme forms of behaviour disorder can resolve without treatment, as these probably only represent enhancement of disturbed behaviour in response to temporary life stress. In contrast, the Isle of Wight Study (Rutter *et al.*, 1970) demonstrated little change in their psychiatrically disordered group between the ages of 10 and 12 years. The only long-term anterospective evidence comes from Brandon (1960) who reports that of the 51 maladjusted children regarded as such before the age of 5, only 10 were classified as normal at 11 years. Rutter *et al.* (1970) argue that as their cases showed disorder of at least three years' duration, another two years for improvement would make for major illness problems which in their own right, at least, merited attempts at amelioration. The crucial question is whether psychiatric help can achieve this (Rutter *et al.*, 1970; Shepherd *et al.*, 1966).

Commentary

An uneasy suspicion has crystallized, based on uninformed criticism, the reviews of Eisenberg (1969) and Levitt (1971) and the research in this country by Shepherd *et al.* (1966*a, b*) that child psychiatric treatment with its cumbersome team, blanket type approach with its aura of mystique has become a sacred cow. Such criticism reaches its apogee in Rehin's (1972) academic and theoretical destructive attack on the child guidance approach. He quotes from Tizard (1966):

... there is widespread failure to tackle the problems of diagnosis and classification, and a lack of realism regarding the effectiveness of treatment. . . . We seem unable to come to terms with the public health problems of child psychiatry, either through epidemiological study . . . or through studies . . . of utilising the scarce resources of child guidance clinics in the most socially useful way.

Rehin himself claims that the child guidance clinics have not been able to demonstrate their effectiveness in a way expected of modern medical care.

Close examination reveals many other contradictions and discrepancies between ideals and realities—administrative dislocation, essential ignorance amid over-abundant theory, wasteful duplication of professional–client relations in circumstances of heavy demands . . . The question of administrative location is the immediate one, but this is part of the larger issue of the allocation and control of limited resources . . . Other interests, professional self image, territory and autonomy, are at stake. Child guidance clinics do not receive much public attention; they often appear highly specialized and mysterious. On all these counts, the policy problem is compounded by irrationalities and ambiguities.

We doubt how valid many of these criticisms actually are, nevertheless it is clear that child psychiatry and child guidance have to meet and answer and not evade these and similar questions. Some of the crucial questions to which the profession has to address itself are:

In relation to the team approach

1. Is it the most effective and sensibly economic use of the highly skilled members of such a psychiatric clinic?

2. For what type of cases does it work best?

3. Do all cases merit the triple sophisticated team assessment?

... Countless extra hours go into interdisciplinary communications in situations where one qualified professional could more effectively manage the problem without ending up talking to himself. More often the 'team' is used as a shibboleth when in fact there is not, and cannot be a team simply by virtue of the relative distributions of time for the various disciplines at the clinic ... The crying need is for rigorous studies evaluating outcome as we introduce new clinics, new services, new health programmes for community mental health [Eisenberg, 1969].

Are role and functioning demarcations too rigidly defined. Is it a flexible enough diagnostic–therapeutic tool (Levy, 1968)?

In relation to the training of the team

There are questions about the need to re-examine the training of each of the three disciplines in relation to their actual professional functions (Eisenberg, 1969).

In relation to clinic policy and therapy

1. How to redeploy our resources and utilize them in the most socially usefully way (Tizard, 1966)?

2. The efficacy of the various therapeutic approaches for psychiatrically disordered children including the different forms of dynamic therapy, behaviour therapy, pharmacotherapy, etc.

3. Questions about the need to re-examine treatment policy of in-patient services including that of waiting-lists.

In relation to administrative organization

Whether, with the reorganization of the health service by the integration of hospital and local authority services, it is going to be possible to achieve more formal collaboration, or even integration between the child guidance and child psychiatric services for a particular area or region.

RESEARCH

We would like to end this paper by providing an account of two pieces of pertinent research. The first is a simple head count about the delivery of child psychiatry services. The second relates to the crucial issue of achieving comparability of disturbance in experimental and control groups in child psychiatry research.

Health service delivery

Introduction and method

In a welfare state it would appear reasonable to assume that the health resources would be reasonably evenly distributed. Many studies have demonstrated that the more educated of the population are aware as to what is available, and how to obtain it, although it is the underprivileged whose needs are greater. Does this apply to child psychiatry in the UK? There is, to our knowledge, no published evidence on this topic. In the north-east of England there is considerable variation in the provision of services, with the most comprehensive and extensive facilities being located in Newcastle in the university hospital group. In this area there is a single large three-team psychiatry department and no private practice. It therefore seemed a reasonable area for a pilot testing for inequalities of service.

We took a series of consecutive cases referred for psychiatric opinion who attended the clinic for the first time in 1972, and worked out their social class distribution. In an overlapping time period, we also surveyed all the cases undergoing regular psychotherapy and case work. We also obtained statistics about all cases admitted to local day or residential maladjusted schools and admitted as day- or in-patients in the local psychiatric hospital.

Our findings are presented in Table 4. We found an excess of new out-patient cases being referred in the upper social class groupings, compared to the distribution described by Neligan in his epidemiological study of three years' births in Newcastle. However, the distribution of cases in the three groupings does not materially differ in relation to regular psychotherapy or admission to hospital. The only other important finding was a steep downward social class gradient of cases admitted to day or residential maladjusted schools.

Commentary

There would therefore appear to be, using social class as an index, some inequalities of health care delivery. It would appear that higher percentages are referred and seen, from the upper social classes and to a lesser extent from the lower social classes, than the middle social class grouping; and furthermore, these two extreme groups are given psychotherapy in similar proportions. But the striking finding necessitating explanation is that the maladjusted schools contain about 50 per cent of children coming from the lower social classes. The explanation is sometimes offered that upper social class families tend to get sufficient relief with regular psychotherapy or short-term hospital admission, not to necessitate maladjusted school placement, while lower social class families do not have the verbal facility to make use of traditional psychotherapy. But there is other evidence which indicates that this is too simple an explanation. In a large-scale study of children attending residential maladjusted schools, Kellmer Pringle *et al.,* (1961) reported that the four adverse conditions often claimed to be associated with 'broken homes' namely divorce, presence of a step-parent, death of a parent, and illegitimacy, affected 60 per cent of the sample. Perhaps it is a combination of low social class and the above indices of serious social disorganization which make for intractable treatment problems necessitating special school placement on a long-term basis. In support of this latter explanation the 1966 RMPA memorandum suggests that many children sent to such residential institutions are not there primarily because of any benefit that would derive from attendance, but rather to remove the child from an unsatisfactory home environment. This is a particularly negative view, and while it may be true of some cases there is no evidence whatsoever that this is true of the majority of cases. Indeed, some would suggest that upper social class families bypass the system and privately arrange for their maladjusted children to attend ordinary boarding schools for the same reasons.

In conclusion, while the higher percentage of upper social class families being referred to the child psychiatry department probably represent higher parental awareness and expectations, the less well off section of the community *after referral* also appear to be getting a fair share of what is available. While we do not believe Newcastle is in any way exceptional compared to other provincial cities in the UK where there is a reasonably comprehensive service but no private practice, the question still remains of whether these findings could be replicated.

Methodology of obtaining matched controls
The problem, method, and findings
In a research project designed to assess the efficacy of different therapeutic regimes with psychiatrically disordered children (whose disturbances are not psychotic or predominantly organic), we were confronted with the problem of selecting a comparable control group of children in the community with disturbance of similar severity but not referred for help to a child guidance or child psychiatry clinic. The methodological techniques of ascertainment to obtain comparability (Shepherd *et al.,* 1966) are crucial, or else the validity of such research findings are open to question (Rutter, 1969; Rutter *et al.,* 1970).

With our experimental groups we were not troubled by problems of definition of psychiatric disorder as this was implicit in the very nature of the children we were studying. In fact it was a simple administrative definition in that all the children in the study had been referred to psychiatric units. Thus our experimental group consisted of children who were basically being managed in a variety of psychiatric or maladjustment settings. Their disorders were of such a severity in terms of causing distress to them, their families or the community, and handicapping them to such a degree that they merited special therapeutic management. They were divided according to administrative convenience into the following groups: children admitted to residential schools for the maladjusted, admitted as in-patients to hospital-based units; admitted on a daily basis to hospital or school units and those receiving regular psychiatric help on an out-patient basis.

There was already evidence (Mitchell and Shepherd, 1966; Rutter *et al.,* 1970) that parents' and teachers' perception of psychiatric disorder are dissimilar and only marginally overlap. Certain researchers have utilized one or other of these screens and have accepted as being psychiatrically disordered those uncovered by the screens used. For instance, Brandon (1960) used information deriving from health visitor (nurse) inquiries, and others (Kellmer Pringle *et al.,* 1966; Chazan and Jackson, 1971) have exclusively used teacher questionnaires as screens; and Atkins and Kolvin (1972) used the thorough, but time-consuming, technique of gathering information both from parents and teachers and additionally interviewing all the children. The most elegant technique was devised for the Isle of Wight Study (Rutter *et al.,* 1970) where only those children uncovered using parent and teacher screens were subsequently examined psychiatrically and their mothers interviewed.

In this research our problem was different from that of an epidemiological case-finding study, in that our main objectives were to find control cases comparable with out clinic cases both in a clinicalseverity sense and in a quantitative sense. Initially we thought that a psychiatric interview alone as a screening technique would suffice in uncovering cases of similar clinical severity relying on the clinician's judgement, but it soon became evident that while cases with a severe degree of psychiatric disorder were recognized without difficulty, the nature and extent of severity for many could only be gauged by gleaning additional evidence from the home and the school. Moreover, there were a number of marginal cases whose final classification was also going to be dependent on this additional evidence.

A brief description is necessary of the three screen techniques used. The first psychiatric interview follows that outlined by Rutter and Graham (1968) with each child being rated for the presence, dubious presence, or absence of a designated number of features. The teacher questionnaire designed by Rutter is fully described by him (Rutter, 1967). Finally, the parents were interviewed using a semi-structured interview (Kolvin *et al.,* 1972) which indirectly derives from Wolff's (1967) modification of the behaviour questionnaire designed by MacFarlane and colleagues (1954).

It was therefore decided to use the psychiatric interview as the initial screen and to follow this up with teacher questionnaires and parental interviews of all cases where severe or moderate emotional disturbance was suspected.

Each child obtained a summed score on each of the three instruments. It remained to be determined how, and with what weight, the three summed scores should be combined for the purpose of selecting comparison groups. This was a fundamental and crucial part of the exercise. The question arose whether to use equal weights in adding the three scores or to weight one of these scores more than the others. As we had no adequate information on which to base a differential weighting system, it was decided to adopt equal weighting by using the usual procedure of adding standardized scores (see addendum).

Our technique simply consisted of using statistical extremes of behaviour as indicators of psychiatric abnormality. Other techniques of defining abnormal behaviour in terms of deviation from prevailing norms have been developed by Shepherd *et al.* (1971) and Lapousse *et al.* (1965). Shepherd *et al.* decided that any item of behaviour which occurred at an intensity or frequency of 10 per cent or less in relation to sex and age, would be designated deviant and given a weighting of 1. Such deviance weightings were added to construct a total index of deviance. Shepherd points out that similar crude techniques have been used in physical disease (MRC, 1966) in screening instruments like the Cornell Medical Index (Goldberg, 1969) and children's behaviour (Douglas, 1964; Glidewell *et al.,* 1957).

The first step was to find schools with a social class distribution reasonably similar to our administratively maladjusted sample and with this in mind, officials from the local education department were consulted. The schools chosen contained a spread of families throughout the social classes but with a majority falling into the Registrar-General's Social Classes III and IV. In these schools we surveyed all the children within the age range under study (7 years to 12 years 11 months). We then took the first 250 completed cases consisting of separate groups of children. Firstly those who were administratively designated as being psychiatrically disordered ($N = 116$) and secondly those additional children moderately or seriously disturbed using the psychiatric screening technique ($N = 134$) described above.

Table 6 demonstrates that the scores of the total 'administratively maladjusted' groups were higher than those of the groups deemed moderately or seriously psychiatrically disturbed using the psychiatric screen (ie the 'screened groups' in Table 6). The residential and in-patient maladjusted children scored particularly highly, but this is to be expected on two counts. Firstly, it is very likely that there will be a 'halo' effect as a result of parents or teachers scoring these children highly on a number of associated features, and secondly it is likely that there is a tendency for the

Table 6. *Results of selection exercise.*

Group	Number	Means of combined standard scores
'Administratively maladjusted' groups		
Residential maladjusted	40	30·8
Day maladjusted	17	29·8
In-patients	32	30·8
Out-patients	27	29·9
Total	116	30·5
Residential only	72	30·8
Day only	44	29·9
Hospital patients only	59	30·4
Screened groups		
1. Ordinary day schools	39	28·6
(a)†	29	29·6
(b)‡	18	30·3
2. Remedials		
Original sample*	26	28·4
(a)†	20	28·8
(b)‡	9	30·7
3. Day ESN		
Original sample*	45	30·0
(a)†	39	30·4
(b)‡	36	30·6
4. Residential ESN		
Original sample*	24	29·9
(a)†	22	30·1
(b)[8]	21	30·2
5. Total of all screened groups		
Original sample*	134	29·3
(a)†	110	29·8
(b)‡	83	30·5

* Original sample: cases moderately or severely disturbed at psychiatric interview.

† Residual sample: excluding cases below $1\frac{1}{2}$ SD from out-patient group mean.

‡ Residual sample: excluding cases below $1\frac{1}{2}$ SD from severely disturbed maladjusted group mean.

more maladjusted children to gravitate to residential maladjusted situations. This is particularly evident when we take a look at the controls where those children in ordinary schools score rather low, whereas those in residential or day-schools for the educationally subnormal (ESN) score highly.

To restate the objective, the aim was to obtain groups comparably disturbed both in the clinical (qualitative sense) and a quantitative sense. The scores in Table 6 reveal that the screened groups were not quantitatively identical to our 'administratively maladjusted' groups. The solution we arrived at to achieve comparability was to exclude the less disturbed of the screened group so that the mean of the remaining children approximated to the mean of the 'administratively maladjusted' groups. In the case of the day-school sample, it was felt that we should seek equivalence with the maladjusted children who had been treated without residential placement; for the residential school population equivalence should be sought with the hospital or residential school maladjusted samples. It was found that when all those screened maladjusted children who scored less than $1\frac{1}{2}$ standard deviations below the means of the two clinical groups described were excluded, then the appropriate mean became approximately equal. In effect, this meant a more extreme cut-off was used (28·26) for those screened who were attending residential situations, and a second, a more mild cut-off (27·8) for those attending day schools (see addendum). Table 6 also indicates the results of this new exclusion procedure. We have already offered explanations for the fact that fewer cases had to be excluded in the ESN group.

In passing it should be noted that although we were not using a random school population, but rather supposedly representative schools in Newcastle, that over this wide age range we obtained higher prevalance figures than in our prevalence study of infant school children, despite the introduction of more rigorous ascertainment techniques. In the ordinary school sample the prevalence of psychiatric disorder was 14·6 per cent. In those attending remedial classes the prevalence was 15·3 per cent. Nevertheless, it is interesting to note that the incidence of cases falling above 'extreme' cut-off points and therefore constituting a more severely disturbed group is much less, ie 9 per cent. In these circumstances we have found, in admittedly a less scientific study than the Isle of Wight, that more than a half of our 'control maladjusted' attending ordinary schools are as disturbed, in a quantitative sense, as those in special residential maladjusted settings. This has very important planning and service implications. However, this needs to be tempered by some common sense.

For most cases the method works adequately. But in some cases, despite arithmetical equivalence, our subjective clinical impression was that, in certain qualitative ways our comparison gropups of maladjusted children were not in fact very comparable. This is partly as a result of the instruments used, which are essentially symptom counts, and which are not sensitive to the severity of individual symptoms. Thus a child with one *incapacitating* symptom may obtain a low score. This may be the reason for Shepherd *et al.* (1971) excluding the most severely disturbed children from their clinical group.

Commentary

The method we have used is a group matching technique designed to make group means much the same. Such a technique is, of course, less precise than the matching of individuals to form like pairs.

If groups of children are to be compared in relation to their improvement or reduction of maladjustment, then it is important that the mean initial levels of maladjustment of the groups should be much the same. This is because of regression to the mean whereby, for purely statistical reasons, the more maladjusted tend to improve more than the less maladjusted (Garside, 1956). It is true that if initial means are not the same, then statistical rather than experimental controls may be used by carrying out an analysis of covariance. But such statistical control is indirect and involves assumptions that may not be met in practice.

SUMMARY

1. In discussing the organization and provision of services for psychiatrically disordered children and adolescents, the dichotomy of ministerial responsibility which has led to some inco-ordination of previous planning is alluded to.

2. Though there are still serious staff shortages, a dramatic improvement in the situation has occurred over the last twelve years. Three levels of recommendations concerning staffing are tentatively proposed: a realistic minimum, a sensible compromise, and an ideal.

3. An examination of the work in child guidance and psychiatry departments leads to the view that the work of the child psychiatrist should be more varied (with built-in evaluation) and also extended (for example into the community).

4. Grave shortages are highlighted of day and residential accommodation and associated staffing for all children, but especially for adolescents.

5. It is thought that the advantages arising from the reorganization of the health services may be counterbalanced by disadvantages in terms of divisive influences.

6. A review of evaluative research in relation to hospital and local education authority services, with their mostly negative findings is undertaken.

7. The current practice of child psychiatry and child guidance is discussed both from a constructive and questioning standpoint with emphasis on the need for critical re-examination and research.

8. A pilot study of the delivery of health services in a region where there is no private practice is reported, which suggests that inequalities of delivery within the health service are minimal *after referral*.

9. Finally, one of the methods dealing with the central problem of selecting comparably maladjusted controls for operational research is discussed.

Acknowledgements

The final part of this paper (on research methodology) was supported by a grant from the Department of Education and Science. However, all the views expressed elsewhere in this paper are entirely personal and are unrelated to the above research.

We would like to thank Miss E. Palframan and Mrs M. Blackburn for their diligent secretarial help, Mrs L. Mein for help with the references, and Mrs D. Muckle for her assistance with statistics.

ADDENDUM

Technique of obtaining mean summed standard scores and cut-off points for groups

This technique was carried out on the first completed 250 cases. Of these 116 were children who were 'administratively maladjusted', the remaining 134 were those felt to be 'moderately disordered' by the psychiatrist interviewing them with the Rutter screening instrument.

The data was subjected to the following procedures:

1. The mean and the standard deviation of the 250 cases for each instrument, ie Rutter Teacher's Questionnaire, Behaviour Instrument, and the psychiatric interview, were calculated.

2. For each of these, a standard or z score for each individual was calculated, using the following equation:

$$Z = \frac{x - \bar{x}}{SD}$$

x = individual's raw score
$\bar{x}$ = mean of group
SD = standard deviation of group.

3. To remove negative scores, each of the individual's three standard scores had 10 added, which meant the range of scores was approximately 7 to 13.

4. Differential weighting of each of the three instruments was considered in view of the greater efficiency of the parent interviewing technique in any case finding exercise (Rutter *et al.,* 1970). However, as we had no adequate information upon which to base differential weighting, it was decided that equal weighting should be given to the three instruments.

5. The three standard scores, each with 10 added, were thus summed to obtain a summed standard score for each individual.

6. These individual scores were then summed over individuals and a group mean obtained.

7. Two cut-off points were then selected: a 'mild' cut-off and an extreme' cut-off. The 'mild' cut-off point was $1\frac{1}{2}$ standard deviations below the mean of the summed scores of the out-patient clinical group. The

'extreme' cut-off point was $1\frac{1}{2}$ standard deviations below the mean of the summed scores of the more severely disturbed group consisting of those in designated day or residential maladjusted settings.

Severely disturbed: $30 \cdot 801 - 2 \cdot 174 = 28 \cdot 627$.
Mildly disturbed: $29 \cdot 981 - 2 \cdot 174 = 27 \cdot 807$.

8. The standard scores for all subsequently completed cases were derived using the same means and standard deviations derived from the first 250 cases.

REFERENCES

Ackral, M., Kolvin, I., and Scott, D. McI. (1968). 'A post registered course in child psychiatry for nurses', *Nursing Times* (April), 53–55.

Atkins, M., and Kolvin, I. (1973). 'An analysis of behaviour and temperament in seven-year-old children' (in preparation).

Balbernie, R. (1966). *Residential Work with Children* (Oxford: Pergamon Press).

Bartlett, E. F. (1970). 'Survey of day units for the maladjusted child', unpublished dissertation for Diploma in Special Education: University College of Swansea.

Blacker, C. P. (1946). *Neurosis and the Mental Health Service* (London: Oxford University Press).

Brandon, S. (1960). 'An epidemiological study of maladjustment in childhood', unpublished MD thesis: University of Durham.

British Paediatric Association (1960). 'Report: psychiatric services for children', *Br. med. J.* **2**, 795–6.

Brothwood, J. (1971). 'A survey of units in England for mentally ill and seriously maladjusted children' (for presentation).

Buckle, D., and Lebovici, S. (1960). *Child Guidance Centres* (Geneva: WHO).

Chazan, M., and Jackson, S. (1971). 'Behaviour problems in the infant school', *J. Child Psychol. Psychiat.* **12**, 191–210.

Cummings, J. D. (1944). 'The incidence of emotional symptoms in school children', *Br. J. Educ. Psychol.* **14**, 151–61.

Department of Education and Science (1968). *Psychologists in Education Services* (Summerfield Report), (London: HMSO).

Department of Health and Social Security (1971). *N.H.S. Reorganization: Consultative Document* (DHSS Circular).

Douglas, J. W. B. (1964). *The Home and the School.* (London: MacGibbon and Kee).

Education Act (1944). (London: HMSO).

Eisenberg, L. (1969). 'The post-quarter century', *Am. J. Orthopsychiat.* **39**, 389–401.

Garside, R. F. (1956). 'The regression of gains upon initial scores', *Psychometrika*, **21**, 67–77.

Glidewell, J. C., Mehsh, I. N., and Gildea, M. (1957). 'Behaviour symptoms in children and degree of sickness', *Am. J. Psychiat.* **114**, 47.

Goldberg, D. P. (1969). 'The identification and assessment of non-psychotic illness by means of a questionnaire', DM Thesis: University of Oxford.

Howells, J. G. (ed.) (1965). *Modern Perspectives in Child Psychiatry* (London: Oliver and Boyd).

Kahn, J. H. (1962). 'The local authority—child guidance clinic', *Lancet*, **i**, 959–60.

Kolvin, I. *et al.* (1972). 'Dimensions of behaviour in infant school children' (for presentation).

Lapousse, R., and Monk, M. A. (1958). 'An epidemiological study of behaviour characteristics in children' *Am. J. Publ. Hlth,* **48,** 1134—44.

———— (1959). 'Fears and worries in a representative sample of children', *Am. J. Orthopsychiat.* **29,** 803–18.

———— (1964). 'Behaviour deviations in a representative sample of children: variations by sex, age, race, social class and family size', ibid. **34,** 436–46.

Levitt, E. E. (1971). 'Research on psychotherapy with children', in Bergin, A., and Garfield, S. (eds), *Handbook of Psychotherapy and Behaviour Change,* pp. 474–94 (New York: John Wiley).

Levy, D. (1951). 'Beginnings of the child guidance movement', *Am. J. Orthopsychiat.* **38,** 799–804.

Lewis, W. W. (1965). 'Continuity and intervention in emotional disturbance. A review', *Exceptional Children,* **31,** 465–75.

Lunzer, E. A. (1960). 'Aggressive and withdrawing children in the normal school. I. Patterns of behaviour', *Br. J. Educ. Psychol.* **30,** 1–10.

MacFarlane, J. W., Allen, L., and Honzik, M. R. (1954). *A Developmental Study of the Behaviour Problems of Normal Children Between 21 Months and 14 Years* (University of California Press).

Maclay, I. (1967). 'Prognostic factors in child guidance practice', *J. Child Psychol. Psychiat.* **8,** 3/4, 207–15.

Ministry of Education (1948). Circular 179 (London: HMSO).

—— (1955). *Report of the Committee on Maladjusted Children* (Underwood Report) (London: HMSO).

Ministry of Health (1947). Memoranda RHB 47(13) (London: HMSO).

—— (1964). *In-patient Accommodation for Mentally Ill and Seriously Maladjusted Children and Adolescents,* HM (64) (London: HMSO).

Ministry of Housing and Local Government (1968). *Report of the Committee on Local Authority and Allied Personal Social Services* (Seebohm Report), Cmnd 3703 (London: HMSO).

Mitchell, S., and Shepherd, M. (1966). 'A comparative study of children's behaviour at home and at school', *Br. J. Educ. Psychol.* **36,** 248–54.

Morris, H. H., Escoli, P. J., and Wexler, R. (1956). 'Aggressive behaviour disorders in childhood. A follow-up study', *Am. J. Psychiat.* **112,** 991–7.

National Association for Mental Health (1965). *Child Guidance and Child Psychiatry as an Integral Part of Community Services* (London: NAMH).

Petrie, I. R. J. (1962). 'Residential treatment of maladjusted children: a study of some factors related to progress in adjustment', *Br. J. Educ. Psychol.* **32,** 29.

Pringle, M. L. K., Butler, N., and Davie, R. (1966). *11,000 Seven Year Olds* (London: Longmans).

Rehin, G. F. (1972). 'Child guidance at the end of the road', *Soc. Wk Today,* **2,** 24, 21–24.

Robins, L. N. (1966). *Deviant Children Grown Up* (Baltimore: Williams and Wilkins).

—— (1970). 'Follow-up studies investigating childhood disorders', in Hare, E., and Wing, J. K. (eds), *Psychiatric Epidemiology* (Oxford University Press for the Nuffield Provinical Hospitals Trust).

Roe, M. C. (1965). *Surveys into Progress of Maladjustment Pupils* (London: ILEA).

Royal Medico-Psychological Association (1965). 'Memorandum, the provision of psychiatric services for children and adolescents'.

—— (1956). *In-Patient Accommodation for Children and Adolescent Patients.*

—— Child Psychiatry Section (1966). 'Report on schools and hostels for maladjusted children', *Br. J. Psychiat.* **112,** 484, 321.

—— (1960). 'Memorandum, the recruitment and training of the child psychiatrist'.

—— (1969). 'Memorandum, the report of the Committee on Local Authority and Allied Personal Social Services (the Seebohm Report)', *Br. J. Psychiat.* **115**, 605–11.

Rutter, M. (1967). 'A children's behaviour questionnaire for completion by teachers. Preliminary findings', *J. Child Psychol. Psychiat.* **8**, 1–11.

—— (1970). 'Follow-up studies investigating childhood disorders: Discussion', in Hare, E. and Wing, J. K. (eds), *Psychiatric Epidemiology* (Oxford University Press for the Nuffield Provincial Hospitals Trust).

—— and Graham, P. (1966). 'Psychiatric disorder in 10 and 11 year old children', *Proc. R. Soc. Med.* **59**, 382–7.

—— —— (1968). 'The reliability and validity of the psychiatric assessment of the child: I. Interview with the child', *Br. J. Psychiat.* **114**, 563–79.

—— Tizard, J., and Whitmore, K. (1970). *Education, Health and Behaviour* (London: Longmans).

Ryle, A., Pond, D. A., and Hamilton, M. (1965). 'The prevalence and patterns of psychological disturbance in children of primary age', *J. Child Psychol. Psychiat.* **6**, 101–13.

Shaw, O. L. (1965). *Maladjusted Boys* (London: Allen and Unwin).

Shepherd, M., Oppenheim, A. N. and Mitchell, S. (1966). 'Childhood behaviour disorders and the child guidance clinic. An epidemiological study', *J. Child Psychol. Psychiat.* **7**, 39–52.

—— —— —— (1966). 'The definition and outcome of deviant behaviour in childhood', *Proc. R. Soc. Med.* **59**, 379–82.

—— —— —— (1971). *Childhood Behaviour and Mental Health* (London: University of London Press).

Shields, R. W. (1962). *A Cure of Delinquents—The Treatment of Maladjustment* (London: Heinemann).

Stott, D. H. (1966). *The Social Adjustment of Children* (Manual to the Bristol Social Adjustment Guides) (London: University of London Press).

Tizard, J. (1966). 'Mental subnormality and child psychiatry', *J. Child Psychol. Psychiat.* **7**, 1–15.

Tripartite Committee (Royal College of Psychiatrists, the Society of Medical Officers of Health and the British Medical Association) (1972). *The Mental Health Service after Unification* (London: BMA).

Wardle, C. J. (1970). 'Report on an investigation into recruitment and training for nursing staff on in-patient units for children and adolescents', memorandum prepared for Child Psychiatry Section of RMPA.

Warren, W. (1971). 'You can never plan the future by the past. The development of child and adolescent psychiatry in England and Wales', *J. Child Psychol. Psychiat.* **11**, 241–57.

Wolff, S. (1961). 'Social and family background of pre-school children with behaviour disorders attending a child guidance clinic', *J. Child Psychol. Psychiat.* **2**, 260.

—— (1967). 'Behavioural characteristics of primary school children referred to a psychiatric department', *Br. J. Psychiat.* **113**, 885–983.

9 Evaluating services for adolescents

MARY CAPES

The development of adolescent psychiatry

It is only during the last thirty years or so that adolescent psychiatry has become a subject of special interest, an interest which has been growing very rapidly during the last decade. Previously this area of psychiatry was considered to fall within the purview of child psychiatry for the younger age-group, up to school-leaving age, and of adult psychiatry from that age onwards. Consequently adolescents requiring psychiatric treatment have used either the services provided for children or adults, if they have used any at all. (For the purposes of this paper adolescence is considered from 12 to 19 years.)

No-one questions that the years 12–19 are difficult ones in terms of emotional demands, when many adjustments have to be made within a very short span of time, adjustments to rapid physical development, to changing from school to job or school to university, and to independence and responsibility. It has been well recognized throughout the ages that these major readjustments are frequently associated with turmoil and emotional disturbance but the general view held that these upheavals were part of normal development and would be outgrown by early adult life. Psychiatric intervention has in the past been largely reserved for seriously disordered conduct or more extreme degrees of withdrawal.

Recent studies of normal development by Offer (1969) have cast doubts on the fact that turmoil is an inevitable accompaniment to adolescence in emotionally healthy subjects. Masterson (1967), on the other hand, in a five-year follow-up of seventy-two disturbed young people whose difficulties might have been associated largely with their phase of emotional development, found that 75 per cent of them still had moderate or severe impairment of function at the age of 21.

More persons in the 10–19 age-group in the USA were found to be attending psychiatric out-patient clinics than in any other decade of life according to the National Institute of Mental Health in 1962 and, when it is remembered that 50 per cent of the population is under the age of 24 in the US now, it gives some indication in sheer numbers of the size of the problem if disturbed adolescents are to be given the help they need.

In-patient care

Unlike child psychiatry which originally developed in the community in the child guidance clinics, adolescent psychiatry came to the fore when special adolescent wards or units were first established. Bellevue Hospital Center in New York City opened a ward exclusively for adolescents in 1937 and two units were set up in the UK in the late 1940s. The first evaluations of these were made some fifteen years later.

Annesley (1961) reviewed 362 patients (228 boys, 134 girls) who had been admitted to the adolescent unit at St Ebba's Hospital between 1949 and 1954 and who had been followed up for over two years after discharge. Behaviour disorders accounted for over half the admissions, a quarter were suffering from schizophrenia, the rest from neuroses except for 2 per cent suffering from affective disorders. These patients were between 7 and 18 years of age (most were over 12) and they were all too incapacitated to be treated at home. Their condition at follow-up was compared with that at time of discharge and the prognosis was found to be encouraging in 75 per cent of the anxiety states and neuroses and in the behaviour disorders: of these 38 per cent had a complete remission and 22 per cent had improved, but in schizophrenia, especially in males, the prognosis was relatively poor: 58 per cent showed no change; 15 per cent of those who were originally diagnosed as anxiety states later developed schizophrenia; but in only 1 per cent of behaviour disorders was this so. The over-all picture showed an improvement in approximately 80 per cent with a better prognosis for the adolescent behaviour disorders than in adult psychopaths, but less good for schizophrenia.

Warren (1965) made a similar study of 157 patients (94 boys, 63 girls) whom he followed up five years after discharge from the adolescent unit at the Bethlem Royal Hospital. Their ages ranged from 11 to $19\frac{1}{2}$. The outcome for the neurotic group ($N = 68$) was found to be better at follow-up than had been expected on discharge, particularly among the girls; two-thirds of this whole group had improved. Three-quarters of the mixed neurotic and conduct disorders group ($N = 44$) had also improved, and about half the conduct disorders. In fact a definite shift towards normality was found in all groups except for the psychotic disorders ($N = 27$). The younger patients were found to have done significantly better than the older, except for the few who remained seriously ill throughout. No definite conclusions were drawn as to the relationship between adolescent and adult illness, though some indications emerged, as in the other study, of the likely outcome of further illness or antisocial behaviour as between the broad diagnostic categories.

As a result of the relative success of these and other units and the increasing public pressure against admitting young adolescents into adult wards, the Department of Health and Social Security (formerly the Ministry of Health) advised in 1964 the provision of at least 25–30 beds per million of the population for the short-term treatment of adolescent patients, with 25 beds in each of the fifteen hospital regions for long-term care.

Adolescent units have now been established in many areas of the UK, but the number of beds to date is about 50 per cent of the total recommended. There is considerable variation in these units although most have been set up in separate buildings relatively close to adult psychiatric hospitals; most contain 20–25 beds and admit young people from 12 to 16 years of age, of either sex, though some are single sexed; the treatment given varies considerably. It is not without significance that some of these special units have unoccupied beds whilst others have long waiting-lists; this anomaly seems to be dependent partly on the admission policy, and partly on the treatment given. Some units only admit adolescents who are likely to respond to therapy based on psycho-analytical concepts, and in most units the number of those who are acting-out and who are likely to be disruptive is limited. The figures available show that in 1970 in England and Wales (population 48,815,000) 1,320 adolescents (aged 10–14) and 7,967 (aged 15–19) were admitted to psychiatric hospitals and special units though the number in the different special institutions is not available. No evaluation has been made of the services provided by the units as a group nor has the comparative effectiveness of treatment in units or in adult wards been assessed to date in the UK.

Evaluating different programmes of in-patient care

In the US, however, Lucero and Vail (1970) made a follow-up study of 288 adolescents who were admitted to seven hospitals in Minnesota, with the aim of comparing the effectiveness of traditional, integrated, and separate programmes of treatment. The patients were between 12 and 17 years of age at the time of first admission and their discharge had to be at least two full years before they were reviewed.

In the traditional approach, the adolescents were housed with adult patients, and participated in the same treatment programme except for the addition of school classes, in the integrated system the adolescents had a separate programme from adults but were still housed in adult wards, whereas in the third they lived in completely separate adolescent units. Several of the hospitals used two types, and one all three. They assumed that all the hospitals had a similar responsibility for treating adolescents in their catchment areas, and that each type of programme would be generally similar from hospital to hospital. The effectiveness of the different programmes was measured by the average length of stay out of the hospital during the two years after discharge, and efficiency was measured by the average length of hospitalization on first admisstion. Recidivism was also noted, and defined as the percentage of patients who returned at least once within the two years after their discharge. Chronicity was defined as the percentage of patients who remained in the hospital longer than two years. The diagnoses of the patients were also compared in the three types of programmes. The average length of stay outside the hospital after discharge was twenty-two months for all three and the recidivism rate was almost identical; an average of 20 per cent. The separate programme, however, scored lower on efficiency with an average stay of ten months as compared with four months for the other two.

These findings were contrary to expectation as the local clinicians were all in favour of separate units, given adequate staffing and facilities.

It was also surprising to find a similarity in types of patients in the three programmes; it had been expected that the separate units would admit a lower proportion of psychotic patients.

For the diagnostic groupings they drew sixty patients at random from each type of programme and here again they found no essential differences in distribution between the three.

The number of neurotic patients, however, was extremely small, the majority were labelled as 'acting out', over 50 per cent in all three programmes, and psychotic disorders numbered at least 25 per cent of the total, others were suffering from brain damage or were retarded.

The therapeutic milieu

Other writers have discussed the pros and cons of admitting adolescents into adult wards in more general terms. Hansen (1969) found their presence led to an increased awareness generally of the dynamics of group behaviour, and of the value of family therapy, and, though the adult patients found the rudeness and impatience of the young hard to bear, they (and the staff) highly prized the vitality they injected into the scene.

Barter and Langsley (1968) on the other hand point to the difficulties created by their disruptive behaviour and to their need for special educational facilities not easily fitted into hospitals for adults.

Craft *et al.* (1964) found that the psychopathic youngsters in his unit committed significantly fewer delinquent acts after discharge when treated in a more rigid and authoritarian manner than when treated more permissively. This raises the whole issue of the efficacy of treating a number of young people suffering from very varied syndromes in the same therapeutic milieu.

One hospital board (Wessex) has attempted to resolve this difficulty by setting up two units, one for long-term intensive psychotherapeutic intervention in a more permissive regime, whilst the other unit has a more structured programme and admits the acting-out and psychotic patients in close association with an adult psychiatric hospital.

More attention has been given to in-patient care rather than to other forms of care in the literature but relatively few adolescents are so ill that they require admission to hospital and, for most of these, this only part of a total treatment programme. There is a risk of this facility getting more attention than the many others which form an important part of their treatment needs.

Out-patient psychiatric clinics

A study was carried out in the USA by Rosen, Bahn *et al.* (1965) (in association with the National Institute of Mental Health) of the current utilization of psychiatric clinic services by adolescent patients. Data were obtained on diagnosis, referral sources, type of service, and disposition by sex and two-year age-groups of 54,000 of the adolescents who attended 788 clinics. Of 750,000 patients served in these clinics in 1962, approximately 25 per cent or 194,000 were adolescents; this represented about 6·2 patients per 1,000 adolescents in the population. The largest proportion referred was in the 14–15 year group, the smallest the 18–19-year-olds, with the sex ratio of 2·6 boys to each girl at 10–11 years decreasing to equal numbers by 18–19.

Sixty per cent were suffering from the less severe disorders such as transient situational disorders, psychoneuroses, and psychophysiological disorders, and 16 per cent from psychotic disorders, brain syndromes, and mental deficiency. Personality and psychotic disorders, however, showed a sharp increase in the late teens, with psychoneuroses and depressive reactions increasing, particularly for girls.

Schools and courts were the major sources of referral, the others came from private physicians and families.

A third of the patients received treatment, the remaining two-thirds were given diagnostic evaluations. The average number of interviews was four, which often included parent interviews in the younger age-group, and a third of these adolescents withdrew from the service on their own initiative.

It was not clear to the authors whether the higher number of referrals at 14–15 arose from a greater incidence of emotional disorder at that stage, or whether it stemmed from the increasing anxiety of responsible adults, who felt they were no longer able to cope.

It is not without interest in this context that the peak age for delinquency amongst working-class children in the UK is located in the final year of formal education, ie during the fourteenth year, and was a year younger when the school-leaving age was earlier. This suggests that this transitional period is associated with considerable stress which gets expressed in asocial behaviour. And psychiatric illness, especially the more serious, is more common in the first year at university than in the following years, which is parallel to the pattern of breakdown in the armed forces.

Table 1.

Group I	(anxiety, depression, withdrawal, etc.)	36 boys, 21 girls =	57
Group II	(mostly habit disorders)	20 boys, 12 girls =	32
Group III	(conduct disorders)	35 boys, 20 girls =	55
Group IV	(physical defects and emotional interactions)	8 boys, 1 girl =	9
Total		99 boys, 54 girls =	153

Rosen *et al.* (1965), however, felt the increase in the number of psychotic and psychoneurotic adolescents was in part because the seriousness of the disorder had by then become more evident: there was less state of flux. Referrals from the clinics back to other agencies were mentioned but no figures were given.

Varied facilities

One study, Capes *et al.* (1971)[1] (which was in the nature of a pilot survey), was conducted by a multidisciplinary team consisting of a psychiatrist, psychologist, and sociologist. The primary aim was to ascertain how much psychiatric help a group of disturbed adolescents was receiving, the nature of the facilities used and where these were lacking. In co-operation with child psychiatric services and children's departments (who referred 54 adolescents in care), annual assessments and prognostic evaluations were made of 150 disturbed adolescents (initially aged 12 and 13) over a period of four years. The home and school milieux, early social and developmental history, intellectual potential, and the nature of the maladjustment were first established and then the progress of these youngsters over the years was noted in relation to the facilities which they used.

The group was a varied one, in terms of environment and social class, and the distribution of their IQs (using the WISC Tests) approximated to a normal one; no children were accepted whose IQ was less than 70.

The four main groups into which their disturbances were placed are shown in Table 1.

Their early backgrounds, during the first five years, were assessed on a four-point scale based on factual information such as a history of violence, gross neglect, break-up of home, and prison sentence; the unsatisfactory milieu created by extremely rigid or punitive or over-indulgent parents was listed in a separate category *b*. Fifty-four were found to have spent their first five years in highly unsatisfactory homes, 59 in unsatisfactory ones (40 were of *b* category), 28 homes assumed to have been satisfactory, and no early history was available in regard to 12 others. The facilities used by 139 who remained in the survey throughout are shown in Table 2.

There were 15 suffering from school-phobia, who all showed, serious emotional disturbance; 11 of these spent the rest of their adolescent schooling in special day-schools for the maladjusted, 2 had their schooling

1. This study was supported by the Nuffield Provincial Hospitals Trust.

Table 2.

	Groups				RESULTS			
					Steady progress on the whole		Remaining unsatisfactory	
	I	II	III	IV	Good and hopeful	Fairly hopeful	Doubtful	Poor
Out-patient treatment only (N = 51)	13	17	16	5	28	15	5	3
Out-patient×special day schooling (N = 17)	11	0	3	3	4	9	2	2
Special residential schooling and holiday psychiatric reviews (N = 19)	3	3	11	2	5	6	4	4
In-patient treatment (N = 9)	6	1	2	0	1	2	4	2
Probation (N = 11)	3	1	7	0	6	1	3	1
Remand home, approved schools, etc. (N = 10)	1	1	8	1				
No psychiatric links (N = 22)	12	7	2					
Total (N = 139)	49	30	49	11				

in the in-patient unit to which they were admitted, and 2 continued in ordinary schools whilst they attended for out-patient treatment. All except two were making favourable progress by the end of the survey, in that they were taking higher education or were in steady employment, and were free from overt symptoms.

In regard to the academic achievements of the group as a whole, the number of poor readers was found to be extremely high. Of the 51 children in care, half the poor readers had significantly higher Performance IQs, but this was true of only 15 per cent of the other 88 referred by psychiatrists, yet the latter group contained most of the seriously backward readers. Presumably emotional disturbance rather than any specific disability was the cause of this. School-teachers in their reports had rarely appreciated the true nature of their backwardness.

Of the nineteen whose prognosis remained poor, all had lived in a highly unsatisfactory or unsatisfactory environment when under 5 years of age, all had been identified as severely disturbed at the beginning of the survey and all except two had problems of an antisocial nature. Eighteen received a great deal of psychiatric treatment of varied kinds, at out-patient clinics, in-patient units, or at residential and approved schools; all without success.

Were these children genetically handicapped, irrevocably damaged during their early formative years, or not given the treatment which would have helped them?

One of the most significant facts to emerge from this survey was the very long history of disturbance in many of the cases, and the need for greater investment of treatment resources at an earlier stage. Over half of the 88 psychiatric referrals had been a cause of worry to their parents from before they were 6 and many of the 54 children in care had spent their early formative years in home conditions which were appalling:

Another highly important fact was the role played by child care officers, probation officers, and specially trained school-teachers in helping to resolve the emotional difficulties and maladjustment of these adolescents, who often showed a much greater resilience than had been expected, when placed in a good environment.

The expertise of the psychiatrist in many cases was used in a consultative and advisory capacity with ease of communication between the 'caring' and psychiatric services being the key factor.

From the 'consumer' angle, 60 parents of the 88 families referred by psychiatrists found the facilities helpful, in particular they mentioned the support of the psychiatric social workers; 17 picked out for mention the special educational facilities provided, and 6 the probation service. Fifteen parents remained somewhat critical and these criticisms were almost equally divided amongst the various facilities used. In the case of 13, there was no comment.

Other facilities

The high drop-out rate (50 per cent) of many adolescents, especially from 14 to 17 years, who do not take kindly to investigations and treatment on traditional lines, has led to the improvisation of services such as 'youth consultation centres' and 'walk-in' clinics. These, however, are mostly used by adolescents of 17 or over (Laufer, 1964). This is not surprising since the 14–17-year-olds are only just reaching the stage of grasping abstract theories and concepts (Piaget, 1969) and find it difficult to verbalise about a changing inner state, least of all with adults. Indeed, where verbal communication has always been limited as for those from disadvantaged backgrounds, any co-operation seems best achieved through 'concrete' types of therapeutic intervention and at times of crisis.

Shore and Massimo (1969), for example, base their programme of interventive support on the adolescent's early attempts to enter employment. They offer active help at this stage, then subsequently make themselves available when a crisis occurs. In this way the adolescent is helped to gain insight and learns to identify gradually with an adult. Opportunities for verbal communication on a more abstract level are also increased.

They evaluated their programme of treatment of a group of adolescent delinquent boys of school-leaving age by comparing them with a similar group who received no help. In the treated group, they observed profound changes in ego functioning and a marked decrease in antisocial behaviour. This improvement had been maintained up to two years after treatment had stopped.

A number of imaginative and highly flexible psychotherapeutic services are developing for adolescents of the middle age range which involve them through practical rather than verbal techniques. These are largely supportive and aimed at reducing anxiety and giving insight, but their establishment is too recent for comment as yet.

Discussion

Special psychiatric services for adolescents have been developing rapidly during the last decade, but, owing to the even more rapid increase in the number of young people needing help, much of the clinical work has had to be undertaken in the existing facilities for children and for adults.

Evaluations of differing types of treatment programmes can thus be made, but should the same criteria for efficiency and effectiveness of treatment apply to adolescents as to adults? Whilst the level of impairment of function and presence or absence of symptoms are important, there is also a changing pattern of development towards maturity expressed in age-adequate behaviour which has to be evaluated. To help towards maturity is likely to require treatment in terms of months rather than weeks.

The study of adolescents who attended out-patient psychiatric clinics in the USA yielded valuable information about the sheer size of the problem, the age at which the highest number of referrals were made, and the relatively high self-termination rate (33 per cent). A similar study which included data on patient satisfaction and progress after consultation, treatment sessions, and/or involvement with other agencies would be even more instructive now.

In fact, the setting up of psychiatric registers (as in only a few cities and areas to date) would lead to the assessment of the various services, the extent they were used and the long-term history of the psychiatric illnesses of adolescents which at present are still obscure. And any data-collecting systems and processes through which continuous evaluations can be made not only of immediate problems but of long-range ones must include all the community facilities, special day or residential schooling, foster care, special units for maladjusted children, half-way houses and hostels which all form a crucial part of adolescent services.

The Wessex Study of disturbed adolescents which clearly showed yet again the influence of the emotional climate during the early formative years in creating later disturbances also revealed a rather unexpected but impressive resilience in some of these young people when they were placed in well-chosen normal environments. It was significant that on a number of occasions this was achieved without psychiatric intervention except in the background with a well-co-ordinated consultative service shared with those responsible for their care and their education.

REFERENCES

Annesley, P. T. (1961). 'Psychiatric illness in adolescence', *J. ment. Sci.* **107,** 268–78.

Barter, J. T., and Langsley, D. G. (1968). 'The advantages of a separate unit for adolescents', *Hosp. and Commn. Psychiat.* **19,** no. 8.

Capes, M., Gould, E., and Townsend, M. (1971). *Stress in Youth,* Occasional Hundreds 1 (Oxford University Press for the Nuffield Provincial Hospitals Trust).

Craft, M., Stephenson, G., and Granger, C. (1964). 'A controlled trial of authoritarian and self-governing regimes with adolescent psychopaths', *Am. J. Ortho-psychiat.* **34,** 543–54.

Hansen, S. (1969). 'Impact of adolescent patients on a psychiatric hospital', *Hosp. and Commun. Psychiat.* **20,** no. 11.

Laufer, M. (1964). 'A psychoanalytical approach to work with adolescents: a description of the Young People's Consultation Centre, London', *J Child Psychol. Psychiat.* **5,** 217–29.

Lucero, R. J., and Vail, D. J. (1970). 'A comparison of three types of residential treatment programs for adolescents', *Hosp. and Commun. Psychiat.* **6,** 29–30.

Masterson, J. F., Jr (1967). *The Psychiatric Dilemma of Adolescence* (London: J. & A. Churchill).

Offer, D. (1969). *The Psychological World of the Teenager* (New York and London: Basic Books).

Piaget, J. (1969). 'The intellectual development of the adolescent', in Caplan, G., and Lebovici, S. (eds), *Adolescence—Psychosocial Perspectives* (New York and London: Basic Books).

Rosen, B. M., Bahn, A. K., Shellow, R., and Bower, E. M. (1965). 'Adolescent patients served in outpatient psychiatric clinics', *Am. J. Publ. Hlth,* **55,** no. 10.

Shore, M. F., and Massimo, J. (1969). 'The chronic delinquent during adolescence: a new opportunity for intervention', in Caplan, G., and Lebovici, S. (eds), *Adolescence—Psychosocial Perspectives* (New York and London: Basic Books).

Warren, W. (1965). 'A study of adolescent psychiatric inpatients and the outcome six or more years later. I and II', *J. Child Psychol. Psychiat.* **6,** 1–17; **6,** 141–60.

10 *Evaluating residential services for mentally retarded children*

ALBERT KUSHLICK

Introduction

For the past eight years we[1] have been working on a method of evaluating the effectiveness of different forms of residential care for the mentally retarded.[2] The approach to the problem was first described in *Social and Economic Administration* (Kushlick, 1967). Developments since that date are described in the annual report on our work to the Medical Research Council and Department of Health and Social Security, 1970.

We have tried to combine and extend the epidemiological approach to mental handicap pioneered by E. O. Lewis in his classical survey of 1929, the work of Professor T. McKeown (1961) in his assessment of service needs among people in hospitals and other forms of residential care, the work of Professor Jack Tizard (1960) in his experimental evaluation of an alternative form of care for mentally retarded children, the measurement of the problems of families with a mentally retarded child at home pioneered by Tizard and Jacqueline Grad (1961) from the MRC Social Psychiatry Research Unit in 1961, the evaluation of different policies of existing psychiatric services in Chichester and Salisbury undertaken by Jacqueline Grad and Peter Sainsbury from the MRC Clinical Psychiatric Research Unit (1963), and the work of Tizard, Raynes, King, and Yule (1968) in evolving objective measures of the quality of residential care.

In the past two years we have been greatly influenced and helped by the methods used by Professor Sidney Bijou (1969) to record adult–child relationships in their natural settings and by Bijou's concepts of mental retardation (Bijou, 1968).

We are, ot course, tremendously indebted to our service colleagues, the

1. The team now consists of Mr Paul Williams, Mr Ron Whatmore on the evaluative studies, Mr Roger Blunden who has taken over from Miss Gillian Cox on the epidemiological side of the work, and Mr Barry Sexton the computer scientist.
2. The British Department of Health and Social Security uses the term 'mentally handicapped' as a synonym for the term 'mentally retarded' [Eds].

families of the retarded and to the retarded themselves whose work and whose problems we are privileged to be able to observe.

Summary of the method used and progress to date

Briefly, the method consists of:

1. Assessing the size and nature of the over-all problem by means of an epidemiological survey which covers people, both in residential care (including hospitals), and at home.

2. Advising service personnel, on the basis of the data generated and other data available, to set up, in parts of the epidemiological area, alternative forms of care ('experimental'), which would be predicted to achieve the defined service aims more simply and effectively than existing ('control') services for other areas which are demographically comparable.

This phase involves defining:

(*a*) Service aims which can be measured.

(*b*) Testable hypotheses on how and why the aims are more or less likely to be achieved by using different methods of care.

(*c*) Measurable criteria of the quality of care.

All measures must be reliable (ie replicable), valid (ie they measure the phenomena that they claim to measure), and relevant to both researchers and service personnel.

3. It involves collecting baseline data on 'experimental' and 'control' people and their families before the new service begins so that subsequent changes can be measured.

The method as described, has the serious limitation that the new 'experimental' service has some built-in advantages over the existing 'control': (i) It is new. (ii) Its staff are likely to be enthusiastic, specially selected, and newly trained. (iii) Its policies have been very carefully worked out. (iv) It has prestigious backing. (v) It may have more resources (for example staff) than 'control' services.

A method attempting to reduce the bias inherent in this approach has been devised which also has the advantage that it serves to meet administrative and service needs. This consists of attempting, at the same time, to implement in the 'control' service, the new operational policies defined for the 'experimental' facilities. This:

1. Provides a way of innovating existing services.

2. Avoids isolation of existing services from new, prestigious facilities.

3. Provides, from a research point of view, opportunities for developing scales of quality of care and testing hypotheses on the factors which determine specific components of 'good' or 'poor' care. These factors become more obvious when attempts are made to introduce new standards in existing services.

4. Involves both service and research personnel in the design and implementation of the policy and its operational measurement.

Table 1. *Wessex Survey: grade, social or physical incapacity, and place of care. Rates per 100,000 total population.* *

Age	Grade	Place of care	NA	All SB	SI	CAN	Total
				Incapacity			
Children	SSN	NI	4(1)	4(3)	2(1)	20(17)	30(22)
		I	5	5(2)	3(2)	5(4)	18(9)
	MSN	NI	1	1(1)	1	7(6)	9(7)
		I	—	1	—	1(1)	2(2)
Adults	MSN	NI	6(1)	2(1)	1	45(18)	50(20)
		I	1	14(3)	6(1)	53(19)	80(24)
	SSN	NI	2(1)	—	—	69(10)	75(10)
		I	2(1)	4(2)	1	45(16)	53(18)

* Totals include cases where incapacity is not known. Figures in parentheses are for people receiving training.
Source. Kushlick and Cox (1967).

It can be seen from Table 1 that there were, in a total population of 100,000 about 20 children (18 SSN and 2 MSN) in residential care, mainly in hospitals for the mentally retarded. Five were non-ambulant (NA), the remainder could walk. Of these 6 had severe behaviour disorders (All SB) with or without severe incontinence. A further 3 were only severely incontinent (SI) and the remaining 6 were continent, ambulant, and had no severe behaviour disorders (CAN).

The new units were designed to test the feasibility of meeting all these children's needs in a domestic unit of around 25 places for a population of 100,000. Additional places were to be provided because there was at the time a waiting-list of about 3 places per 100,000 and it can be seen that there is a very severely retarded child living at home (NI) for every one in hospital.

Two other features are: first, the very low proportion of people receiving any formal education or training (the figures in parentheses); second, the very high proportion of SSN adults in hospitals who are CAN. Indeed half of the adults are also able to feed, wash, and dress themselves without help.

The evaluative study

The possibility that the prevalence data could be used in an evaluative study of different forms of residential care for the severely subnormal was outlined in the early stages of the prevalence survey (Kushlick, 1965) and in more detail later (Kushlick, 1967).

In 1966 a Wessex RHB Working Party (Wessex RHB, 1966) proposed that future residential facilities in the Region be provided in small, locally based units serving the mentally retarded from total populations of 100,000 rather than in the form of a large hospital serving a total population of 500,000 or one million. These included a number of children's units of about 25 places, each serving a total population of 100,000. The children's units were to take care of all of the severely subnormal (SSN) children from the population who required institutional care (Table 1).

It was decided to provide these units in such a way that they might be experimentally evaluated. The evaluation was to take the form of a 'feasibility' trial in which the new units serving areas of 100,000 total population would be compared with existing institutional care, serving demographically comparable areas of 100,000 population. The latter would serve as the 'control'. The first two of these new units were planned for Southampton and Portsmouth because they each have total populations of about 200,000. It was decided to divide the towns into two demographically comparable areas, one served by the new unit and the control side served by existing hospital units.

The research design

Since we planned to evaluate the 'effectiveness' of a new type of unit we had first to define this term. We defined the 'effectiveness' of a service as the extent to which its 'aims' were met.

The aims were defined as:[1]

1. Client-oriented (progress of affected subjects and relief of the burdens of their families).

2. Administration-oriented (the delivery of a defined quality of care with 'reasonable' effort and cost).

The criteria of effectiveness were therefore:

1(*a*) Measures of change in the cognitive and social abilities of the subjects.

(*b*) Measures of change in the family problems arising from the impact of the retarded person on the family.

(*c*) Measures of change in the families' experience with the relevant services and of their degree of satisfaction with these contacts.

2(*a*) Measures of change in quality of care.

(*b*) Descriptions and, where possible, measures of administrative problems involved in staffing and servicing.

(*c*) Costs: capital running and, if possible, cost effectiveness (Kushlick *et al.*, 1970).[2]

This paper concentrates on the problems relating to the quality of care in the living units, its measurement and the factors affecting it.

1. See Kushlick (1967) for details.

2. Our report to the MRC and the DHSS, February 1970 (Kushlick *et al.*, 1970), described the research design in terms of a 'feasibility' trial: the new service would be 'feasible' if it was as effective as, or more effective than, existing services with similar administrative effort and costs. A brief description of the feasibility of aspects of the new service will shortly be published (Kushlick, 1972). The need to change the research design by considering the existing service as a second 'experiment' and by attempting to increase some of the resources and organizational characteristics of the existing service in the direction of the new service is described in a second report to the MRC and the DHSS in 1971 (Kushlick, 1971).

We hypothesized that *all* of the SSN children at present in compre-hensive hospitals for the mentally retarded, under continuous medical and nursing care, could be dealt with *at least* as well in locally based units of about 20–25 places serving a total population of 100,000, and staffed by people trained in child care with a short three-months' training in mental handicap. The staff would have the support of a local GP and a consultant in mental handicap. Educational and social work needs would be met from the local authority's services for those children who lived at home with their parents. Specialist medical needs would be met, where appropriate, from the district general hospital in the same way as they were for children at home.

An operational policy was evolved specially for the new units by a regional hospital board working party (Wessex RHB, 1966). This defined the client-oriented aim of ensuring, in the population served by the new unit, the maximum growth and development of the retarded and the relief of the associated burdens borne by their families.

With respect to the administrative aim of achieving high-quality care in the new residential units, we were fortunate that, at that stage King, Raynes, and Tizard (1968) (on the basis of the work of Goffman [1961]) had provided objective measures of 'poor quality care'. The operational policy specified that these were to be *avoided*.

Details of these measures of child management practices and the back-ground to their development, are described in their recently published monograph *Patterns of Residential Care* (King, Raynes, and Tizard, 1971). Briefly the negative qualities to be avoided are:

'Rigidity of the daily routines' (times of waking, dressing, toiletting, feeding, toiletting, school or recreation, toiletting, eating, recreation, toiletting, eating, washing, and going to bed are fixed and remain constant regardless of day of the week, season, etc.).

'Block treatment' (children move through this routine in large groups).

'Depersonalization' (the absence of personal clothes, toys, or effects).

'Social distance' (staff live and eat away from the children and dress differently [for example in uniforms], they have little contact with individual children except to 'process' them, and there is considerable mobility of staff between the living units.

Their comparative studies of 'homes' for deprived children, and hospitals for the mentally or physically handicapped had produced what then appeared to be convincing evidence that the major factors associated with avoiding these features were the formal training of the heads of the units (child care rather than nursing), the content of their job (child care and administration rather than administration alone), a higher degree of 'responsibility' for such tasks as the buying of clothes, the ordering of food and cleaning materials, organizing the staff and children's day. The operational policy therefore involved the creation of a new grade of hospital staff (a warden) with the main qualifications being in child care. A special training course was set up and the staff recruited to start the course three months before the first unit was due to open. The staff were not to wear uniforms and the person in charge (warden) was to be resident. The unit was specially planned to have a 'domestic quality' with 'domestic' furnishing and fittings. The warden and the staff (called 'house parents') were to eat with the children at the tables. They were also to undertake domestic jobs of bed-making, cleaning, cooking, etc., even though special staff (two domestics plus cooks) were to be appointed.

As evidence for this Working Party Report additional observations had been made of a number of comparable existing units (hospital, local authority, and private homes). These were conducted by the research team with the assistance of the Regional Hospital Board's Training Department and Norma Raynes and Roy King (Kushlick, unpublished). The new unit, designed on the basis of these findings, incorporated three play-rooms and a dining-room to avoid 'overcrowding' found in the traditional hospital ward which has only a single day-room (also used as a dining-room), and also to allow their use for small groups of children. There was to be generous cupboard space for toys, generous provision of toilet facilities (including an outside lavatory) for dealing with incontinent children, and a large garden, walled in to allow robust play activities, while, at the same time, preventing the children from wandering off.

To enhance night supervision, microphones were planned for the bedrooms with a loudspeaker in the office. To facilitate the maintenance of personal clothing, large individual wardrobes were planned for each child, and a domestic laundry was to be provided to care for top clothes. A kitchen was included to allow autonomous catering and so that the children might be able to see food being prepared and cooked.

The epidemiological survey (Kushlick and Cox, 1967) allowed us to predict not only the numbers, but also the incapacities of the future residents (see Table 1). As we anticipated about six non-ambulant, incontinent children, we planned a downstairs bedroom for them with an aided bathroom and toilet.

We had fears about the possible disruption to the routine by the four or five ambulant children anticipated to arrive with severe behaviour disorders and severe incontinence. Our hospital colleagues kindly agreed to take them back to the hospital if they proved unmanageable.

Where such transfer of children to existing hospitals proved necessary, we undertook as a research team to investigate which of the behaviours caused the disruption, and to examine how the existing hospitals coped with them. Such transfer has not proved necessary so far.

The work of King, Raynes, and Tizard suggested that the *available level of staffing* was less crucial to the avoidance of the defined anti-therapeutic qualities, than the other factors. Also we had, as yet, no sophisticated means of estimating the numbers of staff on duty at any time from the over-all staff establishment. We also did not know staff ratios of the existing hospitals.

We decided, on the basis of the Home Office recommended ratio for residential children's nurseries, to plan to ensure that at any time of the day there was a minimum of one member of staff to five children. There was to be one member of night staff on duty at any time.

A special administrator (Mr G. Stedman) was appointed to the Coldeast and Tatchbury Mount Group Hospital Management Committee to set up the new units and to administer them in a 'line' separate from the traditional 'line'. A tutor (Mrs G. E. Kushlick) was appointed to train the first recruits. The physician-superintendent of Tatchbury Mount was to take charge of the children and a GP was appointed for front-line medical care.

The local authority support services were planned in advance and the local society for mentally handicapped children was briefed about the experimental design and the operational policy.

After the baseline measures had been made on all known, severely subnormal Southampton children and their families, the parents of the eligible hospitalized children from the east side of the town were visited and offered places for their children in the new unit.

These points are laboured precisely because they illustrate an important problem in the research design, viz. the combination of special factors which were operating around the experimental units and *not* in the so-called 'control'.

•

Setting up the new locally based units

The unit in Southampton (a converted house headed by a warden without special nursing qualifications) has been operational since 1 January 1970. Except for two parents' refusals and a clinical decision in one case, the children who were in existing units, and whose families are resident on the eastern side of Southampton have been transferred to the new unit. All children at home on the eastern side of Southampton who were on the waiting-list for admission to existing hospitals have also been admitted to the new unit. The negative qualities of residential care are being avoided and full use is being made of local authority educational facilities, GP, and district general hospital facilities on the occasions on which these are needed.

A second purpose-built unit headed by a trained nurse, and serving the southern half of Portsmouth, opened in December 1970. *All* children geographically eligible have been admitted. The defined negative qualities of residential care are also being avoided. The same is true of a third unit opened in June 1972 in Poole: this unit is also headed by a trained nurse.

As predicted, the children in each unit include about 7 non-ambulant; 5 with severe behaviour disorders, plus severe incontinence; 4 who are severely incontinent; 2 who are CAN. On the other hand, the control units associated with the comprehensive hospitals for the mentally retarded where the children are under continuous medical and qualified nursing care, show *all* of the 'anti-therapeutic' features of care: 'rigidity', 'block treatment', 'depersonalization', and 'social distance'.

We will not know, until the children and their families have been reassessed and their progress compared, whether the new units have also been more effective on these criteria. We have, however, been able to begin looking at the reasons why the negative qualities occur in existing hospital units but are avoided in the new units.

Evidence of possible reasons began to emerge from our observations of the routines followed in existing units and the first new unit. Then, as a result of the work of the DHSS's Post-Ely Committee which investigated the conditions in hospitals for the mentally retarded, the RHB and HMC adopted for *all* subnormality hospitals in the Wessex Region, the operational policy already accepted for the new units (Wessex RHB, 1970).

It has also become much clearer to us that it is necessary to specify with even greater precision the positive aims of any service for the mentally retarded.

What follows is an attempt to outline some of the paradoxical features of the problem and to attempt some synthesis of them.

The observations we made, using King *et al.*'s child management scale, make it clear that the tasks of providing individual care are being implemented far more on the new units than on the existing wards.

The profound handicaps of the people on the wards are clearly not, by themselves, the major factor. Videotapes have been taken of 'experimental' children, first on the wards and then, very shortly thereafter, in the new units before they would have acquired new abilities. Children who had had to be mechanically restrained (tied to their chairs or a radiator at meal-times) and fed on the wards, are seen on arrival in new units to be feeding themselves without the use of mechanical restraint. Most of the children in the new units came out of existing wards and they were as severely handicapped and behaviour disordered as those in any hospital ward.

Nor does 'overcrowding' or shortage of *trained* nursing or specialist medical staff appear to explain this phenomenon. Only one of the existing children's wards is 'overcrowded' by officially defined standards. Moreover, the new units, which avoid most negative qualities of care, share specialist medical staff with the existing hospitals, and one new unit has *no trained* nursing staff.

We were very fortunate indeed to be able to observe during 1969, the process by which the operational policy for the new units was adopted for all existing hospitals for the mentally retarded by the RHB and the Coldeast and Tatchbury Mount HMC. This process has been reinforced by the publi-cation this year of the Government White Paper *Better Services for the*

Mentally Handicapped (DHSS, 1971). The recognition of the urgent need to implement individual care practices in existing as well as in new locally based facilities, has allowed us to see, with respect to our original research design, that the existing hospitals now constitute another 'experiment' rather than a 'control'. We have been able to observe the extent to which the new policies, which are to be implemented in both new and existing facilities, are accepted or opposed by key management personnel, and the problems of implementing agreed policies in both types of unit.

These opportunities have allowed us to re-examine widely canvassed, but differing views, on the problems of avoiding negative features of residential care.

There are three questions that need answering:

1. Why is it so difficult to avoid negative characteristics of child care in hospitals for the mentally handicapped or long-term hospitals for the physically handicapped?

2. Why have such anti-therapeutic practices persisted for so long unchanged?

3. How can they be changed?

We have begun to focus more attention on the formal aims of the organization, the tasks required to achieve these and the resources needed to carry out the tasks. It has been noted by many students of organizations that top management of organizations which process people (schools, social agencies, hospitals, etc.) seldom, if ever, declare in documents their specific objectives, or the specific tasks which are necessary to ensure that these objectives are to be achieved. If stated at all, the objectives are very *general*, and it appears to be assumed by top management that the specific objectives are not only obvious, and therefore agreed by everyone concerned in the organization, but that the necessary tasks are being carried out as effectively as is possible by all concerned (Scott, 1966; Nokes, 1960). This was also true of our existing hospitals for the mentally retarded. Thus, when the aims and tasks of implementing a new operational policy in these hospitals were first specified and documented in draft form, there was considerable disagreement among top management about both aims and tasks.

It also became apparent that the negative qualities of care (King, Raynes, and Tizard, 1971) in existing hospitals could not be avoided by simply giving the heads of their living units child-care training in order, thereby, to change their roles. Firstly, the new units headed by trained nursing staff also avoid these features. Secondly, to avoid 'depersonalization' of clothing requires basic laundry resources which do *not*, like existing hospital laundries, lose, deform, or destroy clothing, and facilities for storing individual clothing. Thirdly, it became clear that the behaviour of staff on the wards, whatever their training, was limited by policy decisions taken by top management at HMC, RHB, and DHSS levels, remote from the wards. These policy decisions include the allocation and distribution of resources to the wards: personnel as well as material.

Our own detailed observations of ward routines (undertaken largely by Mr Ronald Whatmore) lead us to what may appear a very naïve conclusion; that the negative characteristics have arisen and been maintained from the need of ward staff and the nursing administration to find strategies for coping with long-standing and impossibly severe shortages of staff at ward levels. By staff we mean simply extra pairs of hands, trained or untrained. This staff shortage has been aggravated by impossibly poor material facilities at ward level.

The naïve way in which, after stumbling around, we eventually approached the problem, was to ask the question 'How many incontinent, non-speaking children, of normal intelligence, not to say overactive or destructive, children, could we, or anyone else, possibly be expected to care for in our own reasonably furnished houses, and in a manner remotely regarded as "child-oriented"? How long could we manage to do this?' When I now attend meetings of HMC members, I generally ask them to raise a hand if they have *ever* had to care, on their own, for as many as three such children. I have never seen a man at such a meeting raise his hand. When, on rare occasions, one or two women *do* raise a hand, I ask which of them have ever cared for four such children. I have never had to reach the number five. Birthday parties for older and continent children, generally last two or three hours and are seldom organized by one parent on his or her own.

A mother caring for three children aged under 5 works at a staff ratio of $1 : 3$ until the father returns home, when the ratio might become $1 : 1 \cdot 5$. In the minority of families with as many as seven children, the staff ratio might be $1 : 3 \cdot 5$ when father returns home. In addition, in such a family it would be most unusual, if not impossible, that by the time there were seven children, none were either attending school for substantial parts of the day, were fully continent, could speak or could feed, wash, and dress themselves and even help to care for the more dependent children.

Yet, in England and Wales, there are very few hospitals for the mentally retarded where the effective staff–child ratio (ie staff available at any time during the day), reaches $1 : 5$ (Morris, 1969).

The recently published and important study of our colleagues Roy King, Norma Raynes, and Jack Tizard,[1] ascribed a relatively low importance to the variables of *assigned* staff–child ratios and to the degree of handicaps of the children as factors determining or setting limits to the range of possible management practices of the staff with respect to the residents. Their reported findings raise important methodological problems. Moreover, interpretations of these data might also lead to policy decisions on the

1. See Chapter 11.

relative unimportance of the need to raise the staffing levels in existing or future facilities for the mentally retarded in Britain.

It will be recalled that this study compared the child management practices in 16 living units for mentally retarded children: 8 local authority hostels, 5 wards of hospitals for the retarded, and 3 private homes. The main finding was that the child-management practices in local authority hostels were consistently 'child-oriented' while those in hospital were consistently 'institution-oriented' as scored on the authors' ingeniously designed objective scale.

In a reference to this study in a paper in the *Lancet*, 22 April 1972, Mather says: 'This difference in score was not due to the wards (of the hospitals) having children with more severe handicaps; nor was it due to the proportion of staff to children assigned to the two types of unit.' In a review in *New Society*, 4 November 1971, Meacher says: 'Yet these differences could not plausibly be attributed to the characteristics of the children . . . It did not seem that the . . . staff–child ratios . . . were decisive factors either, in influencing child-management practices.'

Re-analysis (see Tables 2-4) of data from their monograph, together with unpublished data kindly made available to me by these authors, shows that the study does *not* rule out the strong possibility that both the degree of handicap of the children and the *number* of staff *assigned* to the units influence the child-management practices, or at least set crucial limits on whether they can be changed.

The authors (p. 153) illustrate very clearly that the 'effective' staffing ratios are much better in the hostels than in the hospitals. Thus, during morning and late afternoon periods, when all of the children are on the living units of both hostels and hospitals, the number of children being looked after by *any one* member of staff is significantly greater in the hospitals (1 : 8·40 in the morning to 1 : 10·78 in the afternoon; 55 per cent severely incontinent) than in the hostels (1 : 5·58 to 1 : 5·93; 10 per cent severely incontinent).[1]

Yet they argue that the hospitals' lower 'effective' ratios are *not* due to a shortage of 'assigned' staff. They explain that there were no differences, proportionally, in the total numbers of full-time-equivalent staff *assigned* to the units, but that the child-oriented units ensured that assigned staff were

1. In the best staffed of these hospitals these ratios were 1 : 3·94 and 1 : 6·7 (p. 153); on this unit of 26 children, 58 per cent were severely incontinent and 15 per cent had severe behaviour disorders (p. 143). In only one hospital unit was there more than a single day-room which did not have to double as a dining-room for between 26 and 47 children. It is not clear how many of these units, had enclosed gardens. While it is true that, between hospital units, scores on the child management scale were not related to the 'effective' staffing-ratios, it is not unlikely that the ratios were all below the minimum standards required to undertake continuously any child-oriented practices, particularly those which are dependent on other resources over which they have no control such as personal clothes, etc.

Table 2

	(a) Total children	(b) TC attenders	(c)* Percentage of day at TC	(d) Weekday effective children on living unit
Hostels				
1	23	23	48	0+12 = 12
2	41	41	50	0+22 = 22
3	21	21	57	0+ 9 = 9
4	8	8	50	0+ 4 = 4
5	19	19	50	0+10 = 10
6	15	15	50	0+ 8 = 8
7	12	12	51	0+ 6 = 6
8	23	23	50	0+12 = 12
Total	162	162		83
Hospitals				
A	32	16	39	16+10 = 26
B	44	35	37	9+22 = 31
C	41	11	36	30+ 7 = 37
D	26	23	31	3+16 = 19
E	47	25	38	22+16 = 38
Total	190	110		151
Private homes				
X	12	10	32	2+ 7 = 9
Y	18	—	—	18+ 0 = 18
Z	10	4	50	6+ 2 = 8
Total	40	14	35	35

* These data were kindly supplied by Raynes, King, and Tizard.

present at times when they were most needed. On the other hand, the deployment of assigned staff in the hospitals was rendered less effective by the rigidity of the shift systems.

The authors derive the crucial evidence that equivalent staff have been assigned to both hostels and hospitals, by relating the *total number of hours* worked during a five-day week by the child-care staff, to the *total number* of children living on the unit.

However, this calculation overestimates the staff hours *assigned* to hospital children (Table 2). Thus, *all* hostel children go to school. They leave shortly after breakfast and return some six hours later in the mid-afternoon, that is they are all away from the living unit for about 50 per cent of the working week. On the other hand, nearly a *half* of the hospital children never leave the ward. Moreover, those who attend school start later, have their midday meal in the ward and return to the ward in the early afternoon. I have therefore, recalculated the number of children who are effectively on the living unit during the five-day week because *it is among these children that the total number of hours assigned have to be shared.*

1. While there are no significant differences between the hostels and

Table 3.

	(d)	*(e)**	*(f)*	*(g)*	*(h)*
	Weekday 'effective' children on living unit	Percentage of children severely incontinent (SI)	(d)×1+100 Weekday 'effective' children weighted (×1) for SI	(d)×1+100 Weekday 'effective' children weighted (×2) for SI	(a)×1+100 Total children weighted (×2) for SI
Hostels					
1	12	26	15·12	18·24	34·96
2	22	12·2	24·68	27·38	51·00
3	9	33·4	12·00	15·00	35·00
4	4	—	4·00	4·00	8·00
5	10	21	12·10	14·20	26·98
6	8	40·1	11·21	14·42	27·03
7	6	—	6·00	6·00	12·00
8	12	13·1	13·56	15·12	28·98
Total	83	19·1			
Hospitals					
A	26	37·6	35·75	45·50	56·00
B	31	36·4	42·28	53·56	76·03
C	37	63·5	60·46	83·92	92·00
D	19	65·3	31·41	43·81	59·96
E	38	68·0	63·84	89·68	110·92
Total	151	54·7			
Private homes					
X	9	33·3	12·00	15·00	19·92
Y	18	100	36·00	54·00	54·00
Z	8	100	16·00	24·00	30·00
Total	35	80			

* Raynes, King, and Tizard's definition of 'severe incontinence' is *not* the same as that used by Kushlick.

Kushlick = soiling by day or night or wetting by day more than once per week.

Raynes, King, and Tizard = soiling or wetting by day or night more than once per week.

Therefore, children classified as severely incontinent by Raynes, King, and Tizard may have been only night wetters. It is likely that more children from hostels who only wet at night, were labelled 'severely incontinent' than among the hospital children, where children similarly labelled might also have wet or soiled during the day.

hospitals in the hours worked per *total* child (hostels 9·27; hospitals 7·9) the hours available per *effective* child are much greater than in the hostels. (hostels 18·1; hospitals 9·67).

2. While there is no significant Spearman rank correlation between the child management score (CMS) and the hours per *total* child per week ($r_s = -0.177$), there is a significant correlation ($r_s = -0.498$) at the 5 per cent level of significance between the CMS score and the hours per *effective* child per week (Table 3).

Table 4

	(i)* Total hours worked by child care staff during one five-day week	(j) (i)/(a) Staff hours/ total child/ week	(k) (i)/(d) Staff hours/ effective child/ week	(l) (i)/(f) Staff hours/effective weighted children ($\times 1$)
Hostels				
1	136·0	5·91	11·33	8·99
2	219·5	5·35	9·98	8·89
3	366·5	17·45	40·72	30·54
4	133·5	16·69	33·38	33·37
5	213·5	11·21	21·30	17·60
6	151·3	10·08	18·92	13·50
7	119·5	9·96	19·92	19·91
8	162·6	7·07	13·56	12·00
Total	1502·0	$\bar{x} = 9·27$	$\bar{x} = 18·10$	
Hospitals				
A	254·0	7·94	9·77	6·73
B	228·0	5·18	7·35	5·39
C	414·0	10·10	11·19	6·85
D	290·5	11·17	15·29	9·25
E	276·5	5·88	7·28	4·33
Total	1463·0	$\bar{x} = 7·70$	$\bar{x} = 9·67$	
Private homes				
X	157·5	13·13	17·50	13·12
Y	75·0	4·17	4·17	2·08
Z	115·25	11·53	14·41	7·20
Total	347·75	$\bar{x} = 8·69$	$\bar{x} = 9·94$	

* Data kindly supplied by Raynes, King, and Tizard.
Define the comparisons as:
  (i) CMS v (j), ie staff hours/total child/week (five days).
  (ii) CMS v (k), ie staff hours/effective child/week.
  (iii) CMS v (l), ie staff hours/effective child weighted ($\times 1$)/week.
  (iv) CMS v (m), ie staff hours/effective child weighted ($\times 2$)/week.
  (v) CMS v (n), ie staff hours/total child weighted ($\times 2$)/week.

A further modification of the calculation is required to allow for the very much higher proportion of 'severely incontinent' children in hospitals (see Table 4). 'Severe incontinence' here is used as an index of dependency or incapacity. The hospitals' severely incontinent children may well soil and wet frequently during the day, whereas the classification used in the paper would allow the inclusion as incontinent of hostel children who merely wet during the night. Once a child has wet or soiled himself during the day, the one nurse who is supposed to be caring for 8–10 children must necessarily ignore these in order to wash and change the child. When weighted for

Table 4 *(cont.)*

	(m)	(n)	(o)
	(i)/(g)	(i)/(h)	
	Staff hours/effective weighted children ($\times$2)	Staff hours/total weighted children ($\times$2)	Child management score (CMS)
Hostels			
1	7·46	3·89	10
2	8·02	4·30	6
3	24·43	10·47	14
4	33·37	16·69	4
5	15·00	7·89	22
6	10·49	5·60	3
7	19·91	9·96	18
8	10·76	5·61	11
Total			$\bar{x} = 11$
Hospitals			
A	5·58	4·54	47
B	4·26	3·00	37
C	4·93	4·50	45
D	6·63	4·84	45
E	3·08	2·49	41
Total			$\bar{x} = 43·00$
Private Homes			
X	10·50	7·91	14
Y	1·39	1·39	41
Z	4·80	3·84	28
Total			$\bar{x} = 27·67$

Comparisons between all types of accommodation:

	Σd^2	r_s	Significant level for $N = 16$
(i)	798·5	−0·177	NS
(ii)	1016·5	−0·498	5%
(iii)	1105·5	−0·629	1%
(iv)	1111·5	−0·638	1%
(v)	975·5	−0·438	5%

incontinent children, the correlation between staff hours available per child per week and CMS appears to increase (Table 4).

Thus, while above certain levels of staffing, increased *assigned* staff may not 'improve' child management patterns, this study appears to confirm that, compared with hostels, the numbers of staff assigned to hospitals and the high proportion of their children with severe handicaps, place them at a distinct disadvantage which may well affect management practices scored in this study.

The data collected by Mr Whatmore on the details of the routines on living units show that existing hospitals in our study had lower staffing establishments (numbers assigned) than new units, and that the staff numbers assigned often drop still lower when staff are transferred to other wards of the hospital when these experience periodic but recurrent crises of staff shortage. Moreover, so complex are the routines of the living units, that it would be virtually impossible to redeploy existing staff resources towards child-oriented patterns of management *other than by substantially increasing the length of the staff's working day.*

At the same time we noticed that it was not possible to take children who were not toilet-trained to domestically designed toilets either singly or in small groups, unless there were staff available in each of the toilets as well as outside. Living units of existing hospitals had specially designed 'ablution blocks' which enabled the simultaneous supervision by one or two members of staff of up to 40 children of whom 20 could be on toilets while the remaining 20 waited to use them.

It is interesting that neither sociological researchers of psychiatric hospitals, nor the defenders of the existing facilities and their management practices, appear to have highlighted the need for additional 'hands' on the wards. The former have focused attention on the *informal* authority relationships and communications within these hospitals and on their *'latent'* functions (Smith, 1965*a, b*). They have often noted, without comment, the very low staffing ratios and have not related these to the nature of the *formal* task of the facility (ie their *manifest* function).

The defenders of existing practices have either accused the critics of exaggeration, ignorance, and of undermining their difficult tasks, or they have focused attention on the need for more *buildings* on existing sites in order to relieve the overcrowding, or more qualified professional staff (Shapiro, 1970; Bavin, 1971). There is no documented evidence of requests for major staff increases on the wards. There is, however, evidence that in 1968 hospitals for the mentally retarded, in answer to a DHSS survey, reported no or little lack of training or OT facilities for large numbers of people not receiving either (DHSS, 1970).

Another reason may be the misinterpretation of crude staffing ratios. An over-all ratio of 1 : 4 means, in practice, 1 person cares, at any time of the day, for 12 residents, when allowance is made for shifts, holidays, night staff, etc. (An establishment of 5 people, 2·6 day and 2·4 night, is needed to provide *one* person on duty for 24 hours of the day [Kushlick, 1970].)

Thus, in the new unit the staff–child ratios allow one member of staff to every five children at any time of the day, and particularly at 'peak' periods such as waking, dressing, washing and toiletting, eating and going to bed. In no existing unit does the staffing level equal this. Indeed, by tradition in existing units, it may often be much lower at 'peak' times. For example, night staff (ratio 1 : 20 or 50 children) may have to wake, dress, wash, and toilet the children before day staff arrive (in the new unit day staff do this) and staff take their meals off the living unit at the children's meal times (in the new unit staff eat with the children).

Below certain levels of staff there appears to be little margin for flexibility of the routine which remains the same every day of the week and month of the year (rigidity); for acquiring, distributing, maintaining, or processing individual clothes or toys (depersonalization) or for making meaningful relationships with individual children (social distance) because as many as 10–20 children are simultaneously being looked after, washed, dressed, toiletted (block treated) by one member of staff on existing units.

The availability of staff to children also limits the use of available accommodation because simultaneous use of more than one room requires simultaneous availability in each room of staff. Indeed, 'overcrowding' during the day may be the result of lack of staff rather than of accommodation, if children must be maintained in the only staffed rooms.

The limits imposed by staff–child ratio appear to increase with increasing richness and therefore vulnerability of the fabric, furnishings, fittings, decorations, and other contents of the living unit. That is, given a constant number of mobile children, more staff are needed if there are soft furnishings like curtains, carpets, soft armchairs; fittings like book shelves, cupboards; wallpapers, table-cloths; cutlery, crockery, ornaments, and toys. In the absence of staff to protect these objects from exploration by the children, or to prevent the children from injury from some of the contents, one of three strategies may be followed: the child may be moved from the environment, the child may be mechanically restrained within the environment, or the environment may be cleared of vulnerable or dangerous contents.

Since available child-care staff may be diverted from a group of children by having to restrain one particularly 'disruptive' child, or by having to do domestic chores, these factors have to be taken into account in measuring availability. Moreover, since the need to 'attend to' the disruptive behaviours may actually increase their frequency (Bijou, 1968) the sense of frustration of parents or nursing staff in this situation would appear to be overwhelming. The pejorative use of the term 'rejection' to describe their resulting behaviour seems singularly inappropriate.

The admission of children to residential care outside the home can, *at present,* be more usefully understood in this way rather than as a means of instituting therapy. The parents are eventually limited in the extent to which they can denude the home environment or mechanically restrain the child by the needs of other family members and by the neighbourhood norms of child-rearing and house furnishing. The existing hospital units 'cope' with the child within the limits of staff numbers by denuding the environment; by mechanically restraining the child and by means of the 'anti-therapeutic' regime. These strategies have apparently been 'legitimized' as 'inevitable' in hospitals: particularly in those which are remote from population centres. Staff levels in new living units are high enough to avoid these strategies in the presence of the rich environments needed to conform with neighbourhood values.

Thus, it is widely held that 'anti-therapeutic' routines either cannot be avoided in large bureaucratic organizations in general, or in hospitals in particular, or that this can only be done by such methods as retraining staff at living unit level (ward nurses) and 'changing their attitudes' and roles from 'nursing' to 'child care' or 'teaching' personnel.

Our preliminary evidence suggests otherwise. First, in the new unit, specially trained non-nursing staff keep all of the children in one of the three available play-rooms (ie 'block treatment') when the staff–child ratio falls below the average levels. Present staffing levels do not support the laying of tables at meal-times with cutlery and crockery. Second, a trial staff increase during one morning shift on a very poorly designed and equipped hospital ward for 80 adults (36 very SSN) allowed the staff, during the course of that shift, to implement a completely new routine designed by the nursing staff. This considerably reduced the components of 'rigidity', 'block-treatment', and 'social distance'. Avoidance of 'de-personalization' would have required new stocks of personal clothing, etc.

New skills will surely be required by unit level staff to deploy additional resources effectively (management), to implement teaching programmes and care individually for children (child care). But the primary need for new skills rests with senior management who deploy resources, set tasks and monitor their implementation.

The implementation of the new operational policy for *all* hospitals in Wessex will allow us to measure changes in the quality of care on living units and to begin to identify factors encouraging or hindering the introduction of new policies.

There is at least one other feature which appears to encourage 'anti-therapeutic' behaviour on the existing living units, and which could be modified during the course of the trial. It is dealt with in paragraphs 266 and 267 of Cmnd 4683 (DHSS, 1971).

The residents in existing living units do not come from a defined area in which their kin are living. Indeed, many of the people in existing large comprehensive hospitals do not, at present, even come from the larger catchment area the hospital is supposed to serve. This has arisen because, for many years, people have been admitted to a hospital or a living unit where there is an available bed. Collaboration of living-unit staff with local authority agencies (social welfare and education) is rendered logistically very difficult because residents on any living-unit come from many local authority areas. Eleven of the hospitalized children transferred to the first new unit because their families live in the eastern half of Southampton, were found in 7 different living units: 4 of these units were in 2 large hospitals each situated within 5 miles of Southampton. The remaining 3 units, 2 private homes and an annexe of one hospital, are between 30 and 40 miles on either side of Southampton. There is no reason why people in existing units should not be relocated on a geographical basis if this is believed to be in their interest.

Summary

The relationships between the many factors involved appear to be complex.

Given the limits set at any time by staff availability, the location of the living unit (in the middle of a population centre or away from it) and the type of unit (hospital or family home) appear to determine how far the strategies used 'to cope' can 'legitimately' depart from 'normally accepted' standards of child care. The location of the unit may partially determine the availability of child care staff; ie they may be more easily available in the middle of population centres than away from them. The type of unit (hospital or private home) may determine the traditional way in which people relate to one another (staff of different professions, or from different levels in their hierarchy, to one another, or of staff to residents) and the way in which decisions are taken. However, definitions of 'legitimacy', norms of child care, and traditional ways of relating or decision-making can all be changed, provided that there are policies to be carried out and management with the skills and resources to implement them.

We will eventually have data on four new units. These will allow a preliminary comparison of outcome between subjects using new or existing units. They might also allow a comparison of outcomes between the new units themselves.

The implementation of any of the aims of the new operational policy in existing units will enable us to begin to sort out those components of 'poor' care which can be more easily avoided in existing units, from those which appear to require greater effort or a different form of service.

Research design developments

We have had, as a result of our early findings, to re-examine the assumptions basic to our research design. We have concluded that in any comparisons of the relative effectiveness of more than one form of service, it is most useful if the personnel delivering all forms of service have common declared aims (both negative and positive) with respect to a definable morbid condition or group of conditions, within a definable population 'at risk'. The defined objectives should include both 'client-oriented' aims (ie a reduction in mortality, morbidity, incapacity among subjects, and of burdens among their families) as well as, where possible, 'administration-oriented' aims (ie the components of the service being tasted, by which it is predicted that the 'client-oriented' aims will be achieved). The aims and service components under test should also be understood by the research team undertaking the evaluation because the

research team's task is to devise scales for measuring the extent to which
the aims are achieved.

Agreement of the service personnel on the aims and the service
components under test by the service makes it more likely that the
research will produce valid, meaningful answers. Thus, failure to achieve
agreed aims is then more likely to be due to ineffectiveness of the defined
components of the service under test, than from the fact that personnel
delivering the service are either against the defined objectives, or pursuing
other and conflicting aims.

Such agreement seems particularly important when testing the
'feasibility', as defined above, of *new* forms of service by comparing them
with *existing forms.* New forms of service have, in the initial stages,
inherent temporary advantages over existing forms. A reasonably long
period of evaluation may allow time for such advantages as higher morale,
prestigious backing, and publicity to 'wear off'. However, advantages of a
carefully worked out operational policy of staff specially trained to carry
out the policy, or of additional resources, are likely to last longer. Therefore,
where possible, it is important that every effort be made to confer these
additional advantages on existing services during the trial. If, despite active
attempts to do so, it is difficult or impossible during the trial to confer these
advantages on existing units, the features of existing units which appear to
prevent this can also be more closely studied. It is likely, after aims have
been agreed, that administrative and service personnel will observe more
rigorously than otherwise the rules relating to experimental and control
groups during the period of the trial.

Evaluation of Command 4683 locally based units for adults

The Command Paper 4683, *Better Services for the Mentally Handicapped*
(DHSS, 1971), has defined a new comprehensive service based on existing
epidemiological data. A major aspect of this document involves placing the
responsibility for over half of the people at present being cared for in
existing hospitals for the mentally retarded with the local authority departments of social service.

It has been suggested that this document relegates the future role of
hospitals for the mentally retarded to the custodial care of the profoundly
retarded and severely behaviour disordered children and adults for whom
there is neither hope nor therapeutic possibility (Shapiro, 1970). This criticism implies that neither the new locally based, home-like, and therapeutic
hospital units, *nor* the 'sectorized' (ie geographically selected) wards proposed for existing hospitals in Command 4683 are feasible.

Experience so far with such units for children suggests that they are
feasible, and that they present major therapeutic possibilities. However,
there is no documented experience of such units for profoundly retarded or
severely behaviour disordered adults. As these adults out-number the

children by about four to one, an early feasibility trial of such adult units is urgently needed.

The Coldeast and Tatchbury Mount Hospital Management Committee has therefore decided to open such a unit in July 1972. Thus the first 25-place, locally based unit on a district general hospital site in Christchurch will be used for the most profoundly handicapped and behaviour disordered men and women from this area.

The research team has been asked to evaluate the unit. The research design will be the same as that used for the children's units. The control groups will consist of geographically selected adults with similar capacities either in a newly 'sectorized', equally well staffed ward of an existing hospital, or scattered, as at present, in a number of wards of two or three existing hospitals.

Acknowledgement

The work in this paper arises from a collaborative effort between the members of the research team and our service colleagues.

I would like in particular to thank Dr Roy King for making available to me raw data from his published study *Patterns of Residential Care: Sociological Studies in Institutions for Handicapped Children* (King, Raynes, and Tizard, 1971) and Mr Barry Sexton for his statistical analysis of these data.

REFERENCES

Bavin, J. (1971). 'Residential homes, hostels or hospitals?', *Parent's Voice,* **21,** 8–10.

Bijou, S. W. (1968). 'The mentally retarded child', *Psychology Today,* pp. 47–51.

—— Peterson, R. F., Harris, F. R., Allen, K. S. and Johnston, M. S. (1969). 'Methodology for experimental studies of young children in natural settings', *Psychol. Rec.* **19,** 177–210.

Department of Health and Social Security (1970). *The Facilities of Psychiatric Hospitals in England and Wales 1968* (London: Statistics and Research Division).

—— (1971). *Better Services for the Mentally Handicapped,* Cmnd 4683 (London: HMSO).

Goffman, E. (1961). *Asylums: Essays on the Social Situations of Mental Patients and Other Inmates* (New York: Doubleday [Anchor]).

Grad, J., and Sainsbury, P. (1963). 'Mental illness and the family', *Lancet,* **i,** 544–7.

King, R. D., and Raynes, N. V. (1968). 'Some determinants of patterns of residential care', in *Proc. 1st Cong. Internat. Assoc. Sci. Stud. Ment. Defic. Montpellier,* pp. 642–9 (Surrey: Michael Jackson).

—— —— and Tizard, J. (1971). *Patterns of Residential Care: Sociological Studies in Institutions for Handicapped Children* (London: Routledge & Kegan Paul).

Kushlick, A. (1965). 'A plan for experimental evaluation', *Proc. R. Soc. Med.* **5,** 374–80.

—— (1967). 'A method of evaluating the effectiveness of a community health service', *Soc. Econ. Admin.* **1**, no. 4, 29–49.

—— (1970). 'Residential care for the mentally subnormal', *J. R. Soc. Hlth,* **90**, 255–61.

—— (1971). 'Epidemiological studies on and evaluation of services for the mentally subnormal and the elderly', Report to the MRC and DHSS (mimeo).

—— (1972). 'Action for the retarded: the need for residential care', paper presented to the Conference on Action for the Retarded, Dublin, April 1971.

—— and Cox, G. R. (1967). 'The ascertained prevalence of mental subnormality in the Wessex Region on 1st July 1963', in *Proc. 1st Cong. Internat. Assoc. Sci. Stud. Ment. Defic. Montpellier* (Surrey: Michael Jackson).

—— —— Williams, P., and Whatmore, R. (1970). 'Report to the Medical Research Council and the Department of Health and Social Security' (mimeo).

Lewis, E. I. (1929). 'Report on an investigation into the incidence of mental deficiency in six areas, 1925–1927', *Report of the Mental Deficiency Committee,* Part IV (London; HMSO).

McKeown, T., Mackintosh, J. M., and Lowe, C. R. (1961). 'Influence of age on type of hospital to which patients are admitted', *Lancet,* **i**, 818–20.

Morris, P. (1969). *Put Away* (London: Routledge & Kegan Paul).

Nokes, P. (1960). 'Purpose and efficiency in humane social institutions', in *Human Relations* (London: Tavistock Publications).

Scott, W. R. (1966). 'Some implications of organisation theory for research on health services', *Milbank meml Fund q.* **44**, 35–39.

Shapiro, A. (1970). 'The clinical practice of mental deficiency', *Brit. J. Psychiat.* **116**, 353–68.

Smith, Dorothy E. (1965a). 'The logic of custodial organisation', *Psychiatry,* **28**, 311–23.

—— (1965b). 'Front-line organisation of the state mental hospital', *Admin. Sci. Q.* **10**, no. 3, 381–99.

Tizard, J. (1960). 'Residential care of mentally handicapped children', *Br. med. J.* **1**, 1041–6.

—— and Grad, J. C. (1961). *The Mentally Handicapped and their Families: A Social Survey,* Maudsley Monograph no. 7 (London: Oxford University Press).

Wessex Regional Hospital Board (1966). *The Report of the Working Party of the Provision of Further Accommodation for the Mentally Subnormal* (Wessex RHB).

—— (1970). *Measures for Improving Services for the Mentally Handicapped* (Wessex RHB).

11 *Alternatives to the hospital for the residential care of the mentally retarded*

ROY D. KING

In this paper I want to consider some of the contributions of sociological research to the problems of evaluating the quality of residential care for the mentally retarded, and of maintaining or improving its effectiveness. I shall make no attempt to be exhaustive. Instead I shall discuss some findings from recent studies of residential institutions, other than hospitals, for the retarded and especially for retarded children; and I shall confine myself to the framework of services in England and Wales. None the less it is likely that much of what is said here is of more general relevance, for example, for the institutional care of the mentally ill. I shall conclude by indicating what I take to be some of the main issues that need to be resolved, and I shall argue for the adoption of a more theoretically informed approach towards their resolution. But perhaps it is as well to begin with a brief review of the range of institutional provision in the UK and the proposed pattern for the future.

The range of residential provision: present and future

The publicity surrounding the discharge from St Catherine's Hospital, Doncaster, of three elderly 'patients' committed as moral defectives under the Mental Deficiency Act, 1913, provides ample reminder, should it be required, of the legacy of the past in our existing institutional provision, especially for retarded adults (*The Times,* 22 May 1972). The women had been committed to custody after giving birth to illegitimate children more than forty years ago and had remained there ever since: albeit after 1959 on a 'voluntary' basis. Probably many thousands of other patients, admitted to hospitals for 'social' or 'moral' rather than 'medical' reasons, could live elsewhere given suitable accommodation or adequate after-care services in the local community.

The recent White Paper, *Better Services for the Mentally Handicapped*[1]

1. The British Department of Health and Social Security uses the term 'mentally handicapped' as a synonym for the WHO term 'mentally retarded' [Eds].

(DHSS, 1971*a*, Cmnd 4683) reiterated the principles for hospital and community care which had been set down by the Royal Commission (1957, Cmnd 169) fourteen years earlier. But on the basis of evidence accumulated in the interval it also provided estimates of need for services of different kinds, set targets to be achieved, outlined plans of action to improve existing services, and announced greatly increased government expenditure to go some way towards meeting the costs.

What then is the pattern of residential services for the mentally retarded today, and how does it compare with the one envisaged for the future? On the basis of information available in 1969 it was estimated that 12,300 places for children were required of which only 9,300 were then provided; and that of the 63,800 places which were needed for adults only 56,950 were available (Cmnd 4683, Table 5). The waiting-list is still very much with us, but at least as important as the shortfall in places was the imbalance in the distribution of places provided by the hospitals and by the local authorities.

As far as the local authorities are concerned no new policy is involved. What is needed is faster progress to overcome the present deficiencies, and although the Government has allocated an additional £40 million to local authority and hospital services for the years 1971–5 the main responsibility still rests with the local authorities themselves. The target figures discussed in the White Paper are, in many cases, far beyond what the authorities have yet planned to provide.

Local authority provision may be of several kinds: with foster parents or in lodgings, private housing, flatlets, and group homes with social work support; in children's homes or homes for the elderly; or in homes specifically for mentally retarded children or adults (Cmnd 4683, para. 159). This last category, which may involve the local authorities in running homes themselves or paying for beds in homes run by private and voluntary organizations, makes up, at present, the bulk of local authority provision. However, in 1969 this was well below the level required, especially, as one might expect, for adults: nearly three times as many places were needed for children as were provided (4,900 compared to 1,800) while for adults the proportion was nearly seven times (29,400 compared to 4,300). The first two categories, as yet, account for only very small numbers, although it is expected that they will increase in importance in the future. In 1969 only one-tenth of the required places of this type for children were met (100 out of 1,000), while only one-fourteenth of the required places for adults were available (550 out of 7,400).

These national estimates clearly mask regional variations and some authorities will have adequate services much sooner than others. But even allowing for an annual increase in capital expenditure of 2 per cent per annum over the 1971–2 figure of £7 million (the figure for 1959–60 was less than £1 million) there would still be a shortfall of some 550 places in residential homes for children and of ten times that number for adults by 1987. Sceptics may continue to doubt that *these* targets will be achieved unless something more is done to ensure that local authorities publish their plans and actually implement them under the powers which so many have for so long neglected (NSMHC, 1971*a*; Letters, *Guardian*, 26 May 1972).

With regard to the hospital services it is proposed that the specialist hospitals continue to play an important part: but in future this is to be in relation to the treatment, as opposed to the residential care, of patients with mental retardation (Cmnd 4683, para 174).

In 1969 many more hospital places were available (and, of course, occupied) than it was estimated were actually needed. Again, as one might expect, the situation was worse for adults than for children: 6,400 beds were thought to be needed for children whereas 7,400 were provided, while only 27,000 of the 52,100 adult beds would have been required had there been suitable alternatives. In the long term, then, many fewer hospital beds will be required as local authority provision increases, and many of the existing beds will be wrongly sited in isolated, out of date buildings. Regional hospital boards have accordingly been asked to reorganize and redevelop their existing provisions to meet local needs in consultation with the local authorities and their social service committees.

The recent report on *Buildings for Mentally Handicapped People* (DHSS, 1971*b*) recommended that the most economical way of providing improved accommodation was to upgrade existing provisions and to build new facilities for those displaced in the process of reducing overcrowding. Given the differences of opinion about the best size and location of hospitals, the Government has decided to encourage alternative lines of development by regional boards. Certain guidelines have been laid down. In view of the existing stock of large specialist hospitals, no new hospitals of this type may be built, and no existing hospitals of 500 beds or more on the same site are to be enlarged. If new building is required to relieve overcrowding this is to be provided in areas of population elsewhere in the hospital's catchment area. New buildings may be medium-sized, containing 100–200 beds, which could serve districts with a population of about 250,000 without being too isolated from them. Some units may be small in size, and like the local authority provision, situated in residential areas.

Just as one may have doubts about the feasibility of completely phasing out hospitals for the mentally ill (DHSS, 1971*c*) so one can doubt the speed at which the function of hospitals for the mentally retarded will be changed. And, as the White Paper notes (para 184), for those patients who do have treatment in hospital, even for a short admission, the hospital is also their home. Much has already been done to upgrade hospital wards and regional boards are expected to have implemented the programme of 'interim measures' introduced after the Ely Inquiry (NHS, 1969, Cmnd

3975) by 1974–5. But it is difficult to see how the reduction of the residential care function of hospitals for the retarded can be brought about except by the very gradual transfer, or death, of patients over a period of many years. It is equally difficult to see how the existing hospitals will take on the rather romantic role of 'rural communities' which some writers have proposed for them (Bavin, 1971), when it is precisely the quality of their 'community' life that has been so much under attack.

If progress is to be made one can certainly agree with the White Paper (para. 264) that it will take very careful co-ordination of plans between regional boards (and the future reorganized health authorities) and local authorities to achieve it.

The quality of care: alternatives to the large hospital

The systematic study of hospitals and other residential institutions in recent years has certainly enriched our understanding of different patterns of care, and of how the worst abuses may be avoided. Yet it has to be said that there are still forms of care which have received scant attention from research workers and about which we consequently know very little. There are also many areas where our information is patchy; where the evidence is conflicting or confusingly interpreted; or where we need more detailed research before reasonable conclusions can be drawn. As a result, at least some of the 'social engineering' in this field still has to rest on faith as much as it does on knowledge.

So much has been written about the large mental hospital in the UK, that in this paper I will normally refer to it only in so far as this is required for comparison with alternative forms of provision. However, given that the specialized hospital has a significant future role, at least for the mentally retarded, it is worth pointing out that the problems of these institutions are not solved by press publicity, committees of inquiry and their recommendations, nor even by injecting increased resources. Piecemeal solutions designed to meet specific abuses are seldom sufficient: they often only create different problems. For example, the recommendation of the Ely Hospital Report (Cmnd 3975, para. 538) that nurses should not be allowed to eat on the wards may help to eliminate the pilfering of patients' food, but it may also serve to impoverish the experiences of the patients still further by making staff more socially distant (King, Raynes, and Tizard, 1971). The reform of mental hospitals, and the improvement of standards of care, will depend not least upon the systematic reappraisal of operational policies, and a careful evolution of strategies by which they can be implemented, and this will involve the co-operation of all levels of staff and possibly the retraining of many of them (see Chapter 10). Once standards are improved they have to be maintained. As Wing and Brown (1970) have demonstrated, reform has a natural history and institutions can move backwards as well as forwards unless efforts are kept up. One of the most disturbing things about the Whittingham Hospital Inquiry (NHS, 1972, Cmnd 4861), as was acknowledged by the Minister of State, was that it should have been necessary at all so soon after the Reports on Ely and Farleigh (NHS, 1971, Cmnd 4557). The machinery of new Hospital Advisory Service, with its teams of visiting professionals, may well be helpful in monitoring and maintaining standards (DHSS, 1971*d*), but administratively the maintenance of standards constitutes a real dilemma well known to sociologists. Sooner or later new ideas and new policies become regular routines, bureaucratically applied, supervised, and inspected. In the past the hospital service has abounded with bureaucratic systems of reporting and inspection, but these have not always been successful in maintaining standards or even in preventing ill-treatment (King, Raynes, and Tizard, 1971; Brown, 1972). In the long run research and continuous evaluation probably have to be built in to any service if it is not to fall back on old ways of doing things, and there are signs that some authorities at least have recognized this.

In considering the alternatives to hospital care I shall look first at what has been learned from studies of the provisions made by local authorities for the mentally retarded and then go on to examine some of the new developments by the hospital authorities.

There seems to be little or no published research in the UK on the boarding out or fostering of mentally retarded children, or on the use of other community methods involving social work support for adults placed in lodgings, flatlets, or 'group homes'. For our knowledge of fostering we are largely dependent on studies of deprived children (Trasler, 1960; Parker, 1966). There are scattered references in the literature to group homes for subnormals (Craft and Evans, 1970) and for the mentally ill (Fox and Adams, 1968) but for the most part we have to draw on information from other countries, notably Sweden. I can find no studies of the mentally retarded who have been boarded in either homes for normal children or homes for the elderly. Since there are probably fewer than twenty group homes for the subnormal in England and Wales (Campbell, 1972) and since all these forms of care together provided only 550 places for adults and 100 places for children in 1969 they are not numerically important although the numbers will presumably grow in the future.

A good deal more is known about homes or hostels specifically for mentally retarded children or adults. These may be run either by the local authorities themselves or by voluntary or private organizations. Incidentally the term 'home' is used in the White Paper (Cmnd 4683, para. 161) in preference to the term 'hostel' which is said to suggest impermanence and austerity. In fact the *evidence* suggests that this is not the case, as the authors of the White Paper admit. I shall use the term 'hostel' to denote small unit provision, usually of twenty-five beds or less, by the local authorities (and subsequently to describe similar units developed by hospital authorities) and use the term 'home' to describe the provisions of private and voluntary organizations and which appear to vary greatly in size. Whatever the merits and demerits of this terminology it seems to be in accord with common usage.

In the only national survey of institutions for the mentally retarded (Morris, 1969) most attention was devoted to a sample of thirty-four hospitals. Local authority hostels were excluded on the grounds that they were too few in number and too widely scattered to warrant the expenditure of time and resources. At the time that survey was carried out (1965) local authorities provided 1,466 places in hostels for adults and 900 places for children. The local health authorities also supported some 3,526 patients in nursing homes and residential homes run by private organizations and voluntary societies, and these were included in the survey. Since some of these homes took additional patients privately and some had contractual arrangements to provide beds for regional hospital boards, the total numbers in these institutions must be somewhat higher.

The Mental Health Act of 1959 distinguishes between 'mental nursing homes', which are required to provide 'nursing or other medical treatment' and are registered with the local health authority under the provisions of the Public Health Acts, and 'residential homes' which are registered under the provisions of the National Assistance Acts. Although homes are registered with the local health authorities there was, until the National Society for Mentally Handicapped Children launched their *Directory* (NSMHC, 1971*b*), no central register and Morris reported difficulties in compiling an accurate sampling frame for her survey. The same difficulty was encountered two years later in the study by King, Raynes, and Tizard (1971). Morris was able to gather data from the NSMHC, the National Association for Mental Health, and the local authorities on 127 homes with 5 or more patients and from which a sample of 27 homes was selected. She found, however, that 5 homes had either closed or no longer cared for subnormal patients, and 8 were either much larger or much smaller than had been expected. It seems clear that in this sector of provision there are frequent changes and that information can quickly become out of date. In the event, after substitutions, Morris was able to report on 24 homes, which, although not 'truly representative in statistical terms', none the less covered 'a wide cross-section of homes actually in operation at the time' (Morris, 1969, p. 31).

Unfortunately Morris reports her findings in a very sketchy manner and much of the data seem to be based on fairly tentative impressions. She says that because the sample was not 'entirely satisfactory from a methodological point of view' her aim was only to 'draw attention to what appear to be quite major differences' between hospitals and homes (p. 256). It is a pity that such a fetish should be made of 'representativeness' since, whatever its limitations, it is difficult to see how the sample could have been improved in the circumstances; and it is unlikely that an opportunity for direct comparison on such a scale will occur again. For the same reason it seems a pity that the resources could not have been stretched to allow the collection of more systematic data: the researchers spent only a day in all but one of the homes compared with a week to ten days in the hospitals (pp. 32–33) and even an extra day in each home would have helped. As a result it is not possible to compare the homes with the hospitals, nor different types of home with one another, except in the most general way. For example, average over-all staff ratios are quoted for the homes and these are said to be broadly similar to those for the hospitals (1 : 4·9 for mental nursing homes, 1 : 4·5 for residential homes, 1 : 4·7 for the hospitals) although given that the range of variation for the voluntary homes (from 1 : 3 to 1 : 17) was much greater than that for the hospitals (from 1 : 3·17 to 1 : 8·73) this comparison is not very helpful. No information about the numbers of staff actually on duty in the homes is given, although this was supplied for the hospitals and provides, of course, a much clearer indication of the real staffing situation. Again, the homes studied by Morris were of different sizes: one-third had more than 100 patients, another third had between 50 and 99 patients, while the remainder had 49 or less (Table 11.1, p. 259), but no attempt is made to present any of the findings by size of institution (or, with the exception of staffing matters, even by type of institution). Instead we are given rather vague statements such as 'it was usually the smaller nursing homes that had the better staff/patient ratio' (p. 273).

The main conclusions from Morris's study of these homes are as follows. First, that 'patients in homes probably received more individual attention and had a closer personal relationship with the staff than was the case in hospitals' (p. 276). No description of daily life in any of the institutions is given, however, and little evidence is produced to support this conclusion except the fieldworkers' judgements that personal belongings were more in evidence, and games and dances were encouraged by staff as opposed to the watching of television. Second, that 'in most cases the homes were well run and the physical needs of patients were provided for within the limitations of the facilities available' (p. 277). It is not altogether clear what this statement means especially since we are given little information about either the patients or the facilities in different homes; thus the 'scales' which were used to quantify the physical environment and facilities in the hospitals do not appear to have been applied in the homes. Among the other findings it is useful to learn that proportionately more patients in the homes were engaged on domestic tasks, while proportionately fewer were engaged in occupational or industrial training, than was the case in the hospitals. And again that there appear to be few if any differences in the qualifications of staff in the mental nursing homes expected to provide 'nursing or other medical treatment', on the one hand, and those in the residential homes on the other. But since one of the main impressions was that it was difficult to measure the provision of services because of the wide variety of homes sampled, 'the only thing they all had in common being a degree of independence from the state system' (p. 276), this generalized presentation of the findings seems particularly inappropriate.

Recently a series of studies has provided more systematic and more detailed comparisons, but over a more limited range of variables and utilizing many fewer institutions. King and Raynes (1968*a*) provided a descriptive account of the daily life of three groups of severely subnormal children, comparable in terms of age, IQ, and physical handicap, brought up respectively in a hospital ward, a local authority hostel, and a residential home run by a voluntary organization. The living units were similar in size but the patterns of care were very different. Later King, Raynes, and Tizard (1971) examined units for children in 5 NHS hospitals for the subnormal, 8 local authority hostels, and 3 voluntary homes. The hostels were selected randomly from a list provided by the DHSS but the hospitals and voluntary homes were selected more for reasons of their convenient size and location than for their representativeness. Within each institution those units were chosen which provided the closest match in terms of the characteristics of the patients. Again the focus was on the nature and quality of routine life in the institutions and in this study the authors applied a revised version of a Child Management Scale which had been developed earlier (King and Raynes, 1968*b*) and which was based partly on the ideas of Goffman (1961). The scale measured four general areas of life in the living units: *rigidity:* the extent to which the daily routine is flexible from one day to another, and from one child to another; *'block treatment':* the extent to which children were dealt with as groups before, during or after routine activities; *depersonalization:* the extent to which children had opportunities to have personal possessions and personal privacy; and *social distance:* the extent to which the staff world was cut off from that of the children. Units which exhibited high degrees of rigidity, block treatment, depersonalization, and social distance were characterized as institutionally oriented in their pattern of care and units where these features were absent or found only to a lesser degree were characterized as child-oriented.

The results from this study showed that all 5 hospital units were remarkably institutionally oriented while the 8 hostel units were very much more child-oriented, which confirmed the findings of the earlier descriptive studies. What is particularly interesting, in the light of Morris's generalized report of her 24 voluntary homes, was that the 3 voluntary homes studied here scored very differently from each other: 1 was as child-oriented as the average hostel, 1 was as institutionally oriented as the average hospital, while 1 had a score exactly intermediate between these extremes.

The authors concluded that these results, at least for the hospitals and hostels, might be explained by structural factors within each institutional *type,* that is by the typical ways in which staff were deployed in relation to the activities in the unit, the distribution of role activities and responsibilities among different grades of staff, and by the training of the person in charge of the living unit. These factors seemed to be more important than institutional size, which did not influence scale scores among institutions of the same type, size of living units or the over-all staff–patient ratios. In the hostels it was possible to deploy staff more effectively than in the hospitals and more staff were on duty at the times they were needed. The everyday tasks of child care and supervision, domestic and administrative activities were more evenly distributed among the different grades of staff in the hostels than in the hospitals where the division of labour followed the hierarchical structure. As a result it was possible for senior ward staff to spend much of their time in the office and the kitchen and comparatively little time with children, thus increasing the burden on junior staff (cf Coser, 1962). In spite of spending more time in routine reporting and other administrative tasks, ward sisters actually had less control over matters affecting their living units than did the heads of hostels. Such differences as there were among the hostels seemed to be accounted for by the training of senior staff: the five hostels whose superintendants had been trained in child care had significantly more child-oriented units than the three hostels whose superintendents had received a nursing training. Training seemed to be particularly associated with the way staff performed their duties. For example, child-care-trained staff had much higher measured rates of interaction with children, and especially of talking with children, than did nursing-trained staff.

Of the three voluntary homes, one followed the pattern for the hostels in virtually all respects including the child-care training of the person in charge, another followed the hospital pattern in all respects except that the superintendent was quite untrained. The remaining home had some of the characteristics of the hostel pattern and some typical of those found in the hospitals.

It is sometimes argued that hostels are able to operate a more child-centred pattern of care because of the selectivity of their intake, with fewer severely retarded, incontinent, or behaviour-disordered patients than in hospitals. In the study by King, Raynes, and Tizard (1971) there were indeed slight but persistent differences of this kind between the hostels and the hospitals. However, some of the hostel and hospital units were closely comparable and the authors tentatively concluded that 'while certain types of handicaps may mean that perhaps more staff are required to maintain child-oriented patterns of care, handicaps of residents are not an overriding factor in determining child management practices' (p. 194).

It should not be thought that all hostels will necessarily provide more acceptable standards of care than hospitals. Social structures, after all, are not fixed and immutable but subject to modification and change, though some seem more amenable to change than others. Hospitals for the handicapped do not seem to vary much in their social structure, but it is unlikely that all hostels will be organized to a common pattern. And where they do develop along similar lines in relation to staffing and organization, life in the units will not simply be determined by such structural constraints: according to King, Raynes, and Tizard (1971), even the hostels with child-care-trained superintendents did not have uniformly child-oriented patterns of care as measured by their Scale. It is true that none of the hostels overlapped in their Scale scores with any of the hospitals. But it has to be said that most, if not all, of the hostels were recently opened in new or well-adapted buildings, and that a spirit of enthusiasm for new ideas was very much in evidence among their staff. The hospitals were not new, and staff, while not yet dispirited by adverse publicity (the research was carried out in 1967), saw few alternatives to the traditional ways of doing things, or if they did could not see how they might be implemented. Campbell (1971) has shown that there is still room for improvement in the organization of some local authority hostels. Given what has been said earlier about the natural history of reform in hospitals for the mentally ill, could not the same process of declining standards take place in hostels or other forms of community provisions, simply with the passage of time? Mittler (1966) has suggested that hostels can easily become unstimulating places in which to live unless they are well run, and Apte (1968) has indicated that hostels and half-way houses can develop special problems of their own.

Obviously such dangers should be guarded against so far as this is possible. The safeguards need to be approached from two sides. On the one hand we need to identify the practices which are thought to be undesirable, and to develop our understanding of how they arise so that they can be forestalled. On the other hand desirable practices have to be specified together with an assessment of the staffing, organizational structure, and resources required to support them. At the moment we know more about the former than the latter, but even here the problems can too easily be oversimplified and a good deal more research of a rather detailed kind is required. For example, undesirable practices in hospitals are often dismissed as having been developed to facilitate 'the smooth running of an institutional operation' (Goffman, 1961, p. 79), perhaps arising out of staff shortage. At first sight the hospital 'conveyor belt' system of bathing and toiletting children reported by King, Raynes, and Tizard (1971) seems to have this character. But on closer examination it is apparent that the system actually created more problems of supervision than would have been involved had one member of staff kept the children occupied in the day-room while another took them one at a time to the bathroom. It seems probable that such practices can only arise because staff define their situation, and that of their patients, in ways which make these routines acceptable. This may be more likely to occur in situations of staff shortage, but it certainly does *not* arise *only* in situations of staff shortage. Factors such as the arrangement of duty hours in relation to ward routines, the distribution of tasks among members of staff, the relationships of staff to one another, their training, and so on all seem to play a part.

The on-going evaluation of the Wessex Regional Hospital Board's experimental services for the mentally handicapped should throw valuable light on these and other matters (Kushlick, 1967). In an attempt to achieve the aim of high-quality care in the new community-based residential units, Kushlick and his colleagues set up an operational policy specifying the kinds of negative management practices which were to be avoided (Kushlick, 1973). These negative features were largely those described by King, Raynes, and Tizard (1971): namely rigidity, 'block treatment', depersonalization, and social distance. In order to implement the policy as effectively as possible, a new grade of staff, to be known as warden, was created to take charge of hostel units, and a special training course was set up which among other things stressed the need to avoid institutional practices and to strive for a child-oriented pattern of care. By the skilful use of videotapes it has been possible for the researchers to make very sensitive observations, not just of the patients before and after transfer to the new units but also of their hospital and hostel environments. Technologically, at least, we have travelled a long way since Tizard's pioneering study which removed children from the parent hospital to the experimental unit at Brooklands (Tizard, 1960, 1964).

Then, following the work of the Post-Ely Committee, the operational policy for the experimental units was also accepted as policy for all subnormality hospitals in the Wessex Region, and it became apparent that the hospitals constituted another 'experiment' rather than a 'control' (Kushlick, 1973). It is argued that this removes some of the built-in advantages of the experimental units, although it is apparent from the use of the Child Management Scale developed by King and Raynes that the operational policy is being implemented more successfully in the new units than in the existing wards. Kushlick and his colleagues are now addressing themselves to the problem of why this is so.

In Chapter 10 Kushlick concludes that the main reason why the negative features of hospital care have arisen is because of long standing and impossibly severe shortages of staff at ward levels. In reaching this con-clusion Kushlick, in my view mistakenly, criticizes King, Raynes, and Tizard for the interpretations they placed on their data.[1]

Thus Kushlick states that the 'work of King, Raynes, and Tizard suggested that the *available level of staffing was less crucial* to the avoidance of the defined anti-therapeutic qualities, than the other factors'

1. Dr Kushlick revised his manuscript before publication. However, the essence of the important discussion between him and Dr King remains unchanged [Eds].

(the emphasis is Kushlick's). This is, of course, not the case. What they actually suggested was that 'a high staff–child ratio may be a necessary but not a sufficient condition for child-oriented management' (King *et al.*, 1971, p. 149) and that 'even well-staffed units can be run in an institutionally oriented manner if the staff are not properly organised and if they do not receive the right kind of training' (p. 201). However, in an attempt to demonstrate the overriding influence of staffing Kushlick goes on to suggest that all of the hospitals studied by King, Raynes, and Tizard had effective staff–patient ratios 'below the minimum standards required to undertake continuously any child-oriented practices'. He quotes the data in relation to the best staffed of the hospital units, which had a ratio of 1 : 3·94 in the morning peak period and 1 : 6·7 in the afternoon. This ward had 26 children of whom 58 per cent were severely incontinent and 15 per cent were behaviour disordered. Since Kushlick argues that a ratio of 1 : 5 at any one time is appropriate for the Wessex units, it is difficult to see why this ward should not have managed *some* child-oriented practices, at least in the morning. It would be possible, I suppose, to argue that unless staffing levels are maintained at, say, a ratio of 1 : 5 or better at *all* times then staff would manage children only in the ways which they could manage when there were fewest of them on duty. But this would presumably be because staff *expected* good staffing situations to be only temporary rather than because of the staffing situation as such; that is, because of the way the staff *defined their situation*, and this presumably could be modified by training. King, Raynes, and Tizard anticipated as much when they said: 'Obviously there are limits below which staffing cannot be allowed to fall if child-oriented management practices are to be maintained at a meaningful level. On the other hand, the provision of many staff is no guarantee that institutionally-oriented practices will not occur' (p. 195).

The question remains what are the limits for staffing units of different kinds? Kushlick fails to quote data, from the same tables, about one of the hostels, by no means the worst staffed. This unit had 15 children of whom 33 per cent were severely incontinent and a further 20 per cent were behaviour disordered, while the staff ratios were 1 : 5·45 in the morning peak period and 1 : 7·5 in the afternoon. Applying Kushlick's criteria one might have expected this unit to have difficulty in avoiding institutionally oriented practices, but it was in fact the most child-oriented of all the units studied. It is clear that other factors are at work besides staffing in accounting for these results, however important staffing may be: and it was to these factors that King, Raynes, and Tizard largely addressed themselves.

In fact, King, Raynes, and Tizard argued, like Kushlick, that numbers of staff actually available and working in the ward are important. Indeed they hypothesized that *in general* management practices would not be related to assigned staff ratios, that is total numbers of staff allocated to the units (Hypothesis V, p. 122); but that *child-oriented units would be characterized by better effective staff ratios,* that is numbers of staff actually on duty (Hypothesis VI, p. 122, emphasis added). The evidence supported both hypotheses. The problem is how to improve the effective staff ratios in institutionally oriented units. King, Raynes, and Tizard, on the basis of necessarily limited observations suggested that there was scope for reorganizing either staff duty rotas or the ward routine, or both, so as to maximize effective staff coverage. Kushlick and colleagues, on the basis of presumably more detailed observations in different institutions, argue that there was no such scope without extending the length of the working day. Both could be right, but in any case much more work is needed, not just on staffing standards for living units with different facilities and residents with different degrees of handicap and ability, but also on other factors influencing patterns of care.

Some of the evidence cited by Kushlick does not support the criticism he makes of the concepts and findings of earlier studies. Thus Kushlick (1972) points out that one of the new Wessex units is headed by a person with nursing training who has successfully avoided institutionally oriented practices. But I do not think anyone has suggested that nursing trained staff were so rigid that they would never be able to act differently, especially in an experimental study where a special training course was in operation. Again, Kushlick states that even specially trained non-nursing staff 'block treat' children when the staff—child ratio falls below the average levels. It would be really disturbing if they did so when staffing was at above average levels, as happens in some hospitals; but it should be noted that the 'block treatment' here involves the children being kept together in one of three unlocked play-rooms (presumably playing) which is hardly the same as being kept together with nothing to do in a locked sanitary annexe. Finally, a trial staff increase in a hospital ward is said to have produced a 'completely new routine designed by the nursing staff'. But, as Kushlick says, the hospital units had themselves become experimental rather than control units, and the lessons of the Hawthorne experiments are that almost *any* experimental change in which staff are involved can produce surprising results.

In spite of what has been said here it is to be expected that Kushlick's study will eventually provide a very rich source of detailed information about the possibilities of carrying out child-oriented practices in hospitals and in community-based units; about how many staff are required to do so with given numbers of children with identified handicaps; and, not least, about the effects of the staff training scheme. But perhaps its most important contribution will be in the careful evaluation of the results, not just for the residents, but for their families as well.

The need for theoretically informed research

Attention will now be given to some of the more obvious gaps in our knowledge. We know so little about fostering, and about other community methods such as the use of lodgings, flatlets, or group homes in relation to the mentally handicapped that there is a clear need for both research and experiment in these areas. And the studies of private and voluntary homes for the subnormal have produced sufficiently conflicting results to warrant much closer investigation. At the time of writing an account has just appeared of a privately run home in Suffolk, which is licensed under the National Assistance Act to care for twenty-four mentally handicapped children. During the past eighteen years it is said that about a hundred children cared for at the home died, and some recent deaths are alleged to have resulted from hypothermia (*Sunday Times,* 28 May 1972). It may be that the spotlight is about to be turned on these institutions, but until more systematic research is forthcoming it is difficult to assess their contribution to the over-all provision of care.

Little has been said in this review about the effects of different patterns of care on those who experience them. Surveys of the kind carried out by Morris (1969) and King, Raynes, and Tizard (1971) are prevented by their cross-sectional design from contributing to our knowledge here. There is some evidence from earlier studies (Tizard, 1964) that a change from institutionally oriented to child-oriented care has beneficial effects on the development of retarded children, especially in regard to speech. But hardly anything is known about the effects of residential care, as opposed to training, on retarded adults (Campbell, 1971). The present desirability of patient-centred care rests as much on common sense and common humanity as it does on proven efficacy.

As yet there is no well-articulated theory of the social influences on mental retardation, although Tizard (1970) has made a beginning towards this. And there is no English evidence on the relationship between the residential environment and the progress of patients experiencing it which is comparable, for example, to the carefully demonstrated relationship between institutional environment and the clinical condition of schizophrenic patients provided by Wing and Brown (1970). The study by Kushlick and his colleagues in Wessex should go some way towards meeting this need.

This lack of theory is evident elsewhere in a field which has progressed so far in rather an *ad-hoc* way. The study by King, Raynes, and Tizard (1971) has provided some refinement of at least a part of the theoretical scheme outlined by Goffman (1961), but this does not go nearly far enough. At one level it is necessary to link up with organization theory so that what happens in the living unit can be related to the over-all functioning of the organization. As Kushlick (1972) has observed, what happens in the living unit is in part determined by decisions taken by top management in the local authorities, the regional boards, and the DHSS. This carries the important practical implication that if training is to have any effect it should start at the top and not the bottom. At another level research into structural variables must be related to sociological and social psychological theory about human action and behaviour. It is not enough to know about staff ratios and staff duties without also seeking to understand how staff experience their roles and without finding out how they define their own and their patients' situations. To some extent this has occurred in studies of hospitals for the mentally ill (Coser, 1962; Brown, 1972) but not so far in studies of the retarded. What has been said of staff could also be said of patients, but whereas research into mental illness has utilized patient response (Wing and Brown, 1970) few have attempted this with the retarded (Campbell, 1968). Finally, at still another level, there is a need to see residential care in the context of the community as a whole, as a competitor for scarce resources, influencing and influenced by community attitudes. It is at this level that our current concern with evaluation is worked out and takes expression. From time to time we should all take stock of the assumptions on which our evaluative criteria are based.

If a large number of questions remain to be solved, and a great deal of work is still to be done, I believe that we are at least beginning to ask the right questions.

REFERENCES

Apte, R. Z. (1968). *Halfway Houses: A New Dilemma in Institutional Care,* Occasional Papers on Social Administration no. 27 (London: G. Bell).
Bavin, J. (1971). 'Residential homes; hostels or hospitals?', *Parent's Voice,* **21,** 3, 8–10.
Brown, G. W. (1972). 'The mental hospital as an institution', paper read at the World Psychiatric Association, Second Symposium on Psychiatric Epidemiology, Mannheim, 26–29 July 1972.
Campbell, A. C. (1968). 'Attitudes of mentally disordered adults to community care', *Br. J. prev. soc. Med.* **22,** 2.
—— (1971). 'Aspects of personal independence of mentally subnormal and severely subnormal adults in hospital and in local authority hostels', *Internat. J. Soc. Psychiat.* **17,** 4.
—— (1972). Personal communication.
Coser, R. L. (1962). *Life on the Ward* (Michigan: State University Press).
Craft, M., and Evans, E., (1970). 'Small group homes for subnormals', *Soc. Wk Today,* **1,** 9.
Department of Health and Social Security (1971*a*). *Better Services for the Mentally Handicapped,* Cmnd 4683 (London: HMSO).
—— (1971*b*). *Buildings for Mentally Handicapped People* (London: HMSO).
—— (1971*c*). *Hospital Services for the Mentally Ill,* DHSS Circular 61/71 (London: HMSO).
—— (1971*d*). *National Health Service Hospital Advisory Service, Annual Report for 1969–70* (London: HMSO).

Fox, R., and Adams, A. C. (1968). 'The Phoenix Group Homes', *Br. Hosp. J. and Soc. Serv. Rev.* 14 June.

Goffman, E. (1961). *Asylums: Essays on the Social Situation of Mental Patients and Other Inmates* (New York: Doubleday).

King, R. D., and Raynes, N. V. (1968a). 'Patterns of institutional care for the severely subnormal', *Am. J. Ment. Defic.* **72,** 5, 700–9.

—— —— 'An operational measure of inmate management in residential institutions', *Soc. Sci. and Med.* **2,** 1, 41–53.

—— —— and Tizard, J. (1971). *Patterns of Residential Care: Sociological Studies in Institutions for Handicapped Children* (London: Routledge & Kegan Paul).

Kushlick, A. (1967). 'A method of evaluating the effectiveness of a community health service', *Soc. Econ. Admin.* **1,** 29–49.

Mittler, P. (1966). *The Mental Health Services,* Fabian Research Series no. 252 (London: Fabian Society).

Morris, P. (1969). *Put Away: A Sociological Study of Institutions for the Mentally Retarded* (London: Routledge & Kegan Paul).

National Health Service (1969). *Report of the Committee of Inquiry into Allegations of Ill-Treatment of Patients and other Irregularities at the Ely Hospital, Cardiff,* Cmnd 3975 (London: HMSO).

—— (1971). *Report of the Farleigh Hospital Committee of Inquiry.* Cmnd 4557 (London: HMSO).

—— (1972). *Report of the Committee of Inquiry into Whittingham Hospital,* Cmnd 4861 (London: HMSO).

National Society for Mentally Handicapped Children (1971a). 'The residential needs of the mentally handicapped', *Parent's Voice* (December).

—— (1971b). *Directory of Residential Accommodation for the Mentally Handicapped in England, Wales and Northern Ireland* (June) (NSMHC).

Parker, R. A. (1966). *Decision in Child Care: A Study of Prediction in Fostering* (London, George Allen & Unwin).

Royal Commission (1957). *Report of the Royal Commission on the Law Relating to Mental Illness and Mental Deficiency,* Cmnd 169 (London: HMSO).

Tizard, J. (1960). 'Residential care of mentally handicapped children', *Br. med. J.* **1,** 1041–6.

—— (1964). *Community Services for the Mentally Handicapped* (London: Oxford University Press).

—— (1969). 'The role of social institutions in the causation, prevention and alleviation of mental retardation', in Haywood, H. C. (ed.), *Socio-cultural Aspects of Mental Retardation* (New York: Appleton Century Crofts).

Trasler, G. (1960). *In Place of Parents: A Study of Foster Care* (London: Routledge & Kegan Paul).

Wing, J. K., and Brown, G. W. (1970). *Institutionalism and Schizophrenia: A Comparative Study of Three Mental Hospitals 1960–1968* (Cambridge, at the University Press).

Part 4 Evaluating services for the elderly

12 The principles of providing a service for psycho-geriatric patients

SIR MARTIN ROTH

The demographic background

Having regard to the fact that the proportion of those aged 65 and over in the population has been rising steadily in all advanced countries since the beginning of this century, it is surprising that so little attention was paid to their problems by medical men, administrators, or scientists in the interval between 1909 and the end of the Second World War.

The populations of Europe had been characterized, until about 1800, by a high fertility rate and a high death-rate, more or less in equilibrium leading to little expansion of the population (Daric, 1956). Towards the end of the eighteenth century an explosive increase in the population of western Europe began. This was due in large part to the decline in mortality which affected mainly the children. This trend continued, but coincided, towards the end of the last and the beginning of this century, with a drop in the birth-rate which has continued until the temporary upsurge which followed in some countries after the Second World War. It is this declining birth-rate that has caused the ageing of populations of most advanced countries.

Yet the erroneous view persists that the increased proportion of the aged in the population is due to 'medicated survival'. In fact the expectation of life at the age of 65 has changed relatively little. Only a small part of the increase in the relative proportion of the aged can be regarded as a tribute to the advance of medical science.

In Great Britain the absolute number of those aged 65 and over has increased four-fold and of those 85 and over seven-fold since the beginning of the century and similar trends have been apparent in other affluent countries. The increase in the proportion of aged in relation to the young, that has stemmed from declining birth-rates is now reaching its maximum effects in some countries. But mortality among the young will continue to fall and advances in medical science are likely to bring down mortality in middle life and ultimately in old age. Permanent ageing of populations will result from these changes.

Some of the possible social consequences emerge from estimates made from population forecasts of future utilisation of hospital beds. Ashley and Klein (1971) extrapolating from recent trends have estimated that by 1992, 73·5 per cent of all beds currently available for men and 93·7 per cent of non-maternity beds currently available for women could be filled by old age pensioners. Despite the speculative assumptions inherent in such forecasts (and conceded by the authors) the figures deserve to be pondered by planners of the future health and welfare services.

The magnitude of the problem

In considering services for the elderly, the senile, and arteriosclerotic dementias (or the 'chronic brain syndromes' as they have come to be called), merit special attention. Patients with these disorders have been found to occupy a high proportion of the beds in every type of long-stay accommodation investigated: geriatric wards, residential homes, and mental hospital wards allocated to long-stay patients alike (Kay, Beamish, and Roth, 1964). The success of the plan to phase out mental hospitals of the traditional type within the next few decades will be largely decided by the extent to which alternative forms of care can be provided for aged people with chronic mental disorders.

Those in hospital represent only a fraction of the elderly suffering from mental infirmity and illness. A survey of the elderly living at home in Newcastle upon Tyne (Kay, Beamish, and Roth, 1964) revealed a 10 per cent prevalence of organic brain syndromes and about half of these, that is 5 per cent, were 'severe' cases. The findings of different authors working in a variety of cultural settings reflect a wide measure of agreement (Table 1). However, in Newcastle less than one-fifth, even of these severe cases, were being cared for in hospitals or welfare homes.

Moreover, population trends suggest that the demands made by the aged on the health and social services are bound to increase steeply within the next decade. At the present, roughly one out of every eight persons in the population is aged 65 or more. Ten years hence those aged 65 and over will increase by almost one million and of these about half a million will be aged 75 or more (DHSS, 1971).

On 31 December 1967 patients over the age of 65 made up 43 per cent of all residents in psychiatric hospitals (and more than half of the long-stay group). By the end of the next decade, nearly two-thirds of the patients in psychiatric hospitals might be aged 65 or more, if existing trends and current patterns of hospitalization continue.

In Sweden it has been estimated that as a result of ageing of the population alone, the number of places taken up in psychiatric hospitals by elderly people with degenerative cerebral disease will need to be more than doubled between 1960 and 1980 (Larsson *et al.*, 1963). In the Newcastle survey the prevalence of definite cases among those aged 75 and over

Table 1. The prevalence of the main psychiatric syndromes of old age, according to various authors (percentages).

	Sheldon (1948) (N = 369) 65+	Bremer (1951) (N = 119) 60+	Essen-Moller (1956) (N = 443) 60+	Syracuse (1961) (N = 1,592) 65+	Primrose (1962) (N = 222) 65+	Neilsen (1963) (N = 978) 65+	Kay et al. (1964) (N = 297) 65+
Senile and arteriosclerotic psychoses	3·9	2·5	5·0	—	3·6 ⎱ 4·5	3·1	4·6 ⎱ 5·6
Other organic syndromes	—	—	—	—	0·9 ⎰	—	1·0 ⎰
Major functional disorders	—	4·2*	1·1	—	1·4	5·7*	2·4
Psychoses, all forms	3·9	6·7	6·1	6·8	5·9	6·8	8·0
'Mild mental deterioration'	11·7	—	10·8	—	—	15·4	5·7
Neuroses and allied disorders (moderate/severe forms)	9·4 ⎱ 12·6	5·0 ⎱ 17·6	1·4 ⎱ 12·0	—	10·4 ⎱ 12·6	4·0 ⎱ 8·7	8·9 ⎱ 12·5
Character disorders	3·2 ⎰	12·6 ⎰	10·6 ⎰	—	2·2 ⎰	4·7 ⎰	3·6 ⎰

* Includes 'constitutional' and 'psychogenic' psychoses.

Table 2. *Prevalence of main types of chronic brain syndrome by sex and age (Newcastle upon Tyne).*

	Senile		Vascular		Other		Total	
	M	F	M	F	M	F	M	F
65+	0·5	1·0	2·0	0·3	1·0	1·0	3·5	2·4
75+	4·4	9·3	6·7	2·3	1·1	1·2	12·2	12·7
All ages	1·7	4·1	3·4	1·1	1·0	1·1	6·2	6·2

proved to be 12·5 per cent and within the 65–75 age-group approximately 3·5 per cent (Table 2). This suggests that within a decade there will be approximately 80,000 more cases of 'chronic brain syndrome' among the elderly population. What follows will therefore be mainly concerned with the service needs of this group of elderly people.

The relationship between mental illness and duration of stay in hospital and residential accommodation

For the purpose of inquiry into use of beds, subjects were grouped into three broad and mutually exclusive groups: chronic brain syndrome (CBS), functional syndromes (FS) of at least moderate severity, and a group in which no significant psychiatric abnormality was present. The last included lifelong personality disorders and those with functional syndromes of only mild severity. Chronic physical illness and handicap were, of course, relatively common in this last 'normal' group. The 1960 sample was followed up four years later and the 1964 sample $2\frac{1}{2}$–3 years later, with about 5 per cent loss by death and removal in both. Admissions to hospitals, to local authority welfare homes, and to private nursing or residential homes, and the total duration of stay in each, were ascertained both for those who had died and those who had survived. It will be seen (Table 3) that 19 per cent of the normal, 25 per cent of the FS, and 61 per cent of the CBS subjects had been admitted to some kind of institution, the difference between CBS subjects and the other groups being highly significant ($p<0·01$).

The 6·2 per cent of subjects with CBS contributed 46 per cent of patients admitted to geriatric wards and 15 per cent of those entering residential accommodation (Kay *et al.,* 1970).

The three groups are even more strikingly separated in respect of their average length of stay in different types of accommodation (Table 4). The mean length of stay per subject was 0·9 weeks for the normal group, 3·8 weeks for the FS group, and 12 weeks for the CBS group. In fact, a reasonably good prediction of the amount of use of institutional care could have been made on the strength of a definite diagnosis of senile or arteriosclerotic dementia alone. For the 6·2 per cent of the combined samples who were classified as suffering from CBS accounted for 25 per

Table 3. *1964 sample: Numbers of subjects admitted to various types of care during follow up period, according to diagnosis made when first seen (percentages in parentheses).*

	Normals	Functional	CBS	Total
Acute	57 (16·6)	15 (18·8)	6 (23·1)	78 (17·4)
Geriatric	10 (2·9)	4 (5·0)	12 (46·2)	26 (5·8)
Mental	3 (0·9)	3 (3·8)	2 (7·7)	8 (1·8)
Local authority homes	1 (1·5)	2 (2·5)	3 (15·4)	6 (2·4)
Private homes	4	—	2	6
Admitted somewhere	66* (19·2)	20* (25·0)	16* (61·5)	102* (22·7)
Not admitted	277 (80·0)	60 (75·0)	10 (38·5)	347 (77·3)
Total	343(100)	80(100·0)	26(100·0)	449(100·0)

* Some patients admitted to more than one type of care.

cent of those admitted to mental hospital, and 46 per cent of those admitted to geriatric wards.

In the 1964 sample, the 26 subjects with chronic brain syndrome spent a total of 255 weeks in geriatric wards which was 54 per cent of the 473 weeks spent by the whole sample of 449 subjects in that kind of bed. The same group of subjects spent 360 weeks in homes accounting for 57 per cent of the 630 weeks spent there by the whole sample. Had the future use of hospital care of any kind been predicted on the strength of a diagnosis of a chronic brain syndrome alone, it would have been correct in 58 per cent of cases compared with an over-all chance of admission of 22 per cent in the whole material investigated. A prediction of care in some kind of long-stay unit would have been correct in 54 per cent of cases compared with an over-all chance of admission of only 7·3 per cent in the whole domiciliary sample.

Though the subjects in the CBS group were somewhat older than those in the other groups, a comparison (Table 5) with a psychiatrically normal control group matched for age and sex showed them to be two and a half times as likely to be admitted to hospitals or homes where they spent in all six times as long. And despite the markedly abridged life-expectation of the demented subjects, they had spent four times as long in hospital, and ten times as long in homes as the controls; and 47 subjects with CBS in the 'matched' group had occupied beds in hospital for 390 weeks and in homes for 596 weeks or 11½ years.

Detailed information was available about the home circumstances of each subject and no evidence came to light that institutional forms of care were being over-used. Newcastle was relatively deficient in beds and residential places for the aged. More CBS subjects might well have been admitted and some might have been admitted earlier but for a shortage of 200 places compared with national standards. It is possible that the

Table 4. *1964 sample: total and average duration of stay in weeks in different types of care during follow-up period, by diagnosis when first seen.*

Type of care	Normals (N = 343) Total and mean duration in weeks	Total stay N	Functionals (N = 80) Total and mean duration in weeks	Total stay N	CBS (N = 26) Total and mean duration in weeks	Total stay N	Total (N = 449) Total and mean duration in weeks	Total stay N
Acute	194 (3·4)		37 (2·5)		40 (6·7)		271 (3·5)	
Geriatric	73 (7·3)		145(36·3)		255 (21·3)		473(18·2)	
Mental	37(12·3)		124(41·3)		18 (9·0)		179(22·4)	
Total in:								
Hospitals	304 (4·7)	0·9	306(15·3)	3·8	313 (20·9)	12·0	923(15·2)	2·1
Homes	180(36·2)	0·5	90(45·0)	1·1	360 (90·0)	13·8	630(57·3)	1·4
Total	484(40·9)	1·4	396(60·3)	4·9	673(110·9)	25·8	1,553(72·5)	3·5

Table 5. 1960 and 1964 samples: matched groups. Numbers admitted and duration of stay in various types of care during period of follow-up.

	Normal controls (N = 73)			CBS subjects (N = 47)		
	N	Total and mean duration in weeks	Total stay N	N	Total and mean duration in weeks	Total stay N
Acute	15 ⎫	95 ⎫		8 ⎫	43 ⎫	
Geriatric	2 ⎬ 16*	7 ⎬ 102 (6.4)	1.4	19 ⎬ 26*	298 ⎬ 390(15.0)	8.3
Mental	— ⎭	— ⎭		5 ⎭	49 ⎭	
Local authority homes	— ⎫	— ⎫		4 ⎫ 8*	288 ⎫ 596(74.5)	12.7
Private homes	3 ⎬ 3	59 ⎬ 59 (19.7)	0.8	5 ⎭	205 ⎭	
Total	17*	161(9.5)	2.2	28*	986(35.2)	21.0

* Some patients admitted to more than one type of care.

provision of more extensive domiciliary services and alternative forms of care might have postponed admission in some subjects, or, in a proportion, possibly averted it altogether. The feasibility of such alternatives and the extent to which they are applicable demand systematic exploration. Rough guesses about the efficacy of alternatives and about the scale on which they can be provided will not do.

Limits of safety

But precise information is needed about the feasibility of the alternatives for this specific group of disabilities. There is a precarious equilibrium between the large morbidity in the community and the small proportion of it that flows, ever so slowly, into institutional accommodation. The vacation of places by death and discharge, and the provision of services in the form of domiciliary care, out-patients' clinics, and day-hospitals have somehow kept the system going. But it is astonishing that the service can continue to function even at its present level of efficiency.

With improved care the mortality of dements will slowly but surely decline, to a limited extent, with a consequent increase in demand for accommodation. Townsend (1957) found that relatives bore the main brunt of the burden of sickness in old age and a recent survey (Ministry of Pensions and National Insurance, 1966) has shown that local authority home-helps provide less than one-twentieth of the help given to pensioners with preparation of meals and with shopping, and less than a sixth of the help given with housework. It is this very saving clause, the aid given by relatives, that is now imperilled by the increasing mobility of young adults in search of employment, the population shifts caused by industrial changes, by the closure of mines and shipyards and by the improved opportunities for women in full-time employment. Moreover, precise information about the social effects of such changes on old people is lacking.

At the present time, only 5 per cent of people aged 65 and over are resident in some form of institutional accommodation and the pressure on this accommodation is so intense that an increase of 1 per cent might give rise to serious embarrassment. In the light of these facts, the estimate made some years ago, that approximately 75–80 per cent of aged people in this and other countries (Shanas *et al.*, 1965) live with others and often in close contact with children or other relatives, no longer justifies unalloyed satisfaction. A number of imponderable factors are impinging on the precarious balance that somehow continues between family support, on the one hand, and the care provided by the health and welfare services, on the other. In such a situation one should perhaps hesitate to introduce major over-all changes in patterns of care until their effects on a system in a state of uncertain equilibrium are assessed by carefully designed experiments.

Factors influencing admission

In this context, a number of questions arise in relation to hospital usage by subjects with different types of disorder. If subjects with CBS make such heavy demands on institutional places, and if the number of severely demented living in the community far exceeds those who have had to be admitted, what factors determine viability in the community? This would call for careful comparisons between those in and outside institutions and those comparisons have yet to be made.

Information is available only about over-all differences between institutionalized persons of every kind, on the one hand, and the general population of comparable age, on the other. Surveys in different parts of the world have shown that the single, widowed, and divorced made disproportionate demands. Townsend and Wedderburn (1965) found that among old people living in institutions (1) more are unmarried than married, 30 per cent as against 10 per cent; (2) more of the married or widowed lack children, 26 per cent as against 16 per cent; (3) more lack brothers and sisters, 40 per cent as against 22 per cent; (4) more of those with children have only one, 39 per cent as against 26 per cent, and they have sons rather than daughters. It is not known whether subjects with CBS living in and out of institutions, differ in respect of such familial features, but it would be interesting to find out. A high proportion of those in long-term geriatric wards suffer from dementia as well as chronic physical disability, but if it were not for the psychiatric disorder many would be at home. Community studies have repeatedly paid implicit tribute to the fact that families continue to bear great hardships and burdens as a result of physical disablement and long-term emotional disturbance among their elderly relatives.

As far as features relating to admission among those with dementia are concerned, there is little precise information. Those liable to disturbed, aggressive, and persistently confused behaviour, to dangerous conduct within the home, and to persistent incontinence figure prominently. Urinary incontinence is a major problem, particularly in households with limited resources and few families in ordinary homes can cope with it. Admission is often needed as the result of an exacerbation that follows the death of a spouse or complication by some acute physical illness but such disturbances may be transient. There are also step-like changes in the progress of dementia about which little is known. Systematic observations would be of value in paving the way for the development of more clear and consistent criteria for the admission of those with cerebral degenerative disease to institutions for long-term care. The places are few and precious and the establishment of such criteria is an urgent necessity.

Similar questions have to be posed in relation to functional disorder. If the great majority manage to remain at home, what features decide the ultimate institutionalization of a small proportion? Here again only information of a general kind is available. It is known that there is a high prevalence of chronic physical illness among those with functional disorders and that mortality is far in excess of normal expectation (Kay and Bergmann, 1966). It is known also that the combination of physical illness and depression carries a relatively high suicidal risk. But no specific comparisons have yet been made between institutionalized and non-institutionalized groups. This gap needs to be filled because such observations might pave the way for a reduced rate of institutionalization and improvement in the quality of care in the community.

A third question arises about the stage in the development of a senile or arteriosclerotic dementia at which admission to an institution becomes inescapable. Are there any clearly defined features among those who gain. admission? Or is it possible to develop criteria or some system of weighting that would make for consistency in the decision-making that precedes admission to a long-stay unit? Here again there is little factual observation to provide guidance.

Misclassification of individuals requiring long-term care

Although there is some disagreement as to whether misclassification of those admitted for long-term care results in any measurable effect on the outcome of disorders in old age (Mezey *et al.*, 1968) there is little doubt that admission without regard to the kind of disorder that needs management and rehabilitation denies many old people the best available standard of care and frequently it causes wasteful use of scant resources. It cannot be reiterated too often that having regard to the narrow limits of safety discussed in the foregoing section, a place for long-term care is a scarce and precious commodity. Misclassification may be considered under a number of headings.

Mental hospitals

Among patients aged 65 or over admitted to mental hospitals, 14·5 per cent die within three months of admission (M = 20·2 per cent; F = 11·8 per cent) (Brothwood, 1971). This suggests that a number of these patients might have been more appropriately treated in medical or geriatric units.

Geriatric units

As far as geriatric units are concerned, 5·8 per cent of the second Newcastle survey sample (Kay *et al.*, 1970) had been admitted to geriatric wards during the follow-up period of $2\frac{1}{2}$–3 years but, considered from the point of view of duration of stay, their use of geriatric accommodation was more considerable than the small percentage of persons admitted would indicate. The 5·8 per cent (26 persons) had occupied beds for 473 weeks and the average stay per patient was 18·2 weeks.

In the first Newcastle sample a count was made of persons, previously living in the electoral wards chosen for study, who were in various forms of institutional care on one night (1 November 1960) (Kay *et al.*, 1964) suffering from various degrees of psychiatric disorder (54 [out of 154 in care] were in geriatric wards). Twenty-four of them suffered from dementia, 1 from paraphrenia, 20 from brain syndromes and mild forms of neuroses, and 9 from character disorders. A study of Isaacs (1971) has shown that one-third of the patients in the 65 and over age-group could be regarded as 'medicopsychiatric', most of the patients exhibiting states of acute confusion or dementia with severe physical illness. Five per cent of the patients were without significant disability having been admitted on account of self-neglect arising in the course of a purely psychiatric disorder. Some 20 per cent of patients were bedfast. There was, therefore, no serious misclassification in a purely quantitative sense. However, a single confused or aggressive patient may dangerously disturb patients in a geriatric ward who are seriously ill. Moreover, the psychiatric nursing skills required by the high proportion of mentally ill patients to be found on a geriatric ward are not available there nor can an adequate clinical psychiatric service be provided by one or two cursory visits in a week by a psychiatrist.

Welfare homes

An investigation of welfare homes in Newcastle showed one-third of a sample of residents to be mentally normal, 40 per cent to be suffering from mild or advanced dementia, 5 per cent from other psychoses, and 12 per cent from minor emotional disorders. Ten per cent had epilepsy, subnormality, or character disorder (Kay, Beamish, and Roth, 1962). About one-third of these residents may be fully ambulant but 1 in 5 require personal attention and 1 in 12 may be incontinent or mentally disturbed to a degree that makes admission to hospital desirable (Harris, 1968). The limitation of all such cross-sectional surveys is that they provide very little information about the condition of residents at the time of admission. It is not, therefore possible to judge how far admission could have been averted, or in what cases alternative forms of care would have been more appropriate.

All institutions for long-term care

In the Birmingham inquiry (McKeown and Lowe, 1952) into all the city's elderly residents in geriatric wards, general hospitals, special hospitals, or welfare homes, the findings reflected considerable misplacement or overlap in function. Only 59 per cent of patients in geriatric wards were regarded as truly 'long-term'. The remainder required psychiatric nursing (18 per cent) or investigation and treatment of acute illness (6 per cent) or required welfare home rather than hospital accommodation (17 per cent).

Of the patients examined in psychiatric hospitals in 1959, 19 per cent needed basic nursing, 16 per cent could have gone to homes, and 5 per cent required investigation.

As the health service and the social services are exposed to the pressures that were outlined at an earlier stage, in addition to misuse of resources which will always be in short supply within the foreseeable future, they will be increasingly in danger of being overloaded, impeded, and disarranged.

Suggested guidelines for the provision of residential and institutional care in specific forms of psycho-geriatric disorders

The psycho-geriatric population is a heterogeneous group and some confusions in policy are perpetuated through failure to take this sufficiently into account. The subdivision made here has been mainly based upon:

Patients grown old in mental hospitals

In considering future provision the distinction between patients who have grown old in mental hospitals and those admitted *de novo* in old age is important. As the number of the former is diminishing, new accommodation tends to be regarded as unnecessary. This is reasonable provided account is taken of the assumptions implicit in such policies. The most important are that those with chronic schizophrenic psychoses who are at present able to live in the community can continue to survive there indefinitely. The second is that facilities for community care will be expanded to a level that makes community orientated programmes feasible and humane in the long run. The first assumption requires critical evaluation seeing that some two-thirds of the parents on whom chronic schizophrenics were found, in a recent study (Stevens, 1972), to be heavily dependent, proved to be of pensionable age. The second assumption is invalidated (as far as Great Britain is concerned) by the meagre or wholly inadequate provision of facilities for community care by local authorities. Hence, only if practical measures are taken to justify the assumptions made, can beds previously provided for chronic patients who formerly grew old in mental hospitals be omitted from consideration in planning for future services.

Functional disorders

It has already been indicated that elderly patients with all forms of functional disorder make much smaller demands on beds than do those with dementia and it is clear that, with the provision of adequate day-hospital, out-patient, and domiciliary services, this demand could be further reduced. It is, therefore, reasonable to assume that such patients requiring treatment in hospitals will, in future, be cared for within general hospital psychiatric units. However, steps will have to be taken to ensure that this works out in practice. Little difficulty arises in respect of admission in the 65–75-year age-group. But there are many complaints of difficulty in securing a bed for patients who are more than 75 years old, particularly where there is associated physical disease or psychiatric disorder of an atypical or 'mixed' character. The latter groups are prone to be unnecessarily admitted and the special skills needed for the assessment of elderly subjects with psychiatric disorders deserve emphasis in this context. The elderly are entitled to benefit from them.

Dementia without significant physical disease

Dementia without significant physical disease, may be subdivided into 'mild' and 'severe' cases. It is possible that, with the provision of domiciliary services, many of the mild cases will be provided for within the community. However, some are physically infirm, rendered immobile by bone and joint disease, intermittently incontinent, and liable to recurrent infection. As family support declines, need for residential homes for such old people is bound to increase in the next decade. As far as severe dementia is concerned welfare homes, at present, are unwilling to admit severe dements, particularly if incontinent or to keep those who need constant supervision.

Dementia with significant physical disease

If mental hospitals are no longer to cater for long-term care of severe dements, alternative provision will have to be made in the community. And this will need to be planned in such a way that it meets with the material and emotional needs of progressively declining old people. Further reference to this will be made at a later stage. Geriatric departments in Great Britain already carry the main burden in numbers of admissions and of residents as far as those who are demented and have significant physical disease are concerned. However, if this form of provision is to continue, the standard of care requires to be improved. The psychiatric service enjoyed by geriatric departments is often ill-sustained. Attempts at social and psychological rehabilitation and training to an optimal level leave much to be desired. Nurses with psychiatric training are few and far between and geriatric long-stay wards are far too overcrowded, geographically isolated (which curtails visiting by relatives), dreary, and depressing to be acceptable by contemporary standards. This section has focused on institutional needs which, as already indicated, cannot and should not provide for more than a fraction of psycho-geriatric cases. The main emphasis has to be on a preventive approach which will be considered in the section that follows.

Problems in assessment

Any classification that seeks to provide guidelines for practical purposes must be clear and simple. However, to suggest that the scheme outlined below is satisfactory in these respects would gloss over the problems entailed in judging whether dementia is present at all and in grading its severity. What forms of assessment are to be employed for purposes of classification and grading? Clinical assessments have been surprisingly well validated on the whole. But they can prove misleading. A well-preserved facade can conceal advanced intellectual deterioration until the advent of a domestic crisis.

The use of questionnaires and simple psychometric measures such as the shortened version of the WAIS (Britton and Savage, 1966), Memory-Information Tests, and simple questionnaires (Roth *et al.*, 1967; Blessed *et al.*, 1968) may help to minimize diagnostic errors. But psychometric testing may yield misleading results. Within a group of subjects with 'suspected chronic brain syndrome' followed up $2\frac{1}{2}$–4 years later, those with low scores at earlier testing were found on follow-up not to have deteriorated, while those with significantly higher scores had demented further. The former group were of significantly lower social class and poorer initial intellectual endowment (Bergmann *et al.*, 1972; Nunn *et al.*, 1972). The latter are clearly at risk of being incorrectly designated as early dements.

The use of the general criterion of 'significant physical disease' fails to specify what is perhaps the most important single physical criterion, incontinence, that decides where an elderly person can be cared for.

Finally, in relation to this demented group, judgements about the severity of the dementia should not be made without considering the social setting which may support and protect the patient or contribute to rendering him helpless. A spouse, a daughter, or a family may sustain a fairly severe dement at home for a considerable time. But the death of spouse or the loss of a relative by removal may rapidly transform the situation. These social networks which enable an elderly person to continue living at an acceptable standard, at home, for periods of months or years, require further exploration.

Preventive measures and the concept of 'lines of defence'

It will be plain that illness, disablement, and infirmity is so common among elderly people in the community of modern affluent societies that the only realistic approach is one that devotes substantial resources to facilitating life within the community for all but the most severely infirm and demented aged individuals. Such an approach conforms to the wishes of the great majority of the aged and to a large extent of their families also. And the alternative would imply increasing reductions in the resources made available to the remainder of the population, on a scale that is unacceptable.

It is salutary to return to the philosophy expounded within the Sixth Report of the Expert Committee on Mental Health of WHO (1959):

... the size of the problem of mental health among the aged and the rate at which it is growing make it impracticable to consider in terms of hospital beds the care of even the small fraction of cases who become infirm or sick or who belong to the marginal group that hovers between sickness and health. But, even if there were an abundance of places, the old person is, as a rule, better off in his own home, unless illness or serious infirmity afflict him. It is both expedient and humane to maintain the aged person in the community or, if he breaks down, to treat him promptly and return him there before his social roots have been finally severed. The emphasis on social environment as a factor in mental health is growing, and so is the realisation that uprooting an individual may be as important as illness in the long run, in impeding his return to the community.

The policies envisaged in this statement and described in more detail in the Report imply action along three broad lines: (1) political and social reform in an attempt to mitigate the unhappy plight of many old people in modern industrial communities; (2) medical and social measures to reduce the frequency with which old people are uprooted; (3) the 'lines of defence' concept, or the development of a range of services within the community that make for greater flexibility and freedom of choice in selecting a way of life or planning long-term management for aged people. An examination of recent progress in the light of these recommendations is of interest.

The social background of psycho-geriatric problems

The literature that deals with the social aspects of gerontology has during the past few decades brought to light an impressive body of evidence testifying to the under-privileged status of the aged in modern industrial societies. That they are economically deprived is well established (Townsend and Wedderburn, 1965); they constitute an impoverished leisured class. They suffer more from social isolation (Tunstall, 1966) and the effects of this are frequently compounded with the desolation that follows bereavement. They frequently complain of loneliness (Kay *et al.*, 1964). And in modern industrial communities they are deprived of the privilege and dignity which was their lot in civilizations that placed less emphasis on vigour, enterprise, and youth. Townsend (1957) has given a vivid description of the decline in dignity and self-respect that follows, particularly in working-class men, when they cease to be the breadwinners of the family; women are, in contrast, sustained by their role as managers of the household and the influence for cohesion and unity they exert within the family round which daughters and grandchildren tend to cluster.

The case for social reform to mitigate the plight of aged people in contemporary society does not need to be argued; it is widely accepted that radical measures aimed at enhancing the quality of life in old age are an urgent necessity.

However, systematic observations have failed to bring to light any clear or convincing evidence of a relationship between the indices of underprivilege that have been touched upon and the causation of mental disorder in old age. There is no evidence that retirement exerts an adverse effect upon mental health (Richardson, 1964) but much to indicate that those in manual occupations are in ill health at pensionable age and glad to retire. Isolation has proved, in a number of rigorous inquiries (Lowenthal, 1964; Kay *et al.,* 1964; Garside *et al.,* 1965) to be more a consequence than a cause of mental disorder in old age. Loneliness proves to have little relationship with measures of isolation; it is most conspicuous in those with a long history of emotional instability and life-long difficulties in relating to others (Kay *et al.,* 1964, Part II). Bereavement has been shown (Parkes, 1964) to have a clear association with admission to hospital for psychiatric disorder when all stages of the life span are taken together. But recent widowhood has proved to have no clear association with psychiatric illness in old age, either in the Newcastle or in American surveys (Lowenthal, 1964; Garside *et al.,* 1965) although more detailed inquiries are called for. The same statement has to be made in relation to social class and income; no clear correlation with functional or organic mental disorder has emerged (Garside *et al.,* 1965).

Social reform is not, therefore, likely to make much impression on existing prevalence rates. The health and welfare services seem to have accepted that the geriatric problem has a hard refractory core and that social provision has to be made for a high proportion of elderly people unable to sustain an independent life. In Denmark, for example, there are plans for the provision of residential and nursing home accommodation for 4 per cent of the population aged 65 and over. An additional bed per 100 is intended for elderly people with mental disorder who are to be accommodated outside psychiatric hospitals. Units are to be small and home-like and a large part of the accommodation is to be in single and double rooms and small dormitories. Ample facilities for occupational therapy and social activity will be provided and the units are to be within easy reach of the communities from which the disabled people have been drawn. Moreover, provision on this scale is for the immediate future; it is recognized that, within large cities such as Copenhagen, up to 10 per cent may need to be accommodated in the foreseeable future (WHO, 1972).

Even if the enormous cost of provision on this scale were disregarded, the question arises as to whether geriatric services within which institutional care, albeit of high quality, figures so prominently conforms with the aspirations of old people or their relations. In their important Chichester survey, Grad and Sainsbury (1968) found that families with elderly relatives being cared for at home, in the community-orientated services, suffered considerable hardship, some 63 per cent ascribing symptoms of emotional disturbance to the burdens imposed by elderly relatives. Yet many families preferred to have their aged at home. There are two other points that are germane in this context. The first is that, although social influences have not, so far, proved to have a clear relationship to the causation of mental disorders in the aged, their influence on the likelihood that such elderly persons will have to enter an institution for long-term care is indubitable and the evidence bearing on this has already been discussed. Secondly, the effect of community care, including the network of well-developed domiciliary services, on the prolongation of independent social life and the avoidance of institutionalization is in danger of being under-estimated. In Chichester, domiciliary services were less well developed than in some other areas in England and Wales.

The avoidance of uprooting

As the pressure exerted by the geriatric problem increases, the need to deploy scant resources, in the most efficient manner possible, will grow more urgent. The warning against the dangers of uprooting the elderly implicit in the WHO statement quoted above, continues to be timely. Those responsible for admitting elderly people to residential homes exhibit a distinct preference for well-behaved, well-preserved, and continent old people. Yet, with some measure of support most of such elderly people should be capable of maintaining a life in the community. As a matter of policy, they should be protected from the hazards of entry to Part III accommodation, for, as Townsend (1962) pointed out, discharge from Part III accommodation is very uncommon. According to a recent estimate (Moseley, 1968) sheltered housing would have been a satisfactory alternative for at least one in five persons admitted to residential homes. Some ten years ago Townsend showed social factors to have been decisive in the admission of a substantially higher proportion.

In the Newcastle survey, the estimated total prevalence for elderly persons with psychiatric disorder within institutions was 17·1 per 1,000 and of this almost a quarter was made up by people with manic-depressive disorder, paraphrenia, neuroses, and character disorders. With the addition of mild forms of dementia, these groups accounted for 9·3 persons per 1,000, that is, more than half the total prevalence of institutional cases. The possibility of alternative forms of provision within the community for these groups of cases needs to be carefully studied. But in the near future, decisions relating to admission to long-term care should be governed by a carefully worked out system of priorities. For this purpose medical and social indices, validated by operational research, will be needed. They will have to be applied with stringency if limited resources are to be deployed in the most effective manner possible.

'Lines of defence' within the community

In the Report of the WHO Sixth Expert Committee on Mental Health (1959) the main components of the psycho-geriatric preventive services outlined were:

   1. A number of medical and social arrangements in the community

comprising a network of domiciliary services, out-patient clinics designed to provide for the special problems of aged people, day-hospitals, clubs offering facilities for people with differing needs, and aid to foster the growth of voluntary organizations or, in the words of the Report, 'the spontaneous association of citizens for the purpose of bringing relief to those of their fellows in need'. The domiciliary services for the aged were conceived as providing meals-on-wheels, home visiting and nursing, transport to hospitals and clinics, laundry facilities, and mobile physiotherapy services.

2. An administrative structure that would eliminate wasteful overlap, inefficiency and inflexibility, by facilitating the integration of the services of local health authorities, family doctors, and hospitals.

3. 'Guidance centres' which would provide facilities for multidisciplinary investigation of the early phases of mental disorder as well as counselling.

These centres were, therefore, the progenitors of present-day psycho-geriatric assessment units. They were to be located at the general hospital and be closely linked with the long-stay in-patient unit.

Recent years have seen a certain amount of development along these lines. Thus day-hospital attendance by aged people doubled between 1964 and 1968; changes in out-patient attendances have been on a similar scale (Brothwood, 1971) although it would appear that out-patient services tend to be under-used by the aged. Psycho-geriatric assessment units have been developed in several centres either within general or psychiatric hospitals. However, on the whole the development of community services for the aged is patchy and inadequate. Thus, in 1968, only 13 per cent of local health authorities in England and Wales had established day-centres for mentally infirm old people (Wigley, 1968). With the exception of a few examples, based on local initiative, integration is a remote prospect. But the reorganization of the NHS provides fresh opportunities for establishing an integrated administration for geriatric services at district, area, and regional levels.

Needs in the immediate future

In summary, the main ingredients of the present situation as far as the long-term care of geriatric patients is concerned are: (1) an anticipated rise in the decade 1972–81 of almost a million in the number of those aged 65 and over in the general population with a disproportionate increase in the number of the very aged who make the greatest demands on the health and social services; (2) a disproportionate increase in those forms of mental disorder in old age that have far more need for long-term institutional care than any other kind of geriatric disablement; (3) scarcity of accommodation within every type of institution that provides long-term care against a background of rapid social change that may slowly erode the support and services that at present enable the majority of aged people to live out their days in their own homes; (4) health and social services that function within narrow margins of safety and which show signs of strain at the seams with only 5 per cent of people aged 65 and over within institutions; (5) a policy that is intended within a few decades gradually to eliminate the forms of care for psycho-geriatric patients provided by the traditional type of mental hospital.

This situation calls for certain measures in the immediate future. First, facilities for community care for the aged, and the domiciliary services in particular, require immediate expansion if institutions are not to become gravely over-burdened, and serious encroachment upon the services available to the remainder of the population is to be avoided. Secondly, the projected phasing out of traditional mental hospitals cannot be proceeded with until alternative residential accommodation has been provided within the community; here the main need is for a network of small home-like units that are capable of providing satisfactory care for confused, wandering, intermittently disturbed, demented subjects who frequently suffer from incontinence.

Thirdly, further provision should be made of psycho-geriatric assessment units which can be rapidly established at relatively small cost, and in the present situation, make a contribution of particular value in a number of ways. When adequately staffed so that psychiatrists and geriatricians can combine their efforts with those of social workers, psychologists, occupational therapists, and physiotherapists, they are able to undertake the kind of multidisciplinary assessment that has formerly been lacking and that is essential for the planning of a programme of long-term management, tailored to individual needs. In carrying out these tasks the units already established have exerted a valuable integrative influence in bringing together representatives of local authority services, family doctors, with psychiatrists, geriatricians, social workers, psychologists, and other members of the therapeutic team.

When established in a setting free from the stigma of underprivilege and hopelessness that attach to any long-term units, they have been able to attract referrals at an early stage in the development of disability. This is of great importance for a number of reasons. There have, in the past, been very few opportunities for studying, in the early stages of their development disorders that culminate in severe dementia. However, there are compelling reasons for focusing attention on this stage of dementing processes. Although the evidence is not conclusive, it strongly suggests that the main forms of dementia represent a quantitative exaggeration or parody of the ordinary process of ageing. There are, however, threshold effects. The progressive and irreversible phase in the evolution of dementia commences when the aggregate of the damage passes beyond a certain threshold point. (Roth, 1967; Blessed *et al.*, 1968).

The accounts given in textbooks of medicine suggest that the states of dementia sometimes found in association with pernicious anaemia and myxoedema, among other causes, are reversed when the metabolic defect is corrected. In practice, mental deterioration is often little affected. Yet it might have responded at an earlier stage. Early assessment and intervention are also likely to reduce the proportion of 'crisis' admissions which preclude flexibility in making decisions about the long-term care of elderly people. It also reduces the risk that families who care for elderly, unmanageable, and incontinent patients reach such a pitch of strain, before such patients are admitted to hospital, that they are unwilling to contemplate having the old persons back.

Finally, careful screening procedures are essential to ensure that scarce hospital or sheltered accommodation is not taken up by those for whom home-care, backed by community services, would suffice. This is particularly important in cases for whom a place in a long-term unit is being considered. Although the staff of psycho-geriatric units will not be able to assess and plan disposal in every case, they can through their many contacts with local authorities and welfare departments (Kay, Roth, and Hall, 1966) define the criteria to be applied in disposal and disseminate the pattern among their colleagues.

It is relevant in this connection to draw attention to the large error that has emerged from previous surveys that have attempted to identify senile and arteriosclerotic dementia in their early stages. Experience should make it possible to reduce this error in future; the subject has important practical implications.

In a follow-up of 711 people aged 65 years and over, in Newcastle, 20 were found to have developed chronic brain syndromes 2–4 years after the initial interviews. In only 6 of these 20 had an early brain syndrome been originally suspected. In the remaining 14, initial low intelligence combined with a poor educational standard and long-standing personality difficulties had led to the original, probably erroneous suspicion of an early dementia (Table 5).

Inquiries needed for the planning and development of psycho-geriatric services

It is unlikely that any of the measures outlined will be put into effect at more than a moderate pace. In the meantime, it is essential to provide answers, derived from systematic investigation, to certain crucial questions. The results of screening programmes of elderly people and of early ascertainment require to be evaluated. Do they succeed, in the way suggested, in bringing to light disabilities in an early, treatable phase, and in this way reduce the burdens of chronic disablement and long-term institutionalization? Domiciliary services and the other components of 'lines of defence' within the community absorb a vast effort and the results of this demand investigation. It should prove possible, by making appropriate comparisons, to determine how far they succeed in their objectives, of prolonging the period in which disabled old people (and those with dementia in particular) are able to remain in the community and in averting institutionalization.

Finally, the optimum size and placement within the community of residential units for psycho-geriatric patients needs investigation. Most of those who have written on the subject have expressed themselves unequivocally in favour of the small home-like residence for 40–50 people. The advantages are many and obvious but the problems experienced by isolated small units have received too little attention. Diversification is difficult in a small unit, so that those who are quiet and relatively well for much of the time are constantly exposed to the most disturbed and sick. A small unit is unable to mount an adequate range of occupational and other facilities, sickness and absence among a limited staff is liable to precipitate crises and morale is prone to falter for other reasons. So joint staffing arrangements with neighbouring units may prove to be desirable. The problems entailed in organizing a large network of small units are likely to prove formidable; the resources needed, the staffing problems, and the results achieved need to be compared with those of larger *subdivided* units capable of providing for up to about 100 persons. It is accepted that as far as possible, homes should be located within the community; the advantages of some association with a nearby hospital service as well as practitioners tend to be ignored. Yet such an association makes possible more flexible staffing arrangements, crises are more readily dealt with, specialized investigations can be more easily arranged, and temporary transfer to an acute unit may present fewer problems. The possibility of involving helpers in an active way in the work of the different kinds of units also needs to be studied.

Such inquiries would be expensive but it is no exaggeration to say that there is a dire need for them; disablement in old age represents the largest single problem faced by the health and welfare services in affluent societies everywhere.

Psycho-geriatrics as a special branch of psychiatry?
The quality of the care provided by a service is determined to a considerable extent by the quality of the staff recruited to work in it and the extent to which their training has equipped them for their tasks. It is in the light of such considerations that the need for a special discipline of psycho-geriatrics has to be assessed.

A quarter of a century ago there was scepticism in many sections of the medical profession in the UK about the need to create a distinct geriatric branch of medicine. If the specialities recognized at the time had been as capable of dealing with the social challenge for geriatrics as they were skilled in coping with acute episodes of illness among the elderly, the geriatric specialty would probably not have come into existence. In the event, geriatricians have made a contribution of inestimable value in the care of the aged. They have among other things transformed the chronic institutions where old people who were often despondent, hopeless, apathetic, and unoccupied, and waited passively for death, into departments active in treatment, social rehabilitation, and community care.

In attempting to evaluate what has been achieved in the field of psycho-geriatrics in the light of the recommendations made by the WHO Expert Committee on the Mental Health Aspects of Ageing and the Aged, drafted some fifteen years ago, one is made sharply aware of the painful showness of progress. It will be apparent from the evidence presented that it is the organic psychiatric disorders (which create the most compelling demands for long-term care in institutions and which have been largely responsible for the steeply escalating needs for hospital and residential accommodation for the aged), that are likely to show a marked rise in prevalence during the next few decades. If family support declines, the social problem of this group of people will become acute.

Aged people with psychiatric disorder present for the mental health services a variety of issues ranging from clinical diagnosis which requires special skills, together with improved objective measures and the need for early ascertainment and treatment and the evaluation of the results of such endeavours. As far as institutional provision is concerned the present ignorance is also unacceptable for very little is known beyond crude estimates of the numbers of places needed; the type of environment required for the most effective and economic care of forgetful, deteriorating, confused, often incontinent old people needs to be determined with the aid of systematic observations and experiment.

There is also a new knowledge to be derived from the organic and functional disorders of the aged and the borderland between them. For some questions important for general psychiatry can probably be best explored in populations of elderly people with psychiatric disorders and defects. The need for a discipline of psycho-geriatrics will depend to a considerable measure upon the medical and social circumstances within each country and culture, but in the case of the UK there is the force of the example set by some hospitals which have established special departments of psycho-geriatrics to reinforce other arguments in favour of encouraging, at any rate, a proportion of psychiatrists to specialize in problems of the aged.

REFERENCES

Ashley, J. S. A., and Klein, R. E. (1971). 'The challenge of another million by 1991', *Modern Geriatrics,* **1** (5), 320–9.
Bergmann, K., Kay, D. W. K., Foster, E. M., McKechnie, A. A., and Roth, M. (1972). 'A follow-up study of randomly selected community residents to

assess the effects of chronic brain syndrome and cerebrovascular disease', Paper presented at the Fifth World Congress of Psychiatry held in Mexico, November 1971 (in press).

Blessed, G., Tomlinson, B. E., and Roth, M. (1968). 'The association between qualitative measures of dementia and of senile change in the cerebral grey matter of elderly subjects', *Br. J. Psychiat.* **114**, 797–811.

Britton, P. G., and Savage, R. D. (1966). 'A short form of the WAIS for use with the aged', ibid. **112**, 417–18.

Brothwood, J. (1971). 'The organisation and development of services for the aged with special reference to the mentally ill', in Kay, D. W. K., and Walk, A. (eds), *Recent Developments in Psychogeriatrics,* chap. ix, pp. 99–112 (RMPA, Ashford, Kent: Headley Brothers).

Darie, J. (1956). 'Problems of the aged in Europe', *United Nations European Seminar on Social Services for the Aged,* held in Liège, 1955 (Brussels: United Nations).

Department of Health and Social Security (1971). *Psychiatric Hospitals and Units in England and Wales,* Statistical Report Series no. 12 (London: HMSO).

Garside, R. F., Kay, D. W. K., and Roth, M. (1965). 'Old age mental disorders in Newcastle-on-Tyne, Part III. A factorial analysis of medical, psychiatric and social characteristics', *Br. J. Psychiat.* **111**, 939–46.

Grad, J. C., and Sainsbury, P. (1968). 'The effects that patients have on their families in a community care and a control psychiatric service. A two-year follow-up', ibid. **114**, 265–78.

Harris, A. (1968). *Social Welfare for the Elderly: A Study in Thirteen Local Authority Areas,* vol. 1, Government Social Survey, SS 366 (London: HMSO).

Isaacs, B. (1971). *Studies of Illness and Death in the Elderly in Glasgow,* Scottish Health Service Studies no. 17 (Edinburgh: Scottish Home and Health Department).

Kay, D. W. K., Beamish, P., and Roth, M. (1962). 'Some medical and social characteristics of elderly people under state care', in Halmos, P. (ed.), *The Sociological Review Monograph,* no. 5, pp. 173–93 (University of Keele).

—— —— —— (1964). 'Old age mental disorders in Newcastle upon Tyne, Part I: a study of prevalence', *Br. J. Psychiat.* **110**, 146–58.

—— —— —— (1964). 'Old age mental disorders in Newcastle upon Tyne, Part II: a study of possible social and medical causes', ibid. **110**, 668–82.

—— and Bergmann, K. (1966). 'Physical disability and mental health in old age', *J. Psychosom. Res.* **10**, 3–12.

—— —— Foster, E. M., McKechnie, A. A., and Roth, M. (1970). 'Mental illness and hospital usage in the elderly: a random sample followed-up', *Comprehens. Psychiat.* **2**, 26–35.

—— Roth, M., and Hall, M. R. P. (1966). 'Special problems of the aged and the organisation of hospital services', *Br. med. J.* **2**, 967–72.

Larsson, T., Sjögren, T., and Jacobson, G. (1963). 'Senile dementia', *Acta psychiat. Scand.* **39**, supplement 167 (Copenhagen: Munksgaard).

Lowenthal, M. F. (1964). 'Social isolation and mental illness in old age', *Am. soc. Rev.* **29**, 54–70.

McKeown, T., and Lowe, C. R. (1952). 'A scheme for the care of the aged and chronic sick', *Br. med. J.* **2**, 207–10.

Mezey, A. G., Hodkinson, H. M., and Evans, G. L. (1968). 'The elderly in the wrong unit', ibid. **3**, 16–18.

Ministry of Pensions and National Insurance (1966). *Financial and Other Circumstances of Retired Pensioners* (London: HMSO).

Moseley, L. G. (1968). 'Variations in socio-medical services for the aged', *Soc. and Econ. Admin.* **2,** 169–83.

Nunn, C., Kay, D. W. K., Roth, M., Bergmann, K., and Foster, E. M. (1972). 'The prediction of the development of organic brain syndrome and of death in a psychometrically-tested community sample of old people' (to be published).

Parkes, C. M. (1964). 'Recent bereavement as a cause of mental illness', *Br. J. Psychiat.* **110,** 198.

Richardson, I. M. (1964). *Age and Need: A Study of Older People in North-east Scotland* (London: Livingstone).

Roth, M., Tomlinson, B. E., and Blessed, G. (1967). 'The relationship between measures of dementia and of degenerative changes in the cerebral grey matter of elderly subjects', *Proc. R. Soc. Med.* **60,** 254–9.

Shanas, E., Townsend, P., Wedderburn, D., Früs, H., Milhoj, P., and Stenhouwer, J. (1965). *Old People in Three Industrial Societies* (London: Routledge & Kegan Paul).

Stevens, Barbara, C. (1972). 'Dependence of schizophrenic patients on elderly relatives', *Psychol. Med.* **2** (1), 17–32.

Townsend, P. (1957). *The Family Life of Old People* (London: Routledge).

—— and Wedderburn, D. (1965). *The Aged in the Welfare State* (London: G. Bell).

Tunstall, J. (1966). *Old and Alone: A Sociological Study of Old People* (London: Routledge & Kegan Paul).

Wigley, G. (1965). 'Community services for mentally infirm old People', *Lancet,* **ii,** 583–6.

World Health Organization (1959). *Mental Health Problems of Ageing and the Aged,* Sixth Report of the Expert Committee on Mental Health, Technical Report Series no. 171 (Geneva: WHO).

——(1972). 'Report of Working Group on Education and Training in Long-term Care, including Geriatrics', Florence, November 1970 (Geneva: WHO, to be published).

13 *Evaluating a service in Sussex*

PETER SAINSBURY and JACQUELINE GRAD DE ALARCON

Introduction

Surveys and epidemiological studies of mental illness in the elderly have been surprisingly few; they have, nevertheless, not only clearly shown a high prevalence but have drawn attention to the gross lack of hospital beds and other psychiatric services for the care of the aged. Nielsen (1962) in a survey of the prevalence of mental illness during a six-month period in the Island of Samö found that while 3 per cent of the population over 65 were referred for psychiatric treatment during this time, there were in fact 37·8 per cent who suffered from a recognizable mental illness; 6·8 per cent of the aged population were diagnosed as psychotic.

Kay, Beamish, and Roth carried out a similar but more extensive study in the city of Newcastle in 1964. Like Nielsen, they found a high prevalence: 26·3 per cent with a mental disorder of some kind and 8 per cent with a psychosis. They too point out that the number of cases looked after at home far exceeds those under hospital or other institutional care, the ratio of cases at home to institutional cases being 14: 1; fewer than one-fifth of cases with organic brain syndrome, were cared for in an institution.

Community psychiatry is seen by many as a remedy for this situation, and is now widely advocated both in the US and Britain. But this new enthusiasm has been accompanied by very few rigorously designed attempts to evaluate the effects of the new programmes or their effectiveness. Whereas it is generally accepted that drugs should be evaluated in accordance with recognized scientific and ethical principles, new services have not led to a corresponding set of rules for their assessment; even though their clinical effects may be quite as far reaching, and their consequences to others in the community may also be considerable. In this paper, we will attempt to outline the problems of method, and to illustrate them by referring to those that we encountered in an evaluation of a community psychiatric service in Chichester, in Sussex, and by discussing some of our findings.

The general problem of design and methods in evaluating services

The aims of service evaluation may be broadly classified as assessing:

1. What is provided: the number of kinds of sick people who are in contact with the different amenities provided by the services; ie the clinical and social characteristics of patients and their families. This will entail determining rates of referral, discharge, and duration of contacts with the amenities in a population.

2. What is needed: prevalence and incidence studies to assess the numbers of the mentally ill, their needs, those of their families, and of others in the population.

3. The extent to which needs are met: the effectiveness of the services in meeting these needs; and conversely what burdens they place on the patient, his family, and others in the community; studies of who gets treated where, etc.

4. Standards of care: the quality of care provided for different kinds of patients and type of care most appropriate to each; consumer satisfaction and attitude studies.

5. Efficiency of services: ie the adequacy of the service in relation to its resources, in personnel, money, and material provisions, or in terms of cost benefit of the alternative forms of care.

6. Social and clinical outcome: the therapeutic efficacy of different forms of care (cf clinical trials).

7. Service morale: the attitudes, workload, and satisfaction of those providing the service.

The evaluator will usually be asked to assess the effects of introducing new services or new policies on one or other of these aspects. This may not be as straightforward as it sounds, because those innovating new policies, for example, government health departments, do not always define their goals very precisely, or ask questions pertinent to the implications of their policies. So it may fall to the research workers and personnel providing the service to formulate those questions, that are likely to have most social, clinical, or administrative relevance.

In our experience, aims can rather easily get out of hand; they should be stated very precisely and be feasible from the point of view of available research methods and designs. The aims should also be few; many projects become unmanageable because they attempt too much. But once the aims are clear the criteria for selecting cases and the attributes of the service that will need to be studied will follow. Thus, an evaluation may be restricted to samples of patients within defined age, clinical, or social categories; for example, the course of dementia in those over 65 and attending day-hospitals, may be compared with a matched sample being cared for in a mental hospital. Such a comparison is closely analogous to a clinical trial, with type of care instead of drug as the independent variable.

But if the working of the service, as a whole, is aimed at, then the complete range of referred cases will need to be included. To answer such questions as how does the introduction of extramural facilities affect the rates of referral of the elderly; or what categories of the aged is it possible to treat at home; and what are the needs of their families if they are; then every old person seen by the service will have to be included. To answer questions of this kind, the social and demographic characteristics of the population of the area from which the patients are drawn must also be obtained; because only then can the referral and admission rates of the various groups be compared, or the extent to which services are meeting the community's needs assessed. The research worker who wishes to evaluate a service will therefore have to avail himself of the methods of the epidemiologist as well as those developed in clinical trials if the operation of the service as well as the outcome of the patient's illness are his goals.

Criteria of evaluation

First, and most important, in any evaluation the investigators must define the standards by which the service is to be measured. These may be set out in terms of patients' needs; cost efficiency; time spent in treatment; staff satisfaction; consumer or patient satisfaction; clinical outcome or social outcome. Clearly, some of these items are more easily measured than others, but few generally accepted standard measures are available. Thus, which ever aspects are chosen the standards used must be clearly defined by the investigator and this may well involve designing and pretesting new instruments to measure the effectiveness of the service. Here we should note a common source of confusion when the evaluation or comparison of services is being discussed. It is the expectation that an evaluation will demonstrate one service as superior to, or 'better' than, the other, when clearly the real problem and purpose of the evaluator is to determine those social and clinical characteristics of patients and the circumstances of their families that make it possible to predict the type of facility in which a favourable outcome is probable: who, for example, are the sort of patients that do well in hospital and who benefit from home care? It is most unlikely that one kind of care will be consistently superior to another, and it is pointless to attempt to approach the problem in this way. The evaluation must, therefore, be designed to show which category of patient or household benefits from which type of facility.

Setting up a register

In a comprehensive community psychiatric service the cases will be in contact with a variety of facilities: hostels, day-hospitals, domiciliary visits, etc. If each contact is centrally recorded by making returns to a cumulative case-register, this will enable basic identifying, personal, clinical, and social data to be obtained in a standardized form. This invaluable epidemiological tool will avoid duplication of cases; it will also allow details of a subsequent events and contacts with the different facilities within the service to be accumulated; or whatever information is appropriate to the aim of the evaluation such as cost, social welfare needs, and so on.

In addition, a case-register provides a sampling frame, and this has a number of very useful functions: it will enable the investigator to construct stratified samples, or permit random samples to be drawn for more intensive study. In Chichester, for instance, we wanted to examine in detail the effects on the family of an unselected sample of the referrals to the service and then follow these through two years to assess their outcome. Furthermore, the register permits matching of patient groups, which is often essential when comparisons are to be made between patients referred to differing services or between those referred to different facilities within a service; they often need to be matched on severity of illness, for example. How this might be achieved will be dealt with presently.

Selecting a control

A further problem is that of finding some standard against which to compare the service under scrutiny: in other words some form of control. There are three possible alternatives; one is to compare data on patients before and after the introduction of the service. For information that is consistently and reliably recorded, such as patient suicides, or admission and discharge dates, this is an appropriate procedure, and one which we used to assess the effect of the service on the incidence of suicide in elderly patients. But for most purposes the earlier data will not have been consistently recorded in the required form, in which case comparisons must be made either with a service in another district or by dividing the service being evaluated into two, so that one half operates in accordance with the new policy and the other maintains the old one.

This raises another and related matter: the feasibility of using an experimental design customary with a clinical trial, in which cases are randomly allocated to an experimental and control group. In operational research this is very often, but not necessarily, impracticable; and in some circumstances not altogether desirable. There is often a need to study the service under the actual conditions of its operation, that is under real working conditions. The investigator must then devise appropriate strategies for doing this. But in this more complex situation he will need much more data on all the cases in order to be able to parcel out the effects of the many independent variables that may be accounting for any differences he aims to observe between the two forms of care. In our evaluation, therefore, we did our best to include data on those variables, as far as we could anticipate them, which might be determining a difference.

Limiting the variables examined

Next, bearing in mind the aims of the evaluation, there is the problem of selecting and categorizing the items that will be systematically recorded on each patient and ensuring as far as possible that they can be objectively defined and reliably obtained. These requirements will tend to limit what can be usefully recorded and will often mean relinquishing many cherished items. These items will describe the characteristics of the patient and the outcome of his illness; the circumstances of his family; the features of the services; or other variables relevant to the aspect of the services it is intended to assess.

Deciding on methods of recording and analysis

The reliability and objectivity with which information may be obtained are not the only factors that will limit the number and type of items that are included in the evaluation. An essential early step in designing an evaluation is to review the sources that are available for data collection, processing, and analysis. For example, if interviewing and clerical personnel are readily available but computing facilities poor, the investigator should guard against collecting masses of data which he will not be able to analyse. The nature of the final statistical analysis will also determine not only the number of cases (to enable the required breakdown to be made); but also the form of the questions. For example, they will best be rated if a discriminate function is proposed. So statistical decisions have to be taken when the study is being planned, which will place certain limitations on the information recorded.

Administration

Two final points: the first is the need to ensure that the research team undertaking the evaluation is independent of the service personnel providing it. Nevertheless, they need to collaborate harmoniously; which brings us to the other point. A major consideration is the efficient administration and organization of a project of this kind, not only to ensure that the standards of recording and the time schedule of the research are strictly maintained, but also that the willing participation of those providing the service is actively promoted by regular meetings, explanations, and a readiness to meet their criticisms and difficulties.

The service in Sussex

A community psychiatric service was introduced in Chichester in 1958, an administrative district of Sussex with a population of 120,000. Dr Morrissey, the clinical director of the service, summarized its purposes as follows: To reduce admission to the district mental hospital, Graylingwell, which had become overcrowded, and to explore alternatives to admission for the increasing numbers of geriatric patients; next, to reduce institutionalism by facilitating discharge; to select the type of disposition, whether admission or extramural care, best suited to the needs of the patient and his family; and lastly, to test the assumption that treatment given in the patient's usual social or family setting, other things being equal, is beneficial.

Community programmes vary considerably in their objectives and organization. Common to them all is the extension of the psychiatric services of a district to patients outside the mental hospital and their integration with the other medical or social facilities; provision for the early recognition, treatment, after-care, and where possible, prevention of mental illness are the purposes shared by all schemes of community care. The ways, however, in which the hospital, GPs, public health and other welfare services collaborate to ensure continuity of care differ widely. The distinguishing features of the Chichester services were these: It was managed by the staff of the mental hospital; and initially its emphasis was on home and extramural treatment in close collaboration with the GPs, rather than with the local county welfare services; consequently, it has promoted clinical more than social care. All referrals were first seen at home, at the day-hospital or out-patient clinic before a decision was taken to give treatment in hospital or extramurally; but flexibility was maintained so that the disposal would be changed later if clinical or family factors required. The fact that in Chichester the therapeutic emphasis was directed more towards providing *clinical* rather than *social* support to patients and their families may be a regretted shortcoming, but it was an extramural service nonetheless: in Chichester only 23 per cent of all patients over 65 were admitted to the mental hospital at referral compared with 68 per cent in Salisbury.

The aims of the evaluation

These were:

1. To see how the introduction of the service affects who gets referred to the psychiatrist. Are GPs, for example, more ready to refer depressed, elderly patients to a community than a hospital-based service; are there any particular clinical or social groups who benefit by earlier referral to such a service?

2. To examine how the introduction of the service affects who gets admitted and who gets treated extramurally. Are the bed needs for psychiatric patients different in a 'community' service? Are some patients spared admission altogether? Does the hospital now cater mainly for the acutely ill or are short illnesses treated extramurally leaving the hospital with a heavier load of chronic long-stay patients?

3. To examine the extent to which the patient's family is affected by this policy. Treatment in the community introduces a novel element, because

the patient's family and his neighbourhood will now be closely concerned with the patient's care, and affected by it. Consequently evaluative studies will often need not only to assess the effects on *them* as well as on the patient, but also their needs and whether these are met. The problem of evaluating a service is therefore a complex one. Not only do we wish to know whether the new services benefit the patient more than the policy it supersedes, but also whether it burdens those in the community most closely associated with the patient; and his family or household will claim first consideration.

4. To examine the effect of the new policy on the patient's clinical outcome.

Method and design

The design of the study was to compare all patients referred to the different psychiatric facilities in two districts: one with a community service (Chichester) and the other with a more traditional hospital-based service in which the majority of patients were directly admitted (Salisbury). The two populations at risk were demographically similar and the only psychiatric facilities available to each were those provided by their respective services. The resources available to each were also alike.

Since we aimed to study the effects of the service as a whole it was necessary to include all referrals from the catchment area populations. This also allowed us to calculate the rates of referral, of admission, and rates of contact with the different facilities for specific categories of patients and thereby to answer the first two questions by comparing with the control service in Salisbury.

Case-registers were set up and standardized social and clinical data were recorded by the service psychiatrist on all new patients referred to each service during one year. In order to obtain measures of household characteristics and of the family's burden, the homes of a 1 : 3 sample were visited in both services and the effects on selected aspects of the family and household rated. A second visit was made two years later and the changes in the families' burden ratings recorded. The clinical and social outcomes were assessed on a number of measures at the follow-up visit; a record of all contacts with the service during the two years was also accumulated on the case-registers.

Since random allocation of cases to the two services was not a practical proposition, nor could it have been done without affecting the operation of the services being studied, comparisons between them was only possible if enough data was obtained on every referral in order to match them on intervening variable, such as *severity of illness,* which it was particularly important to allow for in assessing outcome. We therefore first compared the referrals to Chichester and Salisbury on severity of illness in the usual way by seeing how well they matched on clinical characteristics. We went

Table 1. *Populations referral and admission rates in the two services.*

	Chichester	Salisbury
All patients referred in experimental period	823	585
Patients aged 65+ referred in experimental period	216	121
Sample aged 65+ for follow-up study	85	34
Cohort aged 65+ surviving after two years	46	19
Annual referral rate per 1,000 aged 65+	8·3	5·7
Annual admission rate per 1,000 aged 65+	3·6	4·2

one step further, however, by obtaining a family problem score for each case on a scale whose reliability had been satisfactorily established. Our assumption was that the number of problems, such as the hours spent nursing the patient, his effects on the family's leisure activities, on children in the household, etc., would relate closely to the severity of illness and afford a more appropriate measure of it. In the event, the Chichester and Salisbury patients, when first seen, were surprisingly closely matched on family problem scores, and so, we inferred, on severity of illness.

Patients were followed up for two years. To assess outcome and thus compare the achievements of the community and the control psychiatric service, we used the following clinical and social measures:

1. Clinical measures:

(a) Mortality rates.

(b) The service psychiatrist's rating of outcome at the end of treatment or at follow-up.

(c) An independent psychiatrist's rating of outcome at a follow-up interview.

2. Measures of consumer satisfaction:

(a) A self-rating of improvement by the patient.

(b) A rating of improvement by the patient's GP.

(c) A rating of improvement by the patient's closest relative.

3. Measures of social cost. A measure of the reduction of problems caused for the family by the patient's illness at the end of the two-year follow-up compared with the situation at referral.

Pilot studies were undertaken to establish the reliability of the clinical data and such family burden ratings as the effects on the occupation of family members, on their income, health, time spent with patient, their welfare needs and other items that could be objectively recorded.

Some results

Effect of the new service on referral rates

To find out what influence community care had on referrals we examined the differences between the rates in Chichester and Salisbury. The annual referral rate to the Chichester service was 8·3 per 1,000 population, whereas in Salisbury it was 5·7 (Table 1). Fig. 1 shows that while the

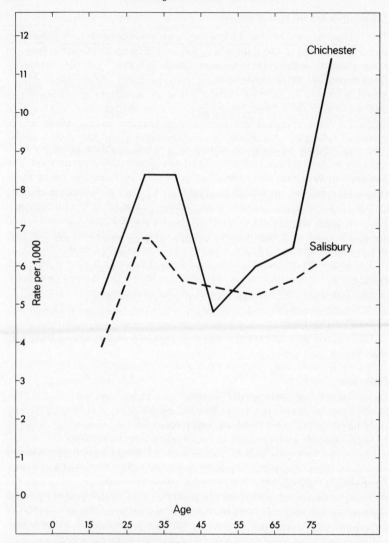

Figure 1. Total referral rates for 1960.

community service had a higher rate for all 10-year age-groups except one. this difference is especially prominent for the aged. Thus the rate for those over 75 years was 11·3 in Chichester and 6·2 in Salisbury. We therefore examined the distribution of clinical and social characteristics that were particularly associated with this higher referral rate in the community service.

Diagnosis and duration of illness

The higher referral rate in Chichester was maintained for all diagnostic categories (Table 2) and therefore was not due to increased referral of more patients with minor disorders. It was, however, particularly marked for depressive illness (endogenous and reactive). There was also a significant trend for patients in the community service to be referred at an earlier stage in their illness than were those in the Salisbury service (see Table 3). While this was not sufficient to account for the whole of the excess of referrals in Chichester, it is nevertheless important in view of the above mentioned preponderance of depressive illness being referred.

Sex and marital state

While the referral rate for both sexes was higher in Chichester than in Salisbury, this difference was not statistically significant except for women aged 75 years and over, where the rate was 12·8 in Chichester and 6·6 in Salisbury. There was no difference between referral rates of married people in Chichester and Salisbury, but the single and widowed had significantly higher rates in the community service, and, again, especially for women (Table 4).

The indications so far are first, that patients are likely to be referred earlier in a community service; secondly, that old women living without the support of a spouse have a greater likelihood of being referred if there is a community service; and thirdly, that this applies particularly to both single men and women suffering from a depression.

Other social factors

Other factors influencing the significantly higher referral rate in the community service were mode of living, social class, and district. Elderly men living alone were referred more often in the community service. Referral rates for elderly males in social classes IV and V were higher also in Chichester and there was also an excess of referrals from urban districts especially from Bognor, a resort town to which the elderly retire. Furthermore, significantly more men over 65 with a diagnosis of depression were referred from Bognor than the other towns. So the community seems to be recruiting more of the underprivileged and lonely old people with psychoses whom the GPs did not previously refer. While the shortage of beds for psycho-geriatric patients is acute in both services, it seems probable that GPs are more likely to refer patients when they know that domiciliary visits and treatment outside the hospital are routinely undertaken for geriatric patients.

Effect of the service on admission rates

The next question was who gets admitted in a community service and who treated at home. We found first, that although the two populations of

Table 2. *Referral rates of patients aged 65 and over per 1,000 population for three diagnostic categories.*

Diagnosis	Chichester	Salisbury
Organic	3·9	3·0
Functional*	3·3	2·1
Neuroses and other*	1·1	0·6
Total†	8·3	5·7

* $p<0.05$, df 1. † $p<0.01$, df 1.

Table 3. *Referral rates of patients with illnesses of differing duration.*

Duration of symptoms before referral	Rate per 1,000 population aged 65+	
	Chichester	Salisbury
0–6 months*	4·8	2·8
6 months–2 years	1·1	0·7
2+ years	2·5	2·0

* $p<0.01$, df 1.

Table 4. *Rates per 1,000 population of referrals aged 65 and over by marital status.*

Marital status	Chichester	Salisbury
Married	5·7	5·5
Single*	12·6	5·8
Widowed*	10·2	5·9
All referrals aged 65 and over*	8·3	5·7

* $p = 0.01$, df 1.

Table 5. *Use of hospital beds by the two services (percentage).*

	Chichester (N = 85)	Salisbury (N = 34)
At referral		
Admitted to mental hospital	23	68
Admitted to other institutions	19	8
Remain at home	57	24
During two-year follow-up		
Ever admitted to mental hospital	52	79
Weeks spent in hospital by admitted patients only (mean)	29	42

Table 6. *Effects on families when patients were first referred (percentage).*

Burden rating	Chichester (N = 85)	Salisbury (N = 34)
None	21	15
Some	39	44
Severe	40	41

elderly patients were comparable clinically, the proportion admitted to hospital from each was affected by the policy of the area psychiatric service. In Chichester, only 23 per cent of all patients over 65 years were admitted to mental hospital at referral, compared with 68 per cent in Salisbury. During a two-year follow-up, this difference decreased but still remained significant, 52 per cent of the original cohort being admitted in Chichester compared with 79 per cent in Salisbury (see Table 5).

Two comments on the more detailed breakdown of the disposal of elderly patients are of interest. The first is that *nursing homes* are used twice as frequently in the community service. Nursing homes will apparently accept mentally disturbed geriatric patients if a psychiatrist is available to visit them. The second is that *treatment at home* with the psychiatrist visiting is used more for geriatrics than any other group of patients, an arrangement which their families usually preferred.

When we came to look at which kind of patient was admitted to hospital, admitted to a nursing home, attended the day-hospital, or treated at home, we found that men, those who are poorest and suffering from organic psychoses are *admitted to hospital;* the elderly widowed with dementias who lived in hotels *go into nursing homes;* the moderately well-off living with their children get *treated at home;* and those aged below 70 who are single, living alone, or with someone other than a relative, and suffering from depressive illness are preferentially *treated in the day-hospital.*

In both areas social as well as clinical factors influenced admission, and one of the most interesting findings was that geriatric patients were preferentially admitted if they lived in hotels and boarding-houses or with non-relatives. This is in accordance with Gruenberg's findings on multi-family dwellings (Gruenberg, 1953). In Chichester, where alternative disposals (day-hospital, domiciliary care, and community nursing homes) were exploited to the fullest possible extent, social factors were more clearly affecting the patient's disposal. Thus males, patients of social classes IV and V, those with low incomes and housing problems, and those who were rated as being a burden on their families, were preferentially admitted. However, elderly patients who lived alone did not have an increased likelihood of entering the mental hospital. Social and family

Table 7. *Specific effects on family at referral of patients aged 65 and over (percentage).*

Effect on family	Families (N = 119)		
	Some effect	Severe effect	Total burden
Mental health	31	32	63
Social and leisure activities	13	37	50
Physical health	35	3	38
Domestic routine	13	23	36
Employment (N = 67)	6	6	12
Income	13	6	19

circumstances that favoured treatment in the community were a satisfactory income, living with relatives, not being over 70, and a depressive illness.

The average number of weeks spent in hospital by the 1 : 3 sample of geriatric patients who survived the two years and were *admitted* during this period was 29 weeks in the community and 42 weeks in the control service; in spite of admitting fewer patients, community care made a short stay possible (see Table 5). Accumulation of long-stay patients: at the end of two years 21 per cent were in hospital and 17 per cent in nursing homes in Chichester, in Salisbury 37 per cent were in hospital.

Effect of the service on families

At referral no differences were found between the burden ratings of families in the two services (Table 6); but in both, the patient was causing very considerable hardship to the others: the health, income, occupation, and domestic routine of the family were all substantially affected. It is therefore clear that families with a mentally ill member who are not receiving medical or social support carry a very heavy burden (Table 7). After two years, however, families had been equally relieved in both services (Table 8); the community service in short was as successful as the control both in relieving families and also in the relief it gave to families when the geriatric patient was treated exclusively in the community throughout the two years. The families' welfare needs were estimated at referral and compared with the social work actually done during the two years (Table 9); we found that the community service was providing less social support than the control, and that failure to relieve the family burden could often be ascribed to this; the psychiatrist making the home visits, while recognizing serious family problems, was failing to notice the less conspicuous ones. It can be inferred from Tables 8 and 9 (and this was confirmed by other data we obtained) that the psychiatrist is able to recognize when a family is severely burdened and deals with this by admitting him; but he fails to make the skilled assessment that enables a

Table 8. *Families relieved after two years* (percentage).*

Rating at referral	Chichester (N = 46)	Salisbury (N = 19)
Some burden	70	92
Severe burden	80	33
		(N = 3)
Any burden	74	80

* Cohort of psycho-geriatric patients still alive with surviving families after two years.

social worker to recognize lesser social stresses in the home. Consequently, these circumstances were usually left unremedied in Chichester with adverse consequences to both patient and family. The comparison between the two services might have favoured Chichester more if social support had been better organized.

Outcome

Mortality

The death-rate over two years was identical in the two services, but the findings on suicides are more important, as a common misgiving about community care is that it may expose the patient to this risk. Walk obtained the incidence of suicide among all geriatric patients within a year of contact with the service. When their suicide rates during the five years before and after the introduction of the community service were compared the incidence of suicide in the elderly had decreased significantly. It would therefore seem that extending psychiatric services to the aged, especially those who were living alone, is protective.

Clinical ratings

Findings of outcome rated by the two psychiatrists and by symptom remission are given in Table 10. According to the psychiatrist's ratings the community service did not achieve as good an outcome for psychogeriatric patients as did the hospital-oriented one. This is a finding which should be accepted with some reservations as, although as far as we were able to judge the two groups were roughly matched on severity of illness at referral, there were in fact significantly more patients aged over 75 in Chichester and these were possibly a more severely ill group to begin with.

This is borne out by the findings on symptom remission. While the community service reported less success with the symptoms of organic deterioration, they were significantly more successful with depression: the symptom, *par excellence*, which psychiatrists would expect to treat successfully in old age.

Table 9. *Social work done in the two services (percentage).*

	Patients 65+ years	
Type of work	Chichester (N = 85)	Salisbury (N = 34)
Social assessment made	5	21
Support, advice, or casework given	7	26
Help with employment problems	0	3
Rehabilitation arranged	0	0
Help with housing or money problems	6	12
Help with children or domestic problems	1	0
Institutional placement	12	6

Table 10. *Clinical outcome (percentage).*

	Chichester (N = 48)	Salisbury (N = 19)
Independent psychiatrist's rating		
Mental illness is absent or mild	56	84
Mental illness is moderate or severe	44	16
Service psychiatrist's rating		
Recovered or much improved	41	63
Unchanged or little improved	58	37
Symptom remission		
Agitation	80	83
Depression	71	39
Retardation	73	83
Loss of concentration	93	83
Insomnia	72	88
Loss of memory	9	40
Confusion	20	60
Disorientation	0	25

Table 11. *Consumer ratings of outcome (percentage).*

	Chichester	Salisbury
Patient's ratings		
Recovered or much improved	63	81
Some improvement or unchanged	37	19
Informant's ratings		
Recovered or much improved	46	55
Some improvement or unchanged	54	45
GP's ratings		
Recovered or much improved	52	63
Some improvement or unchanged	48	36

Table 12. *Outcome of psycho-geriatric patients in Chichester and Salisbury after two years.*

Outcome measures	Findings
1. Research psychiatrist's rating of mental state at follow-up	Better in Salisbury
2. Treating psychiatrist's rating of improvement	Better in Salisbury
3. Patient's rating of improvement	Better in Salisbury
4. Relative's rating of improvement	No difference
5. GP's rating of improvement	No difference
6. Rating of symptom remission	Better in Chichester (more depression remits)
7. Rating by social cost (burden on family)	No difference
8. Death-rate	No difference
9. Suicide rate	Decreased in Chichester

Ratings by patient, family member, and general practitioner (Table 11)

There was also a trend for patients to report more improvement in Salisbury but this was not significant and according to relatives and GPs similar proportions of the patients had improved in both services.

Table 12 summarizes the findings on outcome and leads us to conclude that the community care in Chichester was, on the whole, surprisingly successful with geriatric patients. The increased referral rate of old people and the decrease in their suicide following its introduction are encouraging evidence of the benefits of improved extramural facilities. Moreover, considering how haphazard the organization of social support was in Chichester, patients and their families did surprisingly well; but why they did not do better was also apparent. The Chichester service relied too much on the visiting psychiatrist's assessment of the family situation and too little on the social worker's. Nevertheless, we found the disposal recommended in Chichester was more in keeping with the wishes of families than was the case in Salisbury, and we were impressed by the families' readiness to cope with the old, particularly when arrangements were made to admit her while the family took a holiday.

Conclusions

Our findings draw attention to four aspects in organizing a community psychiatric service. The first is the importance of supplementing clinical care of the patient with regular social support to the family because when the family's problems were recognized, Chichester did as well as the control, but not otherwise. The needs of families must therefore be carefully assessed not only on referral but throughout the course of the patient's illness, otherwise the adverse effects which we had observed on over-burdened families, especially on their mental health, may add to rather than subtract from the community's mental health problem. Given these provisos community care can be as effective as hospital care.

Secondly, it is possible to reduce the number of psychiatric beds in this age-group without necessarily affecting the community adversely according to our measures. This was achieved in Chichester, notably for patients over 65 years, by the ready availability of psychiatrists in the community to visit patients at home and by their close collaboration with GPs. Since the biggest demands on beds is for geriatric patients, and since these patients presented the most severe problems to their families, the success of the Chichester service in reducing this demand without positively increasing family burden is notable.

Thirdly, expanding the extramural services of the district psychiatric hospital leads to an increase in the referral rate of psycho-geriatric patients. This increase in referral is not restricted to patients with milder disorders but, as we have shown, the community service provides for the high-risk groups: more psychotic patients, more socially isolated, and otherwise socially deprived patients appear earlier in their illness for treatment.

Finally, the study of admission rates in the two services has shown that social as well as clinical considerations appear to be important in selecting the most appropriate disposal for different categories of patients. The community-oriented service with its greater flexibility and range of facilities is more able to fit the disposal to the needs of the patient and his family. However, the increased provision for psycho-geriatric patients is only made possible by treating a large proportion of them at home and by giving families the support and practical help they need to do this without being unduly burdened.

14 *Evaluating a service in Lausanne*

J. WERTHEIMER, P. GILLIAND, L. BIRCHER, and M. PERIER

Vaud is a French-speaking, Protestant canton in the western part of Switzerland, with a population of about 500,000, the Lausanne region alone accounting for some 250,000. Geographically, from west to east, we can distinguish three regions: the Jura, constituting the frontier with France; the Plateau, stretching from Lake Geneva to the Lake of Neuchâtel; and the Pre-Alps. The greater part of the territory is devoted to farming and vineyards, with very little industry. Lausanne is essentially a university and tourist centre.

So far as psychiatry is concerned, Vaud has been divided since 1968 into four sectors, each one served by a hospital. The central sector, comprising the Lausanne region, has about 250,000 inhabitants, while the others have about 80,000 each. The sectors are still in the process of organization, with a view to incorporating juvenile, adult, and geriatric psychiatric services. So far as geriatrics is concerned, only the central sector can be regarded as fully organized, since it has a psycho-geriatric hospital and has facilities for specialized consultation.

Psychiatric hospitalization in the canton has been studied from two points of view: detailed analysis of the records of patients discharged in 1950, 1960, and 1966 and a census in 1968 of the patients hospitalized in all the institutions in the canton.

Hospitalization rates are higher in the urban milieu. For every diagnostic group but oligophrenia, they have increased greatly since 1950. The age-related increase has been considerable. The under-hospitalization of women in 1950 has given way to over-hospitalization, as less shame is attached to going to a psychiatric hospital. The records of civil status are revealing, rates being low for married people. Divorce and widowhood have a pronounced effect, especially for men, with rates considerably above average.

A very small number of cases occupy the greatest number of beds. The patient who enters when he is young will either stay for a very short time or will spend the rest of his life in the institution. Elderly patients generally remain for an intermediate period. The comprehensive census revealed that three inhabitants out of 1,000 were in psychiatric institutions. The distribution of beds occupied on a given date in 1968 showed that one-fifth of the cases were psycho-organic.

Ageing of the population has become the essential factor in medical and hospital planning, since elderly people are highly dependent from the medicosocial point of view.

The increasing importance of geriatrics is a direct consequence.

If there were no change in the techniques and means for delivering care, the ageing of the population, for a given number of inhabitants, would result in an increase in the average morbidity rate and call for more and more hospital beds. Ageing modifies the distribution of patients, according to age and the types of service required.

This presents a challenge to the structure of the hospital network. Thus, proceeding from the demographic pattern of 1960 to one which is possible in the next two or three decades, characterized by a life expectancy of 74 years, taking both sexes together, the pressure would theoretically call for more than a two-thirds increase for psycho-organic cases. Furthermore, to avoid institutionalization, the whole concept of the psychiatric hospital network must take into account both therapeutic progress and the structural changes which are now under way. The continuity required in caring for psychiatric patients calls for decentralization of installations, 'sectorization', the setting up of institutions of limited dimensions for chronic patients, extension of home-care and assistance, preventive services, and integration of hospital and ambulatory treatment.

Some of the 1966–8 figures indicate the extent and character of the changing needs:

1. People more than 65 years old constitute about 13 per cent of the total population of Vaud, that is to say, 1 person in every 8.

2. Elderly patients, however, occupy 40 per cent of the beds: 2 beds out of 5.

3. Elderly people require about 1 bed out of every 2 in rest homes, nursing homes, etc.

The average daily rate of occupation of beds by elderly people is four times the average.

The first psycho-geriatric institution to be established by the State of Vaud was the Cery Geriatric Hospital, set up within the framework of the Lausanne Psychiatric Clinic. One-third of this 150-bed institution is devoted to men and two-thirds to women. The minimum age for admission is 65 years. Its purpose, when it was opened, was to provide care for elderly people with psychiatric disorders coming from every part of the canton, its essential role being limited to urgent cases. It very soon fell victim, however, to the generally unsatisfactory condition of the existing infrastructure. Medicosocial institutions accepting difficult cases were and still are rare. From the very outset, therefore, the discharging of dependent patients proved to be difficult. Economic factors were obviously important, since rest homes accepting highly dependent patients often set such high rates that even middle-class families found it difficult to meet them. This imposed additional limits on the possibilities for discharge. Furthermore, when the hospital was established, both general and psychiatric home-care services were inadequate. Abusive hospital admissions were one consequence of this. These fell into two main categories.

The first consisted of essentially social problems which might consist of nothing more than unsatisfactory home conditions. In these situations, analysis of the problem could very well take place outside hospital and lead to a direct solution of the placement problem.

The second category consisted of cases of sub-acute psychic decompensation which could be treated at home if adequate medicosocial support were provided. The geriatric hospital was therefore soon deluged with extremely difficult psycho-organic cases. This made it impossible for the hospital to perform its original role, to take urgent cases only and to carry out intensive readaptation treatment with a view to placement. The resulting paralysis presented the distraught therapeutic team with a disastrous hospital situation: caused by deficiencies external to the hospital.

The creation of a psycho-geriatric out-patient centre in Lausanne in 1968 was designed to provide a partial remedy for this unsatisfactory state of affairs. This polyclinic should be recognized as an indispensable complement to the activity of the geriatric hospital. Its objectives may be summed up as follows:

1. To provide medical and nursing care at home or in medicosocial institutions and contribute to maintaining the patient for as long a time as possible in his own milieu. In this way, hospitalization may either be avoided, postponed, or shortened.

2. To examine applications for admission, in co-operation with the responsible physician, and thereupon to assume responsibility, if necessary, for the medicosocial problems which only a team is equipped to deal with.

3. To encourage the assumption of responsibility for the case by a homogeneous organization which is in charge of both hospital and extra-hospital activities.

4. To contribute to better psycho-geriatric training of residents giving them responsibilities in the hospital and for consultations and home visits. They are thus enabled to follow a patient before, during, and after his stay in the hospital.

To sum up the activity of the Cery Geriatric Hospital, Table 1 recapitulates admissions, discharges, and deaths from 1967 to 1971.

This is the only institution in the canton specializing in psycho-geriatric care. Although it should cover only the central sector, the Lausanne agglomeration, it is also forced to deal with the needs of the other three

Table 1. *Movement of patients at the Cery Geriatric Hospital, 1967–71.*

Year	Admissions	Discharges	Deaths
1967	152	125	69
1968	174	140	80
1969	206	150	95
1970	208	139	107
1971	178	137	93

Table 2. *Distribution of the centre's patients by age-groups (percentage).*

<65 years	8
65–70 years	13
70–80 years	40
>80 years	39

sectors. It comprises 6 divisions of 25 beds each, including 3 divisions for women (2 for intensive care and 1 devoted to stabilized patients), 1 male division for relatively independent patients, and 2 mixed divisions for intensive care. Of the 150 beds, 120 are blocked by chronic patients whom we cannot place elsewhere, for various reasons. Among these reasons are: disorientation with a risk of fugue, necessitating an enclosed milieu; a condition of advanced dementia with complete functional dependence; serious behavioral conditions; incontinence (66 cases as of 31 December 1971).

Our admissions therefore are concerned only with 30 beds, except for those freed by deaths.

As Table 1 shows, the number of admissions increased sharply from 1967 to 1969, going down by thirty between 1970 and 1971. This drop resulted from the fact that an institution for chronic patients, in which we had been placing an average of thirty cases per year, temporarily halted its admissions. We also note that the number of discharges remained relatively stable, but that deaths increased considerably after 1967, due to the overrunning of the hospital by very serious cases.

This study will concern itself with an analysis of the activities of the psycho-geriatric out-patient centre.

The centre occupies a ten-room apartment in the heart of Lausanne. When it was established it employed 1 full-time doctor, 3 part-time doctors, 1 social worker, and 1 secretary. At present, its medical team overlaps with that of the geriatric hospital, most of the doctors working part-time in both services. There are 10 members of the team, including a medical director, an internist serving as a part-time deputy, 2 chief residents, and 6 interns. There are 3 specialized psychiatric nurses who assist the doctors in consultations and who carry out home visits. In addition we have 2 social workers, 2 psychologists, and 2 secretaries. Each of the geriatric hospital's 2 ergotherapists devotes a half-afternoon each week to groups of ambulatory patients.

In principle, the centre should serve only the Lausanne agglomeration, but here again, the three other sectors still lack separate psycho-geriatric services, so the centre must help make up for these deficiencies so far as its resources permit. One decentralized consultation is held for one half-day every week in the eastern zone at Montreux.

Table 3. *Civil status in relation to age.*

Age	Not given	Unmarried	Married	Divorced	Widowed	Separated	Total	%
50–54	—	1	3	1	—	—	5	—
55–59	—	5	17	2	3	1	28	2
60–64	—	9	40	2	16	2	69	6
65–69	—	24	64	13	61	1	163	13
70–74	1	36	85	17	85	4	228	19
75–79	1	38	88	13	106	5	251	21
80–84	1	44	59	13	152	4	273	23
85–89	2	19	17	2	98	—	138	11
90–94	—	12	10	3	26	—	51	4
95–99	—	1	—	—	10	—	11	1
Total	5	189	383	66	557	17	1,217	100
Percentage	—	16	31	6	46	1		100

Since the centre was set up in 1968, it has handled 1,230 cases, 71 per cent women and 29 per cent men. Thus in the ambulatory patients we find the same proportion of sexes as we do in the hospital. The age-groups, as of the time of initial consultation, were as shown in Table 2. Very aged people constitute a majority of the patients.

Table 3 shows the correlations between age and civil status.

Nearly half of our patients have lost their husbands or wives, this proportion increasing progressively with age, from around 25 per cent for those between 60 and 64 to 90 per cent among those over 90. One-third of the patients are married. The over-all proportion of single people is 16 per cent and varies only slightly from one category to another, from 15 to 20 per cent.

Twenty-three per cent of our patients are in medicosocial institutions or hospitals while 77 per cent live at home. The sources of referral for the initial consultation are shown in Table 4.

A very small number of elderly people came on their own initiative. It is noteworthy that the largest proportion were sent to us by physicians, whose co-operation with us has generally been excellent. Furthermore, most of the cases referred by medicosocial institutions and hospitals were sent to us with the agreement of the doctors treating them who welcomed the assistance of a specialized and structured team in solving both the psychiatric problems and their social consequences. The reasons for the initial consultation were evaluated with regard to the major problem presented. This was medical in 891 cases (74 per cent), familial in 110 cases (9 per cent), and social in 202 cases (17 per cent) (see Table 6).

Designation of the various psychiatric conditions was based upon the diagnosis which followed the initial consultation.

The proportion of psychiatric conditions which are organ-related is obtained by adding the number of confusional states to the psycho-organic

Table 4. *Sources of referral for initial consultation (percentage).*

Self-referral by patients	4
Physicians	37
Medicosocial institutions or hospital	26
Social service	17
Family and acquaintances	15
Not given	1
Total	100

Table 5. *Distribution of psychiatric diagnoses.*

Psychiatric diagnosis	N	%
1. No psychiatric indication	51	4
2. Psycho-organic syndromes		
(*a*) Presenile dementia (Alzheimer's dementia, etc.)	14	1
(*b*) Vascular psycho-organic syndromes	133	11
(*c*) Senile degenerative psycho-organic syndromes (senile dementia, Alzheimer-type dementia, dementia in Parkinson's disease)	150	13
(*d*) Mixed psycho-organic syndromes	49	4
(*e*) Psycho-organic syndromes from other causes (inflamatory, traumatic, etc.)	41	4
Total	387	33
3. Confusional states		
(*a*) Simple	98	8
(*b*) Oneiric	19	2
Total	117	10
4. Psychoses		
(*a*) Chronic schizophrenia	16	1
(*b*) Late schizophrenia	52	4
(*c*) Manic-depressive	17	2
(*d*) Senile delirium	29	3
Total	114	10
5. Depressions		
(*a*) Endogenous	16	1
(*b*) Involutional	133	11
(*c*) Mixed	87	7
Total	236	9
6. Neuroses	34	3
7. Reactive conditions		
(*a*) Delirious reaction	36	3
(*b*) Depressive reaction	173	14
(*c*) Other reactions	16	1
Total	225	18
8. Personality disorders (psychopathies, alcoholism, drug dependence, etc.)	39	3

syndromes, giving a total of 504 cases or 43 per cent. These are followed by the depressive conditions, whose total results from the addition of the manic-depressive psychoses, endogenous, involutional, and mixed depressions and the reactive depressions. These add up to 426 cases or 35 per cent of the total. We may also group together under one heading the chronic and late schizophrenias and senile and reactive delirium. This gives us 133 cases or 11 per cent.

In the effort to establish a correlation between the psychiatric diagnosis and the reason for the initial consultation (Table 4), we note that medical reasons predominate in every nosological category. In relation to the aggregate of all the medical reasons, the greatest proportion is of the psycho-organic syndromes (31 per cent) and depressions (23 per cent). It is striking to observe that 41 per cent of the familial reasons relate to reactive conditions and that 40 per cent of the social reasons are con- cerned with psycho-organic syndromes.

The 1,230 patients were given more or less complete physical examinations, as their condition indicated (Table 7).

Among these people whose fundamental problem is psychiatric, we perceive that 81 per cent also suffer from some somatic condition. Cardiovascular disorders largely predominate, followed by neurological and rheumatic conditions. In a second phase of this study, we shall explore the correlations between the psychiatric and physical diagnoses.

The number of contacts with the centre was assessed in terms of the number of consultations and home calls by doctors and also the number of visits by nurses and social workers. One-fifth of the patients were seen only once; one-third had 2 or 3 contacts; one-third had from 4 to 10, while 16 per cent had more than 10 contacts. On the basis of evaluations which it was not always possible to verify, we estimate that hospitalization or institutionalization was avoided or postponed in one-third of the cases dealt with.

During the four-year existence of our centre, 675 patients, half of the total, received care at home. The number of these patients, divided according to the year of entry, is shown in Table 8.

Except for 1968 when the team was still quite limited, the figure remained relatively stable. It might have been larger if we had had more nurses. Furthermore, the table does not take into account the accumulation of cases from year to year. We can gain an approximate impression of this by looking at the total number of home visits made every year by doctors and nurses (Table 9).

Assessment of the catamneses of patients was made for every case at the end of 1971, which means that it covers four years for the cases dating from 1968, three years for 1969 cases, two years for those of 1970, and one year for those of 1971 (Table 10).

The totals show that 27 per cent of the 1,203 cases were still under

Table 6. *Reason for initial consultation, in relation to psychiatric diagnosis.*

Diagnosis	Medical reasons		Family reasons		Social reasons		Total	
	N	%	N	%	N	%	Total	%
1. No psychiatric indication	32	4	4	4	15	8	51	4
2. Psycho-organic syndromes	282	31	25	23	80	40	387	33
3. Confusional states	100	11	7	6	10	5	117	10
4. Psychoses	94	10	3	3	17	7	114	10
5. Depressions	198	23	17	15	21	11	236	19
6. Neuroses	26	3	6	5	2	1	34	3
7. Reactive conditions	138	16	45	41	42	20	225	18
8. Personality disorders	21	2	3	3	15	8	39	3
Total	891	100	110	100	202	100	1,203	100
Percentage	74		9		17		100	

Table 7. *Distribution of somatic diagnoses.*

Somatic diagnosis	N	%
1. No physical anomaly	227	19
2. Neurological conditions	154	13
3. Cardiovascular conditions	423	35
4. Metabolic conditions	60	5
5. Rheumatic conditions	151	12
6. Neoplasms	54	4
7. Other conditions	149	12
Total	1,218*	100

*Some patients suffered from more than one somatic condition.

Table 8. *Patients cared for at home.*

Year	N	%
1968	103	15
1969	180	27
1970	183	27
1971	209	31
Total	675	100

Table 9. *Total number of home visits, by years (doctors and nurses).*

Year	N	%
1968	132	3
1969	648	12
1970	2,184	42
1971	2,210	43
Total	5,174	100

Table 10. *Catamneses as of 30 November 1971.*

	1968		1969		1970		1971 (to 30 November)			
	N	%	N	%	N	%	N	%	Total	%
1. Hospitalization in psychiatric milieu	71	29	87	21	83	23	61	19	302	23
2. Hospitalization in somatic mileu	23	10	42	10	24	7	24	7	113	8
3. Institutional placement	62	26	122	30	104	29	67	21	355	26
4. Deaths	52	21	75	18	53	14	32	10	212	16
5. Still under care on 30 November 1971	35	14	85	21	100	27	141	43	361	27
Total	243	100	411	100	364	100	325	100	1,343*	100
Percentage	18		31		27		24		100	

* The difference between this total and the total of all cases, 1,230, is due to the fact that a number of patients went through two phases, for example, hospitalization followed by institutional placement.

care as of 30 November 1971; that 16 per cent had died; that 31 per cent had been hospitalized either in a psychiatric milieu (23 per cent) or in a somatic milieu (8 per cent), while 26 per cent had been placed in medicosocial institutions. The number of cases remaining under care at the end of the period increased steadily from 14 per cent for those who first came to us in 1968 to 43 per cent for those who came in 1971, whereas deaths diminished from 21 per cent for the former group to 10 per cent for the latter. The rather high over-all proportion of deaths, 16 per cent, resulted from the advanced ages of our patients and their high level of morbidity.

The hospitalization rate, taking into account both psychiatric and somatic milieus, also diminished regularly from 39 per cent for patients under treatment since 1968 to 26 per cent for those who first came to us in 1971. On the contrary, the 21 per cent rate of institutional placement of patients first treated in 1971 appears higher than we might have expected, when compared to cases dating from the earlier years, which remained around 30 per cent.

This analysis of the activity of the Lausanne Psycho-geriatric Out-patient Centre constitutes only a preliminary report on a continuing comprehensive study. It enables us, however, to draw some conclusions. In particular, it has been shown that such an institution, serving as an outpost for a psycho-geriatric hospital, makes it possible to avoid or postpone a substantial number of admissions. Furthermore, as an out-patient service, it provides care at home and in medicosocial institutions which produces real improvement in the condition of patients whose admission to hospital is not absolutely necessary.

Because of the high proportion of psycho-organic cases, of patients suffering both from mental and physical disorders, the team staffing such a centre must have a large enough number of male and female nurses at its disposal so that very burdensome cases will not exhaust the personnel. The abundance of social problems of every kind, ranging from the provision of hot meals at home to the closing up of apartments and the placement of patients, also calls for a sufficient number of social workers. To judge the requirements in this field, we must take into account the many discussions that must be held with the families, the long talks with the elderly patients, the need for frequent contacts, etc. A shortage of social workers will inevitably result in half-way measures whose consequences may be serious.

We should also draw attention to the fact that an out-patient assignment as a complement to hospital work provides to the young doctor completing his training a more vivid and dynamic understanding of psycho-geriatrics than he would otherwise have.

While out-patient centres may resolve some hospitalization problems we must recognize that they also create new problems. Thus, postponing the date of hospitalization means that the case will be a more serious one when the time finally comes. This may also tend to make eventual placement in medicosocial institutions more difficult. On the other hand, this type of polyclinic permits a substantial shortening of the institutionalizing of the less difficult cases.

The method chosen for the analysis of this work opens up some interesting perspectives. It gives us a precise picture of our activities, objectifies certain needs and facilitates planning. We should like, however, to have a more far-ranging longitudinal view of our cases. With this in view, to conduct a satisfactory epidemiological study, it would be very useful both for curative and preventive medicine to establish a comprehensive file covering hospitals, medicosocial institutions, and out-patient services.

15 *Psychiatric morbidity among the physically impaired elderly in the community:* A preliminary report

Introduction

There is now substantial evidence that large numbers of elderly people in the community are suffering from mental illness of a degree which in many instances matches the clinical severity of those admitted to hospitals or institutions (Parsons, 1962; Kay *et al.*, 1964; Stokoe, 1965). Such disorders are often unrecognized by the patients' GPs (Stokoe, 1965) and although frequently associated with serious social impairment are not referred to the mental health and welfare services (Kay *et al.*, 1964). As the number of people aged 65 and over in the population is predicted to increase considerably (Brooke, 1965), the need to establish a means of identifying those elderly patients whose psychiatric disorders are either unrecognized or untreated, in order to mobilize the appropriate community agencies, becomes of great importance. The surveys to date have not indicated how the morbidity is distributed in the community and certain sections of the aged may be at special risk for psychiatric disturbance and need priority in attention.

As large-scale psycho-geriatric screening is likely to pose difficulties to the resources of the GPs who are already committed to an extensive clinical load, the use of alternative medical personnel, such as district nurses or health visitors, as screening agents has been suggested (SHSC, 1970). The district nurse, particularly, seems to be in an advantageous position as her existent close contact with the household provides an opportunity to observe mental disturbance and associated social distress. Furthermore, as there is a close association between physical illness and psychiatric disorder (Kay and Roth, 1955; Kay *et al.*, 1956; Gibson, 1961; Goldfarb, 1961; Simon and Tallery, 1965), the patient population under her care is likely to present an increased vulnerability to mental disorder.

However, the reliability of such ancillary medical staff, who have no specialized psychiatric training as screening agents, has to date not been established and is clearly an essential preliminary before considering the widespread extension of their role to include the detection and notification of psychiatric disorder.

This paper reports the preliminary findings of a study concerned with the former problem, and also with the detection of a high psychiatric morbidity risk group within the aged section of the community.

Design and method

The main aims of the study were to determine the extent and characteristics of psychiatric disorder among the physically impaired elderly patients under the domiciliary care of district nurses, and to assess the reliability of the latter as screening agents for mental disorder in the aged. In addition, it was proposed to examine the social dysfunction that coexists among this group of patients and the need for intervention by the appropriate community health and social services.

The patient population under study comprised all those patients aged 65 and over under the care of district nurses working in liaison with general practices in a south-east London borough. Practices were selected to provide representation of contrasting styles of practice and differing social characteristics of patient populations.

Each nurse was asked to complete a questionnaire on all the elderly patients under her current supervision. This comprised an inquiry about possible behavioural abnormalities and symptoms and was designed to be acceptable in terms of the labour and time needed for its completion, to district nursing personnel who carry a heavy clinical commitment, and at the same time comprehensible to respondents with no specialized psychiatric knowledge. Details of nursing and medical care were also requested and opportunity provided for the nurses to add a brief outline of the case.

All patients recorded as showing psychiatric symptoms were interviewed firstly by the psychiatrist and subsequently by a social research worker. In addition, a number of patients identified as normal by the nurse were also interviewed and, where possible, matched for age, sex, and marital status to provide control data.

The psychiatric assessment was based upon a standardized psychiatric interview schedule designed and tested for use in community work (Goldberg *et al.*, 1970). This was adapted for psycho-geriatric use and incorporated an orientation and memory test, and a Names Learning Test which has been found to discriminate between brain-damaged and non-brain-damaged elderly patients (Irving *et al.*, 1970). Although a physical diagnosis was also sought, emphasis was given to the disabilities, the functional consequences of the underlying illness, based upon an approach of other workers (Bennett *et al.*, 1970: Garrad and Bennett, 1971).

The instrument of social assessment was a modified version of a

Table 1. *Primary causes of physical impairment in forty-eight domiciliary cases of infirm elderly patients.*

	M	F	Total
Locomotor			
Cerebrovascular	1	4	5
Arthritis	5	4	9
Other	2	5	7
Total	8	13	21
Internal			
Cardiovascular	3	7	10
Respiratory	2	0	2
Other	2	4	6
Total	7	11	18
Sensory			
Blindness	0	4	4
Deafness	0	2	2
Other	1	0	1
Total	1	6	7
None	1	1	2

standardized social interview schedule, described elsewhere (Sylph *et al.*, 1969; Cooper *et al.*, 1970). The schedule retained the same framework of inquiry with extended sections on the patient's material circumstances and social dysfunction resulting from both the physical and psychiatric impairment. Detailed inquiry was also made about the services provided for the patient by the local health and welfare departments.

Preliminary findings

At the time of writing (March 1972) the survey is still in progress and as the number of nurses involved to date is small the preliminary results will be considered collectively and not subjected to statistical analysis. The selection of matched cases as controls has been difficult and incomplete, and data in respect of these will be the subject of future publication when the survey has been completed.

Four nurses, working in liaison with 11 GPs, have co-operated to date, and out of a total patient population under nursing care of 165, 124 (75 per cent) were 65 years of age or over and, therefore, acceptable for the study. All patients reported by the district nurses as showing psychiatric symptoms were interviewed in addition to 34 of the 80 reported as normal. No refusals for interview have been encountered.

Physical disorders

The associated primary physical disorders shown in Table 1 have been grouped into three categories on a functional anatomical or pathological

Table 2. *Psychiatric diagnoses of forty-eight cases of physically infirm domiciliary elderly patients.*

	M	F	Total
Dementia			
Mild	2	0	2
Severe	3	12	15
Total	5	12	17
Neuroses*			
Mild	4	15	19
Severe	8	4	12
Total	12	19	31
All disorders	17	31	48

* Includes three personality disorders.

basis and are here termed 'impairments'. In seventeen cases a second or third condition existed and in these instances the impairment contributing most to the patients' disabilities was regarded as primary. Locomotor impairment as indicated by weakness, paralysis, or pain in specified parts of the body concerned with movement, in this group of patients was chiefly associated with cerebrovascular disease or arthritis. The remaining ones in this category comprised disseminated sclerosis, muscular atrophy, and a few instances in which the loss of function of a limb had been due to trauma. Conditions, such as cardiac or respiratory diseases, anaemia, and diabetes were termed 'internal' impairments and accounted for an equivalent number of patients. 'Sensory' impairment apart from one case of peripheral sensory neuropathy were accountable for by blindness and deafness and were less in evidence.

Psychiatric disorders

All 44 patients reported by the district nurse as showing psychiatric symptoms were subsequently confirmed at interview to be psychiatric cases. The mental status of 35 of these was unknown to their GPs and the district nurses' own assessment in these instances could not have been influenced by knowledge from this source. Of the 34 cases assessed by the nurses as being free from psychiatric disorder, 4 (12 per cent) were shown to be incorrect. Three of these were moderately severe examples of dementia and the other a case of mild depression. One of the former had been visited by the district nurse on only two occasions and in the other two instances of dementia, a superficial appearance of joviality had concealed a significant underlying dementing process. Except for the recent arrival to district nursing practice, all of the nurses were well acquainted with their patients, many of whom had been under their care for considerable periods of time.

Table 3. *Analysis by age and sex.*

Diagnosis	65–74 M	F	75+ M	F	Total
Dementia	0	0	5	12	17
Neuroses*	7	10	5	9	31
Total	7	10	10	21	48

* Includes three personality disorders.

Thus, the figures indicate a strikingly high psychiatric morbidity among this group of patients: the minimum estimate would be 38 per cent (ie 48 out of 124), suffering from a formal psychiatric diagnosis selected from the *ICD* classification.

Taking into account the nurses' possible error of 12 per cent with 80 cases regarded as normal, a more likely figure would be 43 per cent. This would represent 0·9 to 1·4 per cent of the collective geriatric population of 4,100 patients of the 11 GPs.

The main diagnostic categories and their analysis by age and sex are shown in Tables 2 and 3.

Virtually two-thirds (31) were functional neurotic disorders. Of these, 24 were categorized as depression, 3 as anxiety states, and 4 as personality disorders, 1 of which was paranoid in type. No example of schizophrenia, 'endogenous' depression, or paranoid psychosis was encountered. The vast majority of cases of depression could be understood as a reaction to physical disability, declining social and leisure outlets, adverse domestic circumstances in the form of interpersonal difficulties within the household, grief following the loss of a spouse, or a variable combination of these. Nearly all the cases of dementia, predominantly arteriosclerotic in nature, were rated as severe, and confined to the older age-groups.

Apart from the severity, a striking feature was the duration of the psychiatric conditions: in well over half the cases the symptoms had been manifest for over a year, a finding generally consistent with the duration of the associated physical disorder. In only three instances had symptoms developed within recent months. For the majority of patients, old age was their first experience of significant mental disorder, and in only 11 cases out of the 48 was there any record of previous psychiatric history.

Disability

Disability is defined in functional terms as 'limitations of performance of one or more activities essential to daily living, such that the person is dependent on others' (Bennett *et al.,* 1970). Impairment, whether it be psychiatric or physical, need not necessarily result in disability. Its assessment was important as, apart from the effect on patients' morale, its nature and severity would indicate the type and amount of care needed from the medical and social services.

Table 4. *Disabilities of a domiciliary group of forty-eight psychogeriatric patients.*

Disability	None/mild M	F	Both	Severe M	F	Both	Total M	F	Both
Mobility	4	8	12	13	23	36	17	31	48
Self-care	11	12	33	6	9	15	17	31	48

Disabilities of the patients in two crucial areas of personal activity, self-care, and mobility, were determined. Mobility comprises such activities as travelling, walking, negotiating stairs, transfer in and out of bed, while self-care involves feeding, dressing, and toilet care. Table 4 indicates that within this particular domiciliary sample of psycho-geriatric patients, disability was widespread and severe. Only a quarter were without significant restriction in mobility and nearly one-third were dependent on others for essential care.

Medical and social care

The main areas of need and the provision of current care of the sample are shown in Table 5.

Medical services

The over-all responsibility for the provision of medical care necessarily lay with the GP, but it was the nurse who was invariably faced with any immediate decisions on management. By virtue of the regular and intimate contact with patients they were well placed to notify the respective doctors of any deterioration in the clinical condition of patients. As already previously indicated, in the majority of instances, the nurses were well aware of the coexistent mental status, but except in situations where the chronic process had finally flared into an acute crisis, usually with associated severe social distress, seldom brought this to the notice of the GPs, who were largely ignorant of this aspect of their patients' conditions. In the context of constant nursing supervision, regular routine visiting by the doctors was not the rule and were made only when clinical changes indicated the need. Virtually all the patients had nevertheless been seen by their GPs at some stage since the onset of the current illness, so failure of recognition was not accountable by lack of opportunity.

The pronounced lack of psychiatric treatment was an inevitable consequence of the over-all unawareness of the family doctors of their patients' mental status. Two-thirds of the patients assessed as being in need of psychiatric treatment were not receiving this, and the psychotropic medication of half of these cases receiving prescriptions was judged to be inappropriate.

In the main, the management of many of the cases was assessed as

Table 5. *Current and unmet care in forty-eight domi-*
cilary psycho-geriatric patients.

	Current care	Unmet care	No unmet needs
Psychiatric			
General practitioner	9	16	11
Specialist	3	9	
Social			
Social work	10	10	
Home-help	19	4	
Social contacts	11	10	10
Miscellaneous	3	11	
Voluntary	11	—	
Physical			
Mobility aids	19	10	19

being within the scope of the GP, given additional help from the appropriate social services. Nevertheless a substantial minority, a quarter, warranted either admission to an in-patient psycho-geriatric unit or attendance at an appropriate psycho-geriatric day-centre. Only three patients had ever seen a psychiatrist during their current illness, and none had ever been an in-patient or out-patient.

A further finding was that although the more severely physically disabled patients were well provided with appropriate aids, 20 per cent were recorded as being in clear need of some type of personal physical appliance, such as a walking aid or wheelchair.

Social needs and care

In addition to assessing material factors, such as housing conditions and finance, the social interviewer made inquiry into the extent of contact and difficulties in interpersonal relationships that patients were experiencing within or beyond the home, with friends, relatives, neighbours, or a spouse. Restrictions of social contact were common, and were by no means confined to those living alone, who comprised two-fifths of the sample. Voluntary agencies usefully helped with this problem by providing visitors, but these, although regular, were too limited in frequency.

Problems in interpersonal relationships featured less but where existent were often severe. In a fifth of the cases, the complexity of the psychosocial problems was assessed as requiring the special skills of a psychiatric social worker. The clinical impression, often pronounced, was that social isolation, or difficult interpersonal relations or a combination frequently contributed to the clinical picture, but the full significance of these factors must await comparison with equivalent data from the control group.

Conspicuous financial difficulties, as indicated by the basic income levels of the DHSS criteria, were little in evidence, but, nevertheless, on the basis of a composite score derived from a detailed assessment of housing conditions, no less than a quarter were rated as having poor or very poor housing conditions which were in clear need of attention.

Although 19 of the 48 psycho-geriatric patients were recorded as being known to workers from the welfare departments at some stage of their illness, in many instances the contacts had been transitory and never subsequently renewed. Only ten cases could be regarded as being under active supervision. The home-help service was well provided and its requirement was a further reflection of the widespread physical infirmity of this group of patients.

The diversity and often multiplicity of needs illustrate the complex issues raised in management, and suggests that the only effective therapeutic approach to this group of psycho-geriatric patients, whose disabilities are associated with physical infirmity should be an integrated one involving all the appropriate medical and social services.

Conclusions

As the sample of the patient population, GPs and district nurses to date is small and derived from an urban area with its own characteristic policies of community care, the findings cannot be assumed to be representative of conditions prevailing elsewhere. Nevertheless, they provide supportive evidence for the existence among the elderly living in the community of a subgroup of high psychiatric morbidity, characterized by chronicity, widespread disability and, in many instances, absence of appropriate medical and social care.

The successful identification by personnel without specialized knowledge of psychiatry of the majority of such cases, many of whom were unknown to the GP, is impressive and encouraging for the prospects of extending their role to the notification of psychiatric disorder in this age-group. Their success largely reflects the strategic advantage of intimate and regular contact with patients in the home environment.

The lack of exploitation by their nurses of their knowledge, except in instances of acute social distress or clinical crises, seemed to derive from an underlying acceptance of psychiatric symptoms as being an understandable reaction to social or physical adversity, or an inevitable accompaniment to old age, for which there was little to be expected from therapeutic intervention.

These aspects emphasize the need for GPs and nurses to be aware of the close relationship between psychiatric disorder and physical illness, particularly as there are large numbers of physically impaired among the elderly in the community (Bennett and Garrard, 1970; Garrard and Bennett, 1971; Harris *et al.*, 1971), and furthermore, that the clinical and social distress in many instances can be alleviated by appropriate action.

The needs of many of the identified cases are complex and diverse, but nevertheless appear manageable in a domiciliary setting, and suggest that such problems in the elderly are best met by a multidisciplinary approach comprising GP, district nurse, social worker, and psychiatrist. Social workers, in addition to providing special skills in psychosocial problems, are well placed to mobilize appropriate social agencies, and can profitably contribute to the management of geriatric problems (Goldberg *et al.*, 1970).

Acknowledgements

The study described in this paper was individual research carried out in the General Practice Research Unit, Institute of Psychiatry, directed by Professor Michael Shepherd and supported by a grant from the Department of Health and Social Security.

I am very grateful to Mrs B. Nurse and Mrs I. Linker who conducted the social interviews, and the district nurses who, in spite of pressure of work, so diligently co-operated.

I am also indebted to the GPs, the borough medical officer of health, the district nursing supervisor for their co-operation, and to the patients, without whose forbearance the survey would not have been possible.

REFERENCES

Bennett, A. E., Garrad, J., and Halil, T. (1970). 'Chronic disease and disability in the community: a prevalence study', *Br. med. J.* **3**, 762–4.

Brooke, E. M. (1965). 'The psychogeriatric patient: some statistical considerations', *Report on World Psychiatric Association Symposium: 'Psychiatric Disorders in the Aged'*, pp. 214–24 (Manchester: Geigy).

Cooper, B., Eastwood, M. R., and Sylph, J. (1970). 'Psychiatric morbidity and social adjustment in a general practice population: a preliminary report', in Hare, E. H., and Wing, J. K. (eds), *Psychiatric Epidemiology*, pp. 299–309 (Oxford University Press for the Nuffield Provincial Hospitals Trust).

Garrad, J., and Bennett, A. E. (1971). 'A validated interview schedule for use in population surveys of chronic disease and disability', *Br. J. prev. soc. Med.* **25**, 97–104.

Gibson, A. C. (1961). 'Psychosis occurring in the senium: a review of an industrial population', *J. ment. Sci.* **107**, 921.

Goldberg, D. P., Cooper, B., Eastwood, M. R., Kedward, H. B., and Shepherd, M. (1970). 'A standardised psychiatric interview for use in community surveys', *Br. J. prev. soc. Med.* **24**, 1.

Goldberg, E. M., Mortimer, A., and Williams, B. T. (1970). *Helping the Aged* (London: Allen & Unwin).

Goldfarb, A. L. (1961). 'Mental health in the institution', *Gerontologist*, **1**, 178–8.

Harris, A. I., Cox, E. and Smith, C. R. W. (1971). *Handicapped and Impaired in Great Britain, Part I*, SS 418. (London: HMSO).

Irving, G., Robinson, R. A., and McAdam, W. (1970). 'The validity of some cognitive tests in the diagnosis of dementia', *Br. J. Psychiat.* **117**, 149–56.

Kay, D. W. K., and Roth, M. (1955). 'Physical accompaniments of mental disorder in old age', *Lancet*, **ii**, 740.

—— Norris, V., and Post, F. (1956). 'Prognosis in psychiatric disorders of the elderly: an attempt to define indicators of early death and early recovery', *J. ment. Sci.* **102**, 129.

—— Beamish, P., and Roth, M. (1964). 'Old age mental disorders in Newcastle-upon-Tyne—Part I: a study of prevalence', *Br. J. Psychiat.* **110,** 146–58.

—— —— —— (1964). 'Old age mental disorders in Newcastle-upon-Tyne—Part II: a study of possible social and medical causes', ibid. **110,** 668–82.

Parson, P. L. (1962). 'A survey of a random sample of the elderly, living in their own homes', MD Thesis (Swansea).

Scottish Health Services Council (1970). *Services for the Elderly with Mental Disorder* (Edinburgh: HMSO).

Simon, A., and Tallery, J. E. (1965). 'The role of physical illness in geriatric mental disorders', *Report on World Psychiatric Association Symposium: Psychiatric Disorders in the Aged,* pp. 154–70 (Manchester: Geigy).

Stokoe, I. M. (1956). 'Physical and mental care of the elderly at home', ibid., pp. 237–46.

Sylph, J., Kedwood, H. B., and Eastwood, M. R. (1969). 'Chronic neurotic patients in general practice: a pilot study', *Jl R. Coll. Gen. Practit.* **17,** 162.

Part 5 *Evaluation of some community services*

16   *Services for the family*

E. MATILDA GOLDBERG

Introduction

The word evaluation is fashionable in British social work today, and can mean almost anything from highly subjective judgements of outcome to descriptive analyses of methods of treatment, to statements of goals in relation to resources. Only very rarely does it concern the objective assessment of the effectiveness of defined methods of social work or of particular measures adopted in the social services.

It is not surprising that evaluation in social work is problematic, since there is so little agreement as to what ills social work is supposed to tackle, what its methods should be and what could legitimately be regarded as success or favourable outcomes.

Objectives

There is first of all the problem of objectives or goals. Who sets them: the public, the agency, the client, or the social worker? It is becoming increasingly apparent that these four groups do not have the same goals. For instance some critics, particularly in the US, have accused social workers of pursuing mistaken objectives, of deploying their resources where they are least needed, of neglecting the poor and the severely disordered, and of 'putting commitment to a method before human need' (Briar, 1968). A recent study of social work clients receiving help at a family welfare agency, suggests that at least some of the social workers' goals are incomprehensible to clients. On the other hand some of the clients' goals seemed unacceptable to the social workers (Mayer and Timms, 1970). The question arises whether successful outcome is more likely when goals are shared by worker and client.

In any case the objectives of social work, particularly when it is concerned with complex family situations in which environmental pressures, interpersonal processes, and personality factors are inextricably interwoven, are often very hard to determine. However, it must also be said that social workers find it difficult to commit themselves to an explicit assessment of their clients' problems and that they shy away even more from the formulation of treatment goals and specific prescriptions. Their aims are often stated in the vaguest terms, such as 'enhanced social functioning', 'greater maturity', and so on. Much social work is based on intuition, empathy, and exploration, following the client through all kinds of mazes and, not infrequently, getting lost with him. Thus, some of the evaluative exercises we shall be considering were almost doomed to produce negative results from the start, because of their lack of specificity in relation to the problems to be tackled, the methods to be adopted, and the objectives to be pursued.

Methods of social work

Secondly we lack systematic descriptions of what social workers actually do. Writings on what are purported to be social work activities are often misleading. Thus, many people believe that social workers are immersed in long-term intensive casework, which is focused on intra-psychic and unconscious conflicts, and that they spend much of their time discussing their clients' early experiences in order to help them towards some insight into the irrational causes of their present maladaptive behaviour.

The few studies which have so far been carried out, show that reality is very different, and more oriented to the external 'here and now' than these notions suggest. Social workers have also been relatively silent about the great amount of practical help and advice they engage in, and about their all-important linking functions with a host of voluntary and statutory agencies in the community.

One of the studies of casework activities aimed at alleviating problems in family relationships was carried out by Reid. He devised an instrument for the study of casework intervention (Reid, 1967), which is much influenced by Hollis's famous typology of casework (Hollis, 1967). Reid's scheme of analysis was applied to 121 tape-recordings of casework interviews, drawn from a random selection of cases in the field experiment to be discussed later. By far the most frequently used technique (46 per cent of the caseworkers' responses) was concerned with 'exploration' of the client's milieu and his relation to it. Twenty-two per cent of the responses were termed 'logical discussion', directed at enhancing the client's understanding of others in his situation. The combination of these two techniques accounted for about three-quarters of the workers' communications in these casework interviews. Somewhat surprising was the relative infrequency (1·4 per cent) of worker responses directed at the client's understanding of intra-psychic causes of behaviour patterns. Only 2 per cent of the caseworkers' formulations were aimed at increasing the client's understanding of childhood origins of current behaviour patterns. Although the percentage of advice-giving was low (4 per cent), this technique was used to a greater extent than any of the insight-oriented techniques. These findings were amply confirmed in a study on marital counselling in which Miss Hollis set out to analyse seventy-five interviews in which marital adjustment was a problem (Hollis, 1968). The profile that emerges from a line by line analysis of clients' and workers' communications is very similar to the one described by Reid. Eighty-seven per cent of the first interview was devoted to exploration, description, and ventilation, and even in the final interviews 63 per cent of the communications consisted of this kind of material. Hollis also found, like Reid, that a very small part of the interviews (1·5 per cent) was taken up by discussion of intra-psychic factors and early life situations. Miss Hollis suggests that a high degree of description and ventilation may be the result of too great passivity on the worker's part. This suggestion is echoed in the findings of the small British study of social work clients (Mayer and Timms, 1970), who were puzzled by the social workers' passive exploratory techniques, which aim at explanation and understanding and which often pay little attention to the client's definition of his problems and his immediate needs.

From these and other studies a profile of the casework process is emerging which is surprisingly constant, variations being more a function of the individual caseworker's style than anything else that could be identified. However, more 'mixed' types of social work which combine practical and psychological help have not been subjected to similar detailed analyses.

Criteria of success and failure

Thirdly, there is the vexing problem of establishing criteria of success or failure of social work. Social workers have traditionally been landed with, or have sought out the 'outcasts in society', and those whose handicaps are long-standing or irreversible. Social workers are concerned with the disabled, the mentally handicapped, the so-called character disorders, the deprived, and the disadvantaged. It is true that social workers have also become increasingly concerned with so-called preventive functions: for example, in child guidance and marriage guidance. However, in these spheres too, they are often dealing with severely disturbed families. How then can we determine criteria of success in such an ill-defined field of social failure and disabilities of all kinds? There are no tests to show, as in some fields of medicine, whether the invading bacilli have been eradicated or the cancerous cells stopped from multiplying. One may even be at a loss how to interpret apparent improvements: intervention may merely cause the underlying pathology of behavioural disorder to choose a different path. Or 'improvement' may set up a chain reaction, which will throw out of balance a long-established social equilibrium.

Another difficulty in defining criteria of success and failure is that theories of social work intervention are based on different sociological and psychological theories of human functioning. The criteria will differ according to whether one considers the subject matter of social work to be one of scarce or maldistributed human and economic resources and of unmet material needs, or whether one thinks that the problems of maladaptation and faulty functioning are largely created by irrational drives and needs within ourselves. There are many positions between these two extremes. For example, field experiments in the US in which casework help was offered to multi-problem families, have shown that many of the major problems experienced by these families were environmental, and often centred around the absence of basic necessities. The authors of one of these studies (Mullen *et al.,* 1970), say:

to the extent that these problems resulted from inadequate information and skill in using community resources, it might be expected that assistance of the kind offered (e.g. casework) in this project would be helpful. However, to the extent that these problems were reflective of difficulties in systems beyond the family and absence of opportunity in the environment for these families we would anticipate a lack of service effectiveness in relation to these problems.

In the field of social psychiatry, a psychiatrist and social worker might consider their work effective if they succeed in maintaining a patient suffering from chronic schizophrenia in employment by supporting him socially and by medication, and by encouraging his parents to tolerate his eccentricities and to see that he takes his medication regularly. Existential psychiatrists would consider this kind of undertaking and its results an abysmal failure of a society which supports an irrational social situation, labels its victims and enforces false values on them.

Leaving aside these basic philosophical and social questions as to what constitutes success and failure in interpersonal helping, even middle range goals present formidable difficulties of how to operationalize and measure criteria of effectiveness. Increased physical and social activity in a case of chronic disability, better marks at school and improvement in parent–child relationships in an anxious and disturbed child, less depression and a higher degree of safety and comfort in an elderly person may be defined as criteria of successful outcome. Do we take the clients' reports as our source material, or the observations of independent assessors, or do we enlist the help of skilled caseworkers who arrive at ratings of social functioning in various aspects of living on the basis of summarized case-records? All these methods have advantages and disadvantages, both as regards reliability and validity of measurement. Then again do we measure and compare the *state* of clients in experimental and control groups at the beginning and at the end of a field experiment? Or do we measure and compare differences in movement within each group?

Some field experiments with no differences in outcomes

How are these problems of aims and methods tackled in actual field experiments which seek to test the effectiveness of social work? The first pioneer experiment I want to consider is *Girls at Vocational High* carried out in New York City in the late 1950s (Meyer *et al.*, 1965). An agency, the Youth Consultation Service in New York which specializes in work with adolescent girls wanted to experiment in a preventive approach, hoping to involve the girls when they were not yet in serious difficulties. The research was based on a Vocational High School in which a pool of potential problem cases was collected by a process of screening school records. From this sample of potential problem cases 200 girls were referred to the Youth Consultation Service and 200 were left as they were. Since the social workers themselves were, as usual, rather vague about their treatment aims, the researchers in consultation with them set up their own criteria of success, spread over many areas of social and psychological functioning.

The great methodological advantage of this study was that the control group was not singled out in any way, as initial and final tests were given to the whole school population and the school data were available anyway. Treatment consisted of individual and group treatment at the Youth Consultation Service with a median number of seventeen contacts.

Few statistically significant results emerged, if one compared the treated and the untreated groups in relation to academic school records, truancy, delinquency, illegitimate pregnancies, personality tests, and social attitude scores. Differences also did not emerge when more clinical indices, such as insight into difficulties, self-conception, sociometric tests, aspirations, and expectations of the future were assessed. The treated showed only small gains in the expected direction. For example, the rate of failures in academic performance decreased more in the experimental than in the control group. There was also a greater decrease in unexcused absences and truancy in experimental than in control cases. In out-of-school behaviour only the slightest advantage was found for experimental cases. The authors conclude that although the effect of treatment was minimal, the results did favour the girls who had the benefit of the treatment programme.

The second field experiment was carried out in Chemung County, New York, in the early 1960s (Brown, 1968). The study dealt with so-called 'multi-problem families'. These were defined as families afflicted by a variety of health and welfare problems, who were chronically dependent on community services, but apathetic towards agency efforts or actually resisting or rejecting the services offered. The objective of this study was to assess the effect of intensive social casework on a group of fifty multi-problem families, in contrast to the effect of normal public assistance services mainly concerned with material help only, given to a control group of fifty similar families. The intensive service (over twice as many contacts as in the control group) lasting thirty-one months was carried out by experienced professionally qualified caseworkers. Caseloads in the demonstration group were limited to less than half the usual number carried by public assistance workers and greater emphasis was put on using other available community services. The essential finding was that while the demonstration group attained a slightly better degree of family functioning its margin of progress over the control group was not significant in the statistical sense, that is the demonstration group's movement could be attributed to chance alone.

It should be added that this study suffered many vicissitudes in relation to staffing, to organizational difficulties in the welfare department and met a very hostile reception in the social work world.

In the third field experiment *Preventing Chronic Dependency* (Mullen *et al.,* 1970), the New York City Department of Social Services and the Community Service Society of New York (a private family casework agency) combined their resources in order to help a group of approximately one hundred families who had become dependent on public assistance for the first time. In addition to being given financial and supportive assistance by the City Department of Social Services, the experimental families received professional social casework services from experienced caseworkers at the CSS for about fourteen months. The objective was to demonstrate the effectiveness of a collaborative approach in preventing individual and family disorganization, as a result of prolonged economic dependence. Families applying to the DSS, for the first time, were randomly assigned to an experimental and control group. Families in the experimental group received both CSS and DSS assistance, while families in the control group received the normal DSS assistance. The data used to evaluate the effects of the experimental service were collected through a structured interview at the end of the project. The respondent, the female head of household, answered questions about the family's experiences since its application for public assistance, and about its conditions and functioning at the time of the interview, ranging from economic status, employment, use of health facilities, and housing to family cohesion and relationships. Since the families came from the same universe and were randomly assigned to the experimental and control groups it was assumed that any differences found between the two groups at the time of the research interview would be the result of the experimental service. The median number of interviews in the experimental group was fifteen and the CSS workers also had many contacts with other organizations, but the close collaboration with the DSS did not materialize and in about one-third of the families there was no face-to-face meeting between the CSS workers and their DSS colleagues.

The results showed only a very moderate success in the experimental group. In the nine areas of family functioning examined, only one area resulted in an experimental control group difference of statistical significance; more experimental families than controls reported having received help in getting medical services, and help with personal or family difficulties. In addition the experimental families showed certain more favourable trends though these did not reach statistical significance. Thus, more experimental than control families were no longer receiving welfare, had completed or were involved in job training and reported receiving help with getting an apartment. The researchers approached the problems of measurement in many ways: for example, by eliminating those experimental families who had not had any contacts with the caseworkers, by only considering those experimental families who had at least five interviews with the CSS workers, by eliminating control families who had received services comparable to those offered by the CSS elsewhere, and so on. But none of these comparisons improved the results appreciably.

Some criticisms of these studies

Both the Vocational High School study and the Chemung County study have been criticized because favourable results could not be expected in a situation where people are not motivated to seek casework. The High School girls were referred for help without necessarily presenting serious overt problems, and many of the girls found it difficult to become involved in individual casework treatment, though they participated more whole-heartedly in the groups. However, in the normal course of events, this particular agency deals with many girls who do not seek treatment themselves but are referred by their parents, courts, and other agencies for difficult behaviour. One could add that most delinquents on probation and many so-called problem families are in the same category. In the Chemung County Study the criticisms about motivation have a different slant. How could one expect to reach these people by relatively permissive casework methods which sought to maximize self-determination? These families, it is pointed out, had for the most part developed negative hopeless attitudes to the agency, would they not be puzzled by the sudden intensive attentions? Were they prepared for this unusual experience? However, in the New York City collaborative study, casework services were offered to families who became dependent on public welfare for the first time with very similar results.

The vaguely defined objectives of treatment have been criticized in both the Vocational High and Chemung County studies. The authors of the collaborative experiment blame the behavioural scientists for 'contributing but limited understanding of the nature of interaction of the varied and complex problems confronting these families, which make it difficult to identify appropriate outcome variables for assessment'.

Criticisms have been made and questions raised about the appropriateness of the treatment offered in these studies. In the Vocational High study the treatment was concentrated mainly on the adolescents themselves, very few parents were seen and the vague aim was to develop more ego strength in the girls to cope with themselves, their difficulties and their often inadequate environment. Apart from general impressionistic accounts and case illustrations there is no systematic and detailed description or conceptualization of the social work input. For these reasons success or failure rates cannot be easily related to different kinds of treatment.

A criticism of the Chemung County Study has been that casework was used as a substitute for much needed material and social resources. Helen Perlman in a spirited attack (Perlman, 1968), asks whether certain minimal conditions should not serve as a floor for such casework efforts. She suggests that 'you cannot expect people to pull themselves up by their boot straps if they have no boots!' Though Mrs Perlman's criticisms seem valid to some extent, they also raise doubts, for she appears to consider casework a 'luxury' only available to those 'who are free to take their eyes off the manifest dangers from outside', rather than part of a comprehensive service.

In the collaborative experiment, the information on what the social workers actually did is also very sparse, apart from the number of contacts with clients and other agencies. And here too, the authors were acutely aware that casework intervention alone cannot alter dysfunctional social systems impinging upon the families, and that it cannot substitute for the absence of adequate employment opportunities, income maintenance for these who cannot work, housing, health and welfare services.

The caseworkers in this experiment raised questions about the research methods, in particular the researchers' complete reliance on the respondents' reports of their problems and the help they received. The caseworkers quote a finding that 'few respondents reported having untreated health problems in either experimental or control groups'. The social workers point out that these families had vast unattended health problems which were in fact one of the major targets of their casework activities. They also felt that casework goals were met in many instances but that these were 'not reflected in the outcome differences between the two groups'. They point to the enormous range of problems these families faced which necessitated a corresponding variety of social work targets, not allowed for in the research design.

The severest criticism of the vagueness of casework aims with the adolescent girls, and the almost exclusive concentration on self understanding and attitudes comes from the authors of *Girls at Vocational High*. They suggest that the professional effort should be directed towards helping clients change their situations and their goals. The authors accept the possibility that psychological changes may be necessary before social and situational changes can be achieved. But it seems equally possible to them that cause and effect occur in the opposite direction. They wonder whether professional effort should not have been directed to the girls' environment, their families and peer groups, to their school and work places which affect their psychological condition. They ask: should we expect weekly interviews with caseworkers, or weekly counselling sessions in groups to have critical effects when situational conditions are hardly touched? They plead for a 'multi-level attack' on the psychological, interpersonal, and environmental levels.

Two field experiments showing differences in outcome

We now turn from field experiments with very heterogeneous groups, ill-defined treatment objectives, and very little information on treatment methods, to two field experiments with more homogeneous groups, more limited treatment goals and more sharply defined and measurable treatment input.

The first field experiment entitled *Brief and Extended Casework* (Reid and Shyne, 1969) (whose social work measurements we have already discussed), aimed at assessing the relative effectiveness of different patterns of casework service in alleviating family problems: planned short-term service limited to eight interviews and open-ended long-term service lasting up to eighteen months. The social workers were six well-qualified and experienced practitioners who started this experiment convinced that open-ended long-term casework was more effective and appropriate in problems of interpersonal relationships. They considered the short-term method second best and found it stressful and challenging to carry out. The criteria for inclusion in the study were that the families should be intact, under 50 years of age, and first-time applicants, experiencing either marital or parent–child problems. A total of 120 families were randomly assigned to these caseworkers for the different service patterns. Independent assessments were carried out by research observers, who were highly experienced caseworkers, at the completion of intake, at the termination of casework service, and six months after termination.

The two sets of families were found to be essentially similar in all characteristics on which measurements were to be carried out. These measurements consisted of sixteen key ratings of family functioning based on clients' reports to the observers. Some of the variables rated were: the family's over-all problem situation, marital problems, parent/child problems, school adjustment of children, functioning as spouse and parent.

To the surprise of everybody the families receiving planned short-term service progressed more than similar families who had long-term treatment particularly those experiencing marital problems, and this held for the follow-up period as well as for the assessment carried out at the end of treatment. The differences occurred mainly in the slightly improved categories, but most remarkably in most of the comparisons a consistently higher proportion of continued service cases showed deterioration. Ten per cent of the short-term clients were rated as having experienced some deterioration compared with 35 per cent for the continued service clients.

The researchers speculate whether long-term clients received an 'overdose' of treatment, leading to diminishing returns when motivation for change is no longer a powerful stimulant.

The analysis of the tape-recorded interviews showed that in short-term treatment social workers used more techniques directed towards promoting change, less passive exploration, and more active intervention than in long-term treatment. The clients preferred the active style and expressed more positive feelings about the social workers in the short-term situations. It must be remembered that the same social workers also carried long-term cases. The authors suggest that the immediacy, sharpness, and urgency of short-term work lead to less improvisation and drift and more selectivity in treatment objectives, more focus on realizable goals and less concentration on unalterable underlying causes than long-term help. Furthermore the 'set' was different from the very beginning: clients accepted that change would occur within a brief period. All the six caseworkers did better with planned short-term service cases than with continued service cases as measured by the key ratings, regardless of their preference. The more stressful pattern to the caseworkers was the more beneficial for the client.

Lastly there is our own field experiment in social work in which we tried to test the effectiveness of social work in the sphere of old age (Goldberg *et al.*, 1970). In this study we aimed:

1. To ascertain the social and medical condition and needs of a sample of old people aged 70 and over, newly referred to a local authority welfare department.

2. To compare services received with services needed.

3. To assess how effective trained social workers were in promoting the welfare of these aged persons.

Hypotheses were formulated about the possible changes which might result from social work in four different areas:

1. Environmental changes in relation to housing, income, and provision of services.

2. Changes in functioning, in personal capacity, in general activities and interests.

3. Changes in subjective attitudes, the amount of depression and loneliness experienced, satisfaction with various aspects of living, including attitudes to the help received.

4. Changes in the extent and nature of the old person's needs, the type and severity of problems experienced and the general contentment conveyed in the interviews.

In short, the criteria ranged from objectively observable and verifiable facts to subjective attitudes and feelings expressed by clients themselves; the criteria also included clinical judgements made by the social work assessors and the medical investigator in relation to disability and the nature and extent of the old people's needs for additional social work help.

The social work assessor, an experienced social worker, and the medical assessor, a social physician, who was also a psychiatrist, assessed the social and medical conditions and needs of a consecutive series of 300 clients, aged 70 and over, who had applied for help to a south London local authority welfare department.

Nearly half of the applicants were over 80, two-thirds lived alone, many in very inconvenient housing, but children and neighbours were in frequent contact.

These welfare clients were more incapacitated than random samples studied in similar age-groups in Britain. A quarter were assessed as suffering from a serious disease which constituted a threat to life, and 15 per cent were suffering from psychiatric disorders. Twenty per cent of these old people experienced frequent and prolonged feelings of depression. The social and medical interviews also revealed many minor medical problems, discomforts, and disabilities which add a great deal to the burden of old age.

Half the sample were already receiving some personal social services before their contact with the welfare department, but many additional medical and social needs were uncovered.

These 300 welfare clients were randomly allocated to a special group and a comparison group, which proved to be reasonably well matched in all important respects, except that there were more men in the special group.

Two trained caseworkers were appointed to take on the social work in the special group while the comparison group remained under the care of the department's welfare officers, none of whom had a professional social work training.

The experimental period of social work lasted for ten and a half months after which the social and medical assessors reassessed all the survivors remaining in their own homes: 110 in the special and 104 in the comparison group. The assessors did not know who was in the special and who in the comparison groups and had no access to their previous assessments.

Differences in input

The input of social work was measured by means of a structured questionnaire interview held with the social workers on every case. These questions aimed to discover the social worker's assessment of the case in terms of the problems observed, the degree of need for social work, and the kind of help indicated at the beginning of the case. Questions followed about the extent and nature of the social work done, the number of visits and interviews that had taken place, what other agencies had been contacted, what practical services had been rendered, and what kind of psychological help had been attempted. We also inquired about the relationship between the client and the worker and about the problems still remaining.

We found that the amount and quality of the social work differed greatly in the two groups. The old people in the special group received twice as much help as those in the comparison group, measured by number of interviews, contacts with other agencies and items of practical help. The trained workers saw more problems and more often combined practical services and casework with both clients and relatives. They worked more closely with medical and voluntary agencies and with volunteers they encouraged more expression of feelings and were more alert to covert depression and more subtle problems in family relationships. They made greater efforts to enrich their clients' lives by introducing them to clubs, encouraging holidays and outings. They were able to use their skills more selectively according to people's needs.

Differences in outcome

Few, if any, changes had occured in the client's material living conditions. The general health of both groups had deteriorated. Their mobility, their capacity to perform basic tasks of everyday living, and contacts with relatives and neighbours had also remained virtually the same. However, both groups had significantly fewer practical needs on reassessment, and this was even more apparent among the clients in the special group resulting in a significant difference between the groups. The clients in the special group had also improved significantly in their 'morale', more of them were attending clubs, had had a holiday, felt satisfied with life at the moment, had a positive attitude towards the world around them, had fewer worries and personal problems than clients in the comparison group. They were significantly more active and less depressed than the comparison group. In addition to these statistically significant differences, we observed movements and differences in outcome, small in range, which consistently favoured the special group. In most respects we could see a close correspondence between the input reported by the social workers and the outcome reported by the clients or the independent assessors. Reduction in practical needs was significantly related to input as measured in number of contacts and items of practical help given. We were not able to identify with similar precision the elements in the casework process which were responsible for changes in attitudes and feelings.

We also tried to get some consumer reactions to the help received. A significantly higher proportion of clients in the special group felt that the social workers' visits had been helpful to them. Clients in the special group mentioned almost three times as many helpful practical services performed by social workers as the clients in the comparison group.

On the whole the results of this study make sense. One would not expect individual social work effort to impinge on broad social conditions such as housing. Nor would one expect any improvements in general health in this very aged group, though it was disappointing that no relief from minor discomforts had been achieved in either group. On the other hand, one did hope that social work would result in the reduction of practical needs and an improvement in social and psychological functioning. The less-trained social workers of the welfare department achieved a good deal, though not as much as their trained colleagues, in alleviating their clients' practical needs. The trained workers also brought about some improvement in their clients' activities and functioning and their feelings and attitudes, and these assessments find confirmation in the clients' own reactions and comments on the help they had received.

Implications of these studies

Critical questions have arisen from both these experiments. For example, the role of the time factor in the Reid and Shyne experiment: were the more favourable results of planned short-term treatment due to assessments being made at the peak point of recovery while clients in long-term treatment were slowing down in their rate of progress? Yet, the proportionately greater improvement of the families who had had short-term service was still maintained six months after termination of treatment; and twice as many families in the continued service group sought further help after social work ceased (44 per cent) than did families in the short-term service group (22 per cent). Caution is indicated of course in generalizing from one specific study which dealt with highly motivated, predominantly lower middle-class intact families, though cost-effectiveness and scarcity of skilled manpower alone demand further study of these findings (1,562 interviews took place in the continued service group compared with 422 interviews in the planned short-term service group). Professor Reid and his colleagues are broadening the context of their work and have developed a conceptual framework for a model of task-oriented short-term treatment (Reid and Epstein, 1972), which they are currently testing with different groups of clients. This approach concentrates on limited achievable goals and pays more attention than is customary in traditional social work to the client's conception of his problems and their solutions.

The underlying theory of this practice model is akin to crisis theory; the temporary breakdown in problem coping triggers off corrective change forces. These forces, it is postulated, operate quickly to reduce problems to a tolerable level after which the intensity and the motivation for further change lessen. Setting limits in advance may increase and quicken these processes of change by providing a deadline against which the client must work and by heightening his expectations that certain changes can occur within the time period.

It is likely that planned short-term intervention will prove inappropriate and ineffective in many chronic and complex situations. But it may be useful to distinguish long-term support or surveillance and help with ongoing management in chronic disability from therapeutic intervention designed to bring about changes in certain specific problem areas. Thus, one could visualize using all kinds of resources: para-professionals, volunteers, community self-help for long-term support, while the professional only intervenes at certain critical points; for instance when a crisis has upset the customary support system, or when the client seems ready to take another hurdle in his developmental journey. Clearly, further imaginative experimenting is required to explore these ideas and we are hoping to do so with groups of social workers in comprehensive social service departments in England.

The field experiment with the aged also raises intriguing methodological questions: for example, are the modest differences between the special and comparison groups due to differences in social work skills brought about by training, or are personality, natural gifts, enhanced motivation, more intensive attention, lower caseloads, and more opportunities for regular team discussions, the crucial ingredients responsible for a more favourable outcome in the special group? There is no finite answer to these questions without further research in which, for instance, caseloads are held constant and methods of intervention varied, or alternatively where methods are held constant and caseloads varied, and so on. At present we can only say that in this first British experiment we wished to find out whether trained caseworkers, under reasonably good conditions, could achieve any different results from untrained workers working in a well-staffed department. It must be remembered that so far no differences had been shown between trained caseworkers and semi-trained welfare officers, despite the fact that in the Chemung County study the trained workers carried half the caseload of the public assistance workers. In the Vocational High School experiment we have an even more extreme situation; there was hardly any difference in outcome between those girls who had skilled help and those who had no help at all. We have argued elsewhere that the richer repertoire of treatment skills of the trained workers in the old age experiment, their wider contacts in the community, their more sharply differentiated help according to the client's specific needs, suggest that skill and training did play a part in achieving these results. We adduced evidence that motivation and the spur of a time-limited experiment probably also contributed. More recently research at the National Institute for Social Work Training on Workloads of Social Workers in Health and Welfare Departments, suggests that size of caseload probably exerts a much smaller effect on what social workers actually do than has hitherto been believed (Carter and Edwards, 1972; Walker *et al.*, 1972).

Perhaps the most important practical implications arising from this field experiment are those related to initial assessment and the subsequent deployment of differential skills in relation to different problems and treatment targets. For instance, the trained social workers in the special group have twice as much help (measured in number of client contacts, contacts with other agencies, and items of practical help), to those clients whose need for social work was judged by the independent assessors to be 'considerable', as they gave to clients whose needs were judged to be 'slight'. The social workers were, of course, unaware of the assessors' judgements. In other words it seemed possible in this group, who ranged from ordinary old people with few practical needs to severely incapacitated persons with complex problems, to assess broadly in one interview the degree and nature of social work need. This finding has considerable implications, in terms of deployment of scarce skilled resources. At the end of the experiment we considered that it was possible to determine the level and type of skill required in the social care of old welfare clients by taking three broad factors into account; their disabilities (physical and mental), their 'morale', and the support they were already receiving. Needless to say, these suggestions need further testing.

There have been other developments in Britain in trying to determine the nature of care, and hence the resources needed for different types of clients. Researchers of the Local Government Operational Research Unit, using a sample of aged welfare clients in a big English local authority, produced, by means of cluster analysis, sixteen groups of related cases. They then chose the most representative member of each group as the 'typical case' (LGORU, 1972). With the help of experienced social workers they then determined the social work needs of these typical cases in two different circumstances: in the community and in residential placements. This enabled the researchers to present to the planners of the social services department estimates of resources required for meeting the needs of their known welfare clients. It should be stressed that the accuracy of the social workers' judgements and the appropriateness of the specific forms of care prescribed by them have not been experimentally tested.

The only possible conclusion one can draw from the social work experiments concerned with the social functioning of families and individuals is that much more remains to be done. A great deal of thought and empirical research will have to go into problem classification and social diagnosis so that we can begin to distinguish more clearly the entities with which we are dealing. The cluster analysis research, just mentioned, is one attempt along these lines. Aims of help will have to be clarified, both theoretically in relation to varying diagnostic circumstances and practically in much closer collaboration with clients, than has hitherto been the custom in social work. Methods of helping will have to be described and conceptualized more succinctly and where possible opened up for objective scrutiny. Finally, many different kinds of assessment of outcome need to be applied from simple 'home-made' monitoring devices to field experiments. Only by devoting attention to all these four aspects of the helping process can we hope to determine the relative effectiveness of different types of intervention in different situations.

REFERENCES

Briar, S. (1968). 'The casework predicament', *Soc. Wk,* **13,** 1.

Brown, G. E. (ed.) (1968). *The Multi-Problem Dilemma, A Social Research Demonstration with Multi-Problem Families* (Metuchen, NJ: Scarecrow Press).

Carver, Vida, and Edwards, J. L. (1972). *Social Workers and their Workloads in Health and Welfare Departments in England and Wales* (Report available from the National Institute for Social Work Training).

Goldberg, E. Matilda, Morthery, Ann, and Williams, B. T. (1970). *Helping the Aged: A Field Experiment in Social Work* (London: Allen & Unwin).

Hollis, Florence (1967). 'Explorations in the development of a typology of casework treatment', *Soc. Casework,* **48,** 8.

—— (1968). 'A profile of early interviews in marital counselling', ibid. **47,** 1.

Local Government Operational Research Unit (1972). *Manchester's Old People,* Report no. C120 (January).

Myer, J. E., and Timms, N. (1970). *The Client Speaks: Working Class Impressions of Casework* (London: Routledge & Kegan Paul).

Meyer, H. J., Borgatta, E. E., and Jones, W. C. (1965). *Girls at Vocational High: An Experimental Study in Social Work Intervention* (New York: Russell Sage Foundation).

Mullen, E. J., Chazin, R. M., and Feldstein, D. H. (1970). *Preventing Chronic Dependency* (New York: Community Service Society).

Perlman, Helen H. (1968). 'Casework and the care of Chemung County', in *The Multi-Problem Dilemma, A Social Research Demonstration with Multi-Problem Families.*

Reid, W. J. (1967). 'Characteristics of casework intervention', *Welfare in Review,* **5,** 8.

——and Epstein, Laura (1972). *Task Centred Casework* (New York: Columbia University Press).

——and Shyne, Ann W. (1969). *Brief and Extended Casework* (New York: Columbia University Press).

Walker, Rea, Goldberg, E. Matilda, and Fruin, D. (1972). *Social Workers and their Workloads in Health and Welfare Departments in Northern Ireland* (Report available from the National Institute for Social Work Training).

17 *The Prevention of suicidal behaviour*

NORMAN KREITMAN

Suicidal behaviours can be taken, for present purposes, to comprise two main classes of self-aggressive acts; completed suicide, and what is still erroneously and lamentably termed 'attempted suicide'. The possibilities for preventive action with each type of behaviour will be discussed briefly, and highly selectively, with particular reference to the problems of evaluation.

Completed suicide

There have probably been more investigations into suicide than any other topic in social psychiatry, and a great deal has by now been documented. There appears to be a reasonable consensus of opinion on the delineation of high-risk groups and also as to the kinds of measures which can be taken in an effort to reduce the suicide rate. These fall into four main classes.

1. Programmes of education for the recognition of the potentially suicidal, and of covert forms of mental illness, directed to the general public, to medical students, to GPs, and to trainee psychiatrists. There are certainly *a priori* grounds for such programmes, including evidence of death occurring in patients whose illness or distress had passed unnoticed, or if recognized, treated incorrectly. The problems of evaluating such activities include the difficulty of identifying the recipients of general educational activities, of the long delay which may be expected in some instances for the effects of such education to become apparent, for example with medical students, and lastly the problems of dealing with self-selected groups when considering the impact of postgraduate training schemes.

2. Public health measures directed to high-risk groups, including the visiting of elderly and isolated members of the community and of the recently bereaved, by district health nurses and the like. Evaluation of this kind of service should be relatively easy in principle. However, no such studies have appeared probably because public health programmes of this kind tend to be patchily implemented, so that evaluation would require the discovery by luck of a particularly good 'natural experiment' or alternatively

that the researcher should have under his virtual control organizational and public health facilities outside the usual range of resources.

3. Further research into the treatment of mental illnesses predisposing to suicide. Although studies from some parts of Britain report that depressive illness is the commonest diagnosis associated with suicide, in other areas of the country it has been found that alcoholism is of at least equal significance. While the treatment of depression, if recognized, is usually satisfactory, the impact of current psychiatric skills on the chronic and socially crippled alcoholic appears to be practically nil. This area therefore represents a research need in its own right, rather than anything which the epidemiologist can currently study in the context of suicide prevention.

4. The use of special agencies has figured prominently in the suicide prevention literature. Such bodies would include the telephone Samaritan organizations in the UK, of which there are about 110, and the Suicide Prevention Centres in the US now numbering close to 200, and similar facilities elsewhere, There seems to be little doubt that such agencies do indeed attract a clientele which is at a relatively high risk for suicide (Barraclough *et al.*, 1970; Wilkins, 1970) but nobody appears yet to have been able to devise an investigation which meets the basic requirements of evaluative research into the efficacy of these organizations. At the time of writing only one study has been published using a comparative method. This was an investigation by Bagley (1968) who compared the rates in cities with and without telephone Samaritan organizations but otherwise matched on a number of relevant criteria. He found a greater decline in the suicide rates of the cities possessing these organizations, dating from the time they were established, but pointed out that although this result was compatible with an interpretation that the agencies are effective, the method does not permit any real certainty on this point. As with many other ecological studies, it is not possible to specify whether the individuals concerned were subjected to the effect of the variables studied, that is, had or had not consulted the telephone Samaritan organization, and moreover various background changes as, for example, of public attitude might have led to both the setting up of the agencies and the effect which was subsequently noted.

The same point may be made, incidentally, about two recent British studies on the efficacy of hospital services in preventing suicide. Both were investigating the effects of the introduction of new services on the suicide rate of their catchment areas and among their referred cases. Ratcliffe (1962) claimed that an open door policy in his area led to a fall in suicides at a time when the national trend was stable, but gives few details. Walk (1967) in a much more sophisticated study on a community care service also came to a favourable conclusion. Incidentally, both authors interpret their findings as largely due to the ability of the services to attract a larger

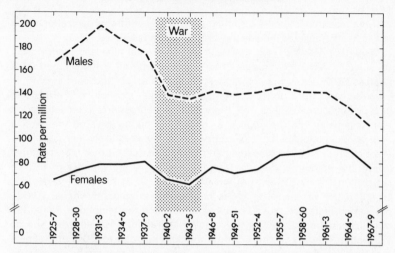

Figure 1. Suicide: crude death-rates per million, England and Wales. *Source.* Registrar-General, 1961.

number of referrals rather than to increased efficiency. Changes in community attitudes in parallel with the setting up of the new services were not considered by either author.

The evaluation of suicide prevention services encounters a number of more or less grave difficulties. In addition to the general problems that arise in connection with any type of preventive activity there are some special features of the suicide problem which deserve mention. One of these is the instability of the base rate. Fig. 1 indicates the trends in suicide as officially reported over the last half-century, and it can be seen that with such striking variations occurring over time any interpretation of secular trends as reflecting prophlactic measures must be viewed with double caution. Moreover, the crude rates illustrated in the figure conceal more than they reveal. Thus, although the over-all rate for men has been falling over the last decade or so, there has been a disturbing increase in the youngest age-groups, as shown in Fig. 2. Preventive services would therefore require to specify their objectives and to evaluate their results in considerable detail before fluctuations in the rate could be interpreted as evidence of success.

It would seem that the only feasible design for demonstrating the efficiency of a preventive service must be the simultaneous study of comparable populations where services are available in one group but not in the other, but where the setting up of the service is not in itself a reflection of a different social ethos. It may be that the difficulty of achieving this situation is one reason for the marked paucity of scientific studies (in contrast to the voluminous impressionistic literature).

Finally, one rather obvious point might be mentioned. There seems to be

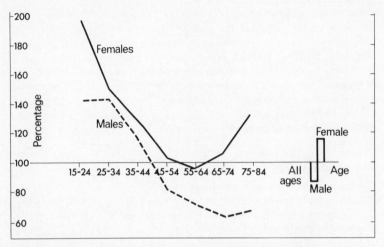

Figure 2. Suicide: average 1966–8 rates compared to average 1950–2 (= 100 per cent), England and Wales.

a peculiar tendency in the literature on suicide prevention to overlook the elementary fact that the work of an organization or of an individual can only be assessed if information is obtained about successes as well as failures. For example, a number of studies have shown that a substantial proportion of suicides intimate their intent to their GPs in the few months preceding their death. It is then implied, if not formally concluded, that GPs (or hospital out-patients or whatever is being investigated) are acting inefficiently. This situation would be precisely analogous to considering the successes of a surgeon solely in terms of the individuals who appear on the post-mortem slab. It is of course true that given greater efficiency in detecting and treating potential suicides the numbers could be substantially reduced, and for this reason it is perfectly rational to seek to improve the skills of all concerned. This should not, however, blind one to the total picture. It is quite possible that GPs and psychiatrists are already operating at a very high level of efficiency in detecting the suicide-prone and that efforts to improve an already high level are unlikely to be rewarding. A much greater pay-off might be obtained, for example, from increasing contact with isolated elderly individuals in the community or by the rehabilitation of social casualties in the middle age-group.

'Attempted suicide' (parasuicide)

Problems of definition and terminology are particularly cogent with the form of behaviour still misleadingly termed 'attempted suicide'. The practice in our group is to consider as falling under this rubric all instances of deliberate self-poisoning or self-injury (Kessel, 1965) without further reference to the intent of the patient. We use the term parasuicide to indicate that there is a *behavioural* analogue between such activity and completed suicide, without any suggestion that there is necessarily a psychological motivation towards death at the time of the act, though this of course is sometimes the case.

The volume of literature on parasuicide is almost as great as that on suicide itself and it will be necessary to limit attention to a few salient problems. Not unnaturally, comment will be partly dictated by the current interests of our unit.

Primary prevention

Clinical exposure to the great variety of individuals who present to psychiatrists[1] following self-poisoning or self-injury rapidly leads to the conclusion that social or interpersonal problems of one kind or another are of relatively greater importance, and that formal psychiatric diagnosis tends to be less valuable, than with many other conditions encountered in the clinic. The conflicts reported by patients may range from relatively minor intrafamilial friction between parents and their children, to rather more severe disorganization of marital and other familial role patterns, and beyond these again to multiple difficulties with almost every kind of relationship. There is evidence that patients are selectively drawn from and share in local subcultures in which self-poisoning or self-injury is a common means of dealing with crisis situations (Kreitman, Smith, and Tan, 1969), and which also have a great deal of 'social disorganization' of many kinds (McCulloch *et al.*, 1967). It is arguable that only a major change in the whole fabric of society, or at least in the relevant subcultures, is likely to make any appreciable difference to the currently very high rates of parasuicide. However, more localized attempts at dealing with the manifest social pathology of these problem areas can be and have been undertaken. One such attempt is currently in progress in Edinburgh; it consists of a multidisciplinary centre in which the activities of some thirty social workers from ten social agencies are co-ordinated under a single director. It was part of the original concept of this centre that evaluative studies should be undertaken of its work but it would be premature to comment on the results to date. Perhaps the important point to be made is that despite the very broad canvas on which such programmes must operate nothing more limited in outlook would be likely to make any impression on the problem with which we are now concerned.

There is, of course, an alternative approach to primary prevention of parasuicide, directed not so much at removing the causes of initial distress

1. A recent study by Kennedy (1971) shows that in Edinburgh about 80 per cent of all self-poisonings and self-injuries (persons, per annum) known to GPs are seen by the hospital service. All referred, including self-referred, cases are admitted.

as in providing distressed individuals with suitably designed services in the hope that their utilization may avert recourse to the dangerous and ineffective problem-solving method represented by the act itself. Once again the agency which comes immediately to mind is the telephone Samaritan organization. We have conducted a number of studies in recent years comparing the clientele of this organization with those who are known parasuicides (Chowdhury *et al.,* 1970, 1971). Over a five-month period all first-ever contacts of the Samaritans, numbering 364, were systematically reviewed. At the same time a series representing all first-ever admissions to the poisoning ward of our local hospital, numbering 225, were also studied. Only individuals from the city of Edinburgh were included. It was found that the Samaritan clients showed a significant (and marked) excess of males when compared to the parasuicide patients. Among the men, clients were less likely to be living with their families or friends although they did not differ in marital status. They tended to be of similar age and social class in the two groups. For women the picture was rather different. Apart. from being under-represented among the clients they also tended to be older than the patients and were more often married or widowed. There were no differences in the proportions living with kin or friends. Various other rather complex similarities and differences concerning the area of residence within the city were also noted for both sexes. An initial conclusion from the survey was that there appeared to be a group of individuals who are 'under-users' of the Samaritan organization from the point of view of parasuicide prevention; in essence they comprise firstly women and especially younger women, and secondly men in selected areas of the city who are still involved with their families (albeit in a highly disruptive manner) rather than the socially isolated.

At this stage, then, it appeared that we had identified groups of individuals who for reasons as yet undertermined were failing to use the service ostensibly designed for their benefit, and that educational campaigns of various kinds might therefore have something to offer. However, an extension to the study caused us to realize that the picture was far more complex. We selected for attention a nuclear group of Samaritan clients who appeared to make optimal use of the service by continuing to work with the Samaritan volunteers and maintaining contact with them over a period of at least two weeks. This sample comprised 121 clients. They were compared with a group of 93 first-ever parasuicides seen at the Regional Poisoning Treatment Centre (RPTC). Both groups were investigated in some detail. In some respects the findings confirmed conclusions already drawn from the first part of the study but some new factors emerged. It was found, for example, that the parasuicides tended to live in a rich, even tumultuous interpersonal environment, while the Samaritan clients tended rather to be isolated, unemployed, and lonely people. Thus, while the client population contained many people apparently seeking someone to whom they could reveal their problems, the parasuicide group already lived in a densely populated world and seeking new contacts seemed a less likely resource for them. The differences in sex-ratio between the two groups we now are inclined to interpret as reflecting a difference between a desire for 'instrumental solutions' to objectifiable difficulties, as displayed chiefly by the men, versus an emotional or 'expressive' activity prompted by a desire for emotional release and favoured particularly by the women. The evidence on which these tentative conclusions are based can scarcely be detailed here, but if substantiated they imply that consultation with the Samaritan organization and parasuicide do not represent *alternatives,* but that the choice of action is an integral part of the outcome which the individual seeks to achieve.

This view was confirmed by another investigation in which a further series of first-ever admissions to the RPTC were specifically questioned as to why they had not chosen to consult some appropriate agency. Interestingly, factual ignorance of the availability of someone whom the patient believed would be prepared to help, a social agency, GP, or the Samaritans, was found in only 15 per cent of the series. It seems evident that elementary dissemination of information has relatively little to offer. Attention was then focused on the attitudes and opinions expressed by patients who were at least factually aware that help-giving resources were indeed available. A number of salient attitudes were identified. The largest group of all claimed they were seeking immediate relief from strain and that this could be most rapidly achieved by self-medication in excessive dosage. Another group believed that although they knew of various benevolently disposed individuals and agencies these in fact, had nothing useful to offer: some patients were speaking from experience of earlier crises. Conceivably for both these groups more satisfactory services of existing types, or a new kind of service specially tailored to meet their needs at an earlier stage could be designed, though the problems would be very formidable. However, it is important to note a number of other categories. There was, for example, a substantial proportion of individuals who simply expressed a wish to die and for whom rescue was precisely what they did not wish to have. Others considered their problems far too personal for ventilation to other people. Another group maintained that their overdose was intended to convey a dramatic message to another person, usually their spouse, and that their purpose could not have been met by anything less flamboyant.

These illustrative findings serve to reiterate the general point made earlier. It is probably inaccurate to think that alternative routes to help are viewed by patients as largely interchangeable. Rather it is the type of eventual outcome which the patient envisages and which in turn is probably linked to his demographic, familial, and social status which determines his choice of action. There is no point in offering alternatives in the way in which a salesman may offer the potential customer different makes of detergent. It seems that the conclusions to be drawn regarding parasuicide prevention at the primary level are not optimistic ones.

Secondary prevention

Repetition of self-aggressive behaviour is a formidable problem in the treatment of parasuicide. Our local experience suggests that approximately 10 per cent of persons admitted to the RPTC will repeat their act within the calendar year and 20 per cent will do so within twelve months of their key admission. Similarly of all admissions within a given year only 60 per cent are first-ever episodes in the lives of the individuals concerned. Evidently the sucessful recognition of the potential 'repeater' and effective methods of preventing repetition are highly desirable from the point of view both of the patient and of the medical services.

There are two distinct problems, the first of these being to predict which individuals are at high risk for a further episode. Such selection is necessitated by the need to focus on a proportion of patients, as the total numbers currently displaying parasuicidal behaviour are too large for universal inclusion in secondary preventive schemes. There are by now a number of studies in the literature distinguishing repeaters from non-repeaters, and the discriminating variables might reasonably be expected to act as predictive indicators for repetition, especially as there is reasonably good agreement between the various studies. There are, however, three points which require some emphasis.

The first is that the supposition that discriminating variables will in fact also be successful predictors is an assumption which requires to be empirically tested. To the best of my knowledge there is only one investigation which has attempted to derive predictive scales which have then been subjected to prospective testing (Buglass *et al.*, 1970). That study illustrated that a retrospectively derived scale could successfully predict repetition in women but that the corresponding scale for men did not hold up. There is clearly a need for further investigations of this kind.

Secondly, there is the general question of *efficiency* of prediction. For practical prophylaxis what is ideally required is not only the designation of high-risk groups but that the groups so defined should contain all, or practically all, the future cases. Preventive programmes often fail to resolve the problem of the large but low-risk categories which in fact yield the majority of patients in time.

Thirdly, it is important to be aware that the characteristics of the parasuicide population may well be changing. Currently the parasuicide rate in Edinburgh is increasing by approximately 10 per cent per annum, and although as far as we can ascertain the characteristics of the patients remain much the same from one year to the other it is difficult to be absolutely certain on this point. Certainly predictive criteria established at one point in time require frequent retesting at later occasions, not only to permit the elimination of purely chance effects but also to keep up to date with a possibly changing population of patients.

The other aspect of secondary prevention is of course the programme of therapy and management which is to be adopted. Evidence on the efficiency of existing services is by no means easily come by. Two studies have suggested in a rather indirect manner that existing patterns of hospital care, including full psychiatric treatment, may be of some value. Thus Greer *et al.* (1971) and Bagley *et al.* (1971) reported that of individuals seen in the casualty department of a large London hospital those who accepted admission and who continued with the planned course of therapy had a lower risk of repetition than individuals who either declined to be admitted or who at some point broke off in their treatment. Similarly, in the general practice survey already referred to (Kennedy, 1971) there was some evidence that patients admitted to the Edinburgh RPTC had a lower rate of repetition than those who were not so admitted; the criterion of success used here was any further episode known to the GP and not simply attempts which came to the notice of the hospital. Both these studies are compatible with the interpretation that the hospital services had something positive to offer. However, neither can furnish conclusive proof. Both studies attempted to identify in their total material those variables associated with subsequent attempts and both demonstrated that the untreated group did not differ from the treated patients on those particular criteria. The objection must remain however, that the untreated group were clearly differentiated from the remainder in some respects, which evidently have eluded analysis, and hence no firm conclusion can be derived.

A more satisfactory design was utilized (Chowdhury, Hicks, and Kreitman, in press) in an investigation designed to test the efficacy of a specially organized after-care service for parasuicides. These workers studied a group of patients admitted to the Edinburgh RPTC who had already made one former 'attempt' within the preceding three years and who were thus expected to contain a reasonably high proportion who would repeat yet again. After excluding a small number of patients on ethical grounds, 155 patients were included in the trial; these were randomly allocated to either the routine after-care service provided by the ward or to a special management regime. This comprised intensive out-patient support with immediate domiciliary visiting if appointments were missed, twenty-four-hour and seven-day a week availability of staff to meet crises, active social work and the deployment of numerous ancilliary agencies where indicated. Patients in the experimental service made extensive use of its facilities, which appeared to be well suited to their needs.

All patients were assessed in detail on admission to the study and again after six months, at which point intensive care was discontinued. The results showed that although the intensely treated group had more satisfactory occupational adjustments and better housing arrangements after the six-month period there was no difference in the proportions in the two groups readmitted for further parasuicide. Similarly no differences were found when various subgroups of patients were considered. It would appear then that an orthodox type of service, however readily available and however carefully designed to meet the requirements of parasuicides, has no demonstrable prophylactic value, at least after the patient's second admission. It is of some interest that the London study just mentioned (Greer *et al.,* 1971) also showed that there was no difference in outcome for patients admitted or not admitted to hospital for their second or subsequent attempt.

So far as one can interpret the exiguous data currently available, it would seem that we need to distinguish two groups of patients from the point of view of secondary prevention. There is firstly the group of individuals, often young women, who make their first attempt in late adolescence or in their early twenties in the setting of a transitory familial disturbance. They appear to have a relatively low risk of repetition and it is possible, though not yet demonstrated, that psychiatric services may reduce this risk still further. Secondly, there is the group of rather older patients often described as personality disorders or psychopaths who tend to make multiple attempts and who accordingly carry a substantial risk both for further parasuicide (and incidentally for suicide too). They are much more difficult to treat, and there is no evidence, direct or indirect, that they benefit from psychiatric attention. We need some radically new notions as to how they should best be handled. This conclusion is apparently shared by the Los Angeles workers (Litman, 1971) who have recently stated that orthodox crisis theory seems to have relatively little to offer for the many individuals among their clientele whose lives are spent in precarious adjustment to society.

Conclusion

It is no part of the epidemiologist's task to bring comfort to anyone. This is just as well so far as the prevention of suicidal behaviour is concerned: for there is no cogent evidence that existing services are having preventive effects to an important degree. In part, this situation simply reflects the difficulty of producing clear evidence in either direction, even when the aims of the service can be specified fairly clearly. The one positive conclusion that can be drawn is that there should be no diminution in the effort to improve existing services and to experiment with radical innovations.

REFERENCES

Bagley, C. (1968). 'The evaluation of a suicide prevention scheme by an ecological method', *Soc. Sci. and Med.* **2,** 1–14.

—— and Greer, S. (1971). 'Clinical and Social predictors of repeated attempted suicide: a multivariate analysis', *Br. J. Psychiat.* **119,** 515–21.

Barraclough, B., and Shea, M. (1970). 'Suicide and Samaritan clients', *Lancet,* **iii,** 868–70.

Buglass, D., and McCulloch, J. W. (1970). 'Further suicidal, behaviour: the development and validation of predictive scales', *Br. J. Psychiat.* **116,** 483–91.

Chowdhury, N., and Kreitman, N. (1970). 'The clientele of the telephone Samaritan organization', *Appl. Soc. Stud.* **2,** 123–35.

—— —— (1971). 'A comparison of parasuicides ("attempted suicide") and the clients of the telephone Samaritan service', ibid. **3,** 51–57.

—— Hicks, R. C., and Kreitman, N. (in press). 'Evaluation of an after-care service for parasuicide ("attempted suicide") patients'.

Greer, S., and Baglhy, C. (1971). 'Effects of psychiatric intervention in attempted suicide: a controlled study', *Br. med. J.* **1,** 310–12.

Kennedy, P. (1971). 'An epidemiological survey of attempted suicide in general practices in Edinburgh', MD thesis, University of Leeds.

Kessel, N. (1965). 'Self-poisoning. The Milroy Lectures', *Br. med. J.* **2,** 1265–70. 1336–40.

Kreitman, N., Smith, P., and Tan, Eng-Seong (1969). 'Attempted suicide in social networks', *Br. J. prev. soc. Med.* **23,** 116–23.

Litman, R. (1970). 'Suicide Prevention Centre clients: a follow-up study', *Bull. Suicidol.* **6,** 12–18.

—— (1971). 'Experience in a Suicide Prevention Centre', in *Suicide and Attempted Suicide* (Skandia Symposium).

McCulloch, J., Philip, A. E., and Carstairs, G. M. (1967). 'The ecology of suicidal behaviour', *Br. J. Psychiat.* **113,** 313–19.

Ratcliffe, R. (1962). 'The open door', *Lancet,* **ii,** 188–90.

Walk, D. (1967). 'Suicide and community care', *Br. J. Psychiat.* **113,** 1381–93.

Wilkins, J. (1970). 'A follow-up study of those who called a Suicide Prevention Centre', *Am. J. Psychiat.* **127,** 155–61.

18 Development of a hospital-centred community psychotherapy service for schizophrenic patients

YRJÖ ALANEN and AIRA LAINE

STARTING POINTS AND THE DEVELOPMENT OF THE SERVICE

Our notions of schizophrenia are still very divided and disintegrated. There is a unanimousness among the investigators primarily only about the view that the aetiology of the disorder is multifactorial. A dividedness of the same kind prevails on the opinions concerning the treatment of schizophrenia. In the frames of community psychiatry, the centre of emphasis has lain in neuroleptic drug treatments and in rehabilitative social services.

It has been known for several decades that a psychotherapeutic relationship can be established with many schizophrenic patients, and that healing and growth of their personality may be possible through such a relationship (for example, Kempf, 1919; Knight, 1939; Federn, 1943; Sechehaye, 1956; Schulz and Kilgalen, 1969). Yet, these experiences are even today left without due attention in the therapeutic encounter with schizophrenic patients. This has perhaps to do not only with the influence exerted by our psychiatric views and traditions but also with the strength of the means of defence which the schizophrenic disorder often tends to activate in other people, both in the individual and community level (see, for example, Alanen, 1972a; Müller, 1972). Those who, like the writers of the present paper, have personal experience of the psychotherapy of schizophrenic patients find it hard to deny either the need for or the justification of this treatment modality (Alanen, 1962, 1972b; Alanen et al., 1970).

By means of the drugs, acute psychotic states can be calmed down, and they also enhance the possibilities of the chronic schizophrenic patient to get along under ambulant treatment. From a psychological standpoint, what takes place can mainly be regarded as an increase in the patient's ability for social adjustment, at the cost of a certain degree of emotional attentuation; in itself such treatment is unlikely to promote the growth of the patient's personality. In the psychosocial treatment sector the patient's problems are often met predominantly as social questions, whereas their personal aspects may be left aside. Only when a psychotherapeutic approach is made an integral part of the treatment of the schizophrenic patient does this treatment become what it should in our opinion be: an activity by means of which an effort is made to help the patient overcome his personal difficulties and to grow as a human being.

It is often felt that the psychotherapy of schizophrenia is excessively time-consuming and expensive. It is thought to be possible only under costly special conditions and to be suitable and profitable only for a few patients. It would seem that such views are associated with a conception of therapy as a prolonged process of interaction between two individuals exclusively, that is, the therapist and the patient. Yet, more than forty years ago Sullivan (1931) already spoke of the significance of a 'socio-psychiatric' programme and environment as a necessary background of the individual psychotherapy of schizophrenia. At present, it seems, insight into the importance of this orientation is rapidly gaining ground among schizophrenia psychotherapists. Psychodynamic research has made us aware of the apparently paradoxical fact that the disorder affecting the autistic schizophrenic patient is particularly strongly dependent on interactional factors (for example, the family studies by Lidz *et al.*, 1965; Bateson *et al.*, 1956; Wynne *et al.*, 1958; Alanen *et al.*, 1966; Stierlin, 1972). Great progress has been made in the family therapy of schizophrenic patients, and it has been also realized how important a part is played by a community-type encounter in the psychotherapy of schizophrenic patients within a hospital setting or within the framework of other therapeutic units. According to our conclusion, there would be every reason to develop treatment communities also in hospitals where the size of staff relative to the number of patients is not very large, that is, in that kind of hospital to which most schizophrenic patients are admitted.

The process of development in Turku, the initial phases of which we will describe here, is based on currents of thought of the above kind. We are making efforts to investigate *the ways in which, and the extent to which, a psychotherapeutically oriented service meant for schizophrenic patients could be evolved within a community psychiatry setting*. The first part of this main question, the evolving of our service, has been our chief concern until now, and the preliminary evaluative study presented in this paper should also be examined on this background.

We are working at the University of Turku Psychiatric Clinic, which at the same time, together with another mental hospital forms the psychiatric part of the hospital system of the municipality of Turku. Our clinic, with 125 beds, was founded in 1967, in premises that had previously accommodated a hospital for chronic psychiatric patients. Two-thirds of the old patients were then transferred to the other psychiatric hospital mentioned, and, interchanging patients, the wards so liberated were filled with acute cases. Because of a difference of psychiatric orientation, this also meant the beginning of a radical change in the treatment of schizophrenic patients in Turku. The great majority of new schizophrenic patients in the catchment area are sent to us, and we also endeavour, as far as possible, to provide our patients with after-care and to readmit them when necessary.

While developing our hospital service, we have followed the working hypotheses, that the symptoms of schizophrenia are both psychologically understandable and communicable, and that the treatment indications should be determined both on the basis of the patient's individual starting-points and the available potential and treatment facilities.

Our hospital is divided in to three sections, or wards. We have made efforts to develop a ward for acute psychotic patients into what we call a 'psychotherapeutic community' (see Alanen *et al.*, 1970; Salonen, 1972). By this concept we do not mean exactly the same thing which is dealt with by the term 'therapeutic community' of Maxwell Jones (1953) and others. Our community is not as structured and maybe not quite as democratic although there also are common meetings preferably in smaller groups including patients and staff members. The main goals of our psychotherapeutic community are: firstly, endeavour to share empathic psychotherapeutic attitude towards the patients; secondly, a common striving of the personnel to open communication and exploration of the attitudes and feelings connected with the patients as well as the interactional problems of the staff; and thirdly, a stimulation of individual psychotherapeutic relationships with the patients, regardless of the formal position of the therapists. We find the use of less educated personnel (social workers and nurses) as therapists important because of the manpower problem. We also think that therapeutic relationships of this kind often come best into existence as a result of a certain spontaneous tendency toward contact between a particular member of the treatment team and a patient. This is in accordance with a psycho-analytic theory of the importance of primary-process level experiences in schizophrenia.

The second ward for acute patients, most of them less disturbed, is run in a more structured way especially as regards group activities and group therapy. The third ward, where the chronic patients were left to stay, is gradually changing to a rehabilitation section of our hospital.

We try to get acquainted with the patients' living conditions immediately after their admission to the hospital. In association with this, the patients' relatives are also met, and in some cases these contacts have been developed into regular family therapy comprising conjoint sessions with the patient and his family members.

The neuroleptic drug treatments have not been used as a mode of treatment antagonistic to a psychotherapeutic orientation, but instead, as an auxiliary means with a place of its own in the totality of treatment. However, we avoid using large dosages, as their effect has been experienced as repressive from the psychotherapeutic point of view.

The personnel–patient ratio in our hospital has been 63 to 100; the members of the treatment staff proper numbered 43 per 100 hospital beds (this year the number increased to 48). These ratios correspond to the average Finnish mental hospitals (the number of doctors, however, being somewhat greater). In 1969, we employed altogether 8 doctors, 1 psychologist, 2 social workers, 14 nurses of the upper and 20 of the lower educational level, 3 occupational therapists, 1 physiotherapists, and 5 hospital aides.

A difficult problem has been constituted by the continuation of the patients' therapies extramurally, following their discharge from the hospital. We have had a lack of extramural treatment staff. The city of Turku has a mental health office, which is operated outside its hospital system, and the work of this office is not psychotherapeutically oriented. We have favoured continuation of therapeutic relationships that have come into being on the ward as much as has been indicated and possible. The psychotherapeutic after-care has thus been supplied with a personnel originally intended for in-patient service exclusively. The number of after-care visits has grown fairly large: in 1971 they totalled 1,373. Besides these, some of our patients have been able to continue their treatment after discharge from hospital as private office patients of some staff members of our hospital.

In the near future, we will be provided with a small open-care unit which hopefully will increase the efficiency of our service. One of the central questions which are in front of us is how to integrate this unit in the best possible way with our in-patient service. We think that with many schizophrenic patients it would be well to continue, in the form of later visits, the therapeutic relationships established on the ward. Other patients, again, could already be brought in contact with the open-care treatment group while in the hospital with a view to arranging their after-care. Moreover, the contribution of the ambulatory treatment group would no doubt even primarily reduce at least to some extent the number of patients needing hospital treatment.

THE 1971 FOLLOW-UP EXAMINATION OF THE 1969 PATIENTS

Aira Laine

Purpose of the follow-up examination

The purpose of this follow-up examination can here be divided into two main parts:

1. A preliminary prognostic assessment of the results of our therapeutic orientation.

2. A preliminary evaluation of the appropriateness and resources of our service, both in regard to the hospital and the ambulatory treatment. This would be of a special current interest for the further development of our service.

The other purposes of this investigation do not belong to the issues of this paper.

Description of the series of patients and the conduct of the follow-up examination

The object of the follow-up examination was formed of the patient under the age of 45 first admitted to our clinic for hospital treatment because of schizophrenia or borderline schizophrenic state during 1969. These patients numbered sixty-eight in all. Viljo Räkköläinen, a psychiatrist member of our staff, then made an extensive clinical and social-psychiatric study (not yet published), covering all these patients, and a psychological study on them was carried out by myself, generally in the phase when the acute psychosis had already subsided and the patient was leaving the hospital. On that occasion comparatively extensive psychological investigation by means of both psychometric and projective methods (WAIS, EPI, Rorschach, ORT) was performed.

A diagnostic distribution of the patients was based on this psychological investigation as well as on the interview connected with it. The distinct cases of schizophrenia, indicating formal thought disorders of typically schizophrenic character were separated from the 'schizo-affective' psychoses and borderline schizophrenics with only slight symptoms.

In 1971 I met sixty-two of the same patients again, approximately in the same order as in 1969, so that the average follow-up period came to be about two years. Two patients refused to come for a follow-up (one of them diagnosed as a typical schizophrenic). In another two cases (neither of them being included in the typical schizophrenia group) I have been in contact with the patient but it has not yet been possible to arrange interviews with them, and two patients (one of them typically schizophrenic) had committed suicide: one while in the hospital for the first time and the other immediately following discharge.

During the follow-up examination, nine of the patients were under hospital treatment.

The diagnostic distribution of the patients met in connection with the follow-up examination is shown in Table 1.

The diagnoses made by Dr Räkköläinen were also at my disposal. There was a 90 per cent agreement between us about the diagnostic distribution presented above. Had a finer classification been used, a slight reduction in agreement would have resulted.

The follow-up examination included a thorough interview, consisting of both structured multiple-choice questions and spontaneous conversation.

Table 1. *Diagnostic distribution of the patient series.*

	M	F	Total
Schizophrenic	16	22	38
Schizophrenic-affective	4	2	6
Borderline	11	7	18
Total	31	31	62

The following areas were covered by the interview: family relationships and interpersonal relationships in general, work, economic position, both the psychic and somatic illnesses from which the patient and his family members had suffered during the follow-up period, the need for hospital treatment and the patient's insight into the pathological nature of his condition in 1969, hospital treatment and after-care, and the patient's present need for treatment. The Rorschach test was readministered on this occasion. For the follow-up I had also formulated questionnaire forms of a kind, by means of which I tried to map out the patient's subjective, conscious experience of his illness, and of his life during hospitalization and after it. Thus, what was concerned was, in a sense, the phenomenology of illness or the examination of certain features of it (Soskis and Bowers, 1969; Stein, 1967).

The examination took about three hours and it was carried out without interruption.

The research results to be reported here are based mainly on the interview stage, because the treatment of the other data is still at its initial phase.

Prognostic criteria

I have conceived of outcome in a broad sense, in such a way that account has been taken both of the patient's total situation and personality and his own appraisals concerning these. The criteria for the assessment of outcome can be classified into the following four groups:

1. The patient's intrapsychic condition and the changes that have occurred in it over the follow-up period. The description will be based on the patient's Rorschach results.

2. Interpersonal relationships; the evaluation will rest both on the interview findings and the ORT results. It should be mentioned that the assessments resting on projective techniques will be carried out not only by the present writer but also by another, independent investigator, who will neither know the patient nor be aware of the stage from which the test results derive.

3. Social adaptation: the writer will assess this on the basis of data on the patient's success in his work or studies since 1969. Use will be made of a four-point scale, in such a way that one point will be scored if the person is comparatively regularly employed and doing work that corresponds to

his schooling or if his success in studies has been normal, two points if he is comparatively regularly employed but the work he does is not wholly consistent with his schooling or if he has fallen behind slightly in his studies, three points if he has made attempts to work and has held a number of posts but the attempts have ended in failure or if he has discontinued his studies, and four points if the patient has been pensioned prematurely or has become otherwise economically dependent upon others (for his living) during the follow-up period. The classification of the patients has been comparatively easy to perform and doubtful cases have been few in number.

4. Clinical condition and changes in it. The description will rest both on the patient's own appraisal and the picture the examiner has received of the patient's behaviour during the follow-up examination. The patient's clinical condition and changes in it will later be also assessed on the basis of the test results. Thus, three different methods will be used in the assessment of the patient's clinical condition and change in it: the patient's own subjective appraisals, the writer's somewhat subjective assessment based on the interview examination situation (year 1971), and the test records (years 1969, 1971), to be interpreted for this purpose by the investigator and by another person independently of each other. At the follow-up stage, the patient was asked whether he felt at present: (*a*) well; (*b*) better than at the time of first admission to the hospital, (*c*) neither better nor worse than at the time of first admission; (*d*) more ill than at the time of first admission.

The scale used by the investigator in assessing the patients on the basis of the interview findings is as follows:

1. Symptom-free, no manifest symptoms.

2. Symptoms (psychotic or seriously neurotic), to a lesser extent than in 1969, the social significance of these symptoms appearing slight.

3. The patient's condition approximately the same as in 1969.

4. The patient's condition worse than in 1969.

In this paper it is possible to consider the results concerning outcome mainly in the light of the last two criteria, that is, the patients' social adaptation and their clinical condition and changes in it, as assessed on the basis of information other than the test results.

Research results

The interelations among the variables have been analysed by means of Pearson's correlations (significance tested by critical ratio) and chi-squared. No statistically significant differences between the typically schizophrenic patient and the borderline group were found as regards age, occupation, marital status, or intellectual ability. Nor were differences found in these variables between men and women.

Evaluation of some community services

Table 2. *The patients' social adaptation.*

	+1	2	3	4—	Total
Number	29	15	6	12	62
Percentage	46·8	24·2	9·7	19·3	100

Social adaptation

The patients' distribution on the adaptation scale is given in Table 2, where both the numerical and percentage frequencies are set out because of the small size of the series.

Social adaptation failed to correlate significantly with age, occupation, intellectual ability, and loss of intellectual abilities (investigated in 1969). On the other hand, there was a highly significant association between social adaptation and the patient's clinical condition as assessed by the investigator ($r = 0.516^{xxx}$) and between the former variable and the length of the first hospital stay ($r = 0.513^{xxx}$): the better the patient's condition at the follow-up stage and the shorter the first hospitalization, the better was his social adaptation.

In the total series, the most frequent length of the first hospital stay was about one to two months. Three of the patients had been discharged only after six months and three others had stayed in the hospital even longer, one of them throughout the follow-up period; thirty had been readmitted during this period, a majority of them to our hospital. Thus, exactly half the patients had not needed renewed hospital care. Of the men, 61 per cent, and of the women 31 per cent had been readmitted ($X^2 = 3.16$; $p < 0.1$). Social adaptation was significantly poorer in cases where the patient had been readmitted, in comparison with cases where the patient had been only once in the hospital.

Clinical condition

In a sense, the patient and the investigator evaluated this by employing the same scale, even though the verbal cues were different. The results of both evaluations are cross-tabulated in Table 3.

The two ratings correlated positively. It should be noted, however, that 15 patients regarded themselves as well, whereas the investigator considered only 6 patients symptom-free. Three patients have not made the evaluation.

When the patients were asked to appraise their own somatic condition, the following was found: the patients who felt that their psychic condition had improved had a tendency to feel that during the two years concerned they had been somatically healthier than previously ($r = 0.539^{xxx}$).

Although there was a distinct association between social adaptation and the duration of the first hospital stay, no corresponding connection was found between the change in the patient's clinical condition, as assessed

Table 3. *The patients' clinical condition evaluated by the investigator and by the patients themselves.*

		Investigator				
		1	2	3	4	
	(0)	(−)	(−)	(3)	(−)	(3)
Patient 1	1	6	8	0	1	15
	2	0	27	9	1	37
	3	0	2	1	1	4
	4	0	0	2	1	3
Total		6	37	15	4	62

$r = 0.496^{XXX}$

by the investigator, and the duration of the first hospital stay. On the other hand, the better the patient's present clinical condition (in the year 1971), the less probably had he been readmitted to the hospital during the follow-up period.

Evaluation of the hospital treatment

As already stated, a short duration of the first hospital stay and good social adaptation were interconnected. Nevertheless, there was no statistically significant association between the length of the first hospital stay and readmissions.

The evaluation of the hospital treatment is a rather diffuse problem area, difficult to approach. An attempt was made to shed some light on this point by inquiring from the patients about their need for treatment and about what in the hospital they felt had been of help. Now, two years afterwards, a majority of the patients (75 per cent) were of the opinion that they had been in need of hospital treatment when they were first admitted. Of the aspects and factors experienced as helpful, conversations were mentioned most often (34 per cent), these including both the conversations with a doctor, psychologist, or another member of the treatment staff, and participation in groups; the stay in the hospital per se was mentioned almost equally often (27 per cent) and so was drug treatment (25 per cent). The percentages have been computed from the total of the factors mentioned and not from the total number of patients. Four of the patients felt that nothing in the hospital had helped them. Also, there was a tendency for those who were well adapted socially to mention a greater number of helpful factors, compared with those who were more poorly adapted.

In order to describe the significance of hospital treatment in another way, I propose to give brief accounts of five cases.

1. Jim was a newly graduated young man aged 23. His father had died in 1965. His admission to the hospital had been preceded by the breaking-off of a prolonged

engagement because the girl had become pregnant by another man. Jim told how his illness broke out one morning: he was unable to walk and he had pain all over his body. On admission the patient was very anxious, agitated, reality testing was deficient (for example, the patient wanted to have his nose reshaped through surgery), and the diagnosis made was a borderline state. The patient only stayed in the hospital for a couple of weeks and then went to serve his time in the army. In the hospital the patient received drugs and conversations were had with him, mainly for examination purposes. The patient himself was very desirous of conservation. After leaving the hospital he discontinued taking his drugs and he had not been under any kind of treatment during the follow-up period. At the time of the follow-up he was very successful in his work and was pursuing postgraduate studies. Outwardly he could have been regarded as symptom-free, even though his excessive self-confidence appeared doubtful.

2. John was a student, aged 25 on admission, married, and the father of two children. He had long been depressed and anxious, began to show paranoid trends and had on a few occasions delusionally heard his name mentioned. He was no longer able to study. In this case, too, the diagnosis was a borderline state. In the hospital John was very tense and withdrawn, and when he moved about, he behaved as if he were all the time careful not to do anything evil. He received drugs, but rather than conversing he for the most part only briefly and slowly answered the questions he was asked. He stayed four weeks in the hospital. In connection with the psychological investigation contact was established with him; both the patient and the psychologist were prepared to continue developing the inchoate therapeutic relationship, and this later led to close frequency psycho-therapy. By the time of the follow-up John had graduated and had received his first post. His therapy had terminated a few months previously.

3. Violet was a housewife aged 28 whose husband was studying. On admission she was gravely psychotic and regressive, the diagnosis being acute schizophrenia. She did not recognize her husband and was seeing her dead relatives on the ward. Violet would have liked to divorce her husband and return to her mother. This she insisted for a long time. Her husband did not, however, consent to divorce her but was able to bear his wife's serious psychotic phase. He came to discuss with the psychiatrist in charge of the ward and conjoint sessions were also held. Violet stayed in the hospital for about two and a half months, and for about a year after being discharged she came a few times a month to discuss either with the psychiatrist or the nurse in charge of the ward. She came for the follow-up from another locality, where her husband had found a job after graduation. Violet herself had been regularly employed for about a year, her work consisting largely in caring for others. She was expecting her first child and the marriage appeared harmonious as a whole.

4. Tom was a 20-year-old student when he was admitted to the hospital. About a year previously he had begun to fall ill, had become inhibited and autistic. He consulted a private practitioner, who referred him to our hospital, where the diagnosis established was hebephrenic schizophrenia. The whole family proved very ill and was found to be collectively psychotic at times. Tom began intensive individual therapy with the psychiatrist in charge of the ward, who also started family therapy. Tom had been in the hospital about half the follow-up period. He continued to be very ill, though not autistic; he did not talk much, but he was clearly in contact with other people. He had developed an intense transference relationship to his therapist, and his world had grown richer and had more content than before. This was also the case with the whole family. Both the individual and family therapies were being continued.

5. Victor was an unmarried labourer aged 37. He came to the hospital direct from

Sweden, where he had been employed. Victor had kept moving from one locality to another all his life. He had been psychotically paranoid for years, but now his delusions of poisoning and homoerotic impulses had grown so strong that suicide was the only alternative he saw to hospitalization. He clearly brought out his need for help. He stayed in the hospital for slightly less than two months, after which he moved away from Turku. At the follow-up stage I went to see the patient at his home. He continued to be very lonesome, but the basic necessities of life were again in order: he had work and a place to live in. After leaving our clinic, he had later gone to another mental hospital, and he was now living in the patient hostel of that hospital. He felt that our clinic had not been able to provide him with any help, but that he had found help in this other hospital.

The above five cases differ widely from one another. In the case of Jim, it seems to me, it is very difficult to determine the part played by hospital treatment. It would seem that the role played by the army had been far more important, in the sense that it helped him disengage from his mother. Jim himself stated that he had never felt less anxiety than when he was in the army. He had had girlfriends, but the relationships had been short-lived. The possibility seems to exist that the next crisis will set in when he begins to keep company with a girl more regularly.

With John, the importance of the hospital may have essentially lain in the fact that it provided him with an opportunity for psychotherapy. Had it been possible to begin the therapy earlier, hospitalization might even have been unnecessary.

Regarding Violet, again, it seems to me that the hospital was of great significance. The hospital was able to encounter her regression but at the same time strongly supported the healthy aspects of her personality. Like a child, Violet wanted to go to the security of her mother, but the hospital provided her with a mother: the nurse in charge of the ward. Security-producing limits were set for Violet.

Tom was one of the most gravely ill of the patients in this series. I would say that the hospital offered him a chance to lead a life, but on the other hand it is hard to know what the hospital's potentialities are. It seems clear, in any case, that without therapy and hospital Tom would have fallen even deeper in his autism. After the follow-up his clinical condition has, as a matter of fact, very much improved. He is not autistic any more and he has less psychotic fantasies.

Victor had lived for years in a psychotically paranoid world involving both sheltering and threatening systems. In the hospital he had a good relationship with the psychiatrist in charge of the ward, he was given a kind of psychotherapeutic help and he received treatment for a skin disorder. I am inclined to believe that this first hospitalization was of some importance to him, even though he failed to see this and felt that his 'difficulties were not taken seriously'. As a matter of fact, our hospital does not have the resources necessary to 'take seriously' a patient like him. We have neither a patient hostel nor other requisite facilities.

Table 4. *The distribution of the long-term psychotherapies.*

Close frequency	Long interval	Family	Group
12	4	2 (1)	3 (1)

The present series included several other patients comparable to Victor, who in our system become forgotten, in a sense: they will either remain in the hospital or leave the hospital to 'live a life all alone'. Often they become ever more regressively dependent on the hospital, their ego functions are not supported, but they are deprived of these, or they will return to drift in life following ways of their own and without finding a place for themselves.

In the statistics the above five cases appear as follows: four patients whose social adaptation was good or moderately good and one patient who was pensioned. The result could be interpreted to show that the hospital had succeeded in four out of five cases. When the cases are scrutinized individually, however, the conclusion proves erroneous. The first hospital treatment in itself may have been of least importance in the case of Jim, John, and Victor and of greatest importance in the case of Violet and Tom. With Violet the situation was good, whereas Tom had not succeeded socially. Still, in my opinion, it would not be justifiable to claim that the hospital failed in its efforts in this case. When the starting points taken into consideration, it would be more legitimate to say that the hospital has done everything possible for Tom.

Ambulatory treatment and psychotherapy

Twenty-nine of the patients had paid visits to the after-care clinic of the hospital, and 15 of them were continuing their visits during the follow-up examination. A further 16 patients were elsewhere under ambulatory treatment, some of them as private office patients of persons working in our hospital. Only 4 patients had not received any sort of ambulatory treatment. Drugs had been taken throughout the follow-up period by 29 patients.

In Table 4, the patients who had been under *psychotherapy* at least for a year are classified according to the type of the therapy. It should be emphasized that all of these therapies had been continued extramurally. In the table, close frequency psychotherapy means a therapy with one session a week or more, and long interval therapy, a therapy with sessions once in two weeks or once a month. Most of the close frequency therapies could be called psycho-analytically oriented and the same is true of the two family therapies. The long interval therapies as well as group therapies could be characterized as supportive contact therapies.

A total of 18 patients had been or were under one type of long-term psychotherapy or another, and 3 patients had simultaneously been under two types of psychotherapy. Except for 5 cases, the psychotherapies were taking place, or had taken place, either at our clinic or the private office of a person belonging to the same treatment system (11 at the clinic and 5 at the private offices; 9 were conducted by the doctors, 3 by the psychologist, 2 by the social workers, and 2 by the nurses). Those patients who have had few therapeutic sessions are not included in the figures of Table 4, despite the fact that such sessions may have been of great importance to the patients. This has apparently been often the case with family therapy. As the family members of all the patients in this series were met, it was perhaps easier than usual to arrange conjoint sessions, and the need for such sessions was easier to perceive than in a situation where there is not contact with the patient's relatives.

DISCUSSION

A follow-up period of two years is very short if we wish to make a prognosis concerning the patient's later course of life or if our aim is to assess the therapeutic results. This should be borne in mind when drawing conclusions.

Of the patients, 71 per cent had adapted well or moderately well socially. The result hardly differs substantially from previous comparable results (for example, Achté, 1967), when the diagnostic distribution of the patients is taken into account.

There was no apparent association between the patient's social adaptation and his age, occupation, or intellectual ability. This may have been partly because the series was rather heterogeneous, but on the other hand, these factors do not seem particularly essential in schizophrenia. The prognosis is likely to depend more on the availability of a symbiotic relationship than on the patient's social status or intelligence.

A fairly interesting finding is, in our opinion, that the patient's and the investigator's assessments regarding the patient's clinical condition were highly similar. It can, or course, be suspected that the patient's appraisals had an effect on the investigator's assessments, and this may in fact have been the case to some extent. However, we do not believe that this is an exhaustive explanation. As we see it, the patient's own opinions about the need for treatment ought to be taken into account more than hitherto. In prescribing drug treatments, for example, the diagnosis ought not to be the only factor taken into consideration.

The findings concerning the length of the patient's first hospital stay and its relation to their clinical condition as assessed during the follow-up study might be of some interest. As could be expected, there was a group of patients whose clinical condition was good and whose first stay in the hospital had been short. But there was also a group whose clinical condition was good but who had had to stay comparatively long in the hospital on first occasion. However we cannot make specific conclusions of this fact at this stage, it might support our hypothesis that some of the patients had benefited precisely by the establishment of therapeutic relationships of comparatively long duration, either in the form of individual psychotherapy or within the framework of the psychotherapeutic community as a whole. As Wing (see Chapter 1) also states, we cannot assume that the reduction in length of the hospital stay means necessarily that the patients had been cured in a shorter period of time. There are studies, for example those of Achté and his co-workers in Helsinki (Achté, 1967; Niskanen and Achté, 1971), which, somewhat surprisingly, indicate that the long-term prognosis of schizophrenia has not improved significantly during the last fifteen years although the length of the hospital periods has grown shorter. We think that some schizophrenic patients need time to be able to return from their withdrawn state and to enter into a therapeutic relationship beneficial for their recovery.

The efficiency of various modes of treatment can scarcely be compared on the basis of this study, because the series is too small and the follow-up period too short for the purpose. We would like to emphasize that it is often very difficult to assess which factors in the treatment or outside it have been helpful to the patient. This is best illustrated by the case-histories included in our paper. It is also very difficult to evaluate the results of psychotherapy solely statistically, without taking into consideration the individual starting-points of the patient and his environment as well as the goals set for the treatment. Even the points of departure seem fallacious and ther seems to be little understanding of the process character of psychotherapy in a method that consists of dividing the patients blindly into a number of groups and applying various modes of treatment to the various groups. A more adequate method in the assessment of the effectiveness of psychotherapy would be the following: an effort is first made to plan the treatment and its modes as openly as possible, within the limits set by the channels that are available when the appeal for the treatment is encountered; and later, after a sufficiently long period of time, an effort is made to examine carefully which factors involved in the treatment process have perhaps been helpful and which have not, and what errors have been committed.

Concerning the resources of our service, the follow-up examination clearly revealed that the need for psychotherapy had been greater than the utilization of it. The follow-up investigator felt that even the fact that most of the patients came for examination surprisingly willingly, was partly due to a need for treatment among them. Eighteen patients had received regular long-term therapy at least for a year, many of them, however, as private office patients. Long-term psychotherapy would not have been either necessary or appropriate with each and every patient in our series. Nevertheless, judging by the picture offered by the follow-up examination, the need for such treatment had remained partly unsatisfied.

The small number of long-term family therapies was especially striking and perhaps somewhat disappointing. This may indicate practical difficulties as far as the continuation of these therapies on an ambulatory basis is concerned; it may also indicate an initial resistance against these therapies among our staff, compared with individual psychotherapy. It may be good to remember, however, that the number of those cases in which we had a family therapy of shorter duration was greater, and also that the amount of family therapies of longer duration has been gradually increasing after 1969. While considering the obvious benefit of these therapies, experienced in practice, one of the conclusions to be made would be an increasing effort to stimulate the family therapeutic approach.

The same would be concluded in regard to the psychotherapeutic relationships conducted by nurses and social workers. Within a community psychiatry setting, psychiatrists and psychologists will be unable to satisfy the need for psychotherapy, even though their number were increased. We have perceived that the use of less-educated personnel as therapists has uncovered therapeutic abilities and potentialities, which would otherwise have remained unutilized. This is, however, not the only important consideration. Another important point is that individual therapeutic contacts, more than anything else, serve to make the members of the various personnel groups open to the problems of the schizophrenic patient. This will turn out to the benefit of the entire treatment community. Development in this direction has also clearly increased the interest of the members of the personnel in their work and enhanced the satisfaction derived from it. The development of such a treatment orientation is not very fast, however, and calls for increased supervisory work. As regards our own service, a lack of supervision has obviously been one of the factors which has especially hampered the continuation of these therapeutic relationships after the patient's discharge from the hospital.

The follow-up examination clearly showed what has been the worst shortcoming of our treatment service its insufficient ambulatory treatment facilities. An efficient and psychotherapeutically oriented open-care treatment group will obviously be of decisive help in meeting the need for after-care services. A further point on which the follow-up shed light was the insufficiency of the social services necessary for schizophrenic patients that our hospital is able to offer. It would be necessary for us to operate a patient hostel, and there is a need for improved forms of social rehabilitation. Instead of reducing the need for such services, the development of the psychotherapeutic service will increase it. That the outcome was favourable in the social respect had in some cases to do with the fact that the patient had a place to go to, while in other cases a poor outcome was due to the very fact that the patient did not have such a place. Social conditions are often of decisive importance, particularly in cases where the preconditions for intensive psychotherapy are unfavourable.

Finally we would like to refer briefly to our further research plans. We intend to evaluate our research by means of long-term follow-up investigations, which are meant to cover both the patients dealt with in this paper and series of patients associated with later phases of development of our treatment service. A series of schizophrenic patients who have received treatment in Turku before the founding of our clinic will also be used for a comparative group. The follow-up examinations will be done by both psychiatrists and pschologists, and we have also become aware of the fact that we must make use of independent evaluators, not belonging to our treatment staff. Besides the histories of treatment, there will be four dimensions of observation: (1) the descriptive-psychiatric (the symptoms); (2) the psychosocial (the social adaptation, history of hospitalizations, etc,); (3) the psychodynamic (the interpersonal relationships and the interpsychic condition); and (4) the phenomenological (the patient's own experience of his illness and treatment). Only after these investigations can we say in which respect we have been able to promote the treatment of schizophrenic patients, if in any.

REFERENCES

Achté, K. A. (1967). 'On prognosis and rehabilitation in schizophrenic and paranoid psychoses', *Acta psychiat. Scand.* **43**, suppl. 196.
Alanen, Y. O. (1962). 'Erfarenheter av supportive psykoterapi med schizofrenipatienter', English summary: 'Experiences from the supportive psychotherapy of schizophrenic patients', *Nordisk. Psykiat. Tidskr.* **16**, 443–56.
—— (1972a). 'On the place of psychotherapy in the psychiatric approach to schizophrenia', in Rubinstein, D., and Alanen, Y. O. (eds), *Psychotherapy of Schizophrenia* (Amsterdam: Exerpta Medica).
—— (1972b). 'The benefits of family psychotherapy in hebephrenic schizophrenia', ibid.
—— in collaboration with Rekola, J., Stewen, A., Takeka, K., and Tuovinen, M. (1966). 'The family in the pathogenesis of schizophrenic and neurotic disorders', *Acta psychiat. Scand.* **42**, suppl. 189.
—— Laine, A., Räkköläinen, V., and Salonen, S. (1970). 'Evolving the psychotherapeutic community: research combined with hospital treatment of schizophrenia'. Paper presented at the conference on Schizophrenia—the Implications of Research Findings for Treatment and Teaching, sponsored by the National Institute of Mental Health and the John E. Fogarty International Center, Washington, DC, 30 May–2 June 1970.
Bateson, G., Jackson, D. D., Haley, J., and Weakland, J. H. (1956). 'Towards a theory of schizophrenia', *Behav. Sci.* **1**, 251–64.
Federn, P. (1943). 'Psychoanalysis of psychoses', *Psychiat. Q.* **17**, 3–19, 246–57, 470–87. Also in Federn, P. (1952). *Ego Psychology and the Psychoses* (New York: Basic Books).
Jones, M. (1953). *The Therapeutic Community* (New York: Basic Books).
Kempf, E. J. (1919). 'The psychoanalytic treatment of dementia praecox. Report of a case', *Psychoanal. Rev.* **6**, 15–58.
Knight, R. P. (1939). 'Psychotherapy in acute paranoid schizophrenia with successful outcome: a case report', *Bull. Menninger Clinic,* **3**, 97–105.

Lidz, T., Fleck, S., and Cornelison, A. R. (1965). *Schizophrenia and the Family.* (New York: International University Press).

Müller, C. (1972). 'The problem of resistance to psychotherapy of schizophrenic patients', in Rubinstein, D., and Alanen, Y. O. (eds), *Psychotherapy of Schizophrenia* (Amsterdam: Excerpta Medica).

Niskanen, P., and Achté, K. A. (1971). 'Prognosis in schizophrenia, and comparative follow-up study of first admissions for schizophrenia and paranoid psychoses in Helsinki in 1950, 1960 and 1965', *Psychiatria Fennica*, pp. 117–26 (Helsinki).

Salonen, S. (1972). 'The psychotherapy of schizophrenia as an individual and community process', in Rubinstein, D., and Alanen, Y. O. (eds), *Psychotherapy of Schizophrenia* (Amsterdam: Excerpta Medica).

Schulz, C. G., and Kilgalen, R. K. (1969). *Case Studies in Schizophrenia* (New York and London: Basic Books).

Sechehaye, M.-A. (1956). *A New Psychotherapy in Schizophrenia* (New York: Grune & Stratton) (French original, *La Réalisation Symbolique* [1947]).

Soskis, D., and Bowers, M. (1969). 'The schizophrenic experience', *J. Nerv. Ment. Dis.* **149,** no. 6.

Stein, W. J. (1967). 'The sense of becoming psychotic', *Psychiatry*, **30,** 262–75.

Stierlin, H. (1972). 'Family dynamics and separation patterns of potential schizophrenics', in Rubinstein D., and Alanen, Y. O. (eds), *Psychotherapy of Schizophrenia* (Amsterdam: Excerpta Medica).

Sullivan, H. S. (1931). 'Socio-psychiatric research. Its implications for the schizophrenia problem and for mental hygiene', *Am. J. Psychiat.* **87,** 977–91. Also in Sullivan, H. S. (1962). *Schizophrenia as a Human Process* (New York: Norton).

Wynne, L. C., Ryckoff, I. M., Day, J., and Hirsch, S. I. (1958). 'Pseudo mutuality in the family relations of schizophrenics', *Psychiatry*, **21,** 205–20.

19 Trials of preventive medication

J. P. LEFF

There is a popular saying that 'prevention is better than cure'. Cure, however, is invariably more dramatic than prevention and has been the focus of attention of scientific workers in medicine for decades. Psychiatric conditions tend to be more chronic or recurrent than those dealt with in the other branches of medicine and hence demand more attention to the preventive aspects of treatment. Up to the 1950s the treatments available for the acute stages of psychiatric illnesses were not appropriate for maintenance therapy, with the exception of lithium. Potent drugs like the phenothiazines and the tricyclic antidepressants then became available, but prior to this there was a change in the attitudes of professional people to psychiatric patients. The belief rapidly grew that patients were better off in the community than in mental hospitals and this social change was soon followed by the introduction of drugs that seemed to make maintenance of psychiatric patients in the community a practical possibility.

The bulk of studies of maintenance therapy have evaluated the phenothiazine drugs and the majority of these have been carried out on hospitalized patients (Good *et al.*, 1958; Shawver *et al.*, 1959; Diamond *et al.*, 1960). Very few have been carried out on patients in the community. One of the most important reasons for this is that it is much easier to study a captive population under constant supervision in hospital than one at large in the community making only periodic contacts with the services. As patients in hospital are shielded from many of the stresses experienced by patients in the community which might precipitate relapse, assessment of out-patients as opposed to in-patients provides a more powerful test of the effectiveness of a drug in preventing relapse.

The earliest studies of maintenance treatment of patients in the community concerned chlorpromazine. Pollack (1958) followed up 316 discharged patients, an attempt being made to continue them all on chlorpromazine. Rather less than half the patients were schizophrenics and the rest represented a variety of diagnoses. All patients were followed for at least six months and some for one year, but only 133 of the 316 continued to take their medication regularly during the total observation period. A marked difference in relapse rates was found between patients who continued regular treatment (20 per cent) and those who did not (43 per cent). This result is open to several interpretations other than the one offered by the author that prophylactic medication is effective in preventing relapse. It is possible that patients who take their drugs regularly differ in important ways from patients who discontinue medication themselves. In fact Leff and Wing (1971) have shown that drug defaulters are likely to be young, unmarried men who have shown a decline in their heterosexual adjustment. An additional possibility is that discontinuation of medication may be itself a premonitory symptom of relapse.

These considerations emphasize the advantages of a placebo-controlled trial over the kind of design employed by Pollack. Although the principles of the double-blind, controlled trial were established twenty years ago (Bradford Hill, 1951), relatively few studies in the field of psychopharmacology since then have employed this method. The theoretical arguments for a matched group of patients maintained on a placebo are unassailable, but many research workers, like Baastrup *et al.* (1970) in the case of lithium, have felt there were strong ethical objections to withdrawing a treatment that seemed from clinical impressions to be effective. However, clinical impressions have been shown in the past to be erroneous, for example with regard to the treatment of schizophrenia with insulin coma (Ackner *et al.*, 1957). In fact, Baastrup and his colleagues eventually overcame their scruples and carried out a placebo-controlled trial of lithium.

There are further defects in the design of Pollack's study that illustrate general problems in the evaluation of preventive medication. His criterion of selection for the study was maintenance with a particular drug, chlorpromazine, and not a specific psychiatric condition. As a result his group of patients includes a variety of conditions, each having its own prognosis, and this clouds the interpretation of his results. Even when a study concentrates on one condition, say schizophrenia, it is rare for the diagnostic criteria to be specified. It is well known that considerable differences exist between psychiatrists in their use of diagnostic labels. These differences are particularly pronounced between American and British psychiatrists (Kendell *et al.*, 1971), so that the results of American studies on specific psychiatric conditions cannot be assumed to apply to the same conditions in England. In fact, most of the studies of preventive medication in schizophrenia were carried out in the US. In view of differing diagnostic habits it is necessary to stipulate the diagnostic criteria used in selecting patients for any future study.

Another point which merits consideration is the unreliability of out-patients in taking their medication. Wilcox *et al.* (1965) showed that about half of all out-patients on chlorpromazine failed to take their medication as judged by urine tests and a similar result was obtained by Parkes *et al.* (1962). This can be anticipated as a problem in trials of oral phenothiazines and anti-depressants, but of course does not apply to trials of long-acting phenothiazine given by injection or trials of lithium, where regular checks on the plasma level of the drug are a routine. A variety of measures are available for checking on reliability in drug-taking and include counting returned tablets, and testing the urine. The relative efficiency of these methods will be discussed later when particular trials are considered.

One of the major practical problems encountered in running a clinical trial is that an initially large population of apparently suitable patients is often reduced to a small fraction when attempts are made to apply experimental procedures. Thus in the study of Leff and Wing (1971), out of a total of 116 schizophrenics judged to be suitable, only 35 (30 per cent) actually entered the trial. A further source of depletion of numbers are the patients who enter the trial and later drop out. In some studies the proportion of drop-outs has been as high as one-third (Diamond *et al.*, 1960; Engelhardt *et al.*, 1960). These two processes of attrition leave a group of highly selected patients who are most unlikely to be representative of the population from which they are drawn.

The multi-centre trial has been proposed as a way of solving the problem of obtaining an adequate number of patients in a reasonable period of time (Shepherd, 1966; Vinar, 1969). Furthermore this method is said to spread the burden of extra work involved in the collection of data. Against these advantages have to be weighed a number of drawbacks of the multi-centre design. Although it may not be difficult to gain the participation of a large number of psychiatrists, only a few of these usually prove sufficiently enthusiastic to make a useful contribution. It is difficult in practice to keep a close check on the work when the participating psychiatrists are widely scattered geographically. Some psychiatrists make personal alterations to the method which may invalidate comparisons of their data with that from other participants. For this reason the criteria for selection for the trial and for relapse of the trial patients have to be clearly stipulated and uniformly adhered to. It is well recognized, however, that psychiatrists vary considerably in their clinical practice and a uniform and consistent method is hard to impose. It is easy to appreciate that the role of co-ordinator in a multi-centre trial is a crucial one.

Enthusiasm for a collaborative trial tends to vary from centre to centre. Participants who take a very active interest in the trial enter relatively large numbers of patients. This may reflect a particular orientation in psychiatry and with it particular attitudes towards diagnosis and physical treatments. Such factors could introduce a bias into the results which is one of the very problems this method seeks to obviate. A single-centre trial is advantageous from the point of view of standardization of procedure and ease of administration but may prove inadequate to provide sufficient patients within a reasonable period. On the other hand a multi-centre trial creates great problems in collaboration. It is preferable to have a small number of highly involved and productive centres than a large number of unreliable and unproductive ones.

Specific trials

Having considered the general problems involved in conducting trials of preventive medication, we can proceed to a discussion of a number of major studies which have been carried out recently concerning lithium, tricyclic anti-depressants, and phenothiazines.

The therapeutic effect of lithium on the acute phase of mania has been known for some time (Schou *et al.*, 1954). However, it is only in the last few years that studies of its prophylactic effect in manic-depressive conditions have been carried out. Most of them have been undertaken by the Danish group headed by Baastrup and Schou. The first systematic study (Baastrup and Schou, 1967) was a non-blind comparison of the frequency of relapses before and during lithium administration in a group of patients suffering from manic-depressive psychosis. This kind of 'mirror-image' design, as it has been called, employs each patient as his own control and thus avoids the use of a placebo. It is based on two assumptions; firstly, that the effect of observer bias and psychological factors are negligible under the circumstances of the trial; secondly, that the course of the disease before treatment can be used as an estimate of the course to be expected during treatment if this is ineffective. It would follow from this that any improvement in course after the start of treatment could be ascribed to the treatment itself. Both these assumptions have been questioned by Blackwell and Shepherd (1968). They criticize the shortness of the follow-up period in the 'mirror-image' study and suggest that this introduces a bias in favour of lithium. A continuous episode of illness can be broken up into an apparently discontinuous set of separate episodes by drug treatment or ECT. This would result in a spuriously large number of episodes during the control period before the prescription of lithium. Patients remaining well after the application of such physical treatments may not be benefiting from lithium but from the treatments themselves. This effect would clearly diminish with an increase in the length of the follow-up period. However, one then encounters another source of bias, namely, the effect of changes in hospital atmosphere and social conditions in the community.

These considerations engender serious doubts about the results of any trial employing a 'mirror-image' design. The Danish workers were convinced enough by the arguments to undertake a double-blind, placebo-controlled trial of prophylactic lithium in manic-depressive and recurrent depressive illnesses (Baastrup *et al.*, 1970). The design provided for discontinuation of lithium in patients who had been receiving it prophylactically for at least one year and up to seven years. The trial involved 84 patients who were paired according to the total number of previous episodes. The partners in each pair were randomly assigned to lithium or placebo and strict precautions were taken to maintain the 'blind' condition of the assessors. A relapse was recorded on the occurrence of a manic or depressive episode of sufficient severity to necessitate either admission to a mental hospital or regular supervision in the home with administration of supplementary drug therapy. Of the 21 relapses that occurred, 17 were admitted to hospital.

The results were unequivocally in favour of lithium in both the manic-depressive and recurrent depressive groups. All the relapses were of patients on placebo. The results of this trial, which was quite rigorously carried out, provide strong evidence for the effectiveness of lithium as a prophylactic agent. However, a number of major criticisms can be levelled at the method. Firstly the diagnostic criteria for inclusion of patients in the trial are not stated. The importance of this omission has been stressed in the first part of this paper. Secondly, it can be argued that selection of patients already maintained on lithium for one year without relapse might have excluded those with the greatest risk of relapse. This general point is discussed further in relation to other drug trials under consideration. Thirdly, it has been pointed out (Blackwell, 1970) that withdrawal of a drug after a patient has been receiving it for some time is not comparable with instituting medication for the first time. Finally, the duration of the follow-up period, five months, was rather short.

The last criticism has been met by the study of Coppen *et al.* (1971). This was a multi-centre trial involving four centres, nevertheless, the total number of patients, 65, is relatively small. The patients suffered from recurrent affective disorders, but once again the diagnostic criteria are not stated, and as discussed above, this is a particularly crucial point in multi-centre trials. A novel feature of the design was that any further treatment other than lithium could be prescribed throughout the trial. To some extent this counters ethical objections to patients being maintained on placebo for any length of time, and in fact the period of the trial lasted more than two years for some subjects.

The patient's mood was rated at each visit and episodes of effective disturbance were inquired about. Stringent precautions were taken to keep the assessors 'blind'. At the end of the trial a record was made of the amount of ECT administered and of the number of weeks on additional anti-depressant and anti-manic medication. The psychiatrist also made a global assessment of the patient's affective state since starting the trial. In terms of each of the measures used, patients on lithium did very much better than patients on placebo.

These two recent studies go a long way towards establishing the effectiveness of lithium in preventing relapses in affective illnesses.

However, the doubt still remains as to the exact nature of the disorders from which the patients in these studies were suffering as insufficient information is given about their clinical state.

The other trial of preventive medication in affective illness to be discussed is the multi-centre study of amitriptyline and imipramine carried out under the auspices of the MRC (Mindham *et al.*, 1972). The trial involved thirty-four psychiatrists from eight different centres. Patients who qualified for the trial had to show full remission of symptoms after treatment with amitriptyline or imipramine for a depressive illness. The patient's illness had to fulfil certain criteria, which were similar to those used in an earlier study of treatments of depressive illness (MRC, 1965). The necessary clinical features of the illness were stipulated, which goes part of the way towards standardization of criteria for entry into a trial. However, the psychiatrists involved were not trained to use these criteria in any uniform way. A total of 211 patients fulfilled the requirements for entry to the preliminary treatment phase of the study. Of these, only 92 (43·6 per cent) responded to treatment and entered the trial. The remainder failed to qualify for maintenance therapy for a variety of reasons; the largest group was excluded because they failed to make a satisfactory response to the preliminary treatment.

Patients were assessed monthly and were regarded as having relapsed when the psychiatrist in charge of their case could no longer continue to give a medication which might be inert. This decision was thus the sole responsibility of the clinician, but various guidelines were laid down to help establish uniformity.

During the trial similar proportions of those on active drug and placebo experienced unwanted effects of medication of some kind. Therefore side effects probably did not affect the 'blindness' of the assessors. An attempt was made to estimate the reliability of patients in taking their drugs by a tablet counting method. This method was not successful because patients frequently failed to comply with the request to return unwanted tablets for a count to be made.

The trial lasted six months for those patients who remained well. In the amitriptyline series patients who received the active drug had a marked advantage in terms of relapse rate over those on placebo. By contrast, in the imipramine series there was no difference in relapse rate between those on active drug and those on placebo. This finding may be due to the relatively small number of patients in the imipramine series. However, there is a possibility that the two populations treated initially with amitriptyline and imipramine were different in some respect which was related to the risk of relapse. The only difference found between the two groups was that the patients on amitriptyline had a higher mean score on 'psychic anxiety' than those on imipramine. In contrast to imipramine, amitriptyline has marked sedative effects, and these rather than its anti-depressant properties may account for its effectiveness as a prophylactic treatment.

The different centres varied considerably in the proportion of patients they contributed to the trial. London contributed 36 patients and Glasgow 31 patients, while the other six centres combined only produced 25 patients. There was considerable variation in the relapse rates in different centres, a hazard of multi-centre trials. The difference between the drug and placebo groups was least in the Glasgow patients and in fact did not reach significance. Nearly all the Glasgow patients were contributed by one psychiatrist and therefore are likely to constitute the least selected group. The difference in results suggests that the other centres were contributing a highly selected group of patients, namely those judged likely to benefit most from maintenance therapy.

This possibility finds strong support in the study by Leff and Wing (1971) of maintenance phenothiazine therapy (chlorpromazine and trifluoperazine) in acute schizophrenics. This trial had a standard double-blind, placebo-controlled design and was similar in its aim and method to the trial of tricyclic anti-depressants discussed above. It differed in involving only one centre and as a consequence the number of patients in the trial was small, only thirty-five. Despite this, a significant advantage was found for active drug over placebo in terms of relapse rates. The criteria for the diagnosis of schizophrenia were carefully laid down and all patients were given a standardized clinical examination. Two main methods were used to check the patients' reliability in taking their medication. One method was the counting of returned tablets, which proved to be just as unsatisfactory as in the anti-depressant trial. The other involved the testing of urine for riboflavine which was incorporated in each tablet as a tracer. This was found to be a reliable method of checking on tablet taking.

Altogether 116 patients were found to be suitable for the trial, but only 35 of these actually entered the trial. The remainder were followed up for the same length of time as the trial patients, namely one year. This provided exceedingly valuable additional information. It was found that two of the main groups of patients who were not entered into the trial comprised (1) those whose adjustment was considered by the clinicians to be too precarious to risk their being given a placebo, and (2) those whose prognosis was considered favourable enough for them not to need maintenance therapy. The follow-up of these groups showed that the clinicians' prognoses were substantially correct. The precarious patients mostly relapsed despite being kept on drugs, whereas those given a good prognosis mostly remained well without any maintenance therapy. It was concluded that the patients who actually entered the trial were intermediate between the other two groups in terms of prognosis and hence were those most likely to benefit from maintenance treatment. It is argued from this that the result of the trial, favouring phenothiazine drugs as preventive medication, cannot be generalized to all acute schizophrenics. This finding provides a plausible explanation of the conflicting results from the different centres in the MRC trial of prophylactic anti-depressant therapy.

The study of Leff and Wing, dealing with patients who had recently recovered from an acute episode of schizophrenia, was followed by another trial in the same unit (Hirsch *et al.*, 1973) of preventive phenothiazine therapy in chronic schizophrenia. This was a double-blind study comparing the effect of fluophenazine decanoate injections with placebo injections of the inert carrier alone. The trial involved 81 patients with chronic schizophrenia; over half of them had been suffering from the illness for more than ten years. The trial lasted nine months and showed a significant advantage for the active drug in terms both of clinical measures, such as readmission or return of schizophrenic symptoms, and of social measures, such as burden on the relatives.

The detailed consideration of the above trials leads us to two main conclusions. The first concerns the design of trials of preventive medication. It is clear that at present there is no design that can compare in effectiveness with the double-blind, placebo-controlled study. Single-centre trials pose less problems in achieving standardized procedures than multi-centre trials, but may sometimes provide inadequate numbers of patients. When a multi-centre trial is obligatory for this reason, a small number of highly motivated centres should be chosen and strenuous efforts should be made to ensure uniformity of the procedures involved. Whether trials involve one or more centres, the clinical characteristics of the patients studied should be recorded in as standard a way as possible. The trial of Leff and Wing has demonstrated the importance of following up patients thought to be suitable for a trial but excluded for various reasons. This additional procedure merits incorporation in the design of any therapeutic trial, otherwise there is a danger of taking too optimistic a view of a positive result.

The second conclusion follows from the results of the trials discussed here. As experimental design has become more rigorous, the evidence has grown stronger for the effectiveness of preventive medication for a variety of psychiatric conditions and a number of different drugs. The principle of preventive medication now seems to be firmly established and demands an expansion of out-patient facilities and ancillary services to exploit to the full this powerful aid to the maintenance of patients in the community.

As mentioned at the beginning of the paper, patients in the community are subject to a variety of social stresses from which patients in hospital are protected. Ideally, drug trials on out-patients should take account of social factors that might be connected with relapse. The importance of the patient's relationship with the people with whom he lives has emerged from the work of Brown and his colleagues. Brown *et al.* (1966) showed that schizophrenic men who returned to live with their wives or parents relapsed more frequently than those who lived on their own in a hostel or lodgings. The important factor in precipitating relapse was found to be a high level of emotional involvement of the patient with his relatives (Brown *et al.,* 1962). Subsequently, Brown *et al.* (1972) have demonstrated that the one crucial measure is the number of critical comments made by the relative about the patient.

In a further series of studies (Brown and Birley, 1968; Birley and Brown, 1970) it has been shown that the onset of relapse in schizophrenics is often shortly preceded by the occurrence of life events. Unfortunately, the design of drug trials is complicated enough without the evaluation of social factors affecting the patient. However, some indication of the interaction between pharmacological and social factors can be obtained from the studies of Brown and his colleagues, even though the prescription of preventive medication was not controlled experimentally. Their findings were that schizophrenics who discontinued or reduced their phenothiazines relapsed in the absence of events, whereas those who had been taking phenothiazines regularly experienced an event shortly before relapse. An attempt was made to substantiate this in the context of a controlled drug trial (Leff, 1972) and the finding was indeed confirmed. The implication is that schizophrenics on no medication can be precipitated into relapse by everyday social interactions, whereas those on preventive medication are protected against the stresses of everyday life but not against the impact of life events.

The interaction between medication, environmental changes, and the emotional tone of relationships is likely to be complex and difficult to unravel, but it is essential to recognize that preventive medication does not operate in a social vacuum.

REFERENCES

Ackner, B., Harris, A., and Oldham, A. J. (1957). 'Insulin treatment of schizophrenia: a controlled study', *Lancet,* i, 607–11.

Baastrup, P. C., Poulsen, J. C., Schou, M., Thomsen, K., and Amdisen, A. (1970). 'Prophylactic lithium: double blind discontinuation in manic-depressive and recurrent-depressive disorders', ibid. ii, 326–30.

—— and Schou, M. (1967). 'Lithium as a prophylactic agent', *Archives Gen. Psychiat.* 16, 162–72.

Birley, J. L. T., and Brown, G. W. (1970). 'Crises and life changes preceding the onset or relapse of acute schizophrenia: clinical aspects', *Br. J. Psychiat.* 116, 327–33.

Blackwell, B. (1970). 'Lithium', *Lancet,* ii, 875.

—— and Shepherd, M. (1968). 'Prophylactic lithium: another therapeutic myth?', ibid. i, 968–71.

Bradford Hill, A. (1951). 'The clinical trial', *Br. med. Bull.* 7, 278–82.

Brown, G. W., and Birley, J. L. T. (1968). 'Crises and life changes and the onset of schizophrenia', *J. Hlth and Soc. Behav.* 9, 203–14.

—— —— and Wing, J. K. (1972). 'Influence on family life on the course of schizophrenic disorders: a replication', *Br. J. Psychiat.* **121**, 241–55.
—— Bone, M., Dalison, B., and Wing, J. K. (1966). *Schizophrenia and Social Care*, Maudsley Monograph no. 17 (London: Oxford University Press).
—— Monck, E. M., Carstairs, G. M., and Wing, J. K. (1962). 'The influence of family life on the course of schizophrenic illness'. *Br. J. Prev. Soc. Med.* **16**, 55–68.
Coppen, A., Noguerd, R., Bailey, J., Burns, B. H., Hare, E. H., Gardner, R., and Maggs, R. (1971). 'Prophylactic lithium in affective disorders', *Lancet,* **ii**, 275–9.
Diamond, L. S., and Marks, J. B. (1960). 'Discontinuance of tranquilizers among chronic schizophrenic patients receiving maintenance dosage', *J. Nerv. Ment. Dis.* **131**, 247–51.
Engelhardt, D. M., Freedman, N., Glick, B. S., Hankoff, L. D., Mann, D., and Margolis R. (1960). 'Prevention of psychiatric hospitalisation with use of psychopharmacological agents', *J. Am. Med. Ass.* **173**, 147–9.
Good, W. W., Sterling, M., and Holtzman, W. H. (1958). 'Termination of chlorpromazine with schizophrenic patients', *Am. J. Psychiat.* **115**, 443–8.
Hirsch, S. R., Gaind, R., Rhode, P., and Stevens, B. C. (1972). 'A clinical trial of long acting fluphenazine in chronic schizophrenics maintained in the community' (to be published).
Kendell, R. E., Cooper, J. E., Gourlay, A. J., Copeland, J. R. M., Sharpe, L., and Gurland, B. (1971). 'Diagnostic criteria of American and British psychiatrists', *Archives Gen. Psychiat.* **25**, 123–30.
Leff, J. P., *et al.* (1973). 'Life events and maintenance therapy in schizophrenic relapse' (to be published in *Br. J. Psychiat*).
—— and Wing, J. K. (1971). 'Trial of maintenance therapy in schizophrenia', *Br. med. J.* **3**, 599–604.
Medical Research Council, Clinical Psychiatry Committee (1965). 'Clinical trial of the treatment of depressive illness', ibid. **1**, 881–6.
Mindham, R. H. S., Howland, C., and Shepherd, M. (1973). 'Continuance therapy with tricyclic anti-depressants in depressive illness', *Lancet,* **ii**, 854–5.
Parkes, C. M., Brown, G. W., and Monck, E. M. (1962). 'The general practitioner and the schizophrenic patient', *Br. med. J.* **1**, 972–6.
Pollack, B. (1958). 'The effect of chlorpromazine in reducing the relapse rate in 716 released patients: study 3', *Am. J. Psychiat.* **114**, 749–51.
Schou, M., Juel-Nielsen, N., Strömgren, E., and Voldby, H. (1954). 'The treatment of manic psychoses by the administration of lithium salts', *J. Neurol. Neurosurg. Psychiat.* **17**, 250–60.
Shawver, J. R., Gorham, D. R., Leskin, L. W., Good, W. W., and Kabnick, D. E. (1959). 'Comparison of chlorpromazine and reserpine in maintenance drug therapy'. *Diseases of the Nervous System,* **20**, 452–7.
Shepherd, M. (1966). 'The method of the multi-centred clinical trial', in *Proceedings of the 5th International Congress of Neuropsychopharmacology*. Excerpta Medica International Congress Series no. 129.
Vinar, O. (1969). 'On-going national collaborative studies in Czechoslovakia', *Psychopharmacol. Bull.* **5**, 2, 10–11.
Willcox, D. R. C., Gillan, R., and Hare, E. H. (1965). 'Do psychiatric outpatients take their drugs?', *Br. med. J.* **2**, 790–2.

20 *Ability and disability in role functioning in psychiatric patient and non-patient groups* [1]

BARBARA SNELL DOHRENWEND, BRUCE P. DOHRENWEND, and DIANA COOK

In 1961 the United States Joint Commission on Mental Illness and Health stated in its final report:

The objective of modern treatment of persons with major mental illness is to enable the patient to *maintain himself in the community in a normal manner.* To do so, it is necessary (1) to save the patient from the debilitating effects of institutionalization as much as possible, (2) if the patient requires hospitalization, to return him to home and community life as soon as possible, and (3) thereafter to maintain him in the community as long as possible [Joint Commission, 1961, p. xvii, italics added].

Investigators attempting to evaluate psychiatric services in terms of this objective will probably encounter little disagreement about what constitute gross departures by patients from normal behaviour in the community, as in the recurrence of bizarre symptoms requiring re-hospitalization (Freeman and Simmons, 1963), or massive failure, as described, for example, by the 'social breakdown syndrome' (Gruenberg, 1967). The problem becomes more difficult when we try to develop a comprehensive definition of functioning 'in a normal manner' in a socially and culturally complex modern industrial society.

To illustrate the nature of the problem, consider how you would evaluate a group with the following characteristics:

... less likely ... to participate in formal, organized social activities ... More ... are outside the mainstream of community life. Not only are they less likely to participate in formal social organizations, including the church, but also they have fewer friends and do less informal visiting. In general, they have few positive, social group experiences or rewarding interpersonal relationships.

1. This work was supported in part by Research Grant MH-10328 and by Research Scientist Award K5-MH-14, 663 from the National Institute of Mental Health, US Public Health Service.

Leisure-time activities...are mostly passive—viewing television, sitting around the house, going to the movies, and so on [Myers and Bean, 1968, p. 191].

You might hazard the guess that the people being described are a group of psychiatric patients living in the community in less than 'a normal manner'. In fact, this is a description of a sample of community respondents from the lowest social class being compared with members of higher social classes in a study conducted in New Haven, Connecticut, by Myers and Bean (1968).

Problem

Most people in the community, regardless of social class, do not suffer from major psychiatric disorders. It seems reasonable to assume, therefore, that the class differences in social performance just described stem more from what John Wing describes as 'handicaps which exist independently of any illness, such as lack of occupational or social skills due to poverty or poor education' than from the 'biological or psychological abnormalities' and related 'maladaptive attitudes and personal habits' that he refers to as primary and secondary components of morbidity (see Chapter 1). We could learn a great deal about the effect of these class differences on patient performance if we had good measures of the functioning of people from higher and lower social classes in the community and of the full range of disabilities exhibited by patients. Moreover, from such normative data we could get a better idea of what might reasonably be meant by maintenance in the community 'in a normal manner' for patients from different social backgrounds. Without these data the psychiatrist dealing with lower-class patients may be hard put to distinguish the need for psychotherapeutic efforts to correct primary and secondary impairments resulting from a patient's psychiatric disorder from the need for political action to correct the tertiary impairments stemming from the social system.

A growing number of studies of psychiatric patients in the community have included questions, observations, and ratings of various aspects of performance (for example, Angrist *et al.,* 1968; Cooper *et al.,* 1970; Gruenberg, 1967; Fairweather, 1964; Freeman and Simmons, 1963; Myers and Bean, 1968; Pasamanick *et al.,* 1967). As far as we know, however, no generally accepted procedures for measuring any but the most grossly impaired aspects of social performance have been developed (see Bahn, 1971; Spitzer, 1971; Katz, 1971; Newbrough, 1971; Dohrenwend, 1971; Clausen, 1971). Moreover, little attention has been given to the problem of how to insure that measures of social performance are reliable for groups that differ in social status and for both patients and samples from the general population.

In this paper, we will describe some of our on-going efforts to build objective, class-comparable measures of social performance and some of the problems of non-comparability that we have encountered. Our focus will be on similarities and contrasts between psychiatric patients and their class counterparts in the general population.

Procedures

Data collection

The data collection instrument on which we will report is the Structured Interview Schedule, a questionnaire modelled on the interview instruments used in epidemiological studies done in Midtown Manhattan, in Stirling County in eastern Canada, and in our own work in Washington Heights, Manhattan. As in these previous instruments, the interview questions and the order in which they were asked were predetermined, and the responses were limited for the most part to fixed categories, such as 'true or false', 'yes or no', or time frequencies. One way in which the Structured Interview Schedule differs from the previous ones, however, is that it includes many more questions on role functioning.

The interviews were conducted by fifteen psychiatrists, all but one of whom had completed his residency training. They received intensive special instruction, averaging thirty hours, in the use of the Structured Interview Schedule together with other research instruments employed in the main study (Dohrenwend *et al.*, 1970). Except with institutionalized respondents, interviews were usually conducted in the respondent's home and the large majority of them were tape-recorded.

As in our previous research, the subjects interviewed came mainly from Washington Heights, a section of Manhattan in New York City. These subjects were chosen to provide strong contrasts in social performance. They consist of patients and convicted prisoners selected to be heterogeneous as to type of disorder; a probability sample of adults from the general population; and community leaders.

The community sample was made up of male household heads, their wives if they were married, and special groups of single female household heads; all were between the ages of 21 and 64 and came from five ethnic groups: white Protestants, Jews, Irish, blacks, and Puerto Ricans. The community sample was stratified on educational level, an indicator of social class, with the aim of balancing the class distribution in each of the five ethnic groups. However, despite our efforts we are short of poorly educated white Protestants and Jews, so that ethnicity and social class are not entirely independent in our community sample.

The patient and prisoner samples were selected from psychiatric out-patient clinics, mental hospital in-patient services, and prisons, the large majority from the first of these sources. The selection process was designed to yield an even distribution of six 'behaviour types' within each of the same five ethnic groups as those sampled from the community. The behaviour types sampled were based on fictitious illustrations of six categories of psychiatric disorder developed by Star and used by her and by

Table 1. *Proportions from patient sample, community resident sample, and community leader sample of three levels of education.**

| | Years of education | | |
Sample origin	<12	12–15	16+
Patients	50·4	42·0	9·1
Community residents	46·0	50·6	47·0
Community leaders	3·5	7·4	43·9
(Number of respondents)†	(113)	(81)	(66)

* Education of respondent in patient or prisoner and in community leader samples; education of head of household in community resident sample.
† See Technical Appendix.

others in studies in public attitudes toward mental illness (for example, Dohrenwend and Chin-Shong, 1967). These categories of psychiatric disorder are: paranoid schizophrenic, simple schizophrenic, anxiety neurotic, compulsive phobic neurotic, alcoholic, and personality disorder of the antisocial type.

Our procedure was to have a patient's therapist or, if the patient was on a waiting-list, his evaluator rank from most to least like the patient cards containing abbreviated descriptions of Star's cases. A patient was then selected to fill the category ranked most like him or rejected if that category had already been filled. Prisoners were included in the sampling in order to obtain a sufficient number of cases in the last category, antisocial personality. Since there were only 11 prisoners by contrast with 33 hospital patients and 60 clinic patients, we will refer to this group of respondents generally as the psychiatric patient sample.

The community leaders were selected on the basis of formal position of influence and on the basis of reputation among other leaders in the Washington Heights area. They included state assemblymen, city councilmen, municipal court justices, school principals, clergymen, and individuals who proved influential in various neighbourhood action groups formed around civil rights issues. All but a few were Jewish, Irish, black, or Puerto Rican. Just as the psychiatric patients are expected to show impaired performance relative to their class counterparts in the community, so are the leaders expected to show effective social performance relative to their class counterparts in the community.

The completed samples of community residents, patients, and community leaders interviewed with the Structured Interview Schedule are shown in Table 1 according to the indicators of social class that we will use in our analysis: years of education of the head of the respondent's family in the community sample, and own education in the patient and leader samples where educational level of male heads of household was not available from females whose spouses were not interviewed.[1] We see that in the last two samples the educational distributions are skewed, with college graduates under-represented in the patient sample and overrepresented in the leader sample, a situation that we will have to take into account in our analysis.

Scale construction and evaluation

The data concerning the social performance of the individual were provided by questions in the Structured Interview Schedule concerning functioning in a number of life roles.[2] As the first step in the construction of scales to assess levels of functioning, therefore, role related items were grouped into the following seven categories in terms of their manifest content: (1) work performance, (2) job morale, (3) marriage, (4) social relations, (5) housework, (6) parenthood, (7) leisure.

In the present report of procedures and problems in constructing class comparable measures we will deal only with the first four categories, namely, work performance, job morale, marriage, and social relations. The items in each of these scales are fully described in the Technical Appendix at the end of this paper. They were made up by us or, more often, adapted from those used by a number of other investigators, especially Bradburn and Caplovitz (1965); Gurin *et al.* (1960); and Spitzer *et al.* (1970).

Responses to these role items were scored so that a high score indicated relatively impaired and a low score relatively effective functioning in the role. An additive scale was formed for each role by summing responses to all items assigned to that role, giving each item equal weight.

The first step in evaluation of these additive scales focused on the question of the relevance of the items to the scale. For this purpose we used coefficient alpha, a measure of the reliability of the scale. On the assumption that a scale is composed of a random sample of items from the hypothetical domain of all relevant items, coefficient alpha represents the 'expected correlation of the [sample of items] with an alternative [sample] containing the same number of items' (Nunnally, 1967, p. 196). To the extent, then, that the items in the scale being evaluated are drawn from several domains rather than from a single homogeneous domain of items the correlation for any given sample size is reduced.

1. Educational level is used as the indicator of social class mainly for two reasons: first, it is usually antecedent to occupation and income and hence less likely to itself be influenced by psychiatric disorder; see, for example, Dunham *et al.* (1966). Second, parental social class, still more antecedent to a person's own occupation and income, is not a good indicator of own social class in either patient or non-patient groups in societies characterized by considerable social mobility; see, for example, Birtchnell (1971).

2. A complete description of the content and scoring of the items used to construct the scales discussed in this paper can be obtained by writing to Dr Bruce Dohrenwend, Social Psychiatry Research Unit, Columbia University, 100 Haven Avenue, New York, NY 10032, USA.

The formula for computing this coefficient is:

$$r_{kk} = \frac{k}{k-1}\left(1 - \frac{\Sigma\sigma_1^2}{\sigma_y^2}\right).$$

where k represents the number of items in the scale, σ_1^2 the variance of a particular item and σ_y^2 the variance of the total scale score. The value of coefficient alpha depends on the correlation among items assigned to the scale, so that to the extent that each item is highly correlated with the rest of the scale, the coefficient approaches one; to the extent that any items are independent of the other items coefficient alpha approaches zero; and to the extent that any items are negatively correlated with the other items in the scale, the value of coefficient alpha approaches minus one. Thus, if the alpha coefficient is low one will probably find that the correlations of one or more items with the remainder of the scale are close to zero or are negative, suggesting that they are not relevant to the scale.

Since we are aiming for scales appropriate to all social classes, we attempted to construct scales that would be reliable in each class. As our criterion we decided to accept scales with modest reliability coefficients, specifically 0·50, since scales at this level of reliability can be used to detect differences between groups even though they cannot, with much confidence, be used to assess individuals. Thus, these moderately reliable scales could be used to evaluate psychiatric services by comparing ex-patients with patients and with other community residents even though it would be inappropriate to use them to evaluate the status of a particular patient or ex-patient.

Since it is possible for a scale to achieve modest reliability even though it contains some items that are uncorrelated with the remainder of the scale, our second step in scale construction involved disposing of uncorrelated items when they occurred in reliable scales. Any given item might be uncorrelated with the remainder of the scale, and thus apparently irrelevant, in only one social class, in two, or in all three of the class categories that we employed. In the last case there was no question but that the item should be dropped from the scale. An item that appeared to belong in the scale in some social classes but not in others, however, presented more of a problem.

One possibility was to keep an item that appeared to be relevant to a particular class in the scale to be used in that class while dropping it from the scale to be used in any class to which it did not appear to be relevant. Arguing against this procedure is the principle that the validity of comparisons across groups is reduced to the extent that measurement instruments vary from group to group. Since our purpose was to develop measures that eliminate this type of invalidity from the evaluation of psychiatric services, we rejected the possibility of using a longer scale in one group than in another.

Given the decision to use the same items in all social classes, the question became whether to retain or to drop items that were not significantly correlated with the remainder of a scale in all three social classes. The issue was whether we would achieve greater validity in our measurement of role impairment by restricting our scales to items that were meaningful indicators of impairment in all social classes, or by extending the scales to include items that provided information about role impairment in only one or two classes. The argument against the latter procedure is that in classes where an item is not relevant its constructual meaning is in doubt. On the other hand, the procedure of dropping all items that are irrelevant to any class has the disadvantage of restricting the range of impairment to that found in all social classes. As a simple analogy, this idea implies using a short stick which may be adequate to differentiate heights within a short population but not within a relatively tall one. In more general terms, which do not involve the assumption of unidimensionality, the restricted scale would exclude attributes that fall within the domain of the role for one class when they do not fall within the domain for all classes. On the judgement that restriction of a scale to the domain common to all classes would probably reduce its sensitivity to differences between patients and non-patients, we retained all items that were correlated with the remainder of the scale in at least one class.

The next major step in evaluation of the scales consisted of testing their ability to discriminate within each social class between groups that could be expected to be functioning at different levels of effectiveness in life roles. Specifically, we assumed that of the groups sampled, the psychiatric patients would on the average reveal the highest level of impairment, community residents a lesser average level of impairment, and community leaders the least impairment. Because of the skewed distribution of educational levels in both the patient sample and the community leader sample, as shown in Table 1, we were limited by the number of available cases to comparisons of two groups within each educational level. In the two lower educational levels we were able to compare patients with community residents, while among college graduates the comparison made was between community residents and community leaders. The most serious omission is lack of a group of psychiatric patients with college graduate backgrounds to compare with the college graduate community sample and community leaders.

Furthermore, an unbalance within the patient sample is shown in Table 2. Mental hospital patients, who are presumably the most seriously impaired, are represented disproportionately in the lowest educational group and clinic patients, who are presumably less impaired, in the middle group. Thus, if a scale were to discriminate between patients and community residents in the lowest but not in the intermediate group this difference in results might be in part a function of the difference in the

Table 2. *Source of patient sample according to educational level.*

| | Years of education | | |
Source	<12(%)	12–15(%)	16+ (N)
Psychiatric clinics	52·6	70·6	(5)
Prisoners	8·8	11·8	(–)
Mental hospitals	38·6	17·6	(1)
(Number of respondents)	(57)	(34)	(6)

composition of the patient sample within the two social classes and a finer breakdown of the patient sample would be in order. The results are such, however, that this problem did not arise.

Results

Work performance scale

The upper part of Table 3 describes the results for the scale that was constructed from all items in the Structured Interview Schedule whose content appeared to be relevant to work performance. The coefficient alpha and the correlation of each item with the remainder of the scale are given for all respondents and for respondents in three educational groups.

We see that this scale was unreliable in the lowest and in the highest educational groups even by the lenient minimum of 0·50 for the coefficient alpha. The correlations of individual items with the remainder of the scale indicate that three items, 'Number of times fired', Number of times laid off', and 'Number of times left a job for other reasons', were major contributors to this unreliability. Each of these items yielded correlation coefficients in the lowest and highest educational groups which were not significantly greater than zero at the 0·10 level of probability. These three items have in common that they involve recall over the entire work history of the respondents. Answers to such questions are subject to distortions. However, there are problems in addition to those of recall with these items.

When we examined transcripts of interviews to see how respondents had answered these items we found, first, that many did not distinguish among being fired, being laid off, and leaving a job for other reasons: perhaps because the distinction itself is sometimes vague and gets vaguer if it has to be recalled over a long period of time. One respondent, for example, reported both that he had been fired four times and that he had been laid off four times, considering both 'in the same category'. When pressed by the interviewer to make the distinction his solution was, 'Let's put it two and two, then'. This kind of confused response probably accounts at least in part for the similarity in the relations between these three items and the remainder of the work performance scale.

The fact that their correlations with other items in the scale were not significantly different from zero is probably due to some extent to our

Table 3. *Coefficient alpha and correlation of each item with remainder of scale for original and revised work performance scales according to years of education of respondent* or head of household† (each item scored on scale of 0–2).*

		Years of education		
Version of scale	All respondents	<12	12–15	16+
Original version				
Coefficient alpha	0·52	0·48	0·69	0·35
	Item correlation with remainder of scale‡			
Number of times in life fired	0·17	*0·06*	0·37	*−0·03*
Number of times in life laid off	0·23	*0·02*	0·45	*0·06*
Number of times in life left for better job	0·27	0·42	0·32	0·31
Number of times left for other reasons	0·20	*0·11*	0·26	0·2
Why left last job: fired, laid off, better job, other reasons	0·27	0·19	0·38	
Current employment status	0·39	0·36	0·53	*0·17*
Length of time unemployed last year	0·49	0·46	0·60	0·22
(Number of respondents)§	(141)	(53)	(44)	(37)
Revised version				
Coefficient alpha	0·63	0·74	0·58	0·74
	Item correlation with remainder of scale‡			
Number of times in life left for better job	0·26	0·45	0·22	0·47
Why left last job	−0·03	*−0·02*	*0·10*	*−0·10*
Current employment status	0·42	0·49	0·33	0·31
Length of time unemployed in last year	0·45	0·62	0·39	*0·16*
(Number of respondents)§	(143)	(54)	(42)	(37)
(Correlation for which $p \leqslant 0·10$ that $r \leqslant 0$)	(0·11)	(0·18)	(0·20)	(0·22)

* Patient and leader sample.
† Community resident sample.
‡ Correlations for which $p > 0·10$ that $r \leqslant 0$ are in italic.
§ See Technical Appendix.

having elicited from a number of respondents incidents that were so early in their long work careers as to be virtually unrelated to their current status. Of two leaders who reported having been fired once, for example, one was a police officer who had been promoted a number of times during his thirty years in the Department and the other a successful lawyer who was satisfied with all aspects of the job at which he had been working for the last thirty-five years. At the other end of the educational scale, a clinic patient who had not finished high school reported twelve job changes prior to his present position as a postal clerk, a position that he had held for the last eleven years. Thus, even though the topic of job changes is obviously relevant to assessment of work performance, the data elicited by the items

Table 4. *Comparison of mean work performance scale scores of presumably more and presumably less impaired respondents from three educational groups.*

Version of scale	All patients	All community residents	YEARS OF EDUCATION					
			<12		12–15		16+	
			Patients	Community residents	Patients	Community residents	Community residents	Community leaders
Original mean	5·51	3·07	5·60	3·47	6·00	3·04	2·33	2·47
df	109		48		40		32	
t	4·60*		2·96*		2·77*			
Revised mean	3·49	2·27	3·90	2·52	3·46	2·15	2·00	2·16
df	108		49		38		32	
t	2·77*		2·06†		1·90†			
						(means reversed)	(means reversed)	

* $p < 0.01$ one-tailed. † $p < 0.05$ one-tailed.

Table 5. *Coefficient alpha and correlation of each item with remainder of scale for original and revised job morale scales according to years of education of respondent* or head of household† (each item scored on scale of 0–3).*

| Version of scale | All respondents | Years of education | | |
		<12	12–15	16+
Original				
Coefficient alpha	0·69	0·64	0·75	0·63
	Item correlation with remainder of scale‡			
Satisfied with present pay	0·51	0·50	0·54	0·34
Satisfied with kind of work	0·65	0·60	0·66	0·67
Satisfied with relations with fellow workers	0·17	*0·12*	0·36	*0·01*
Satisfied with future with job	0·70	0·68	0·76	0·60
How good a job people think you do	0·23	0·25	0·29	*0·11*
Interested in work	0·41	0·52	0·32	0·54
(Number of respondents)§	(150)	(48)	(45)	(51)
Revised				
Coefficient alpha	0·75	0·78	0·74	0·68
	Item correlation with remainder of scale‡			
Satisfied with present pay	0·52	0·58	0·54	0·39
Satisfied with kind of work	0·67	0·67	0·64	0·71
Satisfied with future with job	0·72	0·76	0·78	0·60
How good a job people think you do	0·26	0·38	0·27	*0·09*
Interested in work	0·46	0·62	0·32	0·55
(Number of respondents)§	(154)	(51)	(45)	(52)
(Correlation for which $p \leqslant 0·10$ that $r \leqslant 0$)	(0·11)	(0·19)	(0·20)	(0·22)

* Patient and leader sample.
† Community resident sample.
‡ Correlations for which $p > 0·10$ that $r \leqslant 0$ are in italic.
§ See Technical Appendix.

in the Structured Interview Schedule often were not. Therefore, with the aim of constructing from currently available data a work performance scale that would be reliable in all educational groups we dropped the uncorrelated three items with the results shown in the lower part of Table 2.

Although the revised work performance scale has a satisfactory level of reliability in all educational groups, one item, 'Why left last job', stands out as unrelated to the remainder of the scale. However, deletion of this item, leaving a three-item scale, only reduced the reliability. As a temporary expedient, therefore, we retained the four-item scale shown in the lower part of Table 2 for further analysis.

Table 4 shows that both the original and revised versions of the work performance scale discriminated between presumably more and presumably less-impaired respondents in the two lower educational groups, but not in the college graduate group. We do not know, of course, whether it would have discriminated between college graduate patients and our college graduate community sample. However, the fact that the difference between community sample respondents and community leaders at this educational level was not even in the expected direction does not encourage us to think that this scale will be useful in assessing the work role performance of highly educated people.

Job morale scale

Table 5 shows that, in contrast to the work performance scale, the original job morale scale yielded a coefficient alpha greater than 0·50 in all educational groups. However, the low correlations between the item 'Satisfied with relations with fellow workers' and the remainder of the scale led us to wonder whether we had classified this item properly in terms of subject matter since, after the fact, it seemed to be at least as appropriate to a scale of social relations as to a job morale scale. A check showed that 'Relations with fellow workers' was significantly correlated with the social relations scale at the 0·10 level in the low and intermediate educational groups and fell just short of this level of significance in the highest educational group. This combination of content and correlational evidence led us to remove the item from the job morale scale. The reliability coefficients and correlations of individual items with the remainder of this revised scale are shown in the lower part of Table 4.

Turning to the question of whether the scale discriminated between presumably more and presumably less impaired respondents, we see in Table 6 that it did well with high school graduates and with college graduates, but failed completely in the group with less than a high school education. We will return to the question of why this should be so after discussing the construction of the marital and social relations scales.

Marital scale

Table 7 shows that the marital scale, like the job morale scale was reliable in all educational groups. However, because of its lack of correlation with the remainder of the scale for all respondents we eliminated one item, namely, 'Sexual activities alone or with other than spouse'. Swingers to the contrary, such matters seem highly relevant to the marital role. Unfortunately, however, the question as asked was double-barrelled. By inquiring about both masturbation and adultery in one question we probably confused some respondents and led others to answer one part while ignoring the other. This undesirable form and the resulting ambiguity of response seemed sufficient to justify deleting the item on technical (rather than counter-cultural) grounds. As we would expect, deletion of this one item produced no remarkable changes in the reliability coefficients or in the correlations for individual items.

Table 8 shows that the marital scale did not discriminate presumably more from presumably less-impaired respondents in the highest

Table 6. Comparison of mean job morale scale scores of presumably more and presumably less impaired respondents from three educational groups.

| | | | YEARS OF EDUCATION | | | | | |
| | | | <12 | | 12–15 | | 16+ | |
Version of scale	All patients	All community residents	Patients	Community residents	Patients	Community residents	Community residents	Community leaders
Original mean	4·36	3·51	3·21	3·23	6·08	3·93	3·36	1·60
df	108		42		37		45	
t	0·96		(means reversed)		1·74†		2·38†	
Revised mean	4·09	3·30	3·47	3·09	5·25	3·70	3·13	1·36
df	112		45		37		46	
t	1·17		0·35		4·64*		2·61*	

* $p < 0.01$ one-tailed. † $p < 0.05$ one-tailed.

Table 7. *Coefficient alpha and correlation of each item with remainder of scale for original and revised marital scales according to years of education of respondent* or heard of household† (each item scored on scale of 0–3).*

Version of scale	All respondents	<12	12–15	16+
		Years of education		
Original				
Coefficient alpha	0·81	0·87	0·72	0·79
	Item correlation with remainder of scale‡			
Differ about not showing love	0·47	0·50	0·66	0·57
When quarrel strike each other	0·34	0·52	*−0·07*	0·42
Talk about personal feelings and problems	0·31	0·27	0·52	§
Often feel uncomfortable	0·73	0·84	0·72	0·75
Usually feel affectionate	0·58	0·73	0·25	0·58
Any friends both enjoy	0·38	0·25	0·54	0·74
Think spouse does not love you	0·35	*0·13*	0·54	0·77
Satisfied with marriage	0·62	0·71	0·52	0·71
Spouse satisfied with marriage	0·62	0·86	0·67	0·23
Sexual activities alone or with other than spouse	*0·05*	*0·14*	§	*−0·12*
Marriage breaking up	0·60	0·72	§	0·75
Marriage sexually satisfying	0·71	0·83	0·81	0·30
Frequency of sexual intercourse	0·27	0·35	*0·05*	0·52
(Number of respondents)‖	(114)	(40)	(37)	(34)
Revised				
Coefficient alpha	0·83	0·87	0·72	0·89
	Item correlation with remainder of scale‡			
Differ about not showing love	0·48	0·51	0·60	0·63
When quarrel strike each other	0·31	0·50	*−0·07*	0·31
Talk about personal feelings and problems	0·36	0·28	0·52	0·44
Often feel uncomfortable	0·75	0·86	0·71	0·82
Usually feel affectionate	0·56	0·74	0·26	0·46
Any friends both enjoy	0·41	0·26	0·53	0·81
Think spouse does not love you	0·34	*0·13*	0·53	0·62
Satisfied with marriage	0·69	0·73	0·52	0·80
Spouse satisfied with marriage	0·64	0·84	0·67	0·43
Marriage breaking up	0·56	0·70	§	0·60
Marriage sexually satisfying	0·72	0·82	0·80	0·54
Frequency of sexual intercourse	0·27	0·32	*0·04*	0·52
(Number of respondents)‖	(117)	(40)	(37)	(34)
(Correlation for which $p \leqslant 0·10$ that $r \leqslant 0$)	(0·13)	(0·21)	(0·22)	(0·23)

* Patient and leader sample.

† Community resident sample.

‡ Correlations or which $p > 0·10$ that $r \leqslant 0$ are in italic.

§ Number of positive responses too few to permit computation of correlation.

‖ See Technical Appendix.

Table 8. Comparison of mean marital scale scores of presumably more and presumably less impaired respondents from three educational groups.

| | | | YEARS OF EDUCATION | | | | | |
| | | | <12 | | 12–15 | | 16+ | |
Version of scale	All patients	All community residents	Patients	Community residents	Patients	Community residents	Community residents	Community leaders
Original mean	8·08	2·97	8·25	4·33	7·82	1·43	2·92	2·85
df	80		34		30‡		31	
t	3·31*		1·36†		3·65*		0·04	
Revised mean	7·96	2·92	8·25	4·16	7·82	1·50	2·92	3·57
df	82		35		31‡		32	
t	3·28*		1·48†		3·50*		(means reversed)	

* $p<0.01$ one-tailed test. † $p<0.10$ one-tailed test.

‡ Correction for unequal variances gives $df = 11$; level of significance was unchanged by this correction.

Table 9. *Coefficient alpha and correlation of each item with remainder of scale for social relations scale according to years of education of respondent* or head of household† (each item scored on scale of 0–2).*

		Years of education		
Items in scale	*All respondents*	*<12*	*12–15*	*16+*
Coefficient alpha	0·69	0·76	0·47	0·09
	Item correlations with remainder of scale‡			
Seldom sees anyone	0·36	0·48	0·18	*0·08*
No friends to count on	0·51	0·56	0·27	*0·10*
Does not visit or invite	0·65	0·74	0·48	§
(Number of respondents)	(261)	(91)	(74)	(64)
(Correlation for which $p \leqslant 0·10$ that $r \leqslant 0$)	(0·08)	(0·14)	(0·15)	(0·16)

* Patient and leader samples.
† Community resident sample.
‡ Correlations for which $p > 0·10$ that $r \leqslant 0$ are in italic.
§ Item mean equals zero.

educational group. Since the mean impairment score of the leaders was higher than the mean for their educational peers in the community sample, there was not even a trend in the expected direction. We will consider the implications of this reversal at a later point.

Social relations scale

The reliability of the social relations scale, as indicated in Table 9, was clearly unsatisfactory in the highest educational group and just short of the criterion of 0·50 in the intermediate group. Only in the least educated group did reliability reach a satisfactory level. The fact that the three items used to compose this scale did not even come close to forming a unitary whole in the highest educational group suggests the possibility that social relations with friends and social relations with relatives outside the nuclear family, which were combined in this scale, may not be in the same domain for highly educated people in this urban setting.

Consistent with this lack of reliability, we see in Table 10 that the scale failed to discriminate between presumably more and presumably less impaired respondents in this college graduate group. It did, however, discriminate in the intermediate group despite the unsatisfactory reliability. Thus, it is possible that by adding more items we could achieve a scale that is satisfactory both in terms of reliability and power to discriminate in the expected way in the middle group. In the least educated group, where the level of impairment was relatively high, even this very short scale was adequate both in terms of reliability and in terms of its power to discriminate between presumably more and presumably less impaired respondents.

Table 10. Comparison of mean social relations scale scores of presumably more and presumably less impaired respondents from three educational groups.

| | | YEARS OF EDUCATION | | | | | |
| | | <12 | | 12–15 | | 16+ | |
	All patients	All community residents	Patients	Community residents	Patients	Community residents	Community residents	Community leaders
Mean	1·25	0·43	1·51	0·65	1·18	0·29	0·27	0·28
df		189		84		66		57
t		4·91*		2·57*		3·39*		(means reversed)

* $p < 0.01$ one-tailed.

Table 11. *Summary for final versions of four role performance scales of reliability and ability to discriminate between presumably more and presumably less impaired respondents in three educational groups.*

	YEARS OF EDUCATION		
	<12	12–15	16+
	Reliability *(Values of $\alpha<0\cdot50$ in parentheses)* *Scale*		
Work performance	+	+	+
Job morale	+	+	+
Marriage	+	+	+
Social relations	+	(0·47)	(0·09)

For above educational levels: discrimination at $p<0\cdot10$ or better between:

	Patients and community residents	*Patients and community residents*	*Community residents and leaders*
community			
Work performance	+	+	—
Job morale	—	+	+
Marriage	+	+	—
Social relations	+	+	—

Discussion

Table 11 summarizes the results of our attempt to build four role scales that are reliable and discriminate between groups selected to contrast in levels of social performance. To the extent that these scales were reliable and discriminated as expected within each social class we have evidence that they are valid indicators of handicaps over and above those associated with a particular class.

Except for a possible question about reliability of the social relations scale, all four scales are valid by these criteria in the middle group. Given this consistently positive evidence of validity across scales, the fact that, though generally reliable, none of the scales discriminated as expected in both the lower- and upper-class groups might be explained in either substantive or methodological terms. First, where a scale failed to discriminate between groups that were chosen on *a-priori* grounds to contrast in levels of role functioning it is possible that our *a-priori* assumptions were wrong. This possibility implies, specifically, that a failure of a role scale to discriminate in the lowest educational group indicates that impairment in that particular role in the lowest class is entirely class related with no increment due to psychiatric disorders. On the other hand, failure to discriminate in the highest educational group implies that we were in error in assuming that community leaders function at a higher level in a particular social role than their educational peers in a cross-section of community residents. In contrast, the methodological explanation of a failure to discriminate is that the scale in question is insensitive in a particular class to a difference in level of role functioning that actually exists.

Comparison of the results obtained with the work performance and the job morale scales suggests that, for these scales, the methodological is the more reasonable explanation of the failures to make the expected discriminations. Recall that the work performance scale did not discriminate in the college graduate group. As noted earlier, possibly it would have discriminated between a patient sample and a community sample if the former had been available in this educational group. Even allowing this possibility, it is disturbing that the scale presents community leaders as, if anything, more impaired in work performance than their educational peers among community residents. How did these people become leaders if they did not perform outstandingly in their work role? We find it difficult to accept this result at face value.

If, however, we consider the possibility that the scale is not an adequate measure of work performance in high status groups, the question we have just asked suggests its own answer: specifically, that this scale does not tap the positive behaviour that makes work performance outstanding. This hypothesis is supported by a review of the items in the scale. Only one in either the original or revised versions, namely, 'Number of times left for a better job', might tell us anything about the advances and achievements of an individual who was highly successful in his work. The other items merely recorded an absence of failure.

The job morale scale contrasts with the work performance scale in that it failed to discriminate patients from community sample respondents in the lowest social class, while its greatest success was among high status respondents. It is, in fact, the only scale we have that discriminated the leaders from their educational peers in the community sample.

Comparing the mean scores of the three social classes in the community resident sample on the job morale scale we find that the least educated had a slightly lower mean impairment score than either of the two better-educated groups. Furthermore, among patients the less educated had a considerably lower impairment score, 3·47, than the better educated high school graduates whose mean was 5·25. Thus, the failure of the job morale scale to discriminate in the lowest social stratum occurred as part of a picture of relatively low impairment in job morale in this poorly educated group, a picture which does not make particularly good sense.

This picture of a relatively high level of satisfaction with their job situations among the least educated becomes somewhat comprehensible if we assume that the very fact of having a job in a market of limited opportunity provides satisfaction for persons with few skills (cf. Myers and

Bean, 1968, p. 165). But are we willing to assume also that the handicap associated with low education is so powerful that it overrides any handicap related to job morale that might be associated with psychiatric disorder? This is one possible implication of the failure to make the expected discrimination in this group. Contrariwise, perhaps it makes more sense to question the adequacy of the scale in relation to the concerns and sources of dissatisfaction of the employed lower class person who, numerous studies have suggested (Dohrenwend and Dohrenwend, 1969, p. 142), tends to be oriented primarily toward security rater than toward achievement in his work. A review of the contents of the items in the job morale scale suggests that none, except possibly 'Satisfied with future with job', directly tapped concerns about security. If we were to expand the job morale scale in this direction we would expect to find differences between lower class patients and community residents on the hypothesis that, within the range of jobs occupied by the least skilled, patients are likely to hold the most undesirable, least secure positions.

Thus, a review of the results obtained with the two scales related to the work role suggests that these scales, each in a different way, were too narrowly conceived. Since they did not include the full range of class-related behaviours and styles of functioning in this role, they were, between them, sensitive to impairment in this functioning only in the middle group. These scales, we suggest, should be extended so that each includes both the security-oriented behaviours and concerns of the lower class and the achievement-oriented behaviours and concerns of the higher status groups.

Both the marital and social relations scales failed to discriminate in the highly educated group. Since the social relations scale was also unreliable in this group, however, its failure to discriminate merely confirmed the need for the reconstruction of this scale if we are to have a measure with which to compare college graduates with less educated people.

In contrast, the marital scale was highly reliable in all three classes but, even so, failed to discriminate between the community residents and community leaders at the highest educational level. We do not know, of course, whether it would have discriminated between college-educated patients as against community residents if we had been able to make this comparison. However, even if we make the optimistic assumption that it would have discriminated, we still have to decide whether the relatively high mean impairment score of the leaders suggests that the scale is invalid as an indicator of marital role impairment.

From a survey of a systematic sample of the population of the US, Gurin *et al.* concluded that '. . . the findings with respect to education suggest that the more educated respondents are more sensitive to both the positive and negative aspects of the marriage relationship' (1960, p. 113). This sensitivity to negative factors might explain why the mean impairment score on the marital scale for the college graduate group in the community sample was nearly twice that of the high school graduates. Extrapolating from this difference, perhaps the sensitivity is even more acute among college-educated community leaders compared to their educational peers among community residents. If this interpretation is correct, it raises a serious question about the validity of the marital scale, since it implies that impairment scores reflected aspirations more closely than actual experience.

This interpretation of the meaning of the marital role scores is not consistent, however, with the fact that the least-educated respondents in the community resident sample had a mean impairment score that was higher than that of the college-educated community leaders. The relationship between sensitivity to marital problems and education inferred by Gurin and his colleagues was, as you would expect, assumed to be lowest among the least educated. The question is, then, whether we should go to the unparsimonious length of explaining the observed curvilinear relation between social status and marital role scores in terms of sensitivity to marital problems at the upper end of the social scale and truly impaired marriages at the lower end. Examination of the transcripts of high and low status respondents who had high marital role impairment scores suggested that this expedient is unnecessary, for their comments suggest that the high-scoring college graduates' marriages were as truly impaired as those of the high-scoring respondents in the least educated group. Thus, for example, one leader reported that she was living with her husband only until the children were grown and another described in strong terms his wife's appearance and vocal style, concluding that he found both 'very revolting'. The only obvious differences revealed by the transcripts are the more elaborated and colourful descriptions provided by unhappily married high status respondents and the more frequent mention of alcoholism in connection with unhappy low status marriages. Thus, rather than deciding that the scale is deficient we are inclined to take the results at face value. After the fact, we see no reason why community leaders should have more successful and satisfactory marriages than their educational peers among community residents.

Conclusions

We have shown that it is possible to construct reliable role measures that differentiate the social performance of psychiatric patients from their class counterparts in community samples drawn from the general population. There are, however, serious limitations in the particular measures described in this paper. Although they were based on what we took, perhaps wrongly, to be conventional wisdom, none of the scales met the criterion of reliability in all subgroups and also discriminated as we thought it should. After the fact, we hope we have gained sufficient wisdom about class-related differences in role behaviours and orientations to expand the work-related scales so that they will discriminate in all social classes. At the same time, it is clear that the critical test of the ability of the scales to discriminate within the college-educated stratum requires that we add a group of patients at this educational level to the presently available comparison groups.

Although we have dealt so far only with social class, other normative sources of variability in social performance require similar attention. Of these, ethnicity, sex, and age seem most important. Each refinement of control on status variables, will, of course, complicate the measurement problem. However, each solution of a measurement problem should not only sharpen the precision of the instruments but also increase our understanding of normative differences in role behaviours associated with various social statuses.

With improved scales we can ask more specific questions about the relation of degree and type of role impairment to different types of psychiatric disorder. We would expect to find some differences since, for example, Birtchnell (1971) has shown that degree of downward mobility and, by inference, impairment in the work role, varied according to type of psychiatric disorder even when social factors were controlled.

Thus, as refined scales are developed, measurement of role impairment as a function of specific types of psychiatric disorders within particular social groups will provide the basis for more precise evaluation of the social effectiveness of psychiatric services. The test would be whether these services decrease differentials in social performance that, even with the relatively primitive scales developed here, can be shown to exist for patients by contrast with their status counterparts in the general population. In the context of evaluative research, improved measures of role performance will give operational definition to what can reasonably be meant by the statement that 'The objective of modern treatment of persons with major mental illness is to enable the patient to maintain himself in the community in a normal manner' (Joint Commission, 1961, p. xvii).

TECHNICAL APPENDIX

Frequency of scale and item responses

Looking at the *N*s reported on tables for the frequency of respondents completing different scales and items, the reader will notice considerable variation from the *N* for the total sample 269. Not only are *N*s for each scale less than the total in our sample, but the number of respondents varies from scale to scale.

There are two reasons for this fluctuation. For many respondents scores on some role scales will be inapplicable. The marriage scale, for instance, applies only to married respondents; the job morale and work history scores are computed only for respondents in the job market.

Another reason for the discrepancy of scale frequencies and sample totals is the number of missing data scores for respondents completing our questionnaire. Respondents who failed to answer one or more items from any scale—whether because the role was not applicable, or because they refused to answer or did not complete the questionnaire—were not included in our analysis of scale scores and reliability. Eventually scores for respondents who failed to complete the entire scale will be prorated. At this time, however, we felt that it was important to establish the reliability of scores without including any incomplete measures since we wished to avoid constructing an unreliable measurement, which would occur if the prorated scores introduced a bias in our measurement, or if the prorating were an inaccurate estimate of the respondent's 'true' score.

REFERENCES

Angrist, S., Lefton, M., Dinitz, S., and Pasamanick, B. (1968). *Women After Treatment: A Study of Former Mental Patients and Their Normal Neighbors* (New York: Appleton Century Crofts).

Bahn, A. K. (1971). 'A multi-disciplinary psychosocial classification scheme', *Am. J. Orthopsychiat.* **41**, 830–8.

Birtchnell, J. (1971). 'Social class, parental social class, and social mobility in psychiatric patients and general population controls', *Psychol. Med.* **1**, 209–21.

Bradburn, N. M., and Caplovitz, D. (1965). *Reports on Happiness* (Chicago: Aldine Publishing Co.).

Clausen, J. A. (1971). 'Psychosocial diagnosis: what and why?' *Am. J. Orthopsychiat.* **41**, 847–8.

Cooper, B., Eastwood, M. R., and Sylph, J. (1970). 'Psychiatric morbidity and social adjustment in a general practice population', in Hare, E. H., and Wing, J. K. (eds), *Psychiatric Epidemiology*, pp. 299–309 (Oxford University Press for the Nuffield Provincial Hospitals Trust).

Dohrenwend, B. P. (1971). 'Notes on psychosocial diagnosis', *Am. J. Orthopsychiat.* **41**, 846.

—— and Chin-Shong, E. (1967). 'Social status and attitudes toward psychological disorder: the problem of tolerance of deviance', *Am. Sociol. Rev.* **32**, 417–33.

—— —— Egri, G., Mendelsohn, F. S., and Stokes, J. (1970). 'Measures of psychiatric disorder in contrasting class and ethnic groups. A preliminary report of on-going research', in Hare, E. H., and Wing, J. K. (eds), *Psychiatric Epidemiology*, pp. 159–202 (Oxford University Press for the Nuffield Provincial Hospitals Trust).

Dunham, H. W., Phillips, P., and Srinivasan, B. (1966). 'A research note on diagnosed mental illness and social class', *Am. Sociol. Rev.* **31**, 223–7.

Fairweather, G. W. (1964). *Social Psychology in Treating Mental Illness: An Experimental Approach* (New York: John Wiley).

Freeman, H. E., and Simmons, O. G. (1963). *The Mental Patient Comes Home* (New York: John Wiley).

Gruenberg, E. M. (1967). 'Social breakdown syndrome—some origins', *Am. J. Psychiat.* **123**, 1481–9.

Gurin, G., Veroff, J., and Feld, S. (1960). *Americans View their Mental Health* (New York: Basic Books).

Joint Commission on Mental Illness and Health (1961). *Action for Mental Health* (New York: Basic Books).

Katz, M. M. (1971). 'Problems of training in the application of a new system of classification for the psychosocial disorders', *Am. J. Orthopsychiat.* **41,** 841–3.

Myers, J. K., and Bean, L. L. (1968). *A Decade Later: A Follow-up of Social Class and Mental Illness* (New York: John Wiley).

Newbrough, J. R. (1971). 'Behavioral perspectives on psychosocial classification', *Am. J. Orthopsychiat.* **41,** 843–5.

Nunally, J. C. (1967). *Psychometric Theory* (New York: McGraw-Hill).

Pasamanick, B., Scarpitti, F. R., and Dinitz, S. (1967). *Schizophrenics in the Community* (New York: Appleton Century Crofts).

Spitzer, R. L. (1971). 'A response to the threat of a classification scheme for the psychosocial disorders: some specific suggestions', *Am. J. Orthopsychiat.* **41,** 838–40.

—— Endicott, J., Fleiss, J. L., and Cohen, J. (1970). 'The Psychiatric Status Schedule: a technique for evaluating psychopathology and impairment in role functioning', *Archives of Gen. Psychiat.* **23,** 41–55.